Instructor's Guide

Human Anatomy
Third Edition

Gail C. Turner, Ph.D.

Virginia Commonwealth University

An imprint of Addison Wesley Longman, Inc.

San Francisco • Boston • New York
Capetown • Hong Kong • London • Madrid • Mexico City
Montreal • Munich • Paris • Singapore • Sidney • Tokyo • Toronto

Publisher: Daryl Fox

Senior Project Editor: Kay Ueno

Senior Developmental Editor: Mark Wales

Research Assistant: Jessica Freeman

Publishing Assistant: Richard Gallagher

Managing Editor: Wendy Earl

Production Supervisor: David Novak

Production Editor: Bettina Borer

Composition: Brad Greene, Greene Design

Manufacturing Coordinator: Stacey Weinberger

Marketing Manager: Lauren Harp

Copyright © 2001 by Benjamin Cummings, an imprint of Addison Wesley Longman, Inc.

Many of the designations used by manufacturers and sellers to distinguish their products are claimed as trademarks. When such a designation appears in this book and Benjamin Cummings was aware of a trademark claim, the designation has been printed in initial capital letters (e.g., Macintosh).

All rights reserved.

Printed in the United States of America. This publication is protected by Copyright and permissions should be obtained from the publisher prior to any prohibited reproduction, storage in a retrieval system, or transmission in any form or by any means, electronic, mechanical, photocopying, recording, or likewise. For information regarding permission(s) write to: Permissions Department.

ISBN 0-8053-4931-6

1 2 3 4 5 6 7 8 9 10–VG–04 03 02 01 00
www.awl.com

Preface

This instructor's guide accompanies the textbook *Human Anatomy*, Third Edition, by Elaine N. Marieb and Jon Mallatt. Unlike previous editions, this instructor's guide is devoted solely to supplying teaching suggestions and resources that augment the use of the textbook in the classroom. The chapter tests and final examinations that formerly were included within the instructor's guide now appear in a revised printed and electronic test bank. Please contact your Benjamin Cummings representative for copies of the test banks.

ORGANIZATION AND FEATURES

The *Instructor's Guide* follows the organization of *Human Anatomy*, Third Edition, chapter for chapter. Within each chapter you will find the following new and revised resources grouped in five sections: (1) Lecture and Demonstration, (2) Art Resources, (3) Supplemental Course Materials, (4) Answers to Textbook Questions, and (5) Supplemental Student Materials.

- **Lecture and Demonstration** The opening section of each chapter in the *Instructor's Guide* is devoted to helping you structure and augment your classroom lectures and activities. Five features are offered.

  Student Objectives The objectives are reprinted from the chapter openers of the textbook and focus on the principal themes and topics to be mastered in each chapter.

  Suggested Lecture Outline The outlines generally correspond to the sequence of headings that appear in each textbook chapter. Key page, figure, and table numbers appear next to most of the entries in each outline.

  Lecture Hints This new feature is composed of a list of key lecture points, which follows the order of the suggested lecture outline. In addition to calling attention to the main concepts of each chapter, the lecture hints identify ideas or topics that students may have difficulty mastering in their reading or during lecture.

  Classroom Discussion Topics and Activities This popular feature from the last edition consists of activities, demonstrations, and discussion topics that can be used to augment and enliven your anatomy lectures and laboratories.

  Clinical Questions This section of each chapter provides additional clinically focused, critical reasoning questions like those that appear at the end of each textbook chapter. The answers follow each question.

- **Art Resources** New to this edition of the *Instructor's Guide*, this section is provided to help you utilize the greatly improved illustration program in the third edition of *Human Anatomy* in your classroom teaching. This section includes:

Transparency List This list details which figures in the chapter are available in the new color transparency package. (Call your Benjamin Cummings representative for information about how to obtain the transparency package.) More than double its size from the previous edition, the transparency package includes enlarged and color-enhanced versions of most of the illustrations in the textbook.

Teaching with Art This new section is designed to facilitate your lecture presentations about key figures in each chapter, and it is also aimed at encouraging students to become actively engaged with the textbook illustrations in order to strengthen their understanding of major topics. Each *Teaching with Art* section consists of a checklist of major discussion points about a figure and a list of concepts that students sometimes find difficult to understand or fail to perceive when they interpret a figure on their own. Finally, this section includes an art-based exercise that is designed to help students to better understand the anatomy depicted in a figure. *Teaching with Art* concludes with a visual critical reasoning challenge in which students are asked to synthesize a response based on the visual evidence presented in a figure.

- **Supplemental Course Materials** This section of each chapter of the Instructor's Guide consists of materials that you may use to augment your classroom presentations or assign for student completion. This section consists of:

    Library Research Topics These term paper or report topics can be assigned for extra credit or to help deepen students' understanding of anatomy.

    Audiovisual Aids/Computer Software Revised and updated, this section lists software, videotapes, and CD-ROMs in addition to those offered by Benjamin Cummings. A key to the abbreviations used to identify the audiovisual and electronic media distributors in each list can be found immediately following the table of contents.

    Suggested Readings Revised and updated for this edition, this feature lists classic readings, advanced anatomy textbooks, and current journal articles. This bibliography can be used to introduce your students to scientific literature and to the research process in addition to enhancing their knowledge of human anatomy.

- **Answers to Textbook Questions** This section provides answers to the Short Answer and Essay Questions section and the Critical Reasoning and Clinical Applications Questions section, both located at the end of each textbook chapter.

- **Supplemental Student Materials** This new feature consists of a student-oriented introduction to the mission of each chapter and a description of the practical importance of its coverage. An extended series of learning checkpoints follows that students may use to chart their progress while reading the chapter. This feature is formatted to be easily photocopied and distributed to your students.

GUIDE TO SUPPLEMENTS ACCOMPANYING THE TEXTBOOK

The suite of supplementary materials developed by Benjamin Cummings for the third edition of *Human Anatomy* is more innovative and thorough than ever before—in print, on CD-ROM, and on the Web—for you and your students alike. Here is a description of the new electronic and printed supplements that are specifically dedicated to the textbook.

New Electronic Media Supplements

The Anatomy & Physiology Place (www.anatomyandphysiology.com) From the home page of the Anatomy & Physiology Place, you and your students can access a Special Edition for *Human Anatomy*, Third Edition, which features the following resources and activities:

- 50-question practice quizzes in every chapter
- interactive clinical case studies with labeling and matching exercises
- illustrated bone anatomy quiz
- web research activities
- on-line histology tutor
- pronunciation glossary with an audio feature
- anatomy-related news articles

You will find a useful Syllabus Manager to help organize your course, plus access to the *Benjamin Cummings Digital Library* (discussed next). A free 12-month subscription to this powerful web site is included with each new student copy of the textbook. As an instructor, you will receive a 6-month subscription, which can be renewed free of charge. A 7-day trial option is also available at the web site. Web site access directions along with password and PIN code numbers are attached inside the front cover of the textbook.

Benjamin Cummings Digital Library for *Human Anatomy*, Third Edition (0-8053-6159-6) The *Digital Library* is a CD-ROM featuring all of the illustrations (excluding photomicrographs) from the book—approximately 650 images in all. This important new teaching tool includes a presentation program that can be used for designing a customized slide show of images. You may edit labels, import illustrations and photos from other sources, and export figures to other software programs such as PowerPoint. For increased flexibility, the *Digital Library* presents art in three formats: art with leaders and labels, art with leaders only, and art without leaders and labels. A helpful topic and keyword search function makes it easy to locate the illustrations you need without consulting figure numbers in the textbook.

Study Partner CD-ROM This helpful new interactive learning tool is designed to engage your students as they study and review the main concepts of anatomy. The *Study Partner* contains 53 interactive, illustrated exercises along with quizzes for each chapter. A random-testing feature allows students to construct tests that cover multiple chapters, with the total score revealed at the end of the test. Students can also access a comprehensive Pronunciation Glossary with audio feature. Study Partner icons appearing within the book's end-of-chapter summaries alert students to specific, related exercises on the *Study Partner*. A copy of the *Study Partner* is attached to the inside back cover of the student and instructor versions of each textbook.

Electronic Test Bank (cross-platform CD-ROM: 0-8053-4930-8) Revised by Robin McFarland, Cabrillo College; Temma al Muhktar, San Diego Mesa College; James T. Wetzel, Presbyterian College; and Jon Mallatt, University of Washington. The revised test bank accompanying the third edition offers two 25-question multiple-choice exams per chapter as well as two final exams, each consisting of over 200 multiple-choice questions. Approximately one third of the questions are new to this edition. The electronic test bank is formatted in TestGen-EQ. This versatile new software allows instructors to generate tests via a user-friendly interface in which they can easily view, edit, sort, and add questions. QuizMaster-EQ makes testing even easier for instructors. This free and fully networkable program enables the instructor to create and save tests and quizzes using TestGen-EQ so that students can take tests or quizzes on a computer network. The program automatically grades exams and allows the instructor to view or print reports for individual students, classes, or courses. The test bank also is available in a printed version (0-8053-4937-5).

A.D.A.M.® Interactive Anatomy Student Package (Win: 0-8053-6075-1; Mac: 0-8053-6076-X) *A.D.A.M.® Interactive Anatomy (AIA)*, version 3.0, is now available packaged with Lafferty and Panella's *A.D.A.M.® Interactive Anatomy Student Lab Guide (0-8053-4350-4)* for a special reduced price. With over 20,000 dissectible, atlas, and 3-D anatomy images, AIA also features female and male anatomical structures; cadaver dissections; and 3-D models of the heart, skull, and lungs. AIA icons appearing within most of the textbook's end-of-chapter summaries provide specific directions for locating related images on the A.D.A.M.® Interactive CD-ROM. What is more, AIA-related anatomy review questions are located at the conclusion of most chapters of the textbook. Ask your Benjamin Cummings representative for more information about this special package.

A.D.A.M.® Anatomy Practice (cross-platform CD-ROM: 0-8053-9680-2) This CD-ROM is designed to augment your students' laboratory experience. *Anatomy Practice* features 500 pinned anatomical images, and it includes more than 15,000 practice test questions. Students will find a wide variety of options to review anatomical images and take randomly generated tests with time limits, just like they do in the lab.

Course Management Systems and Special Student Services

WebCT and Blackboard Both course management systems are useful for developing and managing on-line distance learning courses. They are available by themselves or packaged with the textbook. The content provided with either system includes selections from *The Anatomy & Physiology Place* as well as the entire computerized test bank. Contact your Benjamin Cummings representative for more information about how to link your course to WebCT or Blackboard.

AWL Anatomy and Physiology Tutor Center Free tutoring is available to students who purchase a copy of *Human Anatomy*, Third Edition. The AWL Tutor Center is staffed by qualified anatomy instructors who can tutor students on all the material covered in the textbook, including the art and the multiple-choice/matching questions at the end of each chapter. Tutoring content is restricted to textbook material, and tutors will only discuss answers that are provided in the textbook. Students can contact the Tutor Center by phone, fax, or e-mail Sunday through Thursday, between 5:00 PM and 12:00 AM EST. You must authorize access to the Tutor Center for your students. To do so, please contact your local Benjamin Cummings sales representative for information or visit the Tutor Center web site at www.awl.com/tutorcenter.

New and Revised Printed Supplements

Full-color Transparency Acetates (0-8053-4929-4) We are greatly pleased to have more than doubled the number of transparency acetates available with the third edition—approximately 450 in all—which has enabled the authors to include virtually every key illustration in the book (except for photomicrographs). The illustrations in every transparency have been color enhanced and then enlarged for easy viewing in the classroom. The acetate package is available free to adopters of the textbook.

Atlas of the Human Skeleton (0-8053- 4988-X) This new photographic atlas of the human skeleton is an indispensable reference for the laboratory and the classroom. You will find approximately 102 four-color images, with labels and leaders, all beautifully photographed by Ralph T. Hutchings. The Atlas is packaged free with each new textbook.

Human Anatomy Laboratory Manual (0-8053-4968-5) Elaine N. Marieb's widely used *Human Anatomy Laboratory Manual with Cat Dissection*, Third Edition (2001), accompanies this textbook. The manual contains 29 gross anatomy and histology exercises for all major body systems. Illustrated in full color, with a convenient spiral binding, the lab manual has an accompanying *Instructor's Guide* by Linda Kollett of Massasoit Community College.

Additional Supplements Available from Benjamin Cummings

For the Classroom and Laboratory:

Histology Slides for the Life Sciences by Bell and Eroshenko (0-8053-4286-9)

Human Cadaver Dissection Videos by Rose Leigh Vines, et. al.
    Human Musculature Video (0-8053-0106-2)
    Human Cardiovascular System: The Heart Video (0-8053-4289-3)
    Human Cardiovascular System: Blood Vessels Video (0-8053-4297-4)
    Experiments on Hormonal Action Video (0-8053-4155-2)
    Human Digestive System Video (0-8053-4823-9)
    Human Reproductive System Video (0-8053-4914-6)
    Human Urinary System Video (0-8053-4915-4)
    Human Respiratory System Video (0-8053-4822-0)
    Human Nervous System: Human Brain and Cranial Nerves Video (0-8053-4012-2)
    Human Nervous System: The Spinal Cord and Nerves Video (0-8053-4013-0)

Student Video Series for Anatomy and Physiology, Volume I (0-8053-4110-2)

Student Video Series for Anatomy and Physiology, Volume II (0-8053-6115-4)

For Your Students:

The Anatomy Coloring Book, Second Edition by Kapit and Elson (0-06-455016-8)

Anatomy Flashcards by Glenn Bastian (0-8053-0887-3)

Bassett Atlas of Human Anatomy by Robert Chase (0-8053-0118-6)

A Color Atlas of Histology by Dennis Strete (0-673-99190-3)

Many thanks to Mark Wales, senior developmental anatomy and physiology editor, and Jon Mallatt, anatomist extraordinaire, and thanks to Mike and Turbo, too!

Gail C. Turner, Ph.D.
Virginia Commonwealth University

Contents

	Key to Audiovisual Distributors	xi
1	The Human Body: An Orientation	1
2	Cells: The Living Units	11
3	Basic Embryology	23
4	Tissues	33
5	The Integumentary System	47
6	Bones and Skeletal Tissues	59
7	Bones, Part 1: The Axial Skeleton	71
8	Bones, Part 2: The Appendicular Skeleton	83
9	Joints	93
10	Muscle Tissue	105
11	Muscles of the Body	117
12	Fundamentals of the Nervous System and Nervous Tissue	129
13	The Central Nervous System	141
14	The Peripheral Nervous System	159
15	The Autonomic Nervous System and Visceral Sensory Neurons	171
16	The Special Senses	187
17	Blood	201
18	The Heart	213
19	Blood Vessels	225
20	The Lymphatic and Immune Systems	237
21	The Respiratory System	251
22	The Digestive System	267
23	The Urinary System	281
24	The Reproductive System	293
25	The Endocrine System	311
26	Surface Anatomy	325

Key to Audiovisual Distributors

ACC Anatomical Chart Company
8221 Kimball Avenue, Stokie, IL 60076-2956
(800) 621-7500; www.anatomical.com

ACPB The Annenberg/CPB Project; The Corporation for Public Broadcasting
901 E. Street NW, Washington, DC 20004-2037
(800) 532-7637; www.learner.org

ADAM A.D.A.M.
1600 Riveredge Parkway, Suite 800
Atlanta, GA 30328
(800) 755-2326; Fax: (770) 955-3088
www.adam.com

AIMS AIMS Multimedia
9710 DeSoto Avenue, Chatsworth, CA 91311-4409
(800) 367-2647; www.aims-multimedia.com

AMA American Medical Association
Distributed by DGI

BC Benjamin/Cummings Publishing Company
1301 Sansome St., San Francisco, CA 94111
(800) 284-8292; www.awl.com/bc

BIO Biodisc, Inc.
6963 Easton Court, Sarasota, FL 34238-2610
(800) 453-3009; Fax: (941) 921-3009
www.biodisc.com; info@biodisc.com

CAP The Center for Anatomy and Physiology
PO Box 9, 102 Highway 81 North
Calhoun, KY 42327-0009
(800) 962-6662; www.nimcoinc.com

CBSC Carolina Biological Supply Company
2700 York Road, Burlington, NC 27215
(800) 334-5551; Fax: (800) 222-7112

CDL Cambridge Development Laboratory, Inc.
86 West Street, Waltham, MA 02154
(800) 637-0047

CEI Cyber Ed, Inc.
PO Box 3037, Paradise, CA 95967-3037
(888) 318-0700; Fax: (530) 872-2555
www.cyber-ed.com; cybered@cyber-ed.com

CM Concept Media
PO Box 19542, Irvine, CA 92623-9542
(800) 233-7078; www.conceptmedia.com

COR Coronet/MTI Film and Video
168 Wilmont Road, Deerfield, IL 60015-9990
(312) 940-1260; (800) 621-2131

CRM CRM/McGraw-Hill Films
PO Box 641, 674 Via de la Valle
Del Mar, CA 92014
(800) 628-7748; FAX: (800) 355-6813

CVB Connecticut Valley Biological
82 Valley Road, Southampton, MA 01073
(800) 621-7748; Fax: (800) 355-6813

DGI Denoyer-Geppert International
5225 Ravenswood Avenue
Chicago, IL 60640-2028
(800) 621-1014; Fax: (773) 561-4160
denoyer@aol.com

EAI Educational Activities, Inc.
1937 Grand Avenue, Baldwin, NY 11510
(516) 223-4666; (800) 645-3739
Fax: (516) 623-9282

EBEC Encyclopedia Britannica Educational Corporation
425 North Michigan Avenue, Chicago, IL 60611
(800) 554-9862; Fax: (312) 347-7903

EI	Educational Images Ltd. PO Box 3456, West Side Station Elmira, NY 14905 (607) 732-1090; (800) 527-4264 Fax: (607) 732-1183	**IM**	Insight Media 121 West 85th Street New York, NY 10024-4401 (212) 721-6316; (800) 233-9910
ESI	Educational Software Institute 4213 South 94th Street, Omaha, NE 68127 (800) 955-5570; FAX: (402) 592-2017	**KSU**	Kent State University Audiovisual Center Kent, OH 44242 (216) 672-FILM; (800) 338-5718 Fax: (216) 672-3463
FAD	F.A. Davis Co. 1915 Arch Street, Philadelphia, PA 19103	**LOG**	Logal 125 Cambridgepark Drive Cambridge, MA 02140 (888) 564-2999; www.logal.com
FHS	Films for the Humanities and Sciences PO Box 2053, Princeton, NJ 08543-2053 (800) 257-5126; Fax: (609) 275-3767 www.films.com; custserv@films.com	**MBS**	Micron Biosystems, now: Visible Productions 201 Linden Street, Suite 301 Fort Collins, CO 80524 (800) 685-4668; Fax: (970) 407-7248 www.visiblep.com
FREY	Frey Scientific, Beckley Cardy Group 100 Paragon Parkway, Mansfield, OH 44903 (999) 222-1332; FAX (888) 454-1417		
FSC	Flinn Scientific Co. PO Box 219, Batavia, IL 60510 (800) 452-1261; Fax: (630) 879-6962 flinnsci@aol.com	**MBV**	Media Basics Video Lighthouse Square, PO Box 449 Guilford, CT 06439-0449 (800) 542-2505; (203) 458-2505 Fax: (203) 458-9816 www.mediabasicsvideo.com
FSE	Fisher Scientific Education 485 S. Frontage Road, Burr Ridge, IL 60521 (800) 955-1177; Fax: (800) 955-0740 fishered@ix.netcom.com	**MCG**	McGraw Hill Films PO Box 641, 674 Via de la Valle Del Mar, CA 92014 (800) 628-7748; Fax: (800) 355-6813
GA	Guidance Associates PO Box 1000, Mount Kisco, NY 10549-0010 (800) 431-1242; Fax: (914) 666-5319 from Alaska, call collect (914) 666-4100	**MOS**	Mosby, Inc. 11830 Westline Industrial Drive St. Louis, MO 63146-3318 (800) 685-4668; Fax: (303)393-7499
GSM	Gold Standard Multimedia, Inc. 3825 Henderson Blvd., Suite 200 Tampa, FL 33629 Fax: (813) 287-1810	**NASCO**	NASCO 901 Janesville Ave. Ft. Atkinson, WI 53538-0901 (920) 563-2446; Fax: (920) 563-8296
HCA	Health Care Advances PO Box 9, 102 Highway 81 North Calhoun, KY 42327-0009 (800) 962-6662; www.nimcoinc.com	**NCHCA**	The National Center for Health Care Advances A Division of NIMCO, Inc. PO Box 9, 102 Highway 81 North Calhoun, KY 42327-0009 (800) 962-6662; Fax: (502) 273-5844 www.nimcoinc.com
HRM	Human Relations Media 175 Tempkins Avenue, Pleasantville, NY 10570 (800) 431-2050; (914) 769-6900 Fax: (917) 747-0177		

NGF National Geographic Films, Karol Media
22 Riverview Drive, Wayne, NJ 07470
(201) 628-9111

NGS National Geographic Society
1145 17th Street, NW
Washington, DC 20036-4688
(800) 368-2728; Fax: (515) 362-3366

NIMCO The Center for Anatomy and Physiology
A Division of NIMCO, Inc.
PO Box 9, 102 Highway 81 North
Calhoun, KY 42327-0009
(800) 962-6662; Fax: (502) 273-5844
www.nimcoinc.com; support@nimcoinc.com

QUEUE Queue, Inc.
562 Boston Avenue, Bridgeport, CT 06610

PBS PBS Video
1320 Braddock Place, Alexandria, VA 22314
(800) 424-7963; www.pbs.org

PLP Projected Learning Programs, Inc.
PO Box 3008, Paradise, CA 95967-3008
(800) 248-0757; (916) 877-0603
Fax: (916) 877-0573

SKBL Science Kit and Boreal Laboratories
777 East Park Drive
Tonawanda, NY 14150-6787
(800) 828-7777; Fax: (800) 828-3299
www.sciencekit.com

STI SciTech International, Inc.
5225 N. Elston Avenue, Chicago, IL 60647-2003
(800) 290-6057; Fax: (733) 486-9237
www.academic@scitechint.com

SVE Society for Visual Education
6677-North Northwest Highway
Chicago, IL 60631-1304
(800) 829-1900; Fax: (800) 624-1687
www.SVEmedia.com

TF Teaching Films, Inc.
930 Pitner Avenue, Palo Alto, CA 94304

TVC Teachers Video Company
PO Box SCG-4455, Scottsdale, AZ 85261
(800) 262-8837; Fax: (602) 860-8650

UCEMC University of California Extension Media Center
2000 Center St., Fourth Floor
Berkeley, VA 94704
(510) 642-4124; Fax: (510) 643-9271

VTC Victory Technology, Inc.
793 Broadway, Sonoma, VA 95476
(888) 368-3475

VWRSP VWR Scientific Products
PO Box 5229, Buffalo Grove, IL 60089-5229
(800) 727-4367; Fax: (800) 676-2540
www.Sarwel@sargentwelch.com

WARD Ward's Biology
PO Box 92912, Rochester, NY 14692-9012
(800) 962-2660; Fax: (800) 635-8439
www.wardsic.com

WBS W.B. Saunders Co.
The Curtis Center, Independence Square West
Philadelphia, PA 19106-3399
(800) 523-1649; Fax: (215) 238-8483
wbs-support@wbsaunders.com

WCB William C. Brown Publishers
2460 Kerper Blvd., Dubuque, IA 52001

WW Williams and Wilkins
351 West Camden Street
Baltimore, MD 21201-2436
(410) 528-4000

CHAPTER 1

The Human Body: An Orientation

LECTURE AND DEMONSTRATION
Student Objectives

1. Define *anatomy* and *physiology*. Describe the subdivisions of anatomy.
2. Name (in order of increasing complexity) the different levels of structural organization that make up the human body, and explain their relationships.
3. List the organ systems of the body, and briefly state the main functions of each system.
4. Classify the levels of structural organization in the body according to relative and actual size.
5. Give an example of anatomical variation.
6. Define the anatomical position.
7. Use anatomical terminology to describe body directions, regions, and planes.
8. Describe the basic structures that humans share with other vertebrates.
9. Locate the major body cavities and their subdivisions.
10. Name the nine regions and four quadrants of the abdomen, and name the visceral organs associated with these regions.
11. Explain how human tissue is prepared and examined for its microscopic structure.
12. Distinguish tissue viewed by light microscopy from that viewed by electron microscopy.
13. Describe six medical imaging techniques used to visualize structures inside the body.

Suggested Lecture Outline

I. *An Overview of Anatomy (pp. 2–4)*

    A. Anatomical Terminology (p. 2)

    B. Branches of Anatomy (pp. 2–3)

        1. Gross Anatomy

        2. Microscopic Anatomy

        3. Other Branches of Anatomy

    C. The Hierarchy of Structural Organization (pp. 3–4, Figs. 1.1 and 1.2)

    D. Scale: What Size Is It? (p. 4)

    E. Anatomical Variability (p. 4)

II. Gross Anatomy: An Introduction (pp. 4–16)

A. The Anatomical Position (pp. 4–8, Fig. 1.3)

B. Directional and Regional Terms (pp. 8–10, Table 1.1 and Fig. 1.4)

C. Body Planes and Sections (pp. 10–12, Figs. 1.5 and 1.6)

D. The Human Body Plan (pp. 12–13, Fig. 1.7)

E. Body Cavities and Membranes (pp. 13–15), Figs. 1.8, 1.9, and 1.10)

  1. Dorsal Body Cavity

  2. Ventral Body Cavity

  3. Serous Cavities

  4. Other Cavities

F. Abdominal Regions and Quadrants (pp. 15–16, Figs. 1.11 and 1.12)

III. Microscopic Anatomy: An Introduction (pp. 16–18, Fig. 1.13)

A. Light and Electron Microscopy (pp. 16–17)

B. Preparing Human Tissue for Microscopy (pp. 17–18)

C. Scanning Electron Microscopy (p. 18)

D. Artifacts (p. 18)

IV. Clinical Anatomy: An Introduction to Medical Imaging Techniques (pp. 19–23)

A. X Rays (p. 20, Fig. 1.14)

B. Advanced X Ray Techniques: CT, CAT, DSR, Xenon CT (pp. 19–20, Fig. 1.15)

C. DSA (p. 20, Fig. 1.16)

D. PET (p. 21, Fig. 1.17)

E. Sonography (pp. 21–22, Fig. 1.18)

F. MRI (pp. 22–23, Fig. 1.19)

Lecture Hints

1. Discuss the terms *anatomy* and *physiology*. Describe how scientists use these terms.

2. Establish the significance of anatomical terminology at the beginning of the course. Students should understand they are learning a "new language" and will be successful academically only if they master this language.

3. Teach students word origins (Greek and Latin roots) as much as possible. Use terms with which they are familiar, for example: "hand" > *manus* > "manual."

4. Point out that the language of anatomy is redundant and that multiple terms exist for some anatomical structures (e.g., eustachian tube, auditory tube, pharyngotympanic tube, otopharyngeal tube). Explain that some anatomical terms are structural designations while others are functional. Finally, explain that some terms are eponyms that denote the discoverer's name (e.g., Bartholin's gland).

5. Explain to students how the terms *superior/inferior, anterior/posterior,* and *dorsal/ventral* refer to different areas for humans and four-legged animals. Point out that more than one word can be used to correctly describe the position of a structure.

6. Remind students that most body cavities are potential spaces that are filled with viscera, tissues, and fluids.

7. In addition to the dorsal and ventral body cavities, cite other cavities such as the oral cavity, the nasal cavity, and the pericardial cavity.

8. Contrast the types of images obtained with X-rays machines, CT scans, MRI scans, and ultrasonography. Show actual examples of X rays, if possible, and keep in mind the potential use of X rays to demonstrate anatomy in other chapters.

9. List five examples of anatomical structures that exhibit anatomical variation.

Classroom Discussion Topics and Activities

1. Have students discuss the relative vulnerability of the organs in the dorsal and ventral body cavities by asking, "Why do you think a dog instinctively curls over and protects its abdomen when that body region is threatened by a blow or even during play?"

2. Ask students to write down 12 body parts that consist of three letters (e.g., eye, ear, leg), referring to their text if necessary. Follow up with the anatomical term for each part (e.g., "arm"—"brachium").

3. Demonstrate preserved human specimens if available. A simple statement, "This is a heart (or kidney or brain or bone)" is all that is necessary. Ask the class what the specimens have in common. Muscles? Nerves? Blood?

4. Assume the anatomical position and ask the students how that position differs from the "usual" standing position.

5. Call out regional terms (e.g., buccal, femoral) and have the students (as a group) point out the named regions on their own bodies.

6. Placing a chair in front of the class, ask a volunteer to show how the chair would be cut along the sagittal, frontal, and transverse planes. Ask the volunteer to choose which of these planes would yield a usable seat.

7. Use a dissectible model of a human torso to point out the dorsal and ventral body cavities and the main organs in each cavity.

8. Remove all the viscera from the ventral body cavity of a model of the human torso. Ask for volunteers or assign students to return them to their proper anatomical locations. As each organ is properly repositioned, the rest of the students are to call out its name and to say which organ system it belongs to.

9. With the naked eye, view plastinated sections of the human body, which are available for purchase. Or project them on an overhead projector for viewing by the entire class.

10. Use a balloon to illustrate the two layers of the serous membrane.

11. Explain to the class how tissues are cut into thin sections. This can be explained in a general way or by obtaining a microtome and demonstrating how a paraffin-embedded rat liver is sectioned. Remind students that their glass slides possess only a small, thin slice of an organ.

12. Obtain slides to show the types of stains used for light microscopy, such as hematoxylin and eosin, Sudan black B, and methylene blue.
13. Show the class transmission electron micrographs, scanning electron micrographs, and light micrographs. Have the students explain how to tell these apart.

Clinical Questions

1. A surgeon removed a section of tissue along a transverse plane for microscopic examination. What would the section be called?

    Answer: A cross section.

2. Which medical imaging technique has been studied most extensively for its effects on human health?

    Answer: The traditional X-ray technique, because it has been used the longest. MRI and ultrasound are such new techniques that long-term studies of their effects have not yet been possible.

ART RESOURCES
Transparency List

Figure 1.1   Levels of structural complexity.

Figure 1.3   The anatomical position.

Figure 1.4   Regional terms.

Figure 1.5   Planes of the body.

Figure 1.7   Basic human body plan.

Figure 1.8   Dorsal and ventral body cavities and their subdivisions.

Figure 1.9   The serous cavities: pericardial, pleural, and peritoneal.

Figure 1.10 Other body cavities: Oral, nasal, orbital, and middle ear cavities.

Figure 1.11 Nine abdominal regions.

Figure 1.12 Four abdominal quadrants.

Teaching with Art

Figure 1.9a–d   The serous cavities: pericardial, pleural, and peritoneal.
Textbook p. 15; transparencies; Digital Archive CD-ROM.

Checklist of Key Points in the Figure

- In each part, indicate that the visceral layer is in direct contact with the surface of an organ and that the parietal layer is in contact with the body cavity.
- Comment on the function of fluid in the cavities.
- Relate the pericardium to the heart, the pleura to the lungs, and the peritoneum to the abdominal organs.

Chapter 1: *The Human Body: An Orientation* 5

- Point out that in addition to lining the abdominal cavity, the visceral peritoneum and parietal peritoneum form a framework of double-layer folds called mesenteries.

  Display Figure 22.26d, Sagittal section of abdominal cavity of a male. Demonstrate mesenteric folds.

- In (d) explain how mesenteries support abdominal organs.

Common Conceptual Difficulties Interpreting the Art

- Explain the differences between mucous membranes and serous membranes.
- Explain why the pleural and pericardial cavities are "potential spaces." Tell students that the art exaggerates the space between the membranes and that, in a healthy body, only a thin layer of fluid separates the two membranes.
- In (d) explain the difference between an abdominal and retroperitoneal organ.

  Display Figure 22.5a,b, The peritoneum and the peritoneal cavity, to demonstrate how organs become retroperitoneal. Display Figure 23.22a, Position of the kidneys within the posterior abdominal wall, for a detailed view of retroperitoneal organs.

Art Exercise

To help students understand the continuity of the parietal and visceral peritoneum, ask students to trace a continuous line around the serous membrane in (d). The same demonstration is possible using the overhead transparency with an overlay and colored marker and using the drawing tool on the Digital Archive CD-ROM.

Critical Reasoning

Pleurisy is an inflammation of the pleural layers characterized by the abnormal production of pleural fluid. Referring to Figures 1.8 and 1.9, ask students where they think the excess pleural fluid might collect.

Answer: The pleural fluid collects by gravity in the space between the diaphragm and the rib cage called the costodiaphragmatic recess. Medical professionals can extract the excess fluid using a syringe.

SUPPLEMENTAL COURSE MATERIALS
Library Research Topics

1. Research the historical development of gross anatomy.
2. Research the historical development of the techniques of microscopy and histology.

Audiovisual Aids/Computer Software

See Preface of the Instructor's Guide for Key to Audiovisual Distributors

Videotapes

1. *The Incredible Human Machine* (CBS/FSE/NGS, 60 min.)
2. *Body Atlas Series* (HCA, 13-part series, 1994)
3. *The New Living Body Series* (FHS, 10-part series, 20 min. each, 1995)
4. *An Overview of Human Anatomy: The Head and Torso* (NS, 40 min.)

Videodiscs

1. *Human Body* (NGS, 3-part series)
2. *Anatomy and Physiology Videodisc* (VI 6, 1994)
3. *The Living Body* (FSH, 1992)
4. *The Human Body: Systems Working Together* (Ward's, 16 min.)

Computer Software

1. *Body Spectrum: Mosby's Electronic Anatomy Coloring Book* (ACC, Disk for Mac/Win)
2. *The Human Body, Part I* (CL, Disk for Apple II/Mac/IBM)
3. *The Human Body, Part II* (CL, Disk for Apple II/Mac/IBM)
4. *The Human Body: An Overview* (CA, BW100, Apple). Graphic view of the systems of the human body.
5. *Human Systems* (EI, C4350, Apple). Review of the body systems.

CD-ROMs

1. *A.D.A.M. Interactive Anatomy* (CBS/CYB, Mac/Win)
2. *A.D.A.M. Essentials* (CBS/CYB/CL, Mac/Win)
3. *A.D.A.M. Practice Practical* (CBS/CYB, Mac/Win)
4. *Anatomical Charts on CD-ROM* (HCA, Mac/Win)
5. *Body Works* (CL/Ward's, Mac/Win)
6. *The Dissectible Human* (ACC/IM, Mac/Win 1996)
7. *The Human Body* (Queue, Win)
8. *Super Anatomy I* (Queue, Win)

Suggested Readings

Appenzeller, T. (Editor) A call for better EMF studies. (An article that considers dangers of MRI scans.) *Science* 253 (July 26, 1991): 371.

Beard, J. Computer maps guide the surgeon. *New Scientist* (March 30, 1991): 37–39.

Birnholz, J.C., and E. Farrell. Ultrasound images of human fetal development. *American Scientist* 72 (1984): 608–613.

Cahill, D.R. *Lachman's Case Studies in Anatomy.* 4th ed. New York: Oxford University Press, 1997.

Clemente, C.D. *Anatomy: A Regional Atlas of the Human Body.* 4th ed. Baltimore: Williams and Wilkins, 1997.

Decker, C. Vibration imaging: Sounding out tumors. *Science News* 137 (March 31, 1990): 196.

Dunning, A. Lessons from the dead. (An article on autopsy.) *New Scientist* (January 30, 1993): 44–47.

Geller, S.A. Autopsy. *Scientific American* 248 (March 1983): 124–129.

Johns Hopkins University. MRI, the movie. *Breakthroughs in Health and Science* (February 1991): 58.

Moore, K.L., and Arthur F. Dalley, II. *Clinically Oriented Anatomy.* 4th ed. Philadelphia: Lippincott Williams and Wilkins, 1999.

Morris, D. *The Naked Ape.* New York: McGraw-Hill Book Company, 1968.

Smith, C.E. Abdominal assessment, a blending of science and art. *Nursing* 11 (February 1981): 42–49.

Snell, R.S. *Atlas of Clinical Anatomy.* Boston: Little, Brown & Company, 1978.

Spitzer, V.M., and D. Whitlock. High resolution electronic imaging of the human body. *Journal of Biological Photography* 60 (October 1992): 167–172.

Taylor, D.L., et al. New vision of light microscopy. *American Scientist* 80 (July-August 1992): 322.

Webb, J. Fast scanner spots unhealthy hearts. *New Scientist* (September 14, 1991): 26.

Wilson, D.B., and J.W. Wilson. *Human Anatomy.* 2nd ed. New York: Oxford University Press, 1983.

Woodburne, R.T. *Essentials of Human Anatomy.* 9th ed. New York: Oxford University Press, 1994.

ANSWERS TO TEXTBOOK QUESTIONS

Answers for multiple-choice and matching questions 1–11 are located in Appendix B of the textbook.

Short Answer and Essay Questions

12. In the anatomical position the body stands erect, the arms hang at the sides, the palms face anteriorly, the thumbs point away from the trunk, and the feet are flat on the ground with toes forward. It is necessary to use this standard position because most directional terms refer to the body in this position, regardless of its actual position. (p. 8)

13. The electron micrograph (1) provides a sharper image at higher magnification and (2) is always in black and white. The light micrograph, by contrast, will be colored because the stains for light microscopy are colored dyes. (If you see a light micrograph in black and white, it merely means that the colored tissue has been photographed with black and white film.) (p. 10)

14. (a) Bilateral symmetry means that the structures on the right half of the body are essentially mirror images of those in the left half. (b) Examples of segmentation in the human are the repeating vertebrae of the vertebral column, the many pairs of nerves from the spinal cord, the ribs, and the muscles between the ribs. Note that all these are repeating units along the length of the body. (c) Dissection is exposing the internal structures of the body, mostly by removing the connective tissue that holds adjacent organs together. (pp. 2–12)

15. (a) Only CT uses X rays. (b) MRI uses magnetic fields and radio waves. (c) PET uses radioisotopes. (d) CT, PET, sonography, and MRI display body regions in sections; DSA, which is based on traditional X-ray images, does not use sections. (pp. 19–23)

16. (a) arm–brachium. (b) chest–thorax. (c) groin–inguinal region. (d) armpit–axilla. (Figure 1.4)

17. All the photos were taken through a light microscope. This is demonstrated by the fact that they are colored. Also, they show many cells grouped into tissues, so they are low-magnification pictures—the specialty of light microscopy. (pp. 16–18)

18. Liver, stomach, intestines, pancreas, spleen.

19. Here are some examples: The toes are inferior to the knee. The back of the neck is dorsal to the nose. The navel is ventral to the buttocks. The loin is medial to the upper extremity. The

thumb is lateral to the little finger. The skin is superficial to almost everything. The intestines are deep to the ventral body cavity.

20. Here are some examples: abdominal cavity—small intestine, stomach, liver; pelvic cavity—bladder, some sex organs, rectum. (pp 13–16)

Critical Reasoning and Clinical Applications Questions

1. MRI is very effective at peering through bones and at distinguishing tumors from surrounding tissues on the basis of their water content. (CT scans also are used to find tumors.) (p.22)

2. The abdominal organs are susceptible to injury because the walls of the abdomen are not protected by bone as are the thoracic organs (by ribs) and the pelvis (protected by the hip bones). In the automobile accident described here, the seat belts squeezed the children's abdominal viscera upon impact, harming these organs. (p. 13)

3. The inguinal region is the groin, or most inferior part of the anterior abdomen just above the thigh. The lumbar region is the loin or back of the abdomen. The perineum is the region around the anus and external genitalia. (p. 10)

4. The axillary region is the armpit. The coxal region is the hip. The sacral region is in the lower back between the hips. The acromial region is the top point of the shoulder. The peroneal region is the lateral part of the leg (lower leg). (p. 10)

5. The spinal column and spine are the same thing (i.e., the bony vertebral column). The spinal cord, by contrast, is the nerve cord that runs through the dorsal part of the vertebral column.

SUPPLEMENTAL STUDENT MATERIALS TO HUMAN ANATOMY, THIRD EDITION

Chapter 1: The Human Body: An Orientation

To the Student

The concepts in this chapter will orient you to the human body and introduce you to the science of anatomy. Mastering the vocabulary in this chapter will help you to understand basic anatomical relationships and help you to communicate effectively with anatomists and those working in the health care professions.

Step 1: Learn the organ systems of the human body.

- ☐ Name the 12 basic organ systems.
- ☐ Give examples of organs for each system.
- ☐ Which organ systems are located in the head? Thorax? Abdominal cavity? Lower extremity?
- ☐ Do you perceive one system as more important than another? Why or why not?

Step 2: Master the professional vocabulary of the science of anatomy.

- ☐ Describe how a man sitting with hands on his lap moves his body into anatomical position.
- ☐ Using the regional terms and names of specific body areas in Figure 1.4, write comparative statements for the following directional terms: superior/inferior, anterior/posterior, ventral/dorsal, medial/lateral, and proximal/distal. (e.g., "The fingers are distal to the shoulders.")
- ☐ Demonstrate the difference between frontal, transverse, and sagittal planes using your own body.
- ☐ Make vocabulary flash cards.
- ☐ Make copies of text figures without labels for review and test preparation.

Note: Your instructor can print any illustration in the text (except photomicrographs) without labels using the Digital Archive CD-ROM that comes with the instructor's copy of the textbook.

Step 3: Differentiate the major and minor body cavities.

- ☐ Name two major body cavities.
- ☐ List the subdivisions of each cavity.
- ☐ Name the organs associated with each subdivision.
- ☐ Referring to Figure 1.8, identify the distinctive structure that separates the abdominal cavity. from the thoracic cavity.
- ☐ Relate serous membranes and fluids to the subdivisions of the ventral body cavity,
- ☐ Name five minor (smaller) cavities. Which ones are located in the head? Which one has a specialized fluid associated with it?

CHAPTER 2
Cells: The Living Units

LECTURE AND DEMONSTRATION
Student Objectives

1. Define a *cell*, its basic activities, and its three major regions.
2. Describe the composition and basic functions of the plasma membrane.
3. Explain how various molecules move across the plasma membrane.
4. Describe the cytosol.
5. Discuss mitochondria.
6. Compare the structure and function of ribosomes and the endoplasmic reticulum.
7. Describe how the Golgi apparatus relates to the rough endoplasmic reticulum.
8. Compare lysosomes with peroxisomes.
9. Describe the cytoskeleton.
10. Describe the centrosome and centrioles, and explain how they relate to microtubules.
11. Explain the structure of glycogen granules and lipid droplets.
12. Outline the structure and function of the nuclear envelope, chromatin, and the nucleolus.
13. List the phases of the cell life cycle, and describe a key event of each phase.
14. Name some specific cell types, and relate their overall shape to their special functions.
15. Compare theories of cell differentiation and aging.

Suggested Lecture Outline

I. Introduction to Cells (pp. 28–29)

II. The Plasma Membrane (pp. 29–34)

    A. Structure (pp. 29–30), Fig. 2.2)

    B. Functions (pp. 30–33), Figs. 2.3 and 2.4)

III. The Cytoplasm (pp. 34–42)

    A. Cytosol (Cytoplasmic Matrix) (p. 33)

    B. Cytoplasmic Organelles (pp. 33–41, Figs. 2.5–2.16)

        1. Mitochondria

        2. Ribosomes

III. THE CYTOPLASM *(continued)*

    3. Endoplasmic Reticulum

    4. Golgi Apparatus

    5. Lysosomes

    6. Peroxisomes

    7. Cytoskeleton

    8. Centrosome and Centrioles

    9. Vaults

    10. Cytoplasmic Inclusions

IV. The Nucleus (pp. 42–45, Figs. 2.17–2.19)

A. Nuclear Envelope (p. 42)

B. Chromatin and Chromosomes (pp. 42–45)

C. Nucleoli (p. 45)

V. The Cell Life Cycle (pp. 45–48, Figs. 2.20 and 2.21)

A. Interphase (p. 45)

B. Cell Division (pp. 45–48))

    1. Mitosis

    2. Cytokinesis

VI. Cellular Diversity (pp. 48–52)

VII. Developmental Aspects of Cells (pp. 52–53)

A. Youth (p. 52)

B. Aging (pp. 52–53)

Lecture Hints

1. Explain why the cell in Figure 2.1 is described as a "generalized" cell. Emphasize that many body cells have a different structure. (Example: Mature red blood cells are *anucleate*, and skeletal muscle cells are *multinucleate*.)

2. Display slides of electron micrographs to augment text diagrams. Comment on preparation of animal tissues for microscopy and on different types of microscopes.

3. Relate the function of the plasma membrane to its location at the interface between the cell's interior and exterior.

4. Explain diffusion and osmosis. Comment on how diffusion and osmosis differ from active transport mechanisms, such as exocytosis, endocytosis, and phagocytosis.

5. Explain the nature of cytoplasm and make distinctions between cytosol, cytoplasmic organelles, and inclusions.

6. Present a summary list of cellular organelles, and briefly comment on functions of each organelle.

Chapter 2: *Cells: The Living Units*   13

7. Explain the role of mitochondria as the source of most cellular energy. Refer to Figure 2.7.
8. Relate a molecule of glucose (food energy) to ATP production.
9. Using specific cellular examples, comment on why some cells have larger numbers of mitochondria and some have fewer mitochondria.
10. Discuss protein synthesis within cells. Refer to Figure 2.10.
11. Correlate the role of the nucleus as the source of information for protein synthesis with the ribosome as the site of protein synthesis and the Golgi apparatus as the site of packaging and delivery of proteins within cells.
12. Trace the flow of membrane components from the rough ER to the plasma membrane to explain why the rough ER is considered the cell's "membrane factory."
13. List components of the cytoskeleton.
14. Explain how the various elements of the cell's skeleton differ from one another in structure and function.
15. Explain the role of the nucleus as the control center of the cell.
16. Explain the importance of DNA.
17. Point out the relationship of the nuclear envelope to rough ER.
18. Explain differences between chromatin and chromosomes.
19. Point out the difference between *nucleus* and *nucleolus*.
20. Emphasize the cell cycle as a continuous process using the stages as discrete events.
21. Contrast cellular changes during interphase with changes during mitosis.
22. Ask students why telophase is the reverse of prophase.
23. Explain cytokinesis.
24. Point out that mitosis is possible without cytokinesis, using multinucleated skeletal muscle cells for an example.
25. Make sure students understand the difference between genes, chromosomes, DNA, and proteins.
26. Introduce the concept of cellular diversity by relating the shape of a cell to the function of a cell. Figure 2.22 is excellent for this concept.
27. Pique students' interest by discussing topics such as the cell biology of cancer or theories on aging.

Classroom Discussion Topics and Activities

1. Ask students to explain how the plasma membrane is structurally like a chocolate bar with almonds.
2. To explore the fat-protein composition of the plasma membrane, tell students that chloroform, ether, and most anesthetics are fat-soluble substances. Ask them to explain why this chemical characteristic is important to the health professional.
3. Ask students to name common examples of diffusion, osmosis and filtration.
4. Use a plastic model of an animal cell to demonstrate the various organelles and other cell features.

5. Instruct students to list all parts of a generalized cell that are involved in the following functions: respiration, digestion, excretion, transportation, reproduction, food acquirement, energy production, protein formation, and internal support.

6. Instruct the students to construct a chart that lists the membrane-bound organelles in one column, and in another column, the organelles that are not membrane-bound.

7. Use a stack of envelopes to demonstrate the cisterns of the rough endoplasmic reticulum. Paste spherical beads to the external sides of the envelopes to represent the ribosomes.

8. Use a Slinky™ to demonstrate the helical nature of DNA. Demonstrate the relationship between chromatin and the chromosome states by stretching or tightly coiling the Slinky™

9. Beginning with a typical diploid human body cell containing 46 chromosomes, have students identify the number of chromosomes and chromatids present in each stage of mitosis.

10. Use models of chromosomes with detachable chromatids to illustrate mitotic phases. (Make simple models using strands of colored yarn with sewn on snaps or colored pipe cleaners.)

11. Assign the following questions to be answered at the next class meeting:
    a. Why is damage to the heart or brain more damaging than injury to the liver?
    b. Why is precise division of the chromosomes during metaphase of mitosis so important?
    c. Is mitosis without cytokinesis possible? What would be the result?

12. Discuss why certain body cells (e.g., muscle and nerve cells) "lost" their ability to divide.

13. Ask students why they survive despite loss of billions of cells daily.

14. Discuss whether scientific advances will ever be able to greatly extend the human life span.

15. Ask students to consider possibilities of growing organs from "scratch." What ethical issues of tissue engineering and regenerative medicine are involved? Supplemental video: *Spare Parts: Growing Human Organs* (FHS, 26 min., 2000)

Clinical Questions

1. A patient receiving treatment for testicular cancer was told that the chemotherapy drug he received inhibits the division of cancer cells. What could the drug be, and how would it stop cell division?

   Answer: One chemotherapy drug considered in this chapter, vinblastine, inhibits the formation of microtubules and mitotic spindles required for cell division. Since cancer cells divide rapidly, the drug will preferentially affect these cells. Unfortunately, normal cells that divide rapidly will also be affected.

2. A small boy received a cut on his arm and his mother applied hydrogen peroxide to the wound. The wound bubbled! Why?

   Answer: The hydrogen peroxide was degraded to water and oxygen (which bubbled off) by the action of the intracellular enzymes in peroxisomes. (Bacteria in the cut produce a similar enzyme.)

Chapter 2: *Cells: The Living Units* 15

ART RESOURCES
Transparency List

Figure 2.1   Structure of a generalized cell.
Figure 2.2   The plasma membrane.
Figure 2.3   Exocytosis.
Figure 2.4   Phagocytosis and pinocytosis.
Figure 2.5   Receptor-mediated endocytosis.
Figure 2.7   Mitochondria.
Figure 2.8   Ribosomes.
Figure 2.9   Endoplasmic reticulum.
Figure 2.10   Assembly of proteins at rough endoplasmic reticulum.
Figure 2.11   Golgi apparatus.
Figure 2.12   Role of Golgi apparatus in packaging products of the rough endoplasmic reticulum.
Figure 2.14   Cytoskeleton.
Figure 2.15   Centrosome and centrioles.
Figure 2.16   Vaults.
Figure 2.17   Nucleus.
Figure 2.18   Molecular structure of DNA.
Figure 2.20   Cell cycle.
Figure 2.21   Stages of mitosis.
Figure 2.22   Cellular diversity.

Teaching with Art

Figure 2.2   The plasma membrane.
Figure 2.3   Exocytosis.
Figure 2.4   Phagocytosis and pinocytosis.
Textbook pp. 29–31; transparencies; Digital Archive CD-ROM.

Checklist of Key Points in the Figure
- Explain the "fluid" nature of the fluid mosaic model.
- Explain why the fluid mosaic model is a "mosaic."
- Define *intracellular* fluid and *extracellular* fluid.
- Correlate Figures 2.2, 2.3, and 2.4 to differentiate bulk transport concepts, exocytosis, and endocytosis.
- Illustrate the importance of phagocytosis using white blood cells.
- Illustrate exocytosis with the production of salty, protein-containing solution by cells in tear glands when weeping occurs.

Common Conceptual Difficulties Interpreting the Art

- Remind students that Figure 2.2 focuses on the molecular level.
- Parts are recycled and reused.
- Energy is required. Where does it come from?
- Point out relationship of plasma membrane to vesicle formation during endocytosis and exocytosis.

Art Exercise

Using Figure 2.4 for reference, instruct students to represent phagocytosis with a simple drawing. Follow a highlighted segment of plasma membrane to its incorporation into a phagosome. Add lysosomes to the drawing. Ask students where the highlighted membrane finally ends up. A similar demonstration is possible using Figure 2.4 with an overlay and colored marker or using the drawing tool on the Digital Archive CD-ROM.

Critical Reasoning

Ask students why lymph nodes become swollen and tender when there is an infection in the body.

Answer: Lymphocytes are white blood cells that fight infections in the body. A swollen node means a proliferation of lymphocytes and is evidence of the body's fight against infection.

SUPPLEMENTAL COURSE MATERIALS
Library Research Topics

1. Can protein molecules move within the cell membrane? What research supports your findings?
2. Receptor-mediated endocytosis is a highly selective mechanism to ingest molecules. How can it be used to kill cancer cells?
3. Do chemical carcinogens cause all cancers? What other things cause cancer?
4. Review the evidence for and against the theory that mitochondria evolved from bacteria that came to live within primitive eukaryotic cells.
5. Read about the newest research on aging.
6. Research current use of tissue engineering and regenerative medicine.

Audiovisual Aids/Computer Software

See Preface of the Instructor's Guide for Key to Audiovisual Distributors

Slides

1. *Chromosome Movement and Structure Sets* (CBS, 48-1145, 48-1147)
2. *Inside the Cell: Microstructures, Mechanisms, and Molecules Set* (CBS, 48-1127B)
3. *Membrane Set* (CBS, 48-1143A)
4. *Whitefish Mitosis Set* (CBS, 48-1132)

Videotapes

1. *Aging* (*Living Body Series*) (FHS, 28 min., 1991)
2. *An Introduction to Cells* (EI, 60 min.)

Chapter 2: *Cells: The Living Units* 17

3. *An Introduction to the Living Cell* (FHS/CBS, 30 min., 1996)
4. *An Introduction to Living Cells* (IM, 20 min., 1992)
5. *Apoptosis: Cell Death and Cancer* (FHS, 51 min.)
6. *Cancer and Metastasis* (FHS, 37 min.)
7. *Cell Functions: A Closer Look* (FHS, 25 min., 1998)
8. *Cells: An Introduction* (FHS, 25 min., 1998)
9. *Cells: The Basic Units of Life* (HCA/CAP, 23 min., 1994)
10. *Cell Division* (FHS, 15 min.)
11. *The Cell* (FHS, 15 min.)
12. *The Cell* (*Anatomy and Physiology Series*) (HCA/CAP, 28 min.)
13. *The Cell, Part I* (IM, 32 min., 1996)
14. *The Cell, Part II* (IM, 38 min., 1996)
15. *The Structure of the Cell* (CAP/NS, 20 min.)
16. *Understanding Cells* (IM, 3-part series)
17. *Diffusion and Osmosis.* 2nd ed. (EBEC, 14 min.)
18. *DNA: Replication and Mitosis* (FREY, 14 min.)
19. *Mitosis* (HRM, 11 min.)
20. *Mitosis.* 2nd ed. (EBEC, 14 min.)
21. *Proteins* (FHS, 34 min.)
22. *Protein Synthesis* (IM, 18 min., 1990)
23. *Spare Parts: Growing Human Organs* (FHS, 26 min., 2000)

Videodiscs

1. *Aging* (*Living Body Series*) (FHS, 28 min., 1992)
2. *Visualizing Cell Processes* (CBS, 5-part series, 61 min., each)

Computer Software

1. *Mitosis* (EI, C-3025, Apple)
2. *Nucleic Acids* (CBS, 39-8792, Apple)
3. *Protein Synthesis* (CBS, 39-8791A, Apple)

CD-ROMs

1. *The Cell: Examination, Structure and Function* (HCA/CAP, Mac/Win)
2. *Cell Biology, Part 1* (IM, Mac/Win, 1995)
3. *Cell Biology, Part 2* (IM, Mac/Win, 1995)
4. *Cell Biology on CD-ROM, Part 1* (IM/NS, Mac/Win)
5. *Cell Biology on CD-ROM, Part 2* (NS, Mac/Win)
6. *Cell Biology: Complete* (CL, 2 parts, Mac/Win)
7. *Cell Division I: Mitosis, Cell Cycle and Cell Anatomy* (CL, Mac/Win)
8. *Cell Structure and Function* (CAP/CBS/IM, Mac/Win, 1996)
9. *Cell Processes* (IM, Mac/Win, 1997)

Suggested Readings

Alberts, B., et al. *Molecular Biology of the Cell.* 3rd ed. New York: Garland, 1994.

Beardsley, T. Trends in cancer epidemiology: A war not won. *Scientific American* 270 (January 1994): 130–138.

Begley, S., et al. The search for the fountain of youth. *Newsweek* (March 5, 1990): 44–48.

Cavenee, W., and R. White. The genetic basis of cancer. *Scientific American* (March 1995): 72–79.

Cormack, D.H. *Ham's Histology.* 9th ed. Philadelphia: J.B. Lippincott, 1988.

Duke, R.C., D.M. Ojciuis, and J.D.E. Young. Cell suicide in health and disease. *Scientific American* (December 1996).

Fuchs E., and D.W. Cleveland. A structural scaffolding of intermediate filaments in health and disease. *Science* 279 (January 23, 1998): 514–519.

Garavito, R.M., and S.H. White. Membrane proteins. Structure, assembly, and function: a panoply of progress. *Curr Opin Struct Biol* 7 (August 1997): 533–6.

Glick, B.S., and V. Malhotra. The curious status of the Golgi apparatus. *Cell* 95 (December 23, 1998): 883–889.

Goldstein, L., and R. Vale. Motor proteins: A brave new world for dynein. *Nature* 352 (August 15, 1991): 569–570.

Gore, R., et al. The awesome worlds within a cell. *National Geographic* 150 (September 1976): 355–395.

Gourret, J.P. Modelling the mitotic apparatus. *Acta Biotheoretica* 43 (1995): 127–142.

Hartwell, L. and M. Kasten. Cell cycle control and cancer. *Science* 266 (December 16, 1994): 1821–1828.

Hunt, A.J. Molecular motors. Keeping the beat. *Nature* 393 (June 18, 1998): 624–625.

Kabnick, K., and D. Peattie. Giardia: A missing link between prokaryotes and eukaryotes. (Article on the origin of organelles and the nucleus.) *American Scientist* 79 (January-February 1991): 34.

Kiester, E. A bug in the system. (Functions and diseases of mitochondria.) *Discover* 12 (February 1991): 70–76.

Kipling, D., and R.G. Faragher. Telomeres: Ageing hard or hardly ageing? *Nature* 398 (March 18, 1999): 191, 193.

Manuelidis, L. A view of interphase chromosomes. *Science* 250 (December 14, 1990): 1533.

Marx, J.L. Learning how to suppress cancer. *Science* 261 (September 10, 1993): 1385–1387.

Mitchison, T.J. Mitosis. The kinetochore in captivity. *Nature* 348 (November 1, 1990): 14–15.

Mitchison, T.J., and L.P. Cramer. Actin-based cell motility and cell locomotion. *Cell* 84 (February 9, 1996): 371–379.

Murray, A.W., and M.W. Kirschner. What controls the cell cycle? *Scientific American* (March 1991).

Murray, M. Life on the move. *Discover* 12 (March 1991): 72–75.

Nash, J.M. Stopping cancer in its tracks. *Time* (April 25, 1994): 54–61.

Raloff, J. Searching out how a severe diet slows aging. *Science News* 140 (October 5, 1991): 215.

Rusting, R. Why do we age? *Scientific American* 267 (December 1992): 131–141.

Schliwa, M. Molecular motors join forces. *Nature* 397 (January 21, 1999): 204–205.

Scientific American Special Issue. What you need to know about cancer. (September 1996).

Seddon, J., and R. Templer. Liquid crystals and the living cell. (Article on the plasma membrane.) *New Scientist* (May 18, 1991): 45–49.

Spudich, J. How molecular motors work. *Nature* 372 (December 8, 1994): 515–518.

Stossel, T. The machinery of cell crawling. *Scientific American* 271 (September 1994): 54–63.

Suh, Y.A., et al. Cell transformation by the superoxide-generating oxidase Mox1. *Nature* 401 (September 2, 1999): 79–82.

Surridge, C. Molecular motors. Spotting the goods trains. *Nature* 402 (December 9, 1999): 598.

Thweatt, R., and S. Goldstein. Werner syndrome and biological ageing: A molecular genetic hypothesis. *Bioessays* 15 (June 1993): 421–426.

Tomatis, L. (Editor) *Cancer: Causes, Occurrence, and Control.* Oxford University Press, 1991, 368 pages.

Vallee, R. Chromosome kinetics: Movement on two fronts. *Nature* 351 (May 16, 1991): 187–188, 206.

Watts, A. Membrane structure and dynamics. *Curr Opin Cell Biol* 1 (August 1989): 691–700.

ANSWERS TO TEXTBOOK QUESTIONS

Answers for multiple-choice and matching questions 1–13 are located in Appendix B of the textbook.

Short Answer and Essay Questions

14. This sugar coat on the exterior of cells, called the cell coat or glycocalyx, may help bind adjacent cells together. Also, since different cell types have distinct glycocalyces, they act as markers by which cells recognize one another in cell-to-cell interactions. (p. 30)

15. Membrane-lined organelles: mitochondria, rough ER (and nuclear envelope), smooth ER, Golgi apparatus, lysosomes, and peroxisomes (nucleus too). Organelles that have no membrane: centrioles and centrosomes, microtubules, microfilaments, intermediate filaments, and vaults. (p. 40)

16. A nucleolus is a dark-staining structure within a nucleus, much smaller than the nucleus itself. While the nucleus contains many chromosomes, the nucleolus consists of parts of several of these chromosomes that work together to manufacture the basic subunits of ribosomes. (p. 45)

17. (a) In chemotherapy, chemicals that kill cancer cells are administered to the cancer patient. (b) These chemicals target and destroy the most rapidly dividing cells in the body, which do include cancer cells. Unfortunately, the chemicals also destroy normal cells that divide rapidly (those that produce hair, blood cells, and the lining of the digestive tube). (c) Therefore, the side effects of chemotherapy are loss of hair, depression in the number of blood cells, and disruption of digestion (vomiting and nausea). (p. 50)

18. Lysosomal enzymes break down "large biochemical molecules," meaning organic macromolecules. Lysosomes also digest much larger things such as bacteria, worn-out organelles, and

even entire phagocytized cells. Peroxisome enzymes, by contrast, act on free radicals and hydrogen peroxide, which are small molecules. These enzymes also detoxify chemicals such as formaldehyde, phenol, and alcohol, which are small molecules. (p. 38)

19. Mitochondria are the only organelles that have a complex, double-unit membrane, and their own DNA and genes. (Although it was not mentioned, mitochondria also contain their own ribosomes and RNA.) (p. 33)

20. A chromosome is one of 46 long, single molecules of DNA (with the associated protein) in the nucleus of typical human cells. When a cell is dividing, its chromosomes are maximally coiled, so they appear as thick rods. In nondividing cells, the chromosomes are partially uncoiled for transcription (see Figure 2.19).

Critical Reasoning and Clinical Applications Questions

1. Experiments on rats and other animals indicate that slightly underweight and undernourished animals have prolonged life spans. (p. 52)

2. It is lung cancer. As stated in *A Closer Look* (pp. 50–51), lung cancer is the second most common type of cancer, after skin cancer. Since skin cancer is usually curable and lung cancer is seldom curable, lung cancer causes the most cancer deaths.

3. *Hyperplasia* means the cells have proliferated into a thick layer of structurally normal cells; *dysplasia* means that a few of the cells show abnormal size or shape; *lack of neoplasia* means that the cells were not proliferating uncontrollably (no tumor or cancer was evident). Therefore, Kareem did not have cancer of the mouth. (p. 53)

4. G1, S, G2, and M are all phases of the cell life cycle (Figure 2.20). G1 is a growth phase followed by S, the phase in which DNA is replicated in preparation for cell division. G2 is when the final preparations for cell division are made, and M is the mitotic phase leading to division of the nucleus. Clearly, the tumor-suppressor genes are halting various phases of the cell life cycle in precancer cells that would otherwise multiply uncontrollably. (p. 45)

5. Peroxisomes. (p. 39)

SUPPLEMENTAL STUDENT MATERIALS TO HUMAN ANATOMY, THIRD EDITION
Chapter 2: Cells: The Living Units

To the Student

It is essential to understand the cell as the structural and functional unit of all living things. The human body has 50 to 60 trillion cells consisting of some 200 different types that are amazingly diverse in size, shape, and function. Mastery of basic knowledge of the cell leads to fuller understanding and comprehension of tissues, organs, organ systems, and ultimately, the human organism.

Step 1: Learn basic concepts about cells.

- ☐ Define a *cell*.
- ☐ List three major regions of a "generalized" animal cell.
- ☐ Indicate the general function of each region.

Step 2: Correlate plasma membrane structure and function.

- ☐ Describe the composition of the plasma membrane.
- ☐ Relate the composition of the plasma membrane to the movement of substances in and out of the cell.
- ☐ Differentiate between passive and active transport mechanisms.
- ☐ Describe transport processes relative to energy source, substances transported, direction of movement, and mechanisms.

Step 3: Summarize basic structural and functional relationships about the cytoplasm.

- ☐ Describe the composition of the cytosol.
- ☐ List ten organelles, including vaults and inclusions, found in the cytosol.
- ☐ Define *inclusions* and list several kinds.
- ☐ Explain the structure and function of mitochondria.
- ☐ Explain the structure, function, and interrelationships of ribosomes, the endoplasmic reticulum, and the Golgi apparatus.
- ☐ Compare the functions of lysosomes and peroxisomes.
- ☐ Name and describe the structure and function of cytoskeletal elements.

Step 4: Summarize basic structural and functional relationships about the nucleus.

- ☐ Describe the structure and function of the nuclear envelope.
- ☐ Explain the structure and function of chromatin.
- ☐ Explain the structure and function of a nucleolus.

Step 5: Understand events of cell growth and reproduction.
- ☐ List the phases of the cell cycle.
- ☐ Describe the events of each phase.
- ☐ Explain the significance of interphase.

Step 6: Recognize cell diversity.
- ☐ Name specific cell types.
- ☐ Relate the shapes of different cell types to the functions of the cells.

CHAPTER 3
Basic Embryology

LECTURE AND DEMONSTRATION
Student Objectives

1. List the practical and clinical reasons for studying embryology.
2. Distinguish the embryonic period from the fetal period of development.
3. Sketch the basic structural plan of the adult body, which is established during the embryonic period.
4. Describe the earliest stage of development from zygote to blastocyst (week 1).
5. Describe how the embryo becomes a two-layered disc (week 2).
6. Explain gastrulation and the formation of the three germ layers (week 3).
7. Discuss how the body folds from a flat disc into its three-dimensional, tubular shape (week 4).
8. List the main derivatives of each germ layer.
9. Describe the main events of the second month of development.
10. List the major events of fetal development.

Suggested Lecture Outline

I. Introduction to Embryology and Basic Body Plan (pp. 58–59, Fig. 3.1 and 3.2)

II. The Embryonic Period (pp. 59–68)

    A. Week 1: From Zygote to Blastocyst (pp. 59–61, Figs. 3.3 and 3.4a,b)

    B. Week 2: The Two-Layered Embryo (p. 61, Fig. 3.4c–e)

    C. Week 3: The Three-Layered Embryo (pp. 62–65, Figs. 3.5–3.7)

        1. The Primitive Streak and the Three Germ Layers

        2. The Notochord

        3. Neurulation

        4. The Mesoderm Begins to Differentiate

    D. Week 4: The Body Takes Shape (pp. 66–67, Table 3.1, Figs. 3.8 and 3.9)

        1. Folding

        2. Derivatives of the Germ Layers

    E. Weeks 5–8: The Second Month of Embryonic Development (p. 68, Fig.3.10)

III. The Fetal Period (pp. 68–72, Table 3.2, Fig. 3.11)

Lecture Hints

1. Distinguish between the embryonic period and fetal period of development.
2. Compare spermatogenesis and oogenesis.
3. Define *zygote, morula*, and *blastocyst*.
4. Explain the process of fertilization and implantation.
5. Contrast the relative importance of the yolk sac and amniotic sac.
6. Distinguish between monozygotic (*identical*) and dizygotic (*fraternal*) twins.
7. Correlate the basic adult body plan to the three embryonic germ layers.
8. Give examples of major derivatives of the embryonic germ layers.
9. Describe the notochord and explain neurulation.
10. Using Figure 1.7 a, b, and c, point out similarities and differences in the basic body plan between animals and humans.
11. Explain programmed cell death (apoptosis) as a natural part of development.
12. Display Figure 24.10b, Female internal reproductive organs: Midsagittal section, and Figure 24.27, Stages of labor, for uterine size comparison. Point out that a nonpregnant human uterus is approximately 3"×2"×1" and increases in size about 200-fold during pregnancy.
13. Characterize the complex nature of developmental controls.
14. Discuss the structure of the placenta, and discuss which substances readily pass from maternal to fetal blood (e.g., infectious agents, drugs, alcohol, and antibodies).
15. Summarize the human life cycle using the developmental stages of fertilization, cleavage, gastrulation, formation of tissues, organogenesis, and growth, including tissue specialization.

Classroom Discussion Topics and Activities

1. Use embryonic-fetal development models to show cleavage, the blastula, and other stages of development.
2. Show preserved specimens of human embryos or fetuses in various stages of development to illustrate the changes that occur during gestation.
3. Exhibit preserved animal fetuses obtained from a biological supply house.
4. Open a raw egg and point out the small white disc on the yolk as the part of the egg where cleavage occurs.
5. To model the embryonic disc, shape clay into three thin discs: blue clay = ectoderm; red clay = mesoderm; yellow clay = endoderm. Bend the flat disc into the shape of a cylinder (and a tadpole) to show how the body takes shape during the fourth week of development. (Figure 3.8 on p. 66)
6. Bring pieces of pocket (pita) bread to class. (Pocket bread consists of two disc-shaped layers of bread with a space in-between.) Then fill the pocket bread with red jelly to demonstrate how the mesoderm comes to lie in the center of the embryonic disc.
7. Have each student blow up a blue and a yellow balloon. Push the two balloons together so they touch, forming a disc-shaped region. Explain that the blue balloon is the amniotic sac, the yellow balloon is the yolk sac, and the disc formed by the intersection of the balloons represents the bilaminar embryonic disc during the second week of development.

8. Display a sonogram of a fetus for the class.
9. List several features that form early in embryonic development and later in development are lost or converted to new structures (e.g., tail > coccyx).
10. Ask students to compare the similarities and differences of the human life cycle with other animals. Include plants as well if you feel adventurous.
11. Assign the book *A Child is Born*, by Lennart Nilsson, (Dell Publications, revised edition, 1986) as required reading.
12. Discuss the need for sexually active females of childbearing age, whether practicing contraception or not, to maintain a life-style that will enhance, not harm, the developing embryo and fetus should the woman become pregnant. Then list the things a pregnant woman should and should not do.

Clinical Questions

1. Natasha's mother told a neighbor that Natasha was "pregnant in her tubes." Explain what she means. Will Natasha give birth at the end of this pregnancy?

    Answer: The embryo has implanted in one of her uterine tubes, rather than in the wall of the uterus. No placenta can be established, and without treatment, the tube will rupture and cause severe internal bleeding. Tubal pregnancies do not come to term.

2. Lamar and Lamont were twin brothers, and Lorinda and Belinda were twin sisters. Each pair of twins looked alike at birth, but as the boys grew older it became clear that they did not look any more alike than typical siblings; the girls, however, remained so similar that people mixed them up. Explain the differences between the two sets of twins and explain how each act of twinning occurred during embryonic development.

    Answer: The boys are fraternal (dizygotic) twins, meaning their mother released two eggs that were fertilized by two sperm. The girls are identical (monozygotic) twins, meaning that a single morula or blastocyst split into two during the first week of embryonic development.

3. List the four most common types of congenital defects and briefly explain them in your own words.

    Answer: See the table on p. 70 in A Closer Look on birth defects.

ART RESOURCES
Transparency List

Figure 3.1	Prenatal period: embryos and fetuses of different stages.
Figure 3.2	Adult human body plan.
Figure 3.3	Fertilization and events of first 6 days of development.
Figure 3.4	Implantation of the blastocyst.
Figure 3.5	The primitive streak stage.
Figure 3.6	Formation of the mesoderm and notochord.
Figure 3.7	Neurulation and subdivision of the mesoderm.
Figure 3.8	Flat embryo folding into a tadpole shape in week four.
Figure 3.9	Germ layers and their adult derivatives.

Teaching with Art

Figure 3.3 Fertilization and the events of the first 6 days of development. Textbook p. 60; transparencies; Digital Archive CD-ROM.

Checklist of Key Points in the Figure

- Differentiate between the uterus and ovary.
- Explain the anatomy of the uterine tube.
- Focus on the events of fertilization, cleavage, and implantation.
- Explain fraternal and identical twins.
- Point out the open funnel-shaped infundibulum surrounded by the fimbriae of the uterine tube. Explain that this region is unique because this is the only place in the human body where a serous membrane meets a mucous membrane.

Common Conceptual Difficulties Interpreting the Art

- Because the oocyte is released directly into the peritoneal cavity (the uterine tube fimbriae do not touch the ovaries), explain to students how the oocyte is "propelled" into the lumen of the uterine tube.
- Tie in the release of mucus, beating of cilia, and peristaltic contractions to the movement of the egg/embryo within the uterine tube.
- Comment on the pathway sperm had to travel to reach this ultimate destination.
- Explain how the embryo is sustained until implantation by nutrients originally stored in the ovum.
- Describe implantation as an inward erosion process that is in part possible because of the release of digestive enzymes by the embryo.

Art Exercise

Ask students to label an unlabeled copy of Figure 3.3. Follow up with additional diagrams representing events associated with twinning. (Use your copy of the Digital Archive to print copies without labels or leader lines.)

Critical Reasoning

After asking students to recall what they've learned in Chapter 2 about the cell cycle, propose the following question: "Why do you think the embryo does not enlarge in size between fertilization and implantation?"

Answer: The cells of an embryo divide so rapidly during the first 7 days that they do not have time to grow between cell divisions. Hence, the average cell size diminishes by half following each division so that the developing embryo remains relatively constant in size.

SUPPLEMENTAL COURSE MATERIALS
Library Research Topics

1. Research the major birth defects, tabulating them according to the organ systems they affect (e.g., skeletal system, circulatory system).

2. Research the effects of various drugs (illegal and legal) on embryological and fetal development.
3. Research the effects of alcohol on embryological and fetal development.
4. Research the effects of viral and bacterial diseases on embryological and fetal development.
5. Research the types of problems in the fetus and infant that are associated with the mother's life-style (e.g., effects of sexually transmitted diseases, alcoholism, crack addiction, AIDS).
6. Research in vitro fertilization.

Audiovisual Aids/Computer Software

See Preface of the Instructor's Guide for Key to Audiovisual Distributors

Videotapes

1. *A Dozen Eggs: Time Lapse Microscopy of Normal Development* (IM, 46 min., 1991)
2. *A New Life* (*Living Body Series*) (FHS, 28 min., 1990)
3. *A Practical Guide to Sexually Transmitted Diseases* (FSH, 23 min.)
4. *A Woman's Body* (FHS, 49 min., 1990)
5. *The Human Body: The Reproductive System* (Ward's, 15 min.)
6. *Human Embryology Series* (ACG, 6-part series)
7. *Human Reproduction: Ovulation to Birth* (IM, 18 min., 1992)
8. *Human Reproductive Biology: Overcoming Infertility* (FHS, 35 min., 1998)
9. *The Miracle of Life* (CBS, 60 min., 1986)
10. *The Human Reproductive Systems* (BC, 32 min., 1999)
11. *In the Womb* (*Body Atlas Series*) (CAP/HCA, 30 min., 1994)
12. *Life Before Birth* (IM, 25 min., 1988)
13. *The Ultimate Journey* (CBS, 60 min., 1996)

Videodiscs

1. *Coming Together* (*Living Body Series*) (FHS, 28 min., 1989)
2. *Into the World* (*Living Body Series*) (FHS, 28 min., 1989)
3. *A New Life* (*Living Body Series*) (FHS, 28 min., 1989)

Computer Software

1. *The Human Body, Part II* (HCA, Disk for IBM, 1995)
2. *The Human Body, Part II* (CL, Disk for Apple II/Mac/Win)

CD-ROMs

1. *Nine Month Miracle* (CBS, Mac/Win)
2. *Meiosis* (Queue, Mac/Win)

Suggested Readings

Aitken, R. The complexities of conception. *Science* 269 (1995): 39–40.

Balinsky, B.I. *An Introduction to Embryology.* 5th ed. Philadelphia: W.B. Saunders, 1981.

Bower, B. Alcohol's fetal harm lasts a lifetime. *Science News* 139 (April 20, 1991): 244.

Braun, S. New experiments underscore warnings on maternal drinking. *Science* 273 (August 9, 1996): 738–739.

Deutchman, M.E., and E. Sakornbut. Diagnostic ultrasound in labor and delivery. *American Family Physician* 51 (January 1995): 145–154.

England, M.A. *Life Before Birth.* St. Louis: Mosby, 1997.

Ezzell, C. New theory on the origin of twins. *Science News* 142 (August 8, 1992): 84.

Ferrell, J.E., Jr., and E.M. Machleder. The biochemical basis of an all-or-none cell fate switch in Xenopus oocytes. *Science* 280 (May 8, 1998): 895–898.

Fischer, K., and A. Lazerson. *Human Development: From Conception Through Adolescence.* San Francisco: W.H. Freeman, 1984.

Larsen, W.J. *Human Embryology.* New York: Churchill Livingstone, 1993.

Lewis, D.D., and S. Woods. Fetal alcohol syndrome. *American Family Physician* 50 (October 1994): 1025–1032.

Moore, K.L. *The Developing Human.* 6th ed. Philadelphia: W.B. Saunders, 1998.

Satler, T. *Langman's Medical Embryology.* 6th ed. Baltimore: Williams and Wilkins, 1990.

Steinmetz, G. Fetal alcohol syndrome. *National Geographic* (February 1992): 36–39.

Wendell Smith, C.P., and P.L. Williams. *Basic Human Embryology.* 3rd ed. London: Pitman Publishing Limited, 1984.

ANSWERS TO TEXTBOOK QUESTIONS

Answers for multiple-choice and matching questions 1–13 are located in Appendix B of the textbook.

Short Answer and Essay Questions

14. At the primitive streak, epiblast cells migrate inward to form mesoderm and endoderm. As a result of this, the three primary germ layers are present: ectoderm, mesoderm, and endoderm. This occurs during the third week of embryonic development. The primitive node lies at one end of the primitive streak in the third week of embryonic development. At this node, epiblast cells move inward as a rod, pick up some cells from the hypoblast, and thereby form the notochord (primitive version of the backbone). (p. 62)

15. The amniotic sac and the amniotic fluid in this sac surround the developing embryo and fetus. The amniotic fluid serves to cushion the developing human from any physical bumps and jars it might encounter while in the womb. (p. 61)

16. (a) A mesenchyme is any embryonic tissue with actively migrating, star-shaped cells that do not attach to one another. Mesoderm is an example of a mesenchyme, but it is not the only example (neural crest is another). (b) In an epithelium tissue, by contrast, the cells attach

closely to one another to form sheets, and the cells are not star shaped. Epiblast, ectoderm, hypoblast, and endoderm are examples of embryonic epithelia. (pp. 61–62)

17. The flat embryonic disc achieves a cylindrical body shape as its sides fold inward and it lifts up off the yolk sac into the amniotic cavity. At the same time, the head and tail regions fold under. All this folding gives the month-old embryo a tadpole shape. The sequence is illustrated in Figure 3.8 on p. 66.

18. Limb muscles such as the biceps of the arm develop from myotomes, not from splanchnic mesoderm.

19. The neural crest gives rise to the sensory nerve cells, pigment cells, and some skeletal structures and vessels of the head and neck. (Here, for greater precision, the instructor may briefly introduce melanocytes, adrenal medulla for fright and flight, and the skeleton of the larynx.) (Table 3.1 on p. 68)

20. Somites, intermediate mesoderm, limbs. (p. 62)

Critical Reasoning and Clinical Applications Questions

1. Answer (c) is correct, meaning your friend should be aware of the possibility of birth defects. Many harmful substances do pass from mother to fetus, so choice (b) is wrong. The period of maximum danger is from the third to the eighth weeks of development, which includes the period when the friend was taking drugs. Since she continued her drug use past the eighth week of pregnancy, choices (a) and (d) are not correct. (pp. 70–71)

2. The citizens of Nukeville lost their case, because the number of birth defects was no higher than expected in 1000 births in the general population of the country; actually, the number of birth defects in Nukeville was a bit lower than in the general population (2% versus 3%). The percentages of the individual defects (e.g., heart defects, mental retardation, pyloric stenosis, anencephaly, spina bifida) were also very similar to what would be expected in the population as a whole, as indicated by the table in the box on p. 70.

3. Delta, like many people, failed to realize that the human body shape is essentially established by the end of the second month of development. (Figure 3.1 on p. 58)

4. The old idea was wrong, and ethanol freely crosses from mother's blood to the blood of the fetus. Ethanol is a proven teratogen and can lead to fetal alcohol syndrome. Our opinion is that it is good to put up warning signs in bars to discourage pregnant women from drinking —especially from drinking heavily. This is a difficult question to grade, however, because the students may point out that their own mothers and grandmothers drank during pregnancy, without producing any cases of fetal alcohol syndrome of which they are personally aware. (pp. 70–71)

SUPPLEMENTAL STUDENT MATERIALS TO HUMAN ANATOMY, THIRD EDITION
Chapter 3: Basic Embryology

To the Student
Knowledge of basic embryological concepts will enable you to understand the origin of normal adult anatomy and to understand the origin of birth defects. The central challenge of this chapter is to understand how the adult-like body components of a fetus are assembled from a single fertilized ovum.

Step 1: Distinguish between an embryo and a fetus.
- ☐ Define *embryo*.
- ☐ Define *fetus*.

Step 2: Outline early stages of development from zygote to blastocyst.
- ☐ Describe the process of fertilization.
- ☐ Define *zygote*.
- ☐ Relate the anatomy of the uterine tube to the movement of an embryo within it.
- ☐ Describe the process of implantation. Be able to discuss the events depicted in Figure 3.4a–e and name the embryonic tissue structures that form following implantation.

Step 3: Summarize week 2 through week 8 of embryonic development.
- ☐ Describe how the embryo becomes a two-layered disc during week 2. (See Figure 3.5.)
- ☐ Describe the formation of three germ layers during week 3. (See Figure 3.6.)
- ☐ Explain the formation of the neural tube, notochord, and neural crest. (See Figure 3.7.)
- ☐ Explain how the embryo changes shape during week 4. (See Figure 3.8.)
- ☐ List examples of the main derivatives of the embryonic germ layers.
- ☐ Describe the main events of second month of development.

Step 4: List the major events of fetal development.
- ☐ Summarize monthly changes in the fetus until birth. (See Table 3.2.)

CHAPTER 4
Tissues

LECTURE AND DEMONSTRATION
Student Objectives

1. Define *tissue*, and list the four main types of tissue in the body.
2. List several functional and structural characteristics of epithelial tissue.
3. Classify the different epithelia of the body.
4. Describe the apical, lateral, and basal surface features of epithelia and epithelial cells.
5. Define *exocrine* and *endocrine* glands.
6. Explain how multicellular exocrine glands are classified.
7. List the structural elements of loose areolar connective tissue, and describe each element.
8. Describe the types of connective tissue, and explain their main functions.
9. Discuss the structure and function of mucous, serous, and cutaneous membranes.
10. Briefly describe the three types of muscle tissue.
11. Note the general characteristics of nervous tissue.
12. Describe the inflammatory and repair processes by which tissues recover from injury.
13. Indicate the embryonic derivation of each tissue class.
14. Briefly describe age-related changes that occur in tissues.

Suggested Lecture Outline

I. Epithelia and Glands (pp. 76–88)

    A. Special Characteristics of Epithelia (p. 77, Fig. 4.1)

    B. Classification of Epithelia (pp. 77–83, Figs. 4.2, 4.3, and 4.4)

        1. Simple Epithelia

        2. Stratified Epithelia

    C. Epithelial Surface Features (pp. 83–86, Figs. 4.5–4.9)

        1. Apical Surface Features: Microvilli and Cilia

        2. Lateral Surface Features: Cell Junctions

        3. Basal Surface Feature: The Basal Lamina

    D. Glands (pp. 86–88, Figs. 4.10 and 4.11)

        1. Exocrine Glands

        2. Endocrine Glands

II. Connective Tissue (pp. 88–99, Fig. 4.12)

A. Connective Tissue Proper (pp. 88–99, Figs. 4.13–4.15)

  1. Areolar Tissue: A Model Connective Tissue

  2. Other Loose Connective Tissues

  3. Dense Connective Tissue

B. Other Connective Tissues: Cartilage, Bone, and Blood (pp. 98–99, Fig. 4.15)

  1. Cartilage

  2. Bone Tissue

  3. Blood

III. Covering and Lining Membranes (p. 99, Fig. 4.16)

IV. Muscle Tissue (pp. 99–102, Fig. 4.17)

V. Nervous Tissue (p. 102, Fig. 4.18)

VI. Tissue Response to Injury (pp. 102–106, Fig. 4.19)

A. Inflammation (pp. 102–103)

B. Repair (pp. 103–106)

VII. The Tissues Throughout Life (p. 106)

Lecture Hints

1. Define *tissue*.

2. Remind students of cell and organ relationship.

3. List four main tissue types in the human body and give examples.

4. Explain why glands are included with epithelial tissues. A student may not make the connection that liver tissue is of glandular epithelial origin.

5. List six special characteristics of epithelium and explain how these features separate epithelium from other tissue types. Display Figure 4.1.

6. Referring to Figure 4.2:

   a. Classify epithelium based on cell shape.

   b. Classify epithelium based on number of cell layers.

   c. Relate epithelial functions to shape of cell and number of cell layers.

   d. Point out that cell shape of stratified epithelium may vary from layer to layer, and that traditionally, cell shape of stratified epithelium is described according to the *apical* layer.

   e. Mention how pathologists use the tissue level of organization when examining organ biopsies, such as Pap smear examination of cervical stratified squamous epithelium.

7. Differentiate between mesothelium and endothelium.

8. Give specific examples of locations of each type of epithelium.

9. List specialized epithelial surface features.

10. Describe apical surface features: microvilli and cilia.
11. Describe lateral surface features that "glue" epithelial cells together; include specific examples of cell junctions.
12. Describe the function and structure of basal lamina.
13. Describe the function and structure of the basement membrane.
14. Define *gland*.
15. Explain classification of glands as exocrine or endocrine; cite examples.
16. Using Figure 4.10, describe the goblet cell as a very important unicellular exocrine gland due to its mucin production.
17. Review the roles of the rough ER, Golgi apparatus, and secretory vesicles learned in Chapter 2, and apply them to the goblet cell.
18. Classify glands as unicellular or multicellular and include examples. Point out differences in the structure of ducts and secretory units. Refer to Figure 4.11.
19. Define and explain the functions of *connective tissue*.
20. Using Figure 4.13, comment on the simple, basic structural plan of all connective tissues, pointing out three basic elements of connective tissue.
21. Distinguish between ground substance and matrix.
22. Describe how most of the body actually is composed of noncellular (nonliving) material, the extracellular matrix.
23. Explain four main classes of connective tissue and include examples. For each type of connective tissue in the summary outline:
    a. Describe specific examples of connective tissue cells, including origin, function, and mobility.
    b. Describe fibers of connective tissue, including protein structure and mechanical properties.
    c. Discuss properties of the extracellular matrix.
    d. Explain the nature of ground substance.
    e. Include lymph with blood.
24. Explain *fascia* and distinguish between deep fascia and superficial fascia.
25. Discuss covering and lining membranes as a combination of epithelial and connective tissues. Refer to Figure 4.16.
26. Briefly describe the cutaneous membrane (skin) as a combination of epidermis (epithelium) and dermis (connective tissue). Details are covered in Chapter 5.
27. Describe the mucous membrane as a combination of (usually) goblet cell-laden epithelium and lamina propria (connective tissue). More details are presented in later chapters.
28. Describe the serous membrane, introduced in Chapter 1, as a combination of mesothelium and areolar connective tissue.
29. Explain why muscle and nervous tissues may be considered *composite* tissues.
30. List three types of muscle tissue.

31. Using the text and Digital Archive CD-ROM, discuss the histological representations in Figure 4.17 and compare each type of muscle tissue according to the following characteristics:
    a. Description of cells (cell shape, number of nuclei, cell arrangement, striations, and intercalated discs)
    b. Locations
    c. Functions
    d. Voluntary or involuntary nervous control
32. For nervous tissue, give a general description of neurons, locations, and functions.
33. Explain inflammation and repair responses to tissue injury, giving examples of tissues that do not regenerate or repair themselves, i.e., cardiac muscle and most nervous tissue. Refer to Figure 4.19.
34. Explain embryonic origin of each of the four major types of tissue.
35. Name two tissue types that are derived from mesenchyme.
36. Discuss the significance of stem cells.
37. Summarize the effect of aging on tissues and organs.

Classroom Discussion Topics and Activities

1. Obtain or prepare projector slides of all basic tissues, at different magnifications, to help students find the tissues under the microscope.
2. Use simple, three-dimensional models, such as a cube (for cuboidal cells), a fried egg (for squamous cells), and a drinking glass (for columnar cells), to illustrate the shapes of the cells in the various types of epithelial tissues.
3. Ask students to rub the edge of a fingernail along the skin of the forearm, using moderate pressure. Explain that they will see and feel the beginning of an inflammatory response (redness, swelling, irritation).
4. Ask the class to consider how acute inflammation differs from chronic inflammation. How does inflammation caused by an infection (as in a pimple) differ from inflammation caused by a wound (a cut in the skin)?
5. Ask students to explain how nervous and muscle tissues also contain areolar connective tissue.
6. Discuss how the basic structural characteristics of the various classes of epithelia (thickness and cell shape) relate to the specific functions of these epithelia.
7. Discuss how the features of the extracellular matrix of the various connective tissues (dense, loose, bone, cartilage) account for the mechanical properties of each tissue type.
8. Some deep wounds are sutured closed. Ask students why this is necessary (apart from reducing bleeding and preventing infection).
9. Thrust your hand into a flaccid balloon to demonstrate the relationship between the parietal and visceral layers of serosa.
10. Obtain and display fresh tissues, such as a beef joint with tendons and muscles still attached, from a meat packing company or butcher shop.

11. Ask students to design a connective tissue comparison chart. The classification of connective tissues forms the left-hand column. Use the following labels for the comparison columns:
    - Characteristic types of cells
    - Types of fibers
    - Nature of ground substance
    - Nature of matrix
    - Functions
    - Locations
12. Remind students that additional media resources are available at *The Anatomy and Physiology Place* web site, including an interactive multiple-choice quiz and on-line histology tutorial. There is a direct link to this site from the *Study Partner CD-ROM*.

Clinical Questions

1. The following statements are events that occur during tissue repair. Arrange the events in their sequence of occurrence. The initial event, the injury, is already indicated as 1.
    1. The skin receives a cut that penetrates into the dermis; bleeding begins.
    2. Epithelial regeneration and scar formation occur.
    3. Granulation tissue forms.
    4. Blood clotting occurs and stops the blood flow.
    5. Macrophages engulf and clean away cellular debris.

   Answer: 1, 4, 3, 5, 2.

2. A person gets a cut on her hand. After several days, she notices swelling, pain, heat, and redness. Upon opening the wound to relieve the pressure, a yellow pus comes out. What has happened to the wound?

   Answer: The wound is infected. The symptoms indicate acute inflammation. Pus indicates the presence of dead or dying neutrophils, broken-down tissue cells, and living and dead bacteria.

3. When a tendon is torn, it does not heal rapidly. Why?

   Answer: Tendons consist primarily of dense regular connective tissue, which is poorly vascularized. Poorly vascularized tissues heal slowly.

4. What are the signs of inflammation, and why is the inflammatory response beneficial?

   Answer: The four signs of inflammation are swelling, redness, heat, and pain. Swelling, called edema, is beneficial because the increased amount of tissue fluid leaving the capillaries helps to dilute harmful substances that may be present in the connective tissue. It also brings in large quantities of oxygen, nutrients, and white blood cells that are necessary for the repair process.

5. Vitamin C is needed for the proper formation of collagen fibers. Insufficient vitamin C in the diet causes a condition known as scurvy, which is characterized by the general weakening of connective tissues and collagen throughout the body. Keeping in mind that strong connective tissues and collagen are needed to bind body parts together, what might be some of the major symptoms of scurvy?

Answer: The teeth fall out of their sockets, blood vessels rupture, and wounds fail to heal. (Strong collagen is necessary for holding teeth in their sockets, reinforcing blood vessels, and healing wounds.)

ART RESOURCES
Transparency List

Figure 4.1   Special characteristics of epithelium.

Figure 4.2   Classification of epithelia.

Figure 4.5   A cilium.

Figure 4.6   Ciliary movement.

Figure 4.7   Desmosome.

Figure 4.8   Tight junction between epithelial cells.

Figure 4.9   Gap junction between epithelial cells.

Figure 4.10 Goblet cells.

Figure 4.11 Multicellular exocrine glands.

Figure 4.14 Areolar connective tissue: a model connective tissue.

Figure 4.16 Covering and lining membranes.

Teaching with Art

Figure 4.14   Areolar connective tissue: a model connective tissue.

Textbook p. 90; transparencies; Digital Archive CD-ROM.

Checklist of Key Points in the Figure
- Explain why areolar tissue serves a *model* or *prototype* of connective tissue.
- Relate four functions of areolar connective tissue to its structural constituents.
- Explain the origin of tissue fluid and its function.
- Relate macrophages to previous study of endocytosis in Chapter 2.
- Explain extracellular matrix as ground substance + fibers + tissue fluids, except for blood.
- Describe the basement membrane as a combination of epithelium and connective tissue.

Common Conceptual Difficulties Interpreting the Art
- Specialized variations of areolar connective tissue are adipose and reticular tissues. Areolar, adipose, and reticular are all examples of *loose connective tissue*.
- Dense *(fibrous) connective tissue* is similar to areolar but contains more collagen. Give examples.
- Point out similar and dissimilar characteristics of other connective tissues: *cartilage, bone, and blood*.
- The extracellular matrix is *nonliving* and makes up most of the body.
- The matrix largely determines the characteristics of connective tissue.

- All other tissues in the body border or are embedded in areolar tissue. Give examples.
- Connective tissue does not occur on free surfaces.
- Not all connective tissue is highly vascular.

Art Exercise

Display or distribute copies of Figure 3.2, The adult human body plan, on p. 59 of the text. Ask students to identify the dominant tissue types in the organs seen in the diagram. For example, skin is an epithelium and a dense irregular connective tissue, the ribs consist primarily of bone tissue, and the body muscles consist primarily of skeletal muscle tissue.

Critical Reasoning

Display or distribute copies of Figure 21.7, showing the trachea and the esophagus. Ask students to note the different connective tissue structures of these adjacent tube-like structures. What would happen if the trachea were not composed of such massive rings of hyaline cartilage? What might happen if the esophagus were composed of hyaline cartilage like the trachea?

Answer: The trachea is designed to allow the passage of gases, and the esophagus is designed to facilitate the movement of solids and liquids. The hyaline cartilage that encircles the trachea provides stiffness that prevents this tube from collapsing during breathing. If the esophagus were composed of similar amounts of hyaline cartilage, it could not change shape to accommodate the passage of solids.

SUPPLEMENTAL COURSE MATERIALS
Library Research Topics

1. Basement membranes form the interface between epithelia and connective tissues. What is the chemical and fiber composition of this layer, and why is the basement membrane of great interest to cell biologists?
2. Why can some tissues regenerate and others cannot? What advantages and disadvantages are there for either case?
3. Some nutritionists suggest that obesity in later life results from overfeeding during childhood. Review some articles that support and dispute this theory.
4. Research current trends of tissue engineering and regenerative medicine.

Audiovisual Aids/Computer Software

See Preface of the Instructor's Guide for Key to Audiovisual Distributors

Slides

1. *Animal Cells and Tissues, Set 1* (BM). Examines the structure and specialization of epithelial cells and tissues, connective tissue, adipose tissue, cartilage, and bone.
2. *Animal Tissues–Epithelium, Cartilage* (NTA, #50, Microslide Viewer)
3. *Animal Tissues–Muscle, Bone, Connective* (NTA, #51, Microslide Viewer)
4. *Basic Human Histology Set* (CBS, 48-2200). Set of 100 transparencies that cover human histology in a broad sense.

5. *Basic Mammalian Tissue Type Set* (CBS, 48-1754). Thirty-three frames showing the four basic tissues.
6. *Connective Tissue Proper* (CBS, 48-2173)
7. *Connective Tissue Set* (CBS, 48-2116)
8. *Epithelial Tissue Sets* (CBS, 48-2114 and 48-2172)
9. *Histology of Basic Tissue Types* (EI, #611)
10. *Introduction to Mammalian Histology Set* (CBS, 48-1755M). Examines various mammalian tissues.
11. *Skeletal Tissue Set* (CBS, 48-2118)
12. *Striated Muscle Set* (CBS, 48-2134). Eleven frames showing electron micrographs of skeletal muscle and cardiac muscle.
13. *Preparing Tissues for Microscopy* (LPI)

Videotapes

1. *Cells, Tissues, and Organs* (SU, 11 min., VHS). Examines cell differentiation from single cells to tissues to organs.
2. *Cytology and Histology* (EI, SS-0035V, VHS/BETA). Series also available as slide set.
3. *Histology Videotape Series* (BIO). Histology of the human body covered in 26-cassette series.

Videodiscs

1. *Aging (Living Body Series)* (FHS, 28 min., 1992)

CD-ROMs

1. *Histology Collection* (VWR, Mac/Win)
2. *Human Histology* (MOS, Mac/Win, 1997)
3. *The Human Anatomy Project: Basic Human Anatomy—Nomenclature, Systems and Tissues* (NCH, Mac/Win, 1998)
4. *McMinn's Clinical Interactive Anatomy* (DGI, Mac/Win, 1996)
5. *Ward's Histology Collection* (WAR, Mac/Win)

Suggested Readings

Anderson, J.M., and C.M. Van Itallie. Tight junctions: Closing in on the seal. *Curr Biol* 9 (December 16–30, 1999): 922–924.

Aplin, A.E., A.K. Howe, and R. Juliano. Cell adhesion molecules, signal transduction and cell growth. *Curr Opin Cell Biol* 11 (December 1999): 737–744.

Burkitt, H.G., et al. *Wheater's Functional Histology*. 3rd ed. New York: Churchill Livingstone, 1993.

Caplan, A.I. Cartilage. *Scientific American* 251 (October 1984): 84–94.

Cormack, D.H. *Essential Histology*. Philadelphia: J.B. Lippincott, 1993.

Cormack, D.H. *Ham's Histology*. 9th ed. Philadelphia: J.B. Lippincott, 1987.

Dani, C. Embryonic stem cell-derived adipogenesis. *Cells Tissues Organs* 165 (1999): 173–180.

Eroschenko, V. *DiFiore's Atlas of Histology*. 7th ed. Philadelphia: Lea and Febiger, 1993.

Fawcett, D.W. *A Textbook of Histology*. 12th ed. New York: Chapman & Hall, 1994.

Fick, D., and J. Johnson. Resolving inflammation in active patients. *The Physician and Sportsmedicine* 271 (December 1993): 55.

Gartner, L., and J. Hiatt. *Color Atlas of Histology*. 2nd ed. Baltimore: Williams and Wilkins, 1994.

Junqueira, L.C., et al. *Basic Histology*. 9th ed. Stamford, Conn.: Appleton & Lange, 1998.

Kessel, R.G., and R. Kardon. *Tissues and Organs: A Text-Atlas of Scanning Electron Microscopy*. San Francisco: W.H. Freeman & Company, 1979.

Merker, H. Morphology of the basement membrane. *Microscopy Research and Technique* 28 (1994): 95–124.

Mooney, D.J., and A.G. Mikos. Growing new organs. *Scientific American* 280 (April 1999): 60–65.

Parenteau, N. Skin: The first tissue-engineered products. *Scientific American* 280 (April 1999): 83–84.

Robbins, S.L., and V. Kumar. *Basic Pathology*. 6th ed. Philadelphia: W.B. Saunders, 1997.

Ross, M.H., and L. Romrell. *Histology: A Text and Atlas*. 3rd ed. Baltimore: Williams & Wilkins, 1995.

Rubin, E., and J. Farber. *Essential Pathology*. 2nd ed. Philadelphia: Lippincott, 1995.

Walczak, C.E., and D. Nelson. Regulation of dynein-driven motility in cilia and flagella. *Cell Motility and the Cytoskeleton* 27 (1994): 101–107.

Weiss, L. *Cell and Tissue Biology: A Textbook of Histology*. 6th ed. Baltimore: Urban & Schwarzenberg, 1988.

Zaleske, D.J. Cartilage and bone development. *Instr Course Lect* 47 (1998): 461–468.

ANSWERS TO TEXTBOOK QUESTIONS

Answers for multiple-choice and matching questions 1–6 are located in Appendix B of the textbook.

Short Answer and Essay Questions

7. A tissue is a collection of cells of similar structure and function; tissues also contain extracellular material. The four basic types of tissue are epithelial, connective, muscle, and nervous. (p. 76)

8. The classification of multicellular exocrine glands is explained in Figure 4.11 on p. 88. Such a gland is simple if its duct does not branch and compound if its duct branches. It is tubular if its secretory cells are arranged in tubular units and alveolar (acinar) if its secretory cells form hollow balls at the end of the duct system. The main types are simple tubular, simple alveolar, compound tubular, compound alveolar, and compound tubuloalveolar. Specific examples of these gland types are listed in Figure 4.11.

9. (1) loose areolar; (2) elastic; (3) mesenchyme; (4) bone tissue; (5) dense regular; (6) dense irregular; (7) adipose. (pp. 88–99)

10. 1. Support and binding other tissues: This function is performed by fibers in the extracellular matrix, especially by the tension-resisting collagen fibers. 2. Holding tissue fluid derived from

blood capillaries: This function is performed by ground substance in the extracellular matrix, whose molecules act like sponges to hold water. 3. Defending the body against infection: This function is largely performed by a variety of defense cells in the connective tissue, including macrophages, plasma cells, mast cells, and various white blood cells. 4. Nutrient storage, performed by fat cells. (pp. 89–90)

11. (a) Tissue fluid, which occupies the extracellular matrix of connective tissue, is derived from blood and contains the small molecules of blood plasma. (b) The cells of the body obtain their oxygen and nutrients from the surrounding tissue fluid and deposit their wastes into this fluid as well. The tissue fluid is the link between the body cells and the bloodstream. (p. 91)

12. Macrophages are the nonspecific phagocytic cells of our body. That is, they engulf and digest a wide variety of foreign materials, ranging from bacteria to foreign molecules to dirt particles. They also dispose of dead tissue cells. (p. 91)

13. 1. Heat: caused by more blood entering the capillaries of the inflammation site (blood is warm). 2. Redness: also caused by more blood entering the capillaries of the inflammation site (blood is red). 3. Swelling: caused by increased permeability of the capillaries, resulting in increased amounts of tissue fluid in the inflamed connective tissue (edema). 4. Pain: caused by the pressure of edema and by inflammatory chemicals that stimulate nerve endings that mediate pain. (p. 102)

14. (a) Endocrine glands are ductless glands that secrete hormones into the bloodstream. They differ from exocrine glands, which secrete their products onto body surfaces or into body cavities, usually through ducts. (b) Hormones are messenger molecules that travel through the bloodstream, are taken up by specific target organs, and signal the target organs to carry out some characteristic response. For example, endocrine cells in the intestine secrete a hormone that signals the pancreas to release digestive enzymes into the small intestine after a meal. (p. 87)

15. Tissues that regenerate well: epithelial tissues, most types of connective tissue proper (except dense regular connective tissue), bone, blood-cell forming tissue. Tissues that regenerate poorly: cartilage, nervous tissue, cardiac and skeletal muscle. (p. 103)

16. Connective and muscle.

17. Fascia is defined as a fibrous membrane of dense regular connective tissue that wraps around muscles, around groups of muscles, and around large vessels and nerves. (p. 98)

18. The student is referring to the nonliving material between the cells in our tissues, called extracellular material on p. 76. It includes the extracellular matrix of connective tissues. Because the extracellular matrix is more voluminous than the cells in the connective tissues, and because connective tissues are the most abundant tissues in the body, it makes sense to claim that extracellular matrix makes up a greater part of our body than do the cells.

19. Although both are moist membranes within the body, serous membranes line the closed body cavities, whereas mucous membranes line the hollow organs of organ systems that open to the exterior. Furthermore, the epithelium of serous membranes (mesothelium) is invariable and functions only to be slippery, whereas epithelia of mucous membranes vary widely and serve many different functions (e.g., secretion, absorption, ion pumping, protection). (p. 99)

20. (a) dense regular connective tissue. (b) bone tissue. (c) muscle tissue. (d) nervous tissue. (e) elastic cartilage. (f) blood tissue. (g) simple cuboidal epithelium. (Figures 4.3, 4.15, and 4.17)

Critical Reasoning and Clinical Applications Questions

1. Since connective tissue proper is extremely widespread throughout the body, lupus has widespread, not localized, effects.

2. Since scurvy reflects inadequate amounts of vitamin C in the diet, the problem was solved when the sailors started carrying citrus fruits on their voyages. (p. 91)

3. Only the patient with liver damage will gain full functional recovery. This is because nervous tissue and cardiac muscle tissue cannot regenerate, but liver tissue (of glandular, epithelial origin) can. (p. 104)

4. Epithelium does. Recall that a carcinoma is a cancer arising from an epithelium, and an adenocarcinoma is a cancer arising from glandular epithelium.

SUPPLEMENTAL STUDENT MATERIALS TO HUMAN ANATOMY, THIRD EDITION
Chapter 4: Tissues

To the Student

By focusing on the relationship between cellular organization and tissue function, learning the major characteristics of each tissue type is easily accomplished. Since most organs contain all four basic tissue types, understanding tissue interactions permits you to better understand the organization and specific functions of organs and systems in the human body.

Step 1: Distinguish between the four main types of tissue in the human body.
☐ Define *tissue*.
☐ List four main types of tissue and examples of each.

Step 2: Distinguish between the different types of epithelia of the body.
☐ Devise an epithelial classification scheme based on the shape of a cell and the number of cell layers.
☐ Relate cell shape and number of layers to functions of epithelial tissue.
☐ Incorporate specific examples of cell locations into your classification scheme.
☐ List and describe three specific epithelial surface features, including detailed examples of each.
☐ Define *gland*.
☐ Explain why glands are included with epithelium.
☐ Explain the difference between endocrine and exocrine glands, including examples.
☐ Devise a simple classification scheme for glands based on cellularity, including duct structure and secretory units structure. Refer to Figure 4.11.
☐ Describe the goblet cell and its important glandular role.

Step 3: Distinguish between the types of connective tissues.
☐ Name and describe basic components of connective tissue.
☐ List functions of connective tissue.
☐ Devise a summary outline for the four major types of connective tissues, including subtypes.
☐ For each type of connective tissue in your summary outline, list specific associated cells.
☐ For each type of connective tissue in your summary outline, list specific fibers and describe mechanical properties.
☐ Also, for each type of connective tissue, discuss properties of the extracellular matrix and the nature of the ground substance.
☐ Explain tissue fluid.

Step 4: Distinguish between covering and lining membranes.
☐ Define and illustrate *cutaneous membrane*.
☐ Define and give examples of *mucous membrane*.

- ☐ Explain how mucus is moved along the membrane surface.
- ☐ Review the goblet cell and mucus production using Figure 4.10.
- ☐ Review Chapter 2 and summarize the roles of the rough ER, Golgi apparatus and secretory vesicles in goblet cells.
- ☐ Define and give examples of *serous membrane*.
- ☐ Explain the difference between visceral and parietal.
- ☐ Explain how cutaneous, serous, and mucous membranes are compositions of epithelium and connective tissues.

Step 5: Distinguish between three types of muscle tissue.

- ☐ Devise a chart to compare skeletal, smooth, and cardiac tissues in terms of the following characteristics:
  - Cell shape
  - Number of nuclei
  - Cell arrangement
  - Striations present/absent
  - Intercalated discs present/absent
  - Locations in body
  - Functions
  - Type of nervous control

Step 6: Describe the nature of nervous tissue.

- ☐ Define *neuron*.
- ☐ Define *supporting cells*.
- ☐ Explain the function of nervous tissue.

Step 7: Understand tissue response to injury.

- ☐ Explain inflammation.
- ☐ Describe tissue repair.

Step 8: Distinguish the embryonic origins of the four basic tissue types.

- ☐ Name tissues derived from mesenchyme, mostly of the mesoderm germ layer.
- ☐ Name tissues derived from endoderm.
- ☐ Name tissues derived from ectoderm.
- ☐ Discuss the significance of *stem cells*.

CHAPTER 5

The Integumentary System

LECTURE AND DEMONSTRATION
Student Objectives

1. Name the tissue types that compose the epidermis and dermis.
2. Name and describe the functions of the major layers of the epidermis and dermis.
3. Describe the structure and function of the hypodermis.
4. Describe the factors that contribute to skin color.
5. List the parts of a hair and a hair follicle, and explain the function of each part.
6. Explain the basis of hair color.
7. Describe the distribution, growth, and replacement of hairs and how hair changes throughout life.
8. Compare the structure and location of oil and sweat glands.
9. Compare eccrine and apocrine sweat glands.
10. Describe the structure of nails.
11. Explain why serious burns are life threatening and how burns are treated.
12. Differentiate between first-, second-, and third-degree burns.
13. Summarize the characteristics and warning signs of skin cancers, especially melanoma.
14. Briefly explain the changes that occur in the skin from birth to old age.

Suggested Lecture Outline

I. The Skin and the Hypodermis (pp. 112–117, Fig. 5.1)

   A. Epidermis (pp. 113–115, Figs. 5.2 and 5.3)

      1. Layers of the Epidermis

   B. Dermis (p. 115)

   C. Hypodermis (pp. 115–116)

   D. Skin Color (pp. 116–117)

II. Appendages of the Skin (pp. 117–122)

   A. Hair and Hair Follicles (pp. 117–120, Figs. 5.4–5.6)

      1. Hair

      2. Hair Follicles

II. APPENDAGES OF THE SKIN *(continued)*

    3. Types and Growth of Hair

    4. Hair Thinning and Baldness

  B. Sebaceous Glands (pp. 120–121, Fig. 5.7)

  C. Sweat Glands (p. 121, Fig. 5.7)

  D. Nails (pp. 121–122, Fig. 5.8)

III. Disorders of the Integumentary System (pp. 122–124)

  A. Burns (pp. 122–123, Fig. 5.9)

  B. Skin Cancer (pp. 123–124, Fig. 5.10)

    1. Basal Cell Carcinoma

    2. Squamous Cell Carcinoma

    3. Melanoma

IV. The Skin Throughout Life (pp. 124–125)

Lecture Hints

1. Explain how skin and its appendages are *organs* of the integumentary system.
2. List several functions of the integumentary system, emphasizing the amazing diversity of functions.
3. Distinguish between epidermis and dermis, noting the types of tissue present and major layers of each. Use Figure 5.1.
4. Tell students the physical image they project is nothing but *dead cells*.
5. Distinguish between *thick* skin and *thin* skin, indicating which is hairy and which is hairless.
6. Describe functions of each layer of epidermis, specifically including the role of keratinocytes, melanocytes, and cornified cells in discussion.
7. Define *dermis*.
8. Compare human *hide* to animal hide.
9. Distinguish between the two layers of dermis, including structure and function.
10. Because of the popularity of tattoos, students will be interested in *A Closer Look* in Chapter 5.
11. Explain *fingerprints*. Discuss why sanding of fingertips is not a permanent safeguard for criminals.
12. Relate cleavage lines to wound healing and scarring.
13. Describe the structure and function of the hypodermis, noting it is not part of the skin. This layer is also called the superficial fascia and should not be confused with (deep) *fascia*, dense regular connective tissue.
14. List and describe three pigments that contribute to skin color, and comment on reasons for variations in human skin colors.
15. List appendages of skin and point out epidermal and dermal relationships.

16. Describe the structure of hair and follicles. Refer to Figure 5.4.
17. Classify two basic types of hair, using examples.
18. Discuss baldness. If you are vague on the genetics of male pattern baldness, consult a basic genetics text for an explanation.
19. Explain why chemotherapy results in hair loss.
20. Review the structure of sebaceous glands using Figure 4.11d on p. 88.
21. Explain the following familiar circumstances: (a) suntan and why it fades, (b) pimples and blackheads, (c) wrinkled soles and palms after prolonged swimming, (d) greasy hair, (e) dandruff, (f) freckles, (g) bruises, (h) graying hair, and (i) goose bumps.
22. Relate holocrine secretion to sebum production and explain the importance of sebum.
23. Discuss sweat glands, including body distribution, secretory product, and functions.
24. Distinguish between two basic types of sweat glands: eccrine glands and apocrine glands.
25. List and describe examples of modified sweat glands: ceruminous glands and mammary glands.
26. Describe the structure and function of nails.
27. Classify burns by their severity, distinguish between each type, and explain the devastating effects of a burn on skin.
28. Explain conditions defining a critical burn and point out important clinical considerations for burn patients.
29. Using Figure 5.9, explain the purpose of the *rule of nines* with examples.
30. Discuss use of autograft and artificial skin.
31. Emphasize that skin cancer is the most common form of cancer, and exposure to UV sunlight is the primary causative factor.
32. Discuss and distinguish between three important types of skin cancer, and explain the *ABCD rule*.
33. Summarize developmental events associated with skin during development, infancy, adolescence, and old age.
34. Explain why and how skin wrinkles with age, including *photoaging*.

Classroom Discussion Topics and Activities

1. Use three-dimensional models of skin to illustrate the strata.
2. Use a microprojector and microscope slides of skin to illustrate the layers. Use slides of skin from the scalp and palm to show how thin skin differs from thick skin.
3. Provide small glass plates and instruct the students to observe the change in color of their skin while pressing the heel of their palms firmly against the glass. Ask them to explain the reason for the color change and what would happen to their skin cells if the pressure were prolonged.
4. Show the students a photo of a person with a heavily wrinkled face. Ask them to list all the factors that have contributed to the skin deterioration.
5. Discuss the role skin plays in the regulation of body temperature.

6. Ask students why animals with thick fur, such as Alaskan huskies, resist extremely cold air temperatures. How can polar bears and seals survive in near-freezing water temperatures?
7. Humans are often called "naked apes." Ask students why humans lack a full coat of body hair. What are the functions of human body hair? Encourage students to read Desmond Morris' *The Naked Ape* if they have not yet done so.
8. Ask students to compare a snake shedding its "skin" with the process that takes place in humans.
9. Discuss why axillary hair does not grow as long as hair on the scalp.
10. Ask students why it is more difficult to get a suntan during the winter than in summer. Ask why sunlight (and UV rays) is more intense in the tropics than nearer the poles of the earth.
11. Discuss why a suntan eventually fades.

Clinical Questions

1. Jeremy, who is 14 years old, notices that his face is developing many pimples and blackheads. What is causing this problem?

    Answer: Teenagers, because of hormonal changes, frequently have overactive sebaceous glands, whose ducts clog with sebum. This promotes bacterial infection of the clogged gland. Scratching, squeezing, or irritating pimples can aggravate the infection.

2. Albinos commonly contract skin cancer. What seems to be the reason, and what is a way for albinos to avoid skin cancer?

    Answer: The skin of albinos lacks melanin pigment and cannot screen out UV rays from sunlight. As a result, DNA in the living epithelial cells and melanocytes at the base of the epidermis are damaged by radiation, and skin cancer can develop. Covering all body areas with clothing and avoiding bright sunlight can help albinos avoid skin cancer.

3. Mike read in his anatomy book that hair grows in cycles that last about 4 years. He asked why all his hair did not fall out every 4 years, for then he could save money on a barber. How would you answer his question?

    Answer: Individual hairs do fall out every several years, but the growth cycles of the different hairs on the head are not synchronized at all. Therefore, a few dozen hairs fall out each day, but all hairs never fall out together.

4. Ahmed, an anatomy student, was watching an old movie about children in a haunted house. The children saw a ghost and the hair on their heads stood straight up. Is this pure fantasy, or does it have some basis in fact? Explain your answer.

    Answer: Although the ghost movie was greatly exaggerated, fear does cause the arrector pili muscles to pull on the hair follicles so that the hair stands up.

5. Steve went to his 35th high school reunion, the first reunion he ever attended. He was hesitant to go because he had bad acne as a teenager, so he had not been popular in high school. When he arrived at the reunion, his skin looked 10 years younger than that of any of his former classmates. Was there a connection here?

    Answer: Steve has unusually oily skin. This caused pimples when he was a teenager, but the oil keeps his skin from drying, so his skin looks supple and young during middle age.

6. Define the hair matrix. What happens if this matrix is destroyed?

   Answer: The hair matrix is the epithelial layer at the base of a hair follicle, and its epidermal cells divide to induce hair to grow. If the entire matrix of a hair is destroyed (as in a severe burn), that hair is lost and will not regrow.

ART RESOURCES
Transparency List

Figure 5.1   Skin structure.

Figure 5.2   Epidermal cells and the layers of the epidermis in thin skin.

Figure 5.4   Structure of a hair and hair follicle.

Figure 5.8   Structure of a nail.

Teaching with Art

Figure 5.2   Epidermal cells and the layers of the epidermis in thin skin.

Textbook p. 113; transparencies; Digital Archive CD-ROM.

Checklist of Key Points in the Figure

- Distinguish epidermis from dermis.
- The epidermis is excellent example of stratified squamous epithelium.
- Explain why a skin surface composed of stratified squamous epithelium is better than one thicker single layer of columnar epithelial cells.
- Point out four characteristic cell types and comment on their functions.
- Associate stratum basale with cell division and stratum granulosum with initial keratin formation.

Common Conceptual Difficulties Interpreting the Art

- Provide a concrete example of the thinness of *thin* skin; use the thickness of a credit card to approximate 1 mm.
- Emphasize that cells of the stratum corneum are dead because they are too far from life-sustaining capillaries.
- Describe how the production of new cells in the stratum basale literally pushes maturing and dying keratinocytes to the surface.

Art Exercise

Figure 5.2 permits students to choose a keratinocyte in the stratum basale and to diagram its significant cellular events, starting with cell division and ending with its ultimate shedding from the skin surface. Ask students to draw each phase of the cell's life cycle with leader lines connecting to Figure 5.2. Instruct students to incorporate into their drawing a time line based on an average 40-day life of a keratinocyte. Some key events to note are mitosis, pigment deposition, and keratin formation. A similar demonstration is possible using the transparency with an overlay and colored marker or the Digital Archive CD-ROM.

Critical Reasoning

Incorporate two critical reasoning examples into the art exercise.

1. Ask students to indicate the depth at which first-, second-, and third-degree burns are classified.

   Answer: First-degree—only the epidermis; second-degree—epidermis and upper dermis; third-degree—epidermis and dermis.

2. Instruct students to indicate the depths at which originate three types of skin cancer: basal cell carcinoma, squamous cell carcinoma, and melanoma.

   Answer: Basal cell carcinoma—stratum basale; squamous cell carcinoma—stratum spinosum; melanoma—any place there is melanin.

SUPPLEMENTAL COURSE MATERIALS
Library Research Topics

1. What is the difference between A and B types of ultraviolet rays with respect to the types of skin damage they produce?
2. Explore the literature on the latest techniques and materials used in skin grafting (e.g., test-tube-grown skin, synthetic skin, and heterograft skin).
3. The long-term effects of sunburn include severe wrinkling and increased likelihood of skin cancer. What are the latest statistics on this problem, and what has been done to correct it?
4. Although our skin is a barrier to microbes, prepare a list of organisms, such as bacteria, yeast, fungi, protozoans, and arthropods, that may reside on or in our skin.
5. Suggested research topics:
   a. Latest therapies for baldness
   b. New treatments for melanoma that involve immunotherapy
   c. Use of retinoic acid for the treatment of photoaged skin
   d. FDA regulations for the classification of cosmetics and drugs

Audiovisual Aids/Computer Software

See Preface of the Instructor's Guide for Key to Audiovisual Distributors

Slides

1. *First Aid: Newest Techniques, Burns* (SC)
2. *Skin* (NTA, #57, Microslide Viewer)
3. *Skin and Its Function* (EI, 20 slides)
4. *Skin Cancer: The Sun and You* (CBS)
5. *Visual Approach to Histology: Integumentary System* (FAD, 20 slides)

Videotapes

1. *Burns and Heat Stroke* (PLP, 10 min., 1990)
2. *First Aid Video* (ACA, 58 min., 1991)

3. *How the Body Works: Skin, Bone and Muscles* (IM, 19 min., 1996)
4. *Integument* (IM, 29 min., 1990)
5. *The Skin* (*Anatomy and Physiology Series*) (HCA/CAP, 26 min.)
6. *The Skin* (*Body Atlas Series*) (CAP, 30 min., 1994)
7. *The Skin* (*Human Body Live Action Video Series*) (CAP, 28 min., 1993)
8. *Skin* (*New Living Body Series*) (FHS, 20 min., 1995)
9. *Skin Deep* (FHS, 26 min., 1990)

Videodiscs
1. *Skin Deep* (*Living Body Series*) (FHS, 26 min. 1989)

Computer Software
1. *Differential Diagnosis in Dermatology* (WBS, Mac/Win, 1998)
2. *Saunders' Electronic Atlas of Dermatology* (WBS, Mac/Win, 1996)

Suggested Readings

Baran, R., R.P.R. Dauber, and G. Levene. *Color Atlas of the Hair, Scalp and Nails*. St. Louis: Mosby, Inc., 1991.

Barber, P. *Vampires, Burial, and Death*. New Haven: Yale University Press, 1988.

Ceno, R., and W.F. Jackson. *Color Atlas of Allergic Skin Disorders*. St. Louis: Mosby, Inc., 1992.

Cormack, D.H. *Essential Histology*. Philadelphia: J.B. Lippincott, 1993.

Cotsarelis, G., et al. Label-retaining cells reside in the bulge area of pilosebaceous unit: Implications for follicle stem cells, hair cycle, and skin carcinogenesis. *Cell* 61 (June 1990): 1329–1337.

Edelson, L.E., and J. Fink. The immunologic function of skin. *Scientific American* 252 (June 1985): 46–53.

Epstein, E.H., Jr. Molecular genetics of epidermolysis bullosa. *Science* 256 (May 8, 1992): 799–804.

Erickson, D. Beyond sympathy: Growth factors may help heal stubborn wounds. *Scientific American* 265 (December 1991): 141.

Ezzell, C. Skin genes underlie blistering disorder. (An article on epidermolysis bullosa.) *Science News* 146 (September 28, 1991): 197.

Fackelmann, K. 'Vaccine' spurs immune attack on melanoma. *Science News* 137 (March 31, 1990): 197.

Fawcett, D.W. *A Textbook of Histology*. 12th ed. New York: Chapman & Hall, 1994, Chapter 22.

Griffiths, C.E. Drug treatment of photoaged skin. *Drugs and Aging* 14 (April 1999) 289–301.

Harris, M. *Our Kind*. New York: Harper and Row, 1989, p. 112.

Hill, H.Z. The function of melanin or six blind people examine an elephant. *BioEssays* 14 (January 1992): 49.

Holzbecher, J., and D.E. Ryan. Some observations on the interpretation of hair analysis data. *Clin Biochem* 15 (April 1982): 80–82.

Junqueira, L.C., et al. *Basic Histology*. 9th ed. Stamford, Conn: Appleton and Lange, 1998.

Leffell, D.J., and D.E. Brast. Cancer, sunlight and skin. *Scientific American* (July 1996).

McPhail, G. There's no such thing as a healthy glow: Cutaneous malignant melanoma—the case against suntanning. *European Journal of Cancer Care* (Engl) 6 (June 1997): 147–153.

Montagna, W. The evolution of human skin. *Journal of Human Evolution* 14 (1985): 3–22.

Nguyen, Q., et al. Management of acne vulgaris. *American Family Physician* 50 (July 1994): 89–96.

Pennisi, E. Hairy mice offer hope for baldness remedy. *Science* 282 (November 27, 1998): 1617, 1619.

Rosenfeld, A. Some of a body's crucial functions are only skin deep. *Smithsonian* 19 (May 1988): 159–180.

Sheridan, R.L., and R.G. Tompkins. Skin substitutes in burns. *Burns* 25 (March 1999): 97–103.

Sturm, R.A., et al. Human pigmentation genetics: The difference is only skin deep. *Bioessays* 20 (September 1998): 712–721.

Thiboutot, D. New treatments and therapeutic strategies for acne. *Arch Fam Med* 9 (February 2000): 179–187.

Vargo, N.L. The skin cancer success story. *RN* (July 1987): 50–57.

Vines, G. Get under your skin. (A general article about the skin.) *New Scientist* (Inside Science section: January 14, 1995): 1–4.

Weiss, R. Fuzzy science: Researchers brush up on the biology of hair. *Science News* 139 (March 16, 1991): 168–170.

Weiss, R. Wrestling with wrinkles. *Science News* 134 (September 1988): 200–202.

Wickware, P. Progress from a fragile start. *Nature* 403 (January 27, 2000): 466.

Wills, C. The skin we're in. *Discover* (November 1994): 77–81.

ANSWERS TO TEXTBOOK QUESTIONS

Answers for multiple-choice and matching questions 1–10 are located in Appendix B of the textbook.

Short Answer and Essay Questions

11. Generally not. Most "bald" men have fine vellus hairs that look like peach fuzz in the "bald" areas. (pp. 119–120)

12. Thick skin occurs on the palms and soles, body areas that lack hairs. Thin skin covers all other areas of the body, and hair is present on virtually all these areas. (p. 114)

13. First-degree burn: only the epidermis is damaged. Second-degree burn: the apical part of the dermis is damaged, along with the epidermis. Third-degree burn: the entire thickness of the skin is damaged (both dermis and epidermis). (p. 122)

14. Sun exposure (UV light) activates matrix metalloproteinase enzymes in the dermis, which degrade collagen and other components of the dermis, leading to wrinkling, inelasticity, leathery nature, and liver spots in the skin. (p. 117)

15. The stratum corneum cells are dead and cannot divide. (p. 115)

16. (a) When the arrector pili muscles contract to raise the hair, they also dimple the skin to produce "goose bumps." (p. 119) (b) Noninfectious dandruff is the normal shedding of the stratum corneum of the scalp. (p. 115) (c) Stretch marks represent small tears in the dermis, as the skin is stretched by obesity or pregnancy. (p. 115) (d) Fingerprints are films of sweat, derived from sweat glands that open along the epidermal ridges of the hand. (p. 121) (e) The sparseness of hair on the body surface of humans may be an adaptation that allows more efficient sweating in hot climates, for abundant body hair would inhibit the evaporation of sweat. (p. 121) (f) Graying of hair results from decreased melanin production by the hair follicle and from the replacement of melanin by colorless air bubbles in the hair shaft. (p. 117)

17. Pigs and other mammals have far fewer sweat glands in their skin than do humans. Humans sweat more than any other animals, providing an efficient cooling system that allows us to be active on the hottest of days. Other animals pant to rid their bodies of excess heat, but they sweat little. (p. 121)

18. Any three of these: The skin protects, cushions, and insulates deeper structures; helps control body temperature; excretes poisons; screens ultraviolet rays; receives sensory information; and more. (see p. 112)

19. Besides storing fat as a nutrient source, the hypodermis anchors the skin to underlying structures (such as muscles) and allows skin to slide freely over these structures so that some blows just glance off our bodies. It also acts as an insulator against heat loss. (p. 116)

20. (a) Dermis, from the mesoderm, is connective tissue: dense irregular (reticular layer) and loose areolar (papillary layer). (b) Epidermis, from ectoderm, is a stratified squamous epithelium. (c) Hypodermis, from mesoderm, is adipose (and loose areolar) connective tissue. (p. 124)

Critical Reasoning and Clinical Applications Questions

1. The continued loss of skin can result in fluid loss and infection. (p. 122)

2. Dean probably has malignant melanoma. ABCD means that his mole is Asymmetrical, has Border irregularities, contains several Colors, and has a Diameter larger than a pencil eraser. (p. 124)

3. Bedridden patients are turned at regular intervals so that no region of their bodies is pressed against the bed long enough to deprive the blood supply to that skin; thus, bedsores are avoided. (p. 125)

4. When the skin is slit parallel to the cleavage lines like this, it should heal readily with little scarring. (p. 115)

5. The *body* of a nail is the visible, attached part (not its white, free edge). The *root* is the proximal part that is imbedded in skin. The *bed* is the layer of epidermis upon which the nail body lies. The *matrix* is the proximal part of the nail bed and it is responsible for nail growth. The *eponychium* is the cuticle around the perimeter of the nail body. The nail is *not* expected to grow back because its matrix is gone. (p. 121)

6. (a) about 18%. (b) about 18%. (c) about 4.5%. (Figure 5.8 on p. 122)

SUPPLEMENTAL STUDENT MATERIALS TO HUMAN ANATOMY, THIRD EDITION
Chapter 5: The Integumentary System

To the Student

This chapter relates the specifics of skin anatomy to its myriad of functions. Your concept of an organ is broadened to include the skin and its appendages, and what an organ it is! None other is so versatile and familiar to us. Our skin reveals our overall health, age, and emotional state. We are cognizant of our environment, internally and externally. Skin provides protection in numerous ways. What an amazing material it is to resist heat and cold, harsh chemicals, and bacteria. Knowledge of skin structure also will better enable you to understand damage to skin from burns and diseases, such as cancer.

Step 1: Understand the anatomy of the skin and the hypodermis.
- ☐ Distinguish between epidermis, dermis and hypodermis.
- ☐ Identify specific types of tissues associated with the skin and the hypodermis, noting individual functions.
- ☐ Identify specific types of cells associated with skin structure, noting individual functions.
- ☐ Organize the skin and the hypodermis into recognized layers.
- ☐ Explain skin color.

Step 2: Describe the appendages of skin.
- ☐ Name five general skin appendages.
- ☐ For each appendage, describe the structure and relate it to its individual functions.
- ☐ Explain how an appendage is considered as an *organ*.

Step 3: Learn about disorders of the integumentary system.
- ☐ Name two major bodily threats from severe burn.
- ☐ Classify burns by severity.
- ☐ Explain the rule of nines.
- ☐ Identify the major risk factor for skin cancer.
- ☐ Identify three types of skin cancer, indicating degree of occurrence and curability.

Step 4: Summarize the skin throughout life.
- ☐ Identify embryonic origins for the epidermis, dermis, hypodermis, and melanocytes.
- ☐ Describe the skin of a 6-month-old fetus.
- ☐ Describe the skin of old age.
- ☐ Explain factors causing wrinkles.

CHAPTER 6

Bones and Skeletal Tissues

LECTURE AND DEMONSTRATION
Student Objectives

1. Locate the major cartilage elements of the adult human body, and explain the functional properties of cartilage tissue.
2. Compare the structure, functions, and locations of the three kinds of cartilage tissue.
3. Explain how cartilage grows.
4. Explain why bones can be considered organs.
5. Describe the main functions of the bony skeleton.
6. Describe the gross anatomy of a typical long bone and typical flat bone.
7. Explain how bones withstand tension and compression.
8. Describe the histology of compact and spongy bone.
9. Discuss the chemical composition of bone tissue and the functions of its organic and inorganic parts.
10. Compare and contrast the two types of bone formation: intramembranous and endochondral ossification.
11. Describe how endochondral bones grow at their epiphyseal plates.
12. Discuss how bone tissue is remodeled within the skeleton.
13. Explain the steps in the healing of bone fractures.
14. List some symptoms of osteoporosis, osteomalacia, rickets, Paget's disease, and osteosarcoma.
15. Describe how bone architecture and bone mass change from the embryonic period to old age.

Suggested Lecture Outline

I. Cartilages (pp. 130–132)

    A. Location and Basic Structure (p. 130, Fig. 6.1)

    B. Classification of Cartilage (p. 130 and Fig. 4.15h–j on pp. 95–96)

        1. Hyaline Cartilage

        2. Elastic Cartilage

        3. Fibrocartilage

    C. Growth of Cartilage (pp. 130–131)

II. Bones (pp. 132–143)

A. Functions of Bones (pp. 132–133)

B. Classification of Bones (pp. 133–134, Fig. 6.2)

C. Gross Anatomy of Bones (pp. 134–135, Figs. 6.3–6.5)

   1. Compact and Spongy Bone

   2. Structure of a Typical Long Bone

   3. Structure of Short, Irregular, and Flat Bones

   4. Bone Design and Stress

D. Microscopic Structure of Bone (pp. 136–137, Figs. 6.6 and 6.7)

   1. Compact Bone

   2. Spongy Bone

E. Chemical Composition of Bone Tissue (pp. 137–138)

F. Bone Development (pp. 139–140, Figs. 6.8–6.10)

   1. Intramembranous Ossification

   2. Endochondral Ossification

G. Anatomy of Epiphyseal Growth Areas (p. 140)

H. Postnatal Growth of Endochondral Bones (pp. 141–142, Figs. 6.9 and 6.10)

I. Bone Remodeling (pp. 142–143, Fig. 6.11)

J. Repair of Bone Fractures (p. 143, Fig. 6.12)

III. Disorders of Bones (pp. 143–147, Fig. 6.13)

A. Osteoporosis

B. Osteomalacia and Rickets

C. Paget's Disease

D. Osteosarcoma

IV. The Skeleton Throughout Life (p. 147, Fig. 6.14)

Lecture Hints

1. Identify the major locations of cartilage in the human body. Refer to Figure 6.1.

2. For the three major types of cartilage, compare the structure (fibers and matrix), functions and locations.

3. Define *perichondrium*.

4. Explain the two growth patterns of cartilage: *interstitial* and *appositional*.

5. Point out the significance of water to resiliency of cartilage and growth of cartilage. Refer to *A Closer Look: The Marvelous Properties of Cartilage* on p. 132.

6. Define *bone* as an organ.

7. Describe five major functions of the human skeleton and include illustrations.

8. Explain a simple classification system for bones based on shape.

9. Distinguish between *compact* bone and *spongy* (*cancellous*) bone.
10. Describe the gross anatomy of a typical long bone, such as the humerus. Refer to Figure 6.3.
11. Describe the gross anatomy of a typical flat bone, such as a skull bone. Refer to Figure 6.4.
12. Explain how bones withstand tension and compression.
13. Define *osteon* and describe the microscopic structure of compact and spongy bone. Refer to Figure 6.6.
14. Distinguish between the organic and inorganic chemical components of bone tissue, including functions.
15. Define *osteogenesis* and *ossification*.
16. Distinguish between two types of bone formation: *intramembranous* ossification and *endochondral* ossification.
17. Summarize the stages of endochondral ossification of a long bone.
18. Describe the anatomy of epiphyseal growth areas.
19. Explain postnatal growth of a long bone, including how the bone widens.
20. Describe bone remodeling, including comments on *bone deposition* and *bone reabsorption*.
21. Define *fracture* and explain repair of bone fractures.
22. Discuss disorders of bones and comment on the following diseases: osteoporosis, osteomalacia, rickets, Paget's disease, and osteosarcoma.
23. Present a general bone/cartilage timetable that reflects the skeletal events throughout life.

Classroom Discussion Topics and Activities

1. Display examples of human bones illustrating various shapes.
2. Obtain a beef bone from a market and saw it longitudinally to demonstrate the internal structure of long bones. The fresh bone is excellent for demonstrating compact versus spongy bone and red marrow versus yellow marrow.
3. Demonstrate the periosteum by peeling this membrane from the fresh beef bone or the femur of an uncooked chicken leg.
4. Obtain a fresh piece of round steak and point out the marrow in the cut femur.
5. Use a three-dimensional model of compact bone to identify the osteons, lacunae containing osteocytes, lamellae, and canaliculi.
6. As an analogy, hold a bundle of uncooked pieces of spaghetti to show the arrangement of osteons within compact bone.
7. Illustrate the organic and inorganic composition of bone tissue by placing one chicken bone in nitric acid and another in the oven. The acid will leach out the calcium salts (making the bone bendable), and the oven will break down the organic matter (making the bone very brittle). A decalcified fibula can be tied in a knot and will resume its original shape when untied.
8. Obtain a beef elbow joint from a biological supply company. Cut the joint longitudinally to show the epiphyseal line.
9. Obtain X rays of long bones of young children, teenagers, and adults to illustrate the conversion of the epiphyseal plate to an epiphyseal line.

10. Obtain a cleared and stained pig embryo to show the development of bone in the skeleton (available from most biological supply companies).

11. Set up microscopes or use projector slides to demonstrate and contrast endochondral versus intramembranous ossification.

12. Bend a stick of clay to illustrate bending forces typically placed on long bones in the living skeleton. On one side, the clay will tear apart in tension, whereas on the other side it will bunch together in compression; these forces cancel each other out in the center.

13. Break a green twig to illustrate a greenstick fracture. Then break a dry twig to more closely approximate a fracture in an adult.

14. Obtain X rays of limbs whose bones show various types of fractures. If possible, obtain X rays that illustrate healing stages following the fracture.

15. Discuss why infections are more common with compound fractures than simple fractures.

16. Discuss the effects on the skeleton of extended weightlessness in space. How can these effects be minimized or at least reduced?

17. Ask the question, "Why are incomplete or greenstick fractures more common in children, whereas complete breaks are more common in adults?"

18. Explore the statement, "Multiple pregnancies will result in the mother losing all the enamel from her teeth and calcium from her bones." Is this all true, all false, or only partly true?

19. Calcium plays an important role in bone formation. Ask the class what other roles calcium plays in the body.

20. Discuss why fossil remains of vertebrate animals consist almost exclusively of bones and teeth.

21. Ask the class, "If bone tissue is so hard, how can orthodontists move teeth from one location in the jaw to another?"

Clinical Questions

1. Why do many elderly people develop "bowed backs" and appear shorter than they were in younger years?

   Answer: Because of osteoporosis, bone tissue tends to reabsorb faster than it is reformed and the density of the tissue decreases. The bony trabeculae become thin within the bodies of the vertebrae, and thus weakened, they experience numerous microfractures when subjected to the normal weight of the body. This compresses the vertebral bodies, causing the vertebral column to bend forward into a bowshape. The bowed spine accounts for the loss of body height.

2. A 75-year-old woman and her 9-year-old granddaughter were victims of a train crash. In both cases, trauma to the chest was sustained. X rays of the grandmother revealed several broken ribs, but her granddaughter's ribs did not break. Explain these different symptoms.

   Answer: The youngster has relatively more organic material in her bones, which allows them to bend, whereas the grandmother's bones are fully calcified, with less organic material. Furthermore, the grandmother's bones may have been weakened by osteoporosis.

Chapter 6: *Bones and Skeletal Tissues* 63

3. Cyndi fractured the middle of the diaphysis of her right tibia in a skiing accident. The surrounding soft tissue (in the middle of her leg) was also damaged by the force of the accident. After prolonged immobilization of the limb in a cast, it was found that the fracture was not healing. Can you explain why?

Answer: The nutrient artery, which enters near the middle of the diaphysis of a long bone, was destroyed in the accident. Without its blood supply, the shaft of the tibia could not heal.

ART RESOURCES
Transparency List

Figure 6.1	Cartilages in the adult skeleton and body.
Figure 6.2	Classification of bones on the basis of shape.
Figure 6.3	Structure of a long bone (humerus of arm).
Figure 6.4	Structure of a flat bone of the skull.
Figure 6.8	Intramembranous ossification: Development of a flat bone of the skull in the fetus.
Figure 6.9	Stages in endochondral ossification of a long bone.
Figure 6.11	An osteoclast or bone degrading cell.
Figure 6.12	Stages in healing of a bone fracture.

Teaching with Art

Figure 6.3   Structure of a long bone (humerus of arm).

Textbook p. 135; transparencies; and Digital Archive CD-ROM.

Checklist of Key Points in the Figure
- Articular cartilage provides almost frictionless joint surfaces.
- The periosteum is a connective tissue covering of bone. Its superficial layer of dense irregular connective tissue resists tension during bending.
- The deep periosteal layer contains cells that provide lifetime bone remodeling.
- The endosteum covers internal bone surfaces and also contains osteoblasts and osteoclasts.
- Relate bone to other connective tissues using the following concepts: articulations and mobility, prenatal and postnatal growth, support and protection, and nutrition.

Common Conceptual Difficulties Interpreting the Art
- The epiphyseal line is a remnant of the plate of hyaline cartilage that grows to lengthen bone.
- Differentiate between the composition of bone marrow in the long bone of an infant and that of an adult.
- The periosteum provides sites for tendon and ligament attachment.
- Explain that there are separate blood supplies to either side of the epiphyseal line in an adult long bone. (Show Figure 6.9, number 5.)

Art Exercise

1. Instruct students to compare Figure 6.3, Structure of a long bone, with Figure 6.9, Stages in endochondral ossification of a long bone. Instruct students to construct a flowchart summarizing the events that occur from the formation of an epiphyseal plate cartilage to the appearance of the epiphyseal line.

2. Using the Digital Archive CD-ROM, provide copies of Figure 6.3 and Figure 6.9, number 5, with only leader lines. Ask students to associate specific *types* of connective tissue with the anatomical names of bone structures. For example, in addition to labeling the periosteum, a student would indicate that it is also dense irregular connective tissue.

Critical Reasoning

1. Bone tissue does not form the epiphyseal plate. Ask students what tissue does grow and account for lengthening of long bones.

   Answer: Hyaline cartilage.

2. As endochondral ossification occurs, a long bone widens as it grows in length. Ask students how this is accomplished.

   Answer: On the external surface of the diaphysis, osteoblasts in the perichondrium add bone tissue. Internally, osteoclasts in the endosteum remove bone tissue from the inner surface of the diaphysis.

SUPPLEMENTAL COURSE MATERIALS
Library Research Topics

1. How are electrical fields being used to stimulate bone growth and bone repair?
2. Much research is currently being performed to determine the mechanisms by which compression and tension forces on bones stimulate the bone to respond by growing thicker. What are the mechanisms that have been hypothesized?
3. Explore the procedures used in bone-tissue transplants where pieces of bone are removed from one part of the body and implanted into another.
4. What effect does the use of illegal steroids by athletes have on their bone tissue and bone marrow?
5. Research the latest techniques, such as the Ilizarov procedure, used to lengthen bones that have been damaged in accidents or illnesses.

Audiovisual Aids/Computer Software

See Preface of the Instructor's Guide for Key to Audiovisual Distributors

Slides

1. *Specialized Connective Tissue: Cartilage and Bone Set* (CBS, 48-2174)
2. *Systems of the Human Body—The Skeletal System and Its Function Set* (CBS, 48-2065C)
3. *Histology of the Skeletomuscular System* (EI)

Chapter 6: *Bones and Skeletal Tissues*

Videotapes

1. *The Development of Bone* (TFI, 19 min., C, 1988). Step-by-step development, from cartilage to bone.
2. *Bones, Cartilage and Joints* (*Human Body Live Action Video Series*) (CAP, 28 min., 1993)
3. *The Living Body: Growth and Change* (FHS, 28 min., 1990). Explores bone growth and remodeling.
4. *The New Living Body: Bones and Joints* (FHS, 20 min., 1995). Shows bone growth, effects of exercise, injury, and repair.
5. *Skeletal System: the Infrastructure* (FHS, 25 min., 1998). Shows connective tissues.

CD-ROMs

1. *Diagnosis of Bone and Joint Disorders.* 3rd ed. (WBS, 1996, Win/Mac)
2. *The Interactive Skeleton* (DGI, 1996, Win/Mac). Shows dissected bone.
3. *Skeletal Trauma: Fractures, Dislocations, Ligamentous Injuries.* 2nd ed. (WBS, 1998, Win/Mac)

Suggested Readings

Bareggi, R., et al. The growth of long bones in human embryological and fetal upper limbs and its relationship to other developmental patterns. *Anatomy and Embryology* 189 (1994): 19–24.

Beard, J. Injection of starch helps bones to heal. *New Scientist* (July 13, 1991): 27.

Boyan, B. (Chairperson) Symposium on new therapies for age-related bone disease. *Hospital Practice* 26: Supplement 1 (January 1991).

Boyce, B.F., et al. Recent advances in bone biology provide insight into the pathogenesis of bone diseases. *Lab Invest* 79 (February 1999): 83–94.

Byock, J. Egil's bones. (An article on Paget's disease.) *Scientific American* (January 1995): 82–87.

Caplan, A.I. Cartilage. *Scientific American* 251 (October 1984): 84–94.

Cohn, M.J., and P.E. Bright. Molecular control of vertebrate limb development, evolution and congenital malformations. *Cell Tissue Res* 296 (April 1999): 3–17.

Cormack, D.H. *Essential Histology.* Philadelphia: J.B. Lippincott, 1993.

Davies, A. Beads beat bone infection. (An article on osteomyelitis.) *New Scientist* (November 6, 1993): 23.

Frost, H., and S. Webster. Perspectives: A vital biomechanical model of the endochondral ossification mechanism. *The Anatomical Record* 240 (1994): 435–446.

Hayashi, S., et al. Commitment and differentiation of stem cells to the osteoclast lineage. *Biochem Cell Biol* 76 (1998): 911–922.

Horowitz, M. Cytokines and estrogen in bone: Anti-osteoporotic effects. *Science* 260 (April 30, 1993): 626–627.

Iqbal, M.M. Osteoporosis: Epidemiology, diagnosis, and treatment. *South Med Journal* 93 (January 2000): 2–18.

Junqueira, L.C., et al. *Basic Histology.* 9th ed. Stamford, Conn.: Appleton & Lange, 1998.

Kassem, M. Cellular and molecular effects of growth hormone and estrogen on human bone cells. *APMIS Suppl* 71 (1997): 1–30.

Manolagas, S., and R. Jilka. Bone marrow, cytokines, and bone remodeling: Emerging insights into the pathophysiology of osteoporosis. *The New England Journal of Medicine* 332 (February 2, 1995): 305–311.

Mee, A., and P. Sharpe. Dogs, distemper, and Paget's disease. *BioEssays* 15 (December 1993): 783–789.

Notelovitz, M. Estrogen therapy and osteoporosis: Principles & practice. *Am J Med Sci* 313 (January 1997): 2–12.

Pannarale, L., et al. Scanning electron microscopy of collagen fiber orientation in the bone lamellar system in non-decalcified human samples. *Acta Anatomica* 151 (1994): 36–42.

Stolzenburg, W. Hard evidence for bone-building therapy. *Science News* 138 (July 14, 1990): 22.

Zaleske, D.J. Cartilage and bone development. *Instr Course Lect* 47 (1998): 461–468.

ANSWERS TO TEXTBOOK QUESTIONS

Answers for multiple-choice questions 1–14 are located in Appendix B of the textbook.

Short Answer and Essay Questions

15. (a) Cartilage is resilient (springy) because large molecules in its ground substance have a strong attraction for water molecules. When the cartilage is compressed, the water molecules are pushed out of the ground substance, and when the compression lets up, the water rushes back in, causing the cartilage to spring back to its original shape. (b) Cartilage grows quickly because a small amount of its matrix attracts much water, which quickly increases the size of the tissue. Also, cartilage is avascular, so there is no need for the time-consuming process of growing new capillary beds within the growing cartilage tissue itself. (p. 132)

16. Most long bones in the living skeleton are subjected to bending forces, which subject one side of the shaft to extreme tension, the other to extreme compression. These opposite forces cancel each other out in the interior of the diaphysis, so the strongest forces are experienced externally. Placing weak, spongy bone on the exterior would cause this bone to break and crumble very easily when subjected to normal bending stresses. Thus, an imaginary bone with spongy bone on the outside would be of poor mechanical design. (pp. 135–136)

17. The epiphyseal plates close after adolescence, at about age 18 in females and age 21 in males. The plates close because, at this time, the sex hormones signal a slowdown in the division rate of cartilage cells in the plates, and the cartilage is replaced by bone tissue. (p. 135)

18. (a) First decade is the fastest; fourth decade is when skeletal mass starts to decline. (p. 141)
    (b) Elderly people usually experience a loss of bone mass, osteoporosis, and lack of blood supply to bone. This weakens the bones, so they are more easily fractured. (p. 147)

19. Interstitial growth is a *growth from within*, in which the chondrocytes inside a piece of cartilage divide and secrete matrix. Appositional growth, by contrast, is a *growth from outside*, in which cells in the perichondrium around the piece of cartilage produce the new tissue. (p. 130)

20. Membrane bones are the clavicle and the bones of the skull (except some at the cranial base, such as the base of the occiput). All other bones of the skeleton are endochondral. (p. 139)

Critical Reasoning and Clinical Applications Questions

1. In order to remain strong, the bones of the living skeleton must be continually stressed by the weight of the body and by the force of muscles pulling on them. The lower limbs of a paraplegic in a wheelchair experience neither of these forces, so bone tissue is lost. Such bones thin and weaken. (p. 143)

2. The broken bone will heal faster than the torn cartilage. Cartilage cells do not divide after youth, so healing of damaged cartilages is poor in adults. Bone, by contrast, will heal vigorously throughout life. (p. 143)

3. By overdoing his exercise, Carlos had twisted and torn the cartilage in the distal epiphyseal plate of the humerus in his arm. (Recall that cartilage is weak in resisting such twisting stresses: p. 32.) Damage to the epiphyseal plates is common in child athletes (p. 141), but it could not have happened to adult Selena, whose epiphyseal plates have already closed.

4. The epiphyseal plates do grow fast, but the cartilage is replaced by spongy bone tissue at the diaphyseal side as quickly as it grows. Therefore, the plate remains the same width. (pp. 141)

5. Egil is thought to have had Paget's disease, an excessive remodeling of bone dominated by bone deposition (p. 146). For more information on Egil, see pp. 82–87 in the January 1995 issue of *Scientific American* magazine.

6. Bernice had symptoms of osteoporosis. (p. 143)

SUPPLEMENTAL STUDENT MATERIALS TO HUMAN ANATOMY, THIRD EDITION

Chapter 6: Bones and Skeletal Tissues

To the Student

During your study of Chapter 6, you will find out about the amazing structure and functions of bone tissue and cartilage. Together they form your skeleton. You will gain insight as to how an individual bone functions as an organ in its own right. The important relationship of cartilage to bone during development is explained. Understanding the basics in this chapter prepares you for succeeding chapters, where you will learn the bones forming the axial and appendicular skeletons, how joints form, attachments of muscles to bones and movements.

Step 1: Understanding cartilage.

- [ ] Define *cartilage*.
- [ ] Identify major locations of cartilage in the adult human body.
- [ ] Explain the functional properties of cartilage as a tissue.
- [ ] List three major kinds of cartilage tissue.
- [ ] Prepare a comparison chart of the kinds of cartilage, including notes on structure, functions, and locations.
- [ ] Describe how cartilage grows.
- [ ] Define *perichondrium*.

Step 2: Understanding bone tissue.

- [ ] Describe why a bone may be considered an organ.
- [ ] Summarize several main functions of the bony skeleton.
- [ ] Describe the gross anatomy of a typical long bone.
- [ ] Describe the gross anatomy of a flat bone.
- [ ] Explain how bones withstand tension and compression.
- [ ] Draw and label an osteon. Describe histological features.
- [ ] Describe differences between compact bone tissue and spongy bone tissue.
- [ ] Describe the chemical composition of bone and distinguish between its organic and inorganic components.
- [ ] Distinguish between intramembranous and endochondral ossification as types of bone formation.
- [ ] Explain how bone is remodeled in the skeleton.
- [ ] Name some common types of fractures.
- [ ] Explain basic steps in the repair of a fracture.

Step 3: Explore bone disorders and changes of bone tissue throughout life.

- [ ] List symptoms of osteoporosis.
- [ ] Name two ways aged bone differs from young bone.

CHAPTER 7
Bones, Part 1: The Axial Skeleton

LECTURE AND DEMONSTRATION
Student Objectives

1. Define the *axial skeleton* and contrast it with the *appendicular skeleton*.
2. Describe the kinds of markings on bones.
3. Name and describe the bones of the skull. Identify their important markings.
4. Compare the functions of the cranial and facial bones.
5. Define the bony boundaries of the orbit, nasal cavity, and paranasal sinuses.
6. Describe the general structure of the vertebral column, and list its components.
7. Name a function performed by both the spinal curvatures and the intervertebral discs.
8. Discuss the structure of a typical vertebra, and describe the special features of cervical, thoracic, and lumbar vertebrae.
9. Describe the ribs and sternum.
10. Differentiate true ribs from false ribs, and explain how they relate to floating ribs.
11. Describe how the axial skeleton changes as we grow.

Suggested Lecture Outline

I. *The Skull (pp. 154–167)*

   A. Overview of Skull Geography (p. 154)

   B. Cranium (pp. 154–162, Figs. 7.2–7.10)

      1. Frontal Bone

      2. Parietal Bones and the Major Sutures

      3. Sutural Bones

      4. Occipital Bone

      5. Temporal Bones

      6. Sphenoid Bone

      7. Ethmoid Bone

   C. Facial Bones (pp. 162–164, Figs. 7.2–7.4, 7.8–7.10)

      1. Mandible

      2. Maxillary Bones

      3. Zygomatic Bones

I. THE SKULL *(continued)*

    4. Nasal Bones

    5. Lacrimal Bones

    6. Palatine Bones

    7. Vomer

    8. Inferior Nasal Conchae

  D. Special Parts of the Skull (pp. 165–167, Figs. 7.9–7.12)

    1. Orbits

    2. Nasal Cavity

    3. Paranasal Sinuses

    4. The Hyoid Bone

II. *The Vertebral Column (pp. 168–177)*

  A. Intervertebral Discs (pp. 168–172, Fig. 7.14)

  B. Regions and Normal Curvatures

  C. General Structure of Vertebrae (p. 172, Fig. 7.15)

  D. Regional Vertebral Characteristics (pp. 173–177, Figs. 7.16–7.18)

    1. Cervical Vertebrae

    2. Thoracic Vertebrae

    3. Lumbar Vertebrae

    4. Sacrum

    5. Coccyx

III. *The Bony Thorax (pp. 177–179, Figs. 7.19 and 7.20)*

  A. Sternum (pp. 177–178)

  B. Ribs (pp. 178–179)

IV. *Disorders of the Axial Skeleton (p. 179)*

  A. Abnormal Spinal Curvatures

  B. Stenosis of the Lumbar Spine

V. *The Axial Skeleton Throughout Life (pp. 179–182)*

Lecture Hints

1. Distinguish between the axial and appendicular skeletons. Refer to Figure 7.1.

2. List bones of the skull, and indicate significant bone markings.

3. Define *suture* and give several examples using Figures 7.2 and 7.3.

4. Contrast functions of the cranial bones and facial bones.

5. Explain the role of the sphenoid as a *keystone* bone of the cranium.

6. Define the bony framework of the orbit and the nasal cavity.

7. Summarize the structural contents of the orbit: eyeball, muscles, fat, and lacrimal gland.
8. Discuss the functions of the paranasal sinuses of the sphenoid, frontal, ethmoid, and maxillary bones, including the fact they open into the nasal cavity.
9. Using Figure 7.3b, show how the floor of the nasal cavity is the same as the roof of the oral cavity.
10. Remind students that bones vary with individuals and no two skulls will look exactly the same. Point out that humans do not look the same on the outside, so why should they look the same on the inside?
11. Explain the hyoid bone. Refer to Figure 7.12.
12. Describe the general structure of the vertebral column, including regions, curvatures, and intervertebral discs. Include functions.
13. Explain the gross anatomy of a typical vertebra, using features to define cervical, thoracic, and lumbar vertebrae. Refer to Figures 7.15, 7.16, and 7.17 and Table 7.3.
14. Explain the sacrum and coccyx. Refer to Figure 7.18.
15. Define *thorax*.
16. Describe the gross anatomy of the sternum and ribs.
17. Distinguish between *true ribs, false ribs,* and *floating ribs*.
18. Explain the atypical features of ribs 1 and 10–12.
19. Comment on spinal clinical disorders.
20. Describe the gross anatomy of a fetal skull, including fontanels and the frontal (metopic) suture. Remind students of intramembranous ossification. Refer to Figure 7.21.

Classroom Discussion Topics and Activities

1. Demonstrate a complete, articulated skeleton, showing how the skeleton forms the framework of the body and the difference between axial and appendicular skeletons.
2. Demonstrate a skull (with the calvaria cut) and a vertebral column to illustrate how these bones provide protection for the delicate neural tissue of the brain and spinal cord.
3. Using a disarticulated Beauchene skull demo, ask students to list all the bones of the skull and to name all the bones that articulate with each one.
4. Ask students to explain the bony relationships between the ear, the nose, and the throat.
5. Using bone specimens, compare and contrast the structural features of different vertebrae: atlas, axis, cervical, thoracic, lumbar, sacral, and coccygeal vertebrae.
6. Display X rays of spinal columns that exhibit abnormal curvatures, such as scoliosis, lordosis, and kyphosis.
7. Explain in mechanical terms why the vertebral bodies become progressively larger from the cervical to the lumbar regions of the spine.
8. Years ago, students carried heavy books on one arm or the other. Today, most students are using knapsacks (backpacks). Ask students how these different ways of carrying books affect the spinal column.

74 Instructor's Guide for Human Anatomy

9. Various religious writings have suggested that a rib was taken from man to create woman. Ask students if any ribs are missing from the male rib cage.

10. Humans have a short neck, but giraffes have a long one. Ask students if giraffes have more neck vertebrae to accommodate this extra length. Do the rats and cats used in many anatomy courses have more vertebrae and ribs than humans?

11. Discuss what information skeletons provide in forensic medicine.

12. Place a disarticulated bone in a bag and have the students identify it using only their sense of touch.

Clinical Questions

1. During a severe cold accompanied by nasal congestion, Helen complained of a frontal headache and said that the right side of her face ached. What specific bony structures did the cold viruses probably infect?

   Answer: The paranasal sinuses were affected, most specifically the right frontal sinus in the frontal bone.

2. While cleaning out his garage, Otis bent over to lift a heavy box and heard a "pop" in his mid back. Within minutes, he started experiencing waves of severe back pain that forced him seek medical treatment. What may have happened to Otis's back?

   Answer: Most likely, Otis suffered a herniated intervertebral disc of his thoracic spine. The nucleus pulposus of the damaged disc is pressing against the spinal cord or spinal nerve roots, causing the unrelenting pain and discomfort. (See Figure 7.14c.)

ART RESOURCES
Transparency List

Figure 7.1	The human skeleton.
Figure 7.2	Skull.
Figure 7.3	Lateral aspect of the skull.
Figure 7.4	Inferior aspect of the skull.
Figure 7.5	The temporal bone.
Figure 7.6	The sphenoid bone.
Figure 7.7	The ethmoid bone.
Figure 7.8	Detailed anatomy of some facial bones.
Figure 7.9	Bones of the orbit.
Figure 7.10	Bones of the nasal cavity.
Figure 7.11	Paranasal sinuses.
Figure 7.13	The vertebral column.
Figure 7.14	Ligaments and intervertebral discs of the spine.
Figure 7.15	Structure of a typical vertebra.
Figure 7.16	The first and second cervical vertebrae.

Chapter 7: *Bones, Part 1: The Axial Skeleton* 75

Figure 7.17 Posterolateral views of articulated vertebrae.

Figure 7.18 Sacrum and coccyx.

Figure 7.19 The bony thorax.

Figure 7.20 Ribs.

Teaching with Art

Figure 7.9 Bones of the orbit.

Textbook p. 165; transparencies; Digital Archive CD-ROM.

Checklist of Key Points in the Figure

- State that the orbit is roughly conical in shape and that it projects about 2½ inches into the skull's interior.
- Cite the bones and their parts that form the roof, lateral wall, medial wall, and floor of the orbit.
- Explain a suture as a characteristic articulation.
- Emphasize that understanding the orbital articulations increases overall understanding of the very complicated articulations of the skull.
- Point out special features of the orbit for passage of nerves, blood vessels, and ducts, with special attention to the evident foramina and fissures found in the sphenoid bone and between the sphenoid and the maxillary bones.
- Point out the lacrimal fossa and other foramina that border the orbit.
- Mention structures that occupy the orbit: eyeball, muscles, fat, lacrimal gland.

Common Conceptual Difficulties Interpreting the Art

- A colored diagram is necessary to show the difficult-to-distinguish suture lines within the orbit of an actual bony skull.
- When viewing bones of the skull in isolation (e.g., the sphenoid bone), students often fail to appreciate the contribution the bone makes to the construction of the orbits.
- Students may not make the connection between an orbital bone's surface features and their functions, such as a nerve passing through a foramen.

Art Exercises

1. Using the Digital Archive CD-ROM, provide students with unlabeled copies of Figure 7.9b. Instruct them to color and label the surface of each bone that forms a portion of the orbit.

2. Using *A.D.A.M.® Interactive Anatomy*, provide students with copies of a disarticulated sphenoid and a disarticulated maxilla. Ask them to color the portion of each bone that contributes to the formation of the orbit. (This exercise may be expanded to include all the bones of the orbit. A similar demonstration by the instructor is possible using the drawing tool on the Digital Archive CD-ROM.)

3. Ask students to refer to Figure 1.8 and trace the locations of the body cavities on copies of Figure 7.1.

4. Ask students to refer to Figure 1.11 and trace the locations of abdominal regions and quadrants on copies of Figure 7.1.

Critical Reasoning

Ask students to explain why bones have foramina, fissures, passageways, and depressions. Provide a copy of Figure 7.9b and ask students to identify and label several surface markings of the orbit and to indicate the anatomical structures associated with them (e.g., nerves, blood vessels, ducts). Although Table 7.2, Bones of the Skull, lists the specific names of the blood vessels or nerves involved, it is usually sufficient to ask students to focus on general categories of anatomy at this point.

Answer: The following surface features permit passage of cranial nerves and/or blood vessels: supraorbital foramen, infraorbital foramen, infraorbital groove, optic foramen, superior orbital fissure, and inferior orbital fissure. The lacrimal fossa houses the lacrimal sac that helps to drain tears into the nasal cavity.

SUPPLEMENTAL COURSE MATERIALS
Library Research Topics

1. A technique called percutaneous automated discectomy involves back surgery without stitches. How safe is it, and when can it be used? What are some other common techniques used to relieve herniated discs?

2. Spinal deviations such as scoliosis are difficult to repair. What are the current methods of treatment, both invasive and noninvasive?

3. Paleontologists and archaeologists have unearthed many prehistoric skulls and bones of human-like creatures and animals. How can they reconstruct the soft features and tissues of these animals from only their skeletal remains?

4. Trace the origin of congenital disorders of the skeleton, such as spina bifida and cleft palate, starting in the human embryo. What is the explanation for these defects?

Audiovisual Aids/Computer Software

See Preface of the Instructor's Guide for Key to Audiovisual Distributors

Slides

1. *The Skeletal System and Its Function* (EI, SS-03260F, Filmstrips or Slides). Skeletal substructure reviewed.

2. *Introductory Physiology Series: Bones and Muscles* (CRM: McGraw-Hill)

Videotapes

1. *Osteology of the Skull* (TFI, C, VHS/BETA, 1988). An eight-part series covering the anatomy of the skull.

2. *Skeleton* (CBS, 30 min.)

3. *Skeleton, An Introduction* (TFI, 46 min., C, VHS/BETA)

4. *Skull Anatomy Series* (TFI, C, VHS/BETA, 1988). A nine-part series that offers a complete approach to teaching and review of the skull.

5. *Skeletal and Topographic Anatomy Series* (TFI, C, VHS/BETA, 1988). A 30-part series that illustrates the anatomy of the head, neck, thorax, extremities, and other body parts.
6. *Anatomy of the Skull I: Superior, Posterior, and Lateral Views* (BM, 28 min.)
7. *Anatomy of the Skull II: Frontal and Lateral Aspects* (BM, 25 min.)
8. *Anatomy of the Skull III: Basal Aspect* (BM, 40 min.)
9. *Anatomy of the Skull IV: Interior of the Cranial Cavity* (BM, 36 min.)
10. *The Skeleton: An Introduction* (Anatomy and Physiology Series) (HCA/CAP, 29 min.)
11. *The Spine* (*Human Body Live Action Video Series*) (CAP, 28 min., 1993)

CD-ROMs

1. *Body Systems: Interactive Physical Education* (HCA, Mac/Win, 1995)
2. *The Dynamic Human* (ACC/CAP/HCA, Mac/Win)
3. *The Interactive Skeleton* (ACC/ Queue/IM, Mac/Win)
4. *The Interactive Skeleton* (DGI, 1996)
5. *The Ultimate 3-D Skeleton* (DGI, Queue, Mac/Win, 1996)
6. *The Living Body* (Queue, Win)
7. *Virtual Anatomy's 3-D Skeleton* (STI)

Computer Software

1. *Dynamics of the Human Skeletal System* (EI, C-3052, 1988, Apple or IBM)
2. *Bone Probe* (PLP, CH-175027, Apple 64K)
3. *Body Language: Skeletal System* (PLP, Mac/IBM)
4. *The Human Body, Part II* (HAC, 1995)

Suggested Readings

Alper, J. Boning up: Newly isolated proteins heal bad breaks. *Science* 263 (January 21, 1994): 324–325.

Basmajian, J.V. *Grant's Method of Anatomy.* 11th ed. Baltimore: Williams and Wilkins, 1989.

Gilmer, H., et al. Lumbar disk disease: Pathophysiology, management and prevention. *American Family Physician* 47 (April 1993): 1141–1152.

McMinn, R., R. Hutchings, et al. *Color Atlas of Human Anatomy.* 3rd ed. Chicago: Year Book Medical Publishers, 1993.

Moore, K.L. *Clinically Oriented Anatomy.* 34th ed. Philadelphia: Lippincott Williams and Wilkins, 1999.

Pool, R. Coral chemistry leads to human bone repair. *Science* 267 (March 24, 1995): 1772.

Raloff, J. Boning up on biodegradable implants. *Science News* 137 (May 5, 1990): 285.

Romanes, G.J. *Cunningham's Textbook of Anatomy.* 12th ed. Oxford, New York: Oxford University Press, 1981.

Rosse C., et al. *Textbook of Anatomy.* 5th ed. Philadelphia: Lippincott-Raven, 1997.

Williams, P.L., et al. *Gray's Anatomy.* 38th ed. New York: Churchill Livingstone, 1995.

ANSWERS TO TEXTBOOK QUESTIONS

Answers for multiple-choice and matching questions 1–6 are located in Appendix B of the textbook.

Short Answer and Essay Questions

7. At birth, the cranium is huge relative to the face and body. The face (including jaw and nose) enlarges during youth to reach its adult proportions. (p. 180)

8. The normal vertebral curvatures are cervical, thoracic, lumbar, and sacral. The thoracic and sacral curvatures are primary. The cervical and lumbar are secondary. (pp. 172 and 180)

9. Cervical vertebrae possess transverse foramina and have small bodies. Thoracic vertebrae possess facets for the ribs and have circular vertebral foramina. Lumbar vertebrae have massive bodies and blunt, hatchet-shaped spinous processes. (p. 174)

10. (a) The discs act as shock absorbers, bind successive vertebrae together, and allow the spine to flex and extend. They also resist tension forces placed on the vertebral column. (b) The anulus fibrosus is a series of about 12 concentric rings, which contain fibrocartilage and surround the nucleus pulposus. The nucleus pulposus is a sphere of gelatinous substance in the center of each intervertebral disc. (c) The nucleus pulposus herniates in a prolapsed disc. (pp. 168–172)

11. A floating rib (ribs 11 or 12) is a false rib. The definition of a false rib (ribs 8–12) is that it does not attach directly to the sternum. The floating ribs fit this definition because they do not attach to the sternum at all. (p. 178)

12. Cleft palate: a persistent opening in the medial part of the palate that interferes with sucking and can lead to aspiration of food into the lungs. A cleft palate is a common birth defect. (pp. 179–180)

13. In the young adult skeleton, the amount of bone mass is maximal, and the water content in the intervertebral discs is optimal. In old age, the water content of the discs declines, and the discs become thinner and less resilient. The spine is shorter and may assume a flexed arc. All the bones lose mass. The thorax becomes more rigid with increasing age, mainly due to ossification of the costal cartilages. The cranial bones decline in mass less extensively than do the other bones, but the facial contours of the aged change (jaws look smaller, especially if the teeth are lost). (pp. 180–181)

14. Movements allowed by the *lumbar region*: flexion and extension of the spine, but not rotation. Movements allowed by the *thoracic region*: rotation and some lateral flexion, but not flexion or extension. (p. 175, plus Table 7.3 on p. 174)

15. *Anterior cranial fossa*: frontal, ethmoid, sphenoid. *Middle cranial fossa*: sphenoid, temporal. *Posterior cranial fossa*: temporal, occipital (see Figure 7 4b and c, on p. 158). (Despite appearances, the *parietal* bone is not said to contribute to any of the cranial fossae.)

16. Sternum: Its three basic parts are manubrium, body, and xiphoid process. Other important features, as shown in Figure 7.19a, are the jugular notch, clavicular notches, articulations with ribs 1–7, sternal angle, and xiphisternal joint. (pp. 177–178)

17. The vertebral arch is the part of the vertebra defined by the two pedicles and the two laminae. The vertebral foramen is the space within the arch, and the successive vertebral foramina

form the vertebral canal for the spinal cord. The intervertebral foramina are lateral openings between adjacent vertebrae, and they contain spinal nerves. (p. 173)

18. The *anterior fontanel* is between the frontal and parietal bones; the *posterior fontanel* is between the parietal and occipital bones; and the *sphenoidal fontanel* is between the greater wing of the sphenoid and temporal, and parietal and frontal bones. The *mastoid fontanel* is between the occipital, temporal, and parietal bones. (See Figure 7.21 on p. 181.)

19. The spinal cord, not swallowed food, passes through the foramen magnum. (p. 157)

Critical Reasoning and Clinical Applications Questions

1. Frontal, zygomatic, maxillary. (Figure 7.9 on p. 165)

2. A lateral curvature is scoliosis due to an uneven pull of muscles. Since muscles on one side of the body were nonfunctional, those on the opposite side caused an uneven pull and forced the spine out of alignment. (p. 179)

3. Mr. Chester has lordosis, an exaggerated lumbar curvature of the spine. It is caused by the large weight of his anterior abdomen and by the fact that he must continuously thrust his shoulders posteriorly to counterbalance this anterior weight. (p. 179)

SUPPLEMENTAL STUDENT MATERIALS TO HUMAN ANATOMY, THIRD EDITION
Chapter 7: Bones, Part I: The Axial Skeleton

To the Student

Chapter 7 is an introduction to the bones of the axial portion of the human skeleton. Of the 206 total bones in the body, this chapter covers the bones of the skull, vertebral column, and rib cage that form the long axis of the body. The next chapter covers the remaining bones of the appendicular skeleton. In this chapter you will master new terminology and learn how the bones of the skull articulate with one another. Also, you will be introduced to special bone marks and features of the skeletal bones—features that you will relate in later chapters to facts about muscles, tendons, nerves, and blood vessels. For example, remembering that the lesser wings of the sphenoid bone of the skull house the optic foramina will make it easier for you understand the passage of the pair of optic cranial nerves from the eyeball to the base of the brain. The surface markings of bones also relate to the foundations of understanding muscle attachments and movements.

Step 1: Distinguish between the axial skeleton and the appendicular skeleton.
☐ List the bones of the axial skeleton.
☐ List the bones of the appendicular skeleton.
☐ Describe several examples of bone markings and features.

Step 2: Understand general characteristics, bones, major sutures, and cavities of the skull.
☐ List all the bones of the skull and name all the other bones with which each skull bone forms an articulation.
☐ Distinguish between cranial and facial bones.
☐ Describe in detail the bony framework of the orbit and the nasal cavity.
☐ List bones that contain paranasal sinuses. Indicate which are evident in a midsagittal view of the skull.

Step 3: Understand the general structure, functions, and parts of the vertebral column.
☐ Describe the general structure of the vertebral column.
☐ List the bones of the vertebral column.
☐ Explain the functions of spinal curvatures and intervertebral discs.
☐ Describe the general gross anatomy of a typical vertebra.
☐ Distinguish between cervical, thoracic, and lumbar vertebrae by listing special features of each.
☐ Distinguish between the intervertebral foramina and vertebral canal and explain what passes through each.

Step 4: Understand the general structure and functions of the bony thorax.
- ☐ Define *thorax*.
- ☐ List the bones that compose the bony thorax.
- ☐ Describe the gross anatomy of a rib and the sternum.
- ☐ Distinguish between a right rib and left rib.
- ☐ Distinguish between true, false, and floating ribs.

Step 5: Understand general structure of the fetal skull.
- ☐ Define *fetal*.
- ☐ Define *fontanel*.
- ☐ List the fontanels of the fetal skull.
- ☐ Explain the advantages an infant receives from incompletely formed skull bones and fontanels.

CHAPTER 8

Bones, Part 2: The Appendicular Skeleton

LECTURE AND DEMONSTRATION
Student Objectives

1. Name the basic parts of the appendicular skeleton.
2. Identify the bones that form the pectoral girdle, and explain their functions.
3. Identify the important bone markings on the pectoral girdle.
4. Describe the bones of the arm, forearm, wrist, and hand.
5. Name the bones contributing to the hip bone, and relate the strength of the pelvic girdle to its function.
6. Compare and contrast the male and female pelvis.
7. Identify the bones of the lower limb and their important markings.
8. Name the three supporting arches of the foot, and explain their importance.
9. Describe how the lengths of the limbs change, relative to the length of the head and trunk as we grow.

Suggested Lecture Outline

I. *The Pectoral Girdle (pp. 186–189, Figs. 8.1–8.3)*

　A. Clavicles (p. 186)

　B. Scapulae (pp. 186–189)

II. *The Upper Limb (pp. 189–194, Figs. 8.3–8.6 and Table 8.1)*

　A. Arm (pp. 189–190, Fig. 8.3)

　B. Forearm (p. 190, Figs. 8.4 and 8.5)

　　1. Ulna

　　2. Radius

　C. Hand (pp. 190–194, Fig. 8.6)

　　1. Carpus

　　2. Metacarpus

　　3. Phalanges of the Fingers

III. The Pelvic Girdle (pp. 194–199, Figs. 8.7, 8.8, and Table 8.1)

   A. Ilium (p. 194, Fig. 8.7)

   B. Ischium (p. 194, Fig. 8.7)

   C. Pubis (p. 198, Fig. 8.7)

   D. True and False Pelves (pp. 198–199, Fig. 8.8)

   E. Pelvic Structure and Childbearing (p. 199, Fig. 8.8 and Table 8.2)

IV. The Lower Limb (pp. 199–205, Figs. 8.9–8.11, and Table 8.1)

   A. Thigh (p. 199, Fig. 8.9b)

   B. Leg (p. 202, Fig. 8.10)

   1. Tibia

   2. Fibula

   C. Foot (pp. 202–205, Fig. 8.11)

   1. Tarsus

   2. Metatarsus

   3. Phalanges of the Toes

   4. Arches of the Foot

V. Disorders of the Appendicular Skeleton (p. 205)

VI. The Appendicular Skeleton Throughout Life (pp. 205–206)

Lecture Hints

1. Distinguish between basic parts of the appendicular skeleton. Emphasize that the pectoral girdle and pelvic girdle are appendicular because they attach the limb bones to the rest of the skeleton. Students erroneously think "midline" with the pelvic girdle.

2. Using Figure 8.1, identify the bones of the pectoral girdle and explain their functions, pointing out that the clavicle functions as a "prop," and if fractured, the entire shoulder collapses forward.

3. Point out important bone markings on the clavicle and scapula.

4. Encourage students to thoroughly master the scapula to facilitate the future study of shoulder and arm muscles.

5. Explain the articulation between the clavicle and the scapula.

6. Describe how the scapula articulates with the humerus.

7. Explain to students that the word *arm* is used in a strict anatomical sense, referring to only the upper portion of the limb.

8. Emphasize the importance of *anatomical position* to the forearm. Refer to Figure 1.3.

9. Devise a simple mnemonic for the bones of the wrist.

10. Using Table 8.1, identify the bones of the pelvic girdle and explain their functions.

11. Explain the three *separate* bones of the *composite* coxal bone. Refer to Figure 8.7b.

12. Describe how when sitting, the weight of the body is borne by the *ischial tuberosities*, the strongest part of the pelvic girdle.
13. Distinguish between *true* pelvis and *false* pelvis.
14. Distinguish between a male pelvis and a female pelvis. Refer to Figure 8.2.
15. Relate pelvic structure to childbearing.
16. Name and describe the bones of the lower limb. Refer to Figures 8.9–8.11.
17. Explain to students that the word *leg* is used in a strict anatomical sense, referring to only the portion of the lower limb between the knee and ankle.
18. Distinguish between the tibia and fibula in terms of size, location, bony features, functions, and articular surfaces.
19. Explain the importance of arches of the foot and clues provided by a *wet footprint*.
20. Comment on disorders of the appendicular skeleton, including fractures (covered in Chapter 6), hip dysplasia, and clubfoot.
21. Using Figure 8.13, discuss the changes in body proportions throughout life.

Classroom Discussion Topics and Activities

1. Obtain male and female pelvic girdles, and explore the differences.
2. List several skeletal landmarks that are used to guide a nurse or physician in giving shots, locating areas for surgery, and assisting in the diagnosis of internal conditions. (Note that these topics are covered fully in Chapter 26 of the textbook.)
3. Discuss the effects of exaggerated exercise or the complete lack of exercise on bones such as the tibia, femur, and humerus, (a) during childhood and (b) during adulthood. Then explain why the bones of the lower limb are the thickest and heaviest bones in the body.
4. Numerous children are born with a congenital hip defect. Ask students why this area is affected so often and what can be done to correct the defect.
5. Place a disarticulated appendicular bone in a bag and have the students identify it using only their sense of touch.
6. Provide a complete disarticulated skeleton and instruct students to arrange bones in correct positions.

Clinical Questions

1. A group of high school students suffered a serious accident as they drove to the prom. Brad suffered multiple injuries to his lower left limb. Protruding through the skin was a splintered portion of the longest bone in the body. This bone was the (a) ___ . Adrian didn't consider her injuries serious, so she walked several blocks to find help. Then she noticed that her right knee was not functioning normally; examination revealed a fractured kneecap. Another name for the kneecap is the (b) ___ . She also realized she had fractured several toe bones, or (c) ___ . Greg fractured his heel bone, more correctly called the (d) ___ .

   Answers: (a) femur; (b) patella; (c) phalanges; (d) calcaneus.

2. The femur is the strongest bone in the body, but it is also one of the most often fractured bones in the skeleton. How can the strongest bone be broken so often?

   Answer: The neck of the femur is not as strong as its shaft, and it is often weakened in people with osteoporosis. When weakened, the neck of the femur breaks under the weight of the body; this is a broken hip.

ART RESOURCES
Transparency List

Figure 8.1   Overview of the pectoral girdle.
Figure 8.2   The scapula.
Figure 8.3   The humerus of the right arm.
Figure 8.4   Radius and ulna of the right forearm.
Figure 8.5   Details of bones of the forearm and elbow.
Figure 8.6   Bones of the hand.
Figure 8.7   Bones of the pelvic girdle.
Figure 8.9   The right patella and femur.
Figure 8.10 The tibia and fibula of the right leg.
Figure 8.11 Bones of the right foot.
Figure 8.12 Arches of the foot.

Teaching with Art

Figure 8.7   Bones of the pelvic girdle.

Textbook p. 195; transparencies; Digital Archive CD-ROM.

Checklist of Key Points in the Figure

- Explain that a *complete* pelvic girdle contains two coxal bones, as well as the sacrum and coccyx of the vertebral column.
- Point out the sacroiliac joint.
- Relate the strength of the pelvic girdle to its functions.
- Discuss why so many names of bones are used for the *hip* bone and how to distinguish the Y-shaped junction within the acetabulum.
- Point out several prominent bony features, such as the iliac crest, obturator foramen, and acetabulum, and explain functions of each.
- Explain the difference between the false pelvis and the true pelvis.

Common Conceptual Difficulties Interpreting the Art

- A coxal bone is a fusion of three bones with distinguishable sutures in a child but with indistinguishable sutures in the adult.
- The acetabulum and obturator foramen result from the fusion of these three bones.
- A dense, fibrous membrane fills most of the opening of the obturator foramen, leaving room for the passage of blood vessels and nerves.

Art Exercise

1. Using the Digital Archive CD-ROM, provide students with unlabeled copies of Figure 8.7. Instruct students to color the bony pelvic brim to distinguish the upper false pelvis from the lower true pelvis.
2. Using an unlabeled diagram of Figure 8.6a, mark the position of a ring and/or a watch on the figure.

Critical Reasoning

Ask students to name specific organs located in the false pelvis and the true pelvis. Refer to Chapter 1 and Figures 1.8 and 1.11.

Answer: The rectum and anal canal of the large intestine, urinary bladder, and urethra, as well as male and female reproductive organs (male: prostate gland and seminal vesicles; female: ovaries, uterine tubes, and uterus) occupy the true pelvis. Organs found in the false pelvis are portions of the large intestine and small intestine.

SUPPLEMENTAL COURSE MATERIALS
Library Research Topics

1. Research congenital skeletal malformation. Name examples of abnormalities of the appendicular skeleton.
2. Research bipedal locomotion and explore the adaptations that led to this type of movement.
3. Research current trends in bone repair.

Audiovisual Aids/Computer Software

See Preface of the Instructor's Guide for Key to Audiovisual Distributors

Videotapes

1. *Osteology of the Upper Limb* (TFI, 23 min., C, VHS/BETA, 1988)
2. *Skeletal and Topographic Anatomy Series* (TFI, C, VHS/BETA, 1988). A 30-part series that illustrates the anatomy of the head, neck, thorax, extremities, and other body parts.
3. *Anatomy of the Thorax* (BM, 36 min.)
4. *Anatomy of the Upper Limbs* (BM, 52 min.)
5. *Anatomy of the Vertebral Column* (BM, 30 min.)
6. *Skeleton* (CBS, 30 min.)
7. *Skeleton, An Introduction* (TFI, 46 min., C, VHS/BETA)

Computer Software

1. *Dynamics of the Human Skeletal System* (EI, C-3052, 1988, Apple or IBM)
2. *Bone Probe* (PLP, CH-175027, Apple 64K)
3. *Body Language: Skeletal System* (PLP, Mac/IBM)
4. *The Human Body, Part II* (HAC, 1995)

CD-ROMs

1. *Body Systems: Interactive Physical Education* (HCA, Mac/Win, 1995)
2. *The Dynamic Human* (ACC/CAP/HCA, Mac/Win)
3. *The Interactive Skeleton* (ACC/Queue/IM, Mac/Win)
4. *The Interactive Skeleton* (DGI, 1996)
5. *The Ultimate 3-D Skeleton* (DGI, Queue, Mac/Win, 1996)
6. *The Living Body* (Queue, Win)
7. *Virtual Anatomy's 3-D Skeleton* (STI)

Suggested Readings

Katz, R. Carpal tunnel syndrome: A practical review. *American Family Physician* 49 (May 1, 1994): 1371–1379.

McMinn, R., R. Hutchings, et al. *Color Atlas of Human Anatomy*. 3rd ed. Chicago: Year Book Medical Publishers, 1993.

Moore, K.L. *Clinically Oriented Anatomy*. 34th ed. Philadelphia: Lippincott Williams and Wilkins, 1999.

Romanes, G.J. *Cunningham's Textbook of Anatomy*. 12th ed. Oxford, New York: Oxford University Press, 1981.

Scott, S., and D. Winter. Biomechanical model of the human foot: Kinematics and kinetics during the stance phase of walking. *Journal of Biomechanics* 26 (1993): 1091–1104.

ANSWERS TO TEXTBOOK QUESTIONS

Answers for multiple-choice questions 1–4 are located in Appendix B of the textbook.

Short Answer and Essay Questions

5. (a) Stability. (b) To provide stability, the pelvic girdle is fused to the axial skeleton (sacrum), and its socket for articulation with the largest limb bone (femur) is deep. By contrast, the highly movable pectoral girdle is not fused to the axial skeleton (except at the medial part of the clavicle), and its socket for articulation with the largest limb bone (humerus) is shallow. (pp. 186–199)

6. The female pelvic inlet and outlet are wider, the pelvis is shallower, lighter, and wider than that of the male, and the ischial tuberosities are farther apart. Furthermore, the pubic arch forms a larger angle. (Table 8.2 on p. 200)

7. The three arches of the foot function to distribute the weight of the body. (p. 205)

8. Hip dysplasia: the acetabulum is incompletely formed, and the head of the femur slips out of the hip joint. Hip dysplasia is a common birth defect. (p. 205)

9. The true pelvis is the pelvic region inferior to the pelvic brim. The false pelvis, actually part of the abdomen, lies superior to the pelvic brim (and extends to the level of the iliac crest). (p. 199)

10. The correct names are tibia (not fibia) and fibula (not tibula). (p. 202)

11. See Figure 8.1e on p. 187.

12. (a) greater trochanter: femur, superolateral part; (b) linea aspera: femur, posterior part of shaft; (c) trochlea: this is the medial condyle on the distal end of the humerus; (d) coronoid process: ulna, proximal anterior end; (e) deltoid tuberosity: humerus, lateral surface of mid shaft; (f) greater tubercle: humerus, superolateral part; (g) greater sciatic notch: posterior part of the ischium. (Table 8.1, pp. 196–197)

13. (a) The arm is the segment of the upper limb occupied by the humerus—from shoulder to elbow. (b) The medial side of the hand is the side of the fifth ("little") finger (recall the anatomical position).

14. Tom was helping the students learn the obturator foramen in the hip bone.

Critical Reasoning and Clinical Applications Questions

1. Since the clavicles act to hold the scapulae and arms out laterally from the thorax, the shoulder region collapses medially when a clavicle is broken. Malcolm's fracture probably did not damage the subclavian artery posterior to (deep to) the clavicle, because the curves in the clavicle ensure that it fractures anteriorly at its middle third. (p. 186)

2. Flat foot is a depression, or falling, of the arches of the foot. It may result from prolonged standing at a stand-up job or running on hard surfaces, and is most likely to occur after wearing shoes that do not provide proper arch support. (p. 205)

3. These are the symptoms of the repetitive strain disorder called carpal tunnel syndrome. (p. 191)

SUPPLEMENTAL STUDENT MATERIALS TO HUMAN ANATOMY, THIRD EDITION

Chapter 8: Bones, Part 2: The Appendicular Skeleton

To the Student

Chapter 8 is an introduction to the bones of the appendicular portion of the human skeleton. Of the 206 total bones in the body, you mastered all the bones of the skull, vertebral column and rib cage in the preceding chapter. This chapter covers the remaining bones. Continued mastery of new terminology is necessary. Your goal is to understand how individual bones of the appendicular skeleton form the pectoral and pelvic girdles and upper and lower limbs.

Step 1: Distinguish between the axial and appendicular skeletons.
- ☐ Name the bones of the axial skeleton.
- ☐ Name the bones of the appendicular skeleton.

Step 2: Understand the bones that form the pectoral girdle and upper limb.
- ☐ Name the bones that form the pectoral girdle.
- ☐ Explain how bones of the pectoral girdle articulate with each other.
- ☐ Explain the functions of the pectoral girdle.
- ☐ Indicate major bone markings of the bones of the pectoral girdle and upper limb.
- ☐ Describe the bones of the arm, forearm, wrist, and hand, including articulations.

Step 3: Understand the bones that form the pelvic girdle and lower limb.
- ☐ Name the bones that form the pelvic girdle.
- ☐ Explain the articulations between the bones forming the pelvic girdle.
- ☐ List the functions of the pelvic girdle.
- ☐ Indicate major bone markings of the bones of the pelvic girdle and lower limb.
- ☐ Compare and contrast male and female pelves.
- ☐ Describe the bones of the thigh, leg, and foot, including articulations.

CHAPTER 9

Joints

LECTURE AND DEMONSTRATION
Student Objectives

1. Define *joint*.
2. Classify the joints by structure and by function.
3. Describe the general structure of fibrous joints. Provide examples of the three types of fibrous joints.
4. Describe cartilaginous joints, and give examples of the two main types.
5. Describe the structural characteristics shared by all synovial joints.
6. Explain how synovial joints function.
7. List three factors that influence the stability of synovial joints.
8. Define *bursa* and *tendon sheath*.
9. Name and describe the common types of body movements.
10. Name six classes of synovial joints based on the shapes of their joint surfaces and the types of movement they allow. Give examples of joints in each class.
11. Describe the key features of the jaw, shoulder, elbow, hip, knee, and ankle joints.
12. Name the most common injuries to joints, and discuss the problems associated with each.
13. Name and describe the types of arthritis.
14. Describe how joints develop and how their functions may be affected by aging.

Suggested Lecture Outline

I. Classification of Joints (p. 212)

II. Fibrous Joints (pp. 212–213, Fig. 9.1)

    A. Sutures (p. 212)

    B. Syndesmoses (pp. 212–213)

    C. Gomphoses (p. 213)

III. Cartilaginous Joints (p. 213, Fig. 9.2)

    A. Synchondroses (p. 213, Fig. 9.2)

    B. Symphyses (p. 213, Fig. 9.2)

IV. Synovial Joints (pp. 214–234, Figs. 9.3–9.14)

    A. General Structure (pp. 214–218, Fig. 9.3)

    B. How Synovial Joints Function (p. 218)

    C. Bursae and Tendon Sheaths (p. 219, Fig. 9.4)

    D. Factors Influencing the Stability of Synovial Joints (pp. 219–220)

        1. Articular Surfaces

        2. Ligaments

        3. Muscle Tone

    E. Movements Allowed by Synovial Joints (pp. 220–224, Figs. 9.5 and 9.6)

        1. Gliding

        2. Angular Movements

        3. Rotation

        4. Special Movements

    F. Synovial Joints Classified by Shape (pp. 224–226, Fig. 9.7)

        1. Plane Joints

        2. Hinge Joints

        3. Pivot Joints

        4. Condyloid Joints

        5. Saddle Joints

        6. Ball-and-Socket Joints

    G. Selected Synovial Joints (pp. 226–227, Figs. 9.8–9.14)

        1. Temporomandibular Joint (pp. 226–227)

        2. Shoulder Joint (pp. 227–228)

        3. Elbow Joint (p. 227)

        4. Hip Joint (pp. 229–231)

        5. Knee Joint (pp. 231–233)

        6. Ankle Joint (pp. 233–234)

V. Disorders of Joints (pp. 234–238)

    A. Joint Injuries (p. 234)

        1. Sprains

        2. Dislocations

        3. Torn Cartilage

    B. Inflammatory and Degenerative Conditions (pp. 236–238)

        1. Bursitis and Tendonitis

        2. Arthritis

        3. Lyme Disease

VI. The Joints Throughout Life (p. 238)

Lecture Hints

1. Explain the functional and structural classification systems of joints. Refer to Table 9.1 on p. 212.
2. Distinguish between three types of fibrous joints, noting names, structural characteristics, fibers, and mobility.
3. Distinguish between two types of cartilaginous joints, noting names, structural characteristics, types of cartilage, and mobility.
4. Distinguish between six types of synovial joints, noting names, structural characteristics, and mobility.
5. Instruct students to design a work sheet that compares joints based on structure.
6. Explain the general structure of synovial joints.
7. Explain how synovial joints function.
8. Distinguish between bursae and tendon sheaths.
9. Discuss factors that influence the stability of synovial joints.
10. Describe and demonstrate movements allowed at synovial joints.
11. Explain how synovial joints are classified by shape. Refer to Figure 9.7.
12. Describe in detail one or more of the following joints: temporomandibular, shoulder, elbow, hip, knee, and ankle. Refer to Figures 9.8–9.15. Illustrate how anatomical differences between these joints relate to functional differences.

Classroom Discussion Topics and Activities

1. Select a student to illustrate several types of movements, such as abduction and adduction, and flexion and extension. Encourage group participation.
2. Ask a student to crouch into a fetal position with hands forming fists. Instruct the rest of the class to identify the flexed joints.
3. Instruct students to perform an action as the instructor calls it out. The class will look and sound like an aerobics class if done energetically. Be sure to include the command "flex arm" because 95% of the students will flex the forearm instead of the arm.
4. Using a synovial joint model, such as one of the knee, illustrate features of a joint.
5. Use a fresh beef joint to provide an excellent demonstration of joint features: capsule, cavity, ligaments, articular cartilage, periosteum, and articular disc or meniscus. If enough muscle is attached, demonstrate movement by pulling the muscle or the tendon.
6. Use an articulated human skeleton to demonstrate joints such as sutures, cartilaginous joints, gomphoses, and synovial joints. Show how articulating bone surfaces have complementary shapes. Ask students to explain how the shapes of some specific bone surfaces at joints determine the movements possible at those joints. The elbow, jaw, ankle, hip, and hand joints are especially good for this purpose.
7. To illustrate weeping lubrication, use a smooth plastic ball to squeeze soapy water from a stiff sponge.
8. Obtain X rays of patients with osteoarthritis and rheumatoid arthritis.

9. Discuss how shots of an anti-inflammatory hormone, a corticosteroid called cortisone, can readily reduce the swelling that follows joint injuries. Why is it dangerous for athletes to continue getting these shots? (Corticosteroids are discussed in depth in Chapter 25, The Endocrine System, so you may refer students to that chapter.)

10. Ask students why physical therapists suggest that athletes warm up with various stretching exercises before proceeding with rigorous physical activity. Of what value are these exercises for the joint areas?

11. Ask students to make an informal survey of family and friends to find out how many of them have an artificial joint or know of someone who does. The numbers will be surprising. Some individuals may volunteer information about their pets as well. Incorporate *A Closer Look: the Development of Artificial Joints,* textbook p. 238, into the discussion.

12. Ask students how an India rubber man is able to perform his contortions.

Clinical Questions

1. Paul Jones fell off of the staging while painting his house. His left arm and side struck the ground with a good deal of force. When he picked himself up, he felt sharp pain in his left shoulder and was unable to move his left arm. During the examination, his physician recorded that the normal roundness of the left shoulder was absent and there was a bulge inferior to the lateral end of the left clavicle. What is your diagnosis?

   Answer: Inferior and anterior dislocation of the left shoulder.

2. Jenny's father loved to hold his 4-year-old daughter by her hands and swing her around in great circles. One day, Jenny's glee was suddenly replaced with tears, and she screamed that her left elbow hurt. When examined, the little girl was seen to hold her elbow semiflexed and her forearm pronated. What is your diagnosis?

   Answer: The annular ligament around the head of the radius has been torn, and the head of the radius has pulled distally to slip out of this ring. (The swinging accident may also have pulled and injured the child's biceps brachii muscle.)

3. Crazy Legs Girsh, an American League pitcher, had been warming up for an important baseball game. He threw an extremely hard sidearm pitch and felt something "pop" in his shoulder. The trainer said he had injured his rotator cuff. What and where is the injury?

   Answer: The rotator cuff is a collection of muscles and tendons that encircle the shoulder joint and fuse with the articular capsule. The injury probably resulted from stretching and tearing some of these muscles.

4. Amy studied at her desk for 7 straight days for her nursing board exams. Soon, she noticed extreme pain and swelling on the point (olecranon) of both her elbows. What had happened?

   Answer: Amy had developed "student's elbow," or olecranon bursitis. Obviously, she had rested her elbows on the desk as she studied, and the continual pressure eventually irritated the bursa deep to the skin over the olecranon process.

Chapter 9: *Joints*

ART RESOURCES

Transparency List

Figure 9.1   Fibrous joints.

Figure 9.2   Cartilaginous joints.

Figure 9.3   Synovial joints.

Figure 9.4   Bursae and tendon sheaths.

Figure 9.5   Movements allowed by synovial joints.

Figure 9.6   Some special body movements.

Figure 9.7   Synovial joints, classified by the shape of their articular surfaces.

Figure 9.8   The temporomandibular (jaw) joint.

Figure 9.9   The shoulder joint.

Figure 9.10   The elbow joint.

Figure 9.11   The hip joint.

Figure 9.12   The knee joint.

Figure 9.15   The ankle joint.

Teaching with Art

Figure 9.12   The knee joint: (a) Sagittal section; (b) Superior view.

Textbook p. 230; transparencies; Digital Archive CD-ROM.

Checklist of Key Points in the Figure

- Explain that the knee is largest joint in the body.
- Explain the bicondyloid shape of the knee joint.
- Review basic synovial joint structure.
- Point out the menisci and bursae of the joint, explaining their functions.
- Note the intracapsular (cruciate) ligaments, including their attachment points.

Common Conceptual Difficulties Interpreting the Art

- Note that the articular capsule merges with the tissue of the periosteum.
- Explain that the articular capsule is missing anteriorly and replaced with ligaments.
- Point out that the patellar ligament is a continuation of the tendon of the quadriceps femoris group of muscles.
- Explain that there is no common synovial cavity but one consisting of incomplete subdivisions and extensions.

Art Exercises

1. Using the Digital Archive CD-ROM, provide students with unlabeled copies of Figure 9.3c, Synovial joints. Instruct students to add modifications to the drawing that are characteristic of the knee joint, including menisci and intracapsular ligaments. The instructor may perform a similar demonstration in class using the Figure 9.12 transparency with an overlay and a colored marker or using the drawing tool on the Digital Archive CD-ROM.

2. Using the Digital Archive CD-ROM, provide students with copies of unlabeled anterior/posterior views of a skeleton. (See Figure 7.1 or the art in Table 9.2.) Instruct students to label the joints in the illustration that contain hyaline cartilage, fibrocartilage, or fibrous tissue.

Critical Reasoning

Using Figure 9.12, instruct students to study the arrangement of the intracapsular ligaments and to explain which ligament primarily is responsible for the prevention of the following undesirable movements: (a) the forward sliding of the femur, (b) the backward displacement of the tibia when the leg is flexed, (c) anterior sliding of the tibia on the femur when the leg is flexed, (d) hyperextension of the leg at the knee.

Answers: (a) posterior cruciate ligament, (b) posterior cruciate ligament, (c) anterior cruciate ligament, (d) anterior cruciate ligament.

SUPPLEMENTAL COURSE MATERIALS
Library Research Topics

1. Explore temporomandibular joint disorders in more depth. What is known of the causes? What methods of treatment are available and how successful are they?
2. Acknowledge that much controversy surrounds the use of the drug dimethyl sulfoxide (DMSO) for treating joint pains. Why is the Food and Drug Administration so reluctant to provide full approval of DMSO for use in humans when it is widely used in horses?
3. Research the use of arthroscopic surgery to treat disorders of joints other than the knee.
4. Review the literature on the procedures and materials used for joint prostheses. How close are scientists to developing an artificial hip or knee joint that can withstand the demands of a young, active athlete?
5. Point out that rheumatoid arthritis appears to be an autoimmune disease. What are the current methods of treatment, and what are some proposals for providing a cure in the future?

Audiovisual Aids/Computer Software

See Preface of the Instructor's Guide for Key to Audiovisual Distributors

Videotapes

1. *Moving Parts* (FHS, QB-830, VHS/BETA). Discusses muscle coordination and activity, including the role of joints, and shows a human knee joint. Also available as 16-mm film.
2. *Body Atlas Series: Muscle and Bone* (NCHCA, 30 min., 1994). Presents modern imaging techniques used to study muscle and bone.
3. *The Living Body: Growth and Change* (FHS, 28 min., 1990). Covers bone growth and remodeling.
4. *The New Living Body: Bones and Joints* (FHS, 20 min., 1995). Shows bone growth, injury, repair, and effects of exercise.
5. *Movement at Joints of the Body* (FHS, 40 min.). Looks at movements at synovial joints and actions of muscles.

6. *The Video Atlas of the Human Body: Tape 1* (DGI, 2 hr.). Discusses the shoulder, arm, forearm, and hand.

7. *The Video Atlas of the Human Body: Tape 2* (DGI, 2 hr.). Discusses the hip, knee, leg and ankle, and foot.

8. *The Video Atlas of the Human Body: Tape 3* (DGI, 2 hr.). Discusses the spine, thorax, abdomen, and pelvis.

Computer Software

1. *Body on Disc: Muscles and Bones* (NCHCA, 1996). A detailed look at the skeletal and muscular systems.

2. *Diagnosis of Bone and Joint Disorders.* 3rd ed. (WBS, 1996). Bone and joint problems viewed with the latest techniques in medical imaging.

3. *Skeletal Trauma: Fractures, Dislocations, Ligamentous Injuries.* 2nd ed. (WBS, 1998). Covers musculoskeletal trauma injuries.

4. *The Ultimate 3-D Skeleton* (DGI, 1996). A virtual tour of the human skeleton.

5. *Virtual Anatomy's 3-D Skeleton* (STI). A complete look at the human skeleton.

Suggested Readings

Allman, W.F. The knee. *Science 83* (November 1983): 122–123.

American Dental Association. Theme issue on temporomandibular disorders. *Journal of the American Dental Association* 120 (March 1990).

Barinaga, M. Treating arthritis with tolerance. *Science* 261 (September 24, 1993): 1669–1670.

Beck, M., et al. Living with arthritis. *Newsweek* (March 20, 1989): 64–70.

Clayton, J. Confusion in the joints. (Article on rheumatoid arthritis.) *New Scientist* (May 4, 1991): 40–43.

Evans, F.G. *Studies on the Anatomy and Function of Bone and Joints.* New York: Springer-Verlag, 1966.

Frankel, V.H., and M. Nordine. *Basic Biomechanics of the Skeletal System.* Philadelphia: Lea and Febiger, 1980.

Fuss, F.K. The restraining function of the cruciate ligaments on hyperextension and hyperflexion of the human knee joint. *The Anatomical Record* 230 (1991): 283–289.

Harris, C. Osteoarthritis: How to diagnose and treat the painful joint. *Geriatrics* 48 (August 8, 1993): 39–46.

Hecht, J. Cartilage culture mends damaged joints. *New Scientist* (October 29, 1994): 25.

Higging, J.R. *Human Movement: An Integrated Approach.* St. Louis: C.V. Mosby, 1977.

Johnson, G.T. Arthroscopic surgery on the knee. *The Harvard Medical School Health Letter* (March 1982).

Kantor, F. Disarming Lyme disease. *Scientific American* (September 1994): 34–39.

Levy, M. Diagnosing meniscus injuries. *The Physician and Sportsmedicine* 22 (May 1994): 47–54.

Romanes, G.J. *Cunningham's Textbook of Anatomy.* 11th ed. London: Oxford University Press, 1972, pp. 207–258.

Saul, H. Hipbone connected to the titanium implant. *New Scientist* (July 16, 1994): 34–38.

Simon, W.H. *The Human Joint in Health and Disease.* Philadelphia: University of Pennsylvania Press, 1978.

Toufexis, A. Treating an "in" malady. (An article about temporomandibular joint disorder.) *Time* (April 25, 1988): 102.

Valceschini, G. Immediate reduction of shoulder dislocation. *The Physician and Sportsmedicine* 23 (March 1995): 61–65.

Walker, P.S. Joints to spare. *Science* 85 (November 1985): 57.

Weiss, R. Bio-tick-nology yields Lyme disease vaccine. *Science News* 138 (October 27, 1990): 261.

Williams, P.L., et al. *Gray's Anatomy.* 37th ed. New York: Churchill Livingstone, 1989, pp. 459–544.

ANSWERS TO TEXTBOOK QUESTIONS

Answers for multiple-choice and matching questions 1–6 are located in Appendix B of the textbook.

Short Answer and Essay Questions

7. Joints are defined as sites of contact between two elements of the skeleton, usually between two bones.

8. Synovial fluid is derived from the synovial membrane of synovial joints. It is primarily a tissue fluid derived from capillaries in the synovial membrane. It also contains a glycoprotein lubricant that is secreted by fibroblasts in the connective tissue of the synovial membrane.

9. When pressure on a synovial joint pushes the adjacent articular cartilages together, it squeezes synovial fluid from the cartilages onto the cartilage surfaces. This fluid acts as a slippery lubricant, allowing the cartilages to glide across one another without friction. This is weeping lubrication.

10. Flexion and extension refer to decreasing or increasing the angle of a joint, while abduction and adduction refer to moving a part of the body (limb, finger) away from or closer to the midline.

11. *Hinge joint*: elbow and ankle (the knee and temporomandibular joints could be called *modified* hinge joints); *plane joint*: intertarsal, intercarpal, proximal tibiofibular, and sacroiliac joints; *condyloid joint*: atlanto-occipital joint, wrist, and knuckle; *ball-and-socket joint*: shoulder and hip. (Table 9.2)

12. The knee menisci even out the distribution of compressive load and of synovial fluid in the joint cavity; they also help guide movements of the condyles and prevent side-to-side rocking of the femur on the tibia. The cruciate ligaments act to prevent anterior and posterior sliding of the tibia on the femur, and help to secure the joint.

13. These injuries are problematic because they heal poorly. Sprains—tearing of joint ligaments—heal slowly because all ligaments are poorly vascularized. Torn cartilages heal poorly (in adults) because cartilage cells have no ability to divide.

14. (a) The humerus dislocates anteroinferiorly, (b) the ulna dislocates posteriorly, and (c) the femur dislocates posteriorly in car accidents.

15. The sutures on the back of the skull are fibrous joints, as is the distal tibiofibular joint, which also can be seen from a posterior view. The intervertebral discs between adjacent vertebral bodies are fibrocartilaginous joints. Essentially all the other joints visible on the posterior skeleton are synovial and have articular cartilages of hyaline cartilage. (See Figure 6.1 on p. 131, as well as Table 9.2 on pp. 216–218.)

16. (a) interphalangeal joints; flexion and extension. (b) radiocarpal joint; flexion and extension, abduction and adduction, circumduction. (c) temporomandibular joint; hinge action resulting in elevation and depression of mandible, as well as protraction and retraction. (d) sacroiliac joint; slight gliding. (e) metacarpophalangeal joint; flexion and extension, abduction and adduction, circumduction. (pp. 216–218, Table 9.2)

17. (a) The fibrous capsule contains the joint contents and resists tension so the bones of the joint are not pulled apart. (b) Synovial fluid is a lubricant that prevents articular elements from rubbing together and destroying the joint through friction. (c) Articular discs improve the fit between the two bone elements in joints, evenly distributing the load and minimizing wear. They also may allow two different movements at the same joint.

18. A bursa is a thin, fibrous sac of synovial fluid that is lined by a synovial membrane. Bursae function to prevent friction, and are located where ligaments, muscles, or skin overlie and rub against bone. A tendon sheath is essentially an elongated bursa that wraps around a tendon like a bun around a hot dog. Tendon sheaths surround tendons where several tendons crowd together in a narrow space, and they serve to reduce friction between these tendons.

19. (a) acromioclavicular joint. (b) intervertebral joints. (c) sternocostal joints. (d) costovertebral joints. (e) intertarsal joints. (pp. 216–218, Table 9.2)

20. (a) shoulder joint. (b) knee joint. (c) proximal radioulnar joint. (d) elbow joint. (e) ankle joint.

Critical Reasoning and Clinical Applications Questions

1. (a) Dorsiflexion and plantar flexion only (some call these movements flexion and extension) (Table 9.2, pp. 216–218). (b) No: dislocation and spraining do not indicate broken bones. (c) Reduction is returning the dislocated bone ends to their original, proper positions. (d) Sprains heal slowly and need repair to stabilize the joint. (e) In arthroscopic surgery, only small incisions are needed instead of a large surgical wound. There is less chance of infection, and healing of the incision is considerably faster.

2. Dan had dislocated his temporomandibular joint on one side, as this joint can be dislocated anteriorly by a wide, open-mouthed yawn. The dislocated head of Dan's mandible is now located in a position where the main jaw-closing muscle (called the masseter) cannot close the mouth, but only opens it wider. That is why Dan's mouth will be stuck open until he gets treatment.

3. (a) Rheumatoid arthritis, the type that often flares and then fades. (b) It is an autoimmune disease, a disorder in which the body's immune system attacks its own tissues.

4. Her shoulder had been dislocated so that the head of humerus had moved inferiorly. This is the most common type of shoulder dislocation.

5. Jim has all the classical symptoms of osteoarthritis, as described on p. 236.

6. Lyme disease is transmitted by ticks from deer (and other animals) to people.

SUPPLEMENTAL STUDENT MATERIALS TO HUMAN ANATOMY, THIRD EDITION
Chapter 9: Joints

To the Student
Now that you know the names of the bones of the skeleton, it is time to explore the union of bones and how movement of the skeleton is accomplished. Chapter 9 introduces you to the variety of joints (articulations) that form where bone attaches to bone. Although most joints unite bone to bone, some articulations join bone to cartilage. Relate the structure of the joint to the specific type of joint and the degree of mobility permitted. A specific movement is determined by the structure of the joint. When a muscle contracts, movement occurs. Study movements carefully and thoroughly so that your next step, the study of muscles in Chapter 10, will not be difficult to master.

Step 1: Be able to classify joints.
- ☐ Define *joint (articulation)*.
- ☐ Classify joints according to structure.
- ☐ Classify joints according to function.

Step 2: Describe and understand fibrous joints.
- ☐ Describe the general structure of fibrous joints.
- ☐ Give examples of three types of fibrous joints.
- ☐ Describe the mobility of each type of fibrous joint.
- ☐ Point out examples of fibrous joints on a diagram of a skeleton.

Step 3: Describe and understand cartilaginous joints.
- ☐ Describe the general structure of cartilaginous joints.
- ☐ Name two examples of cartilaginous joints.
- ☐ Describe the mobility of each type of cartilaginous joint.
- ☐ Point out examples of cartilaginous joints on a skeletal diagram.

Step 4: Describe and understand synovial joints.
- ☐ List basic structural characteristics of a synovial joint.
- ☐ Explain the mobility of a synovial joint.
- ☐ Explain how synovial joints function, including weeping lubrication.
- ☐ Distinguish between bursae and tendon sheaths and explain their significance within a synovial joint.
- ☐ Name and explain three factors that influence joint stability.
- ☐ Distinguish between gliding, angular, and rotation types of movements.
- ☐ Give examples of gliding joints.
- ☐ Define and give examples of five types of angular movements: *flexion* and *extension*, *abduction* and *adduction*, and *circumduction*. Include the plane of movement for each action.
- ☐ Define and give examples of *rotation*.

☐ Define and give examples of the following special movements: *supination* and *pronation*, *dorsiflexion* and *plantar flexion*, *inversion* and *eversion*, *protraction* and *retraction*, *elevation* and *depression*, and *opposition*.

☐ List and give examples of six structural types of synovial joints.

☐ Distinguish between nonaxial, uniaxial, biaxial, and multiaxial joints.

☐ For each of the following selected synovial joints, name the articulating bones, the structural type of joint, the functional type of joint, and all movements permitted.

- Temporomandibular joint
- Shoulder joint
- Elbow joint
- Hip joint
- Ankle joint

Step 5: Fill in the following joint classification work sheet.

Apply three of the following terms to each of the joints on the numbered list.

Amphiarthrosis	Hinge	Syndesmosis
Diarthrosis	Pivot	Gomphosis
Synarthrosis	Saddle	Fibrous joint
Ball and socket	Suture	Cartilaginous joint
Condyloid	Symphysis	Synovial joint
Gliding	Synchondrosis	

1. Interlocking joint between cranial bones: _____
2. Knee joint: _____
3. Elbow joint: _____
4. Intervertebral joint between articular processes: _____
5. Articulation between tibia and fibula at distal ends: _____
6. Shoulder joint: _____
7. Symphysis pubis: _____
8. Joint between the diaphysis and epiphysis of a long bone of a child: _____
9. Joint between the first metacarpal and carpus (trapezium): _____
10. Wrist (carpals to carpals): _____
11. Ankle (tarsals to tarsals): _____
12. Ankle (talus to tibia): _____
13. Hip joint: _____
14. Axis-atlas rotation: _____
15. Finger joint (between phalanges): _____
16. Phalanges to metacarpals: _____
17. Toe joint (between phalanges): _____
18. Phalanges to metatarsals: _____
19. Teeth and mandible or maxilla: _____

CHAPTER 10
Muscle Tissue

LECTURE AND DEMONSTRATION
Student Objectives

1. List four functional properties that distinguish muscle tissue from other tissues.
2. Compare and contrast skeletal, cardiac, and smooth muscle tissue.
3. Name the layers of connective tissue that occur in and around a skeletal muscle, and briefly describe a muscle's blood and nerve supply.
4. Describe the various ways in which muscles attach to their origins and insertions.
5. Define *muscle fascicles*.
6. Describe the microscopic structure of a skeletal muscle cell (fiber) and the arrangement of its contractile filaments into sarcomeres and myofibrils.
7. Explain the sliding filament theory of muscle contraction. What is the role of titin?
8. Describe the sarcoplasmic reticulum and T tubules in muscle fibers.
9. Compare and contrast the three kinds of skeletal muscle fibers.
10. Compare cardiac (heart) muscle to skeletal muscle.
11. Describe the structure and function of intercalated discs.
12. Compare smooth muscle fibers and skeletal muscle fibers in terms of their structure and functions.
13. Describe how smooth muscle cells form a sheet-like tissue.
14. Explain some symptoms of muscular dystrophy, myofascial pain syndrome, and fibromyalgia.
15. Describe the embryonic development and capacity for regeneration of muscle tissue.
16. Explain the changes that occur with age in skeletal muscle.

Suggested Lecture Outline

I. *Overview of Muscle Tissue* (p. 244)

    A. Functions

    B. Classification

II. *Skeletal Muscle* (pp. 244–254)

    A. Basic Features of a Skeletal Muscle (pp. 244–247, Figs. 10.1–10.3)

        1. Connective Tissue and Fascicles

        2. Nerves and Blood Vessels

II. SKELETAL MUSCLE *(continued)*
      3. Muscle Attachments
    B. Microscopic and Functional Anatomy of Skeletal Muscle Tissue (pp. 248–253, Figs. 10.4–10.9)
      1. The Skeletal Muscle Fiber
      2. Myofibrils and Sarcomeres
      3. Mechanisms of Contraction
      4. Muscle Extension
      5. Muscle Fiber Length and the Force of Contraction
      6. The Role of Titin
      7. Sarcoplasmic Reticulum and T Tubules
      8. Types of Skeletal Muscle Fiber

III. *Cardiac Muscle (p. 254, Figs. 10.10–10.11)*

IV. *Smooth Muscle (pp. 254–257, Fig. 10.12)*

V. *Disorders of Muscle Tissue (pp. 257–259)*
    A. Muscular Dystrophy
    B. Myofascial Pain Syndrome
    C. Fibromyalgia

VI. *Muscle Tissue Throughout Life (pp. 259–261)*

Lecture Hints

1. Discuss four basic functions of muscle tissue.
2. Explain four functional features of muscle tissue that distinguish it from other tissues.
3. Compare and contrast skeletal, cardiac, and smooth muscle tissue, including histological similarities as well as differences. Refer to Table 10.1 on pp. 245–246 in the text.
4. Explain why skeletal and smooth muscle cells are referred to as fibers.
5. Distinguish between sarcolemma and sarcoplasm, including a reference to the plasma membrane and cytoplasm.
6. Remind students that a skeletal muscle, such as the brachialis, is also an organ.
7. Figure 10.1 on p. 246 in the text shows the continuity of tough fibrous connective tissue connecting bone and muscle and provides an excellent illustration of how structure is related to function in the musculoskeletal system.
8. Using Figure 10.1, explain the multilevel relationships of connective tissue to muscle: (a) the covering of bone (periosteum) merges with tendons and ligaments, (b) it forms a structural framework by wrapping muscles and muscle groups, and (c) it also penetrates muscles, providing passage for blood vessels and nerves.
9. Explain the supply of blood vessels and nerves to muscle tissue.

Chapter 10: *Muscle Tissue*

10. Review superficial and deep fascia functions. Refer to Chapter 4, p. 98.
11. Distinguish between the origin and insertion of a muscle.
12. Distinguish between direct and indirect attachment, including definitions of tendon and aponeurosis.
13. Using Figure 10.4, explain the microscopic anatomy of a skeletal muscle fiber by describing the following structural features: fibers, sarcolemma, sarcoplasm, striations, myofibrils, myofilaments, sarcomere, and contractile proteins. Point out the multinucleate characteristic and remind students how that is possible.
14. Describe structural and functional details of a sarcomere.
15. Explain the sliding filament theory of muscle contraction. Refer to Figure 10.6.
16. Explain the source of energy for contraction to occur.
17. Explain the difference between *contraction* of a muscle and *extension* of a muscle.
18. Explain that what is true for a muscle fiber physiologically is true for the entire muscle, and relate this to muscle fiber length and force of contraction.
19. Discuss the physiological role of titin in muscle contraction.
20. Explain the role played by the sarcoplasmic reticulum and T tubules in muscle contraction. Refer to Figure 10.8.
21. Distinguish between three types of skeletal muscle fibers: red slow-twitch, white fast-twitch, and intermediate fast-twitch, including a brief comparison of muscles belonging to a long-distance runner and weight lifter.
22. Describe the anatomy of cardiac muscle, including intercalated discs and respective cell junctions. Refer to Figure 10.10.
23. Review briefly the comparison of cardiac muscle to skeletal muscle.
24. Identify locations of smooth muscle tissue.
25. Describe characteristics of smooth muscle fibers and explain organization of fibers into *sheets*.
26. Explain peristalsis, providing several examples and relating structure to function. Emphasize peristalsis as a recurring topic in the study of anatomy.
27. Comment on disorders of muscle tissue: muscular dystrophy, myofascial pain syndrome, and fibromyalgia.

Classroom Discussion Topics and Activities

1. Obtain three-dimensional models of the three types of muscle fibers (skeletal, cardiac, smooth) to exhibit their histological characteristics. Ask students how a cell can have more than one nucleus.
2. Obtain a three-dimensional model of a sarcomere to exhibit myofilaments and the sliding filament theory of muscle contraction.
3. To demonstrate the sliding filament theory, orient two stools horizontally, feet to feet, hold yardsticks between the stools, and ask students to move the stools together and apart. Each stool represents a Z disc with attached thin filaments, while each yardstick is a thick filament. The same demonstration is possible on a smaller scale using pipe cleaners.

4. Use a microprojector and microslides of skeletal, smooth, and cardiac muscle to compare and contrast these three muscle tissues.

5. So that students do not confuse such similar terms as fiber, fibril, fascicle, and filament, instruct them to list all the levels of organization of a skeletal muscle, from the whole muscle to the molecular level. The list will read as follows: muscle, fascicle, fiber, myofibril, sarcomere, and myofilament.

6. Ask students what "rigor mortis" means. What causes it? What happens approximately 20 hours later to end this physical state?

7. Ask students why they feel fatigue after strenuous exercise.

8. Discuss the consequences of taking anabolic steroids. Refer to *A Closer Look: Anabolic Steroid Abuse* on text book p. 260.

9. Discuss why is it important to keep moving and exercising rather than sitting on the ground, motionless, waiting for rescue if lost in a snowstorm.

10. Discuss muscle atrophy and hypertrophy. Ask students why muscles immobilized for long periods of time, as in a cast, tend to get smaller. What is necessary to revitalize them?

11. Ask students why weightlifters have such enormous muscles, while distance runners have lean muscles.

12. Smooth and cardiac muscle are both resistant to fatigue, but their endurance arises from two different mechanisms. Discuss and contrast the two mechanisms.

13. Ask students what would happen to body functions if intestinal peristalsis were stopped either by infection or injury.

14. Ask students why "warming up" is necessary prior to strenuous exercise and why someone is out of breath afterwards.

15. Students always enjoy a discussion of potential dinner topics. Explain the difference between red meat and white meat. Also, comment on what makes steak tender. And, you may as well tell them what that long white thing is that hangs off a chicken leg.

16. A simple way to demonstrate that muscles shorten when contracted is to ask students to stand on one foot and notice that the leg shortens enough that the other leg has to bend.

17. Remind students that additional media resources are available at *The Anatomy and Physiology Place* web site, including an interactive multiple-choice quiz. There is a direct link to this site from the *Study Partner CD-ROM*.

Clinical Questions

1. What is the immediate cause of death in most people who have Duchenne muscular dystrophy?

   Answer: When the main respiratory muscles weaken, death results from an inability to breathe.

2. Why are elderly people who have intermittent claudication extremely susceptible to developing frostbite in their toes?

   Answer: Since claudication is a restriction of the blood flow to the lower limb, an insufficient amount of warming blood reaches the toes on a cold day.

3. Backaches are among the most common of all maladies. Many people think that most backaches result from herniated intervertebral discs. Is this true?

    Answer: No. Most backaches are caused by strains and spasms in the deep muscles of the back that interconnect the vertebrae. (See the discussion of lower back pain in the Related Clinical Terms section of Chapter 10, p. 261.)

ART RESOURCES
Transparency List

Figure 10.1   Connective tissue sheaths in skeletal muscle.

Figure 10.4   Microscopic anatomy of a skeletal muscle fiber.

Figure 10.6   Sliding filament mechanism of contraction of a skeletal muscle.

Figure 10.8   Sarcoplasmic reticulum and T tubules in the skeletal muscle fiber.

Figure 10.10 Cardiac muscle.

Figure 10.12 Smooth muscle.

Teaching with Art

Figure 10.1   Connective tissue sheaths in skeletal muscle.

Textbook p. 246; transparencies; Digital Archive CD-ROM.

Checklist of Key Points in the Figure

- Demonstrate the sheaths of connective tissue (from external to internal) in a skeletal muscle: epimysium, perimysium, and endomysium.
- Stress that a muscle *fiber* is a *cell*.
- Explain that bundles of fibers form fascicles.
- State that the entire group of fasicles (i.e., the muscle) is an organ.
- The intramuscular connective tissues allow passage for blood vessels and nerves.
- Explain that a skeletal muscle generally has one nerve, one artery, and one or more veins that repeatedly branch within the layers of the intramuscular connective tissue.
- Point out that a tendon attaches muscle to bone (as well as to skin or another muscle).

Common Conceptual Difficulties Interpreting the Art

- Stress the continuity of the system of intramuscular connective tissue. The collagen fibers in the epimysium, perimysium, and endomysium converge at the origin and insertion of a muscle to form a fibrous tendon.
- Point out that a tendon is part of the muscle itself and acts to attach the muscle to the bone. Remind students that bone is covered with periosteum, a connective tissue that joins with the tendon to help anchor the muscle.
- Explain that when a muscle contracts, the connective tissue sheaths are pulled, which in turn applies mechanical force to the bone.

- State that connective tissue sheaths are responsible for muscle elasticity, a property which enables a muscle to resume its resting length.
- Explain the relationship of the epimysium to the deep fascia.

Art Exercise

The following exercises stress the ubiquity of connective tissue in a muscle:

1. Using the Digital Archive CD-ROM, distribute unlabeled copies of Figure 10.1. Instruct students to color or shade all parts of the illustration that represent connective tissue.

   Comment: The ubiquity of connective tissue in a muscle should become evident when everything, except muscle fibers and blood vessels, are colored, including the tendon and bone surface. A very alert student will also color the blood inside the vessels as an example of a very atypical type of connective tissue.

2. Provide a copy of Figure 11.17a, a cross section of the muscles of the arm. Instruct students to color the connective tissues that form the compartments of the arm.

Critical Reasoning

1. Ask students to describe the relationship of the *deep fascia* to the muscles, tendons, and bones in Figure 10.4 and Figure 11.17.

   Answer: Deep fascia, a dense connective tissue, would wrap around the muscle and tendon, separating them from adjacent muscles. Also, deep fascia compartmentalizes and binds muscles forming functional groups, such as the anterior and posterior compartments of the arm.

2. Ask students why the tenderest cut of a steak comes from the center of the belly of the muscle instead of near the ends of the muscle.

   Answer: There is much more connective tissue near the ends than in the belly.

SUPPLEMENTAL COURSE MATERIALS
Library Research Topics

1. What do you think is the functional "reason" why skeletal and cardiac muscle tissues have little or no ability to regenerate? What current research is being done in this area?
2. Investigate the long-term effects of anabolic steroid use on muscle tissue.
3. Why are the Olympic committees so adamant against the use of "performance-enhancing" drugs such as anabolic steroids?
4. Explore the current theories for the causes of muscular dystrophy.

Audiovisual Aids/Computer Software

See Preface of the Instructor's Guide for Key to Audiovisual Distributors

Videotapes

1. *Anabolic Steroids: Quest for Superman* (HRM, 31 min., 1991). Covers the pros and cons of using anabolic steroids.

2. *The Anatomy and Physiology Video Series: The Muscular System* (NIMCO, 25 min.). Discusses the anatomy and physiology of the muscular system and some specific muscles.

3. *Body Atlas Series: Muscle and Bone* (NCHCA, 30 min., 1994). Modern imaging techniques used to study muscle and bone.

4. *Bones and Muscles* (FHS, 15 min., 1990). An in-depth look at bones and muscles and their interactions.

5. *The Human Body: Muscular System* (WARD, 15 min., 1993). A detailed look at the muscular system.

6. *The Human Body Series: Muscles* (NIMCO, 28 min., 1993). Discusses muscle tissue and how different types of muscles work.

7. *The Living Body: Muscle Power* (FHS, 27 min., 1990). A study of muscle at the microscopic level.

8. *Moving Parts* (FHS, 27 min., 1990). Demonstrates how the cerebellum coordinates muscle activity, proprioceptors, and the role of joints.

9. *Muscle Power* (FHS, 27 min., 1990). Demonstrates a microscopic view of how muscles work.

10. *Muscles* (FHS, 20 min., 1995). Covers the general nature of muscles.

11. *Muscular System at Work: The Inner Athlete* (FHS, 25 min.). Studies the roles played by muscle and skin.

12. *The New Living Body: Muscles* (FHS, 20 min., 1997). An in-depth look, from gross structure to detailed microstructure.

13. *Muscle Power* (FHS, QB-829, VHS/BETA). Shows microscopic views of muscles and compares all three types of muscle. Also available as 16-mm film.

14. *Your Body Series—Part 1, Your Muscular System* (PLP, CH-140201, VHS)

15. *What Can Go Wrong? (Muscular-Skeletal System)* (PLP, CH-140503, VHS)

16. *Steroids: Shortcut to Make-Believe Muscles* (CBS, 49-3810-V, VHS)

Computer Software

1. *Skeletal Muscle Anatomy and Physiology* (PLP, R-510001, Apple). Looks at the three categories of muscles, sliding filament theory, and motor units.

2. *Skeletal Muscle Anatomy and Physiology* (QUE, INT4612A, Apple). Covers the main categories of muscle tissue, sliding filament mechanism, motor units, and lever systems.

3. *A.D.A.M. Interactive Physiology CD-ROM: Muscular System* (ADAM). Discusses muscle physiology; interactive.

4. *Biochemistry of Muscle* (CDL). Covers neuromuscular junctions and sarcomeres.

5. *Body on Disc: Muscles and Bones* (NCHCA, 1996). A detailed look at muscular and skeletal systems.

6. *Mechanical Properties of Active Muscle* (MS-DOS). Offers six simulations to explore the mechanical behavior of active skeletal muscle.

7. *Muscle Tutorial* (STI, Mac only). Muscle microanatomy and physiology.

Slides

1. *Histology of the Skeletomuscular System* (EI, 615, Slides). Skeletal muscle, tendons, motor nerve endings, and bone.
2. *Muscular System and Its Function* (EI, SS-0355). Basics of muscular contraction and the significance of skeletal muscle striations.
3. *Muscle Contraction Set* (CBSC, 20 slides)

Suggested Readings

Acsadi, G., et al. Human dystrophin expression in mdx mice after intramuscular injection of DNA constructs. *Nature* 352 (August 29, 1991): 815.

Bower, B. Pumped up and strung out: Steroid addiction may haunt the quest for bigger muscles. *Science News* 140 (July 13, 1991): 30–31.

Brotchie, D., et al. Dual-channel laser scanning microscopy for the identification and quantification of proliferating skeletal muscle satellite cells following synergist ablation. *Journal of Anatomy* 186 (1995): 97–102.

Brown, S., and J. Lucy. Dystrophin as a mechanochemical transducer in skeletal muscle. *BioEssays* 15 (June 1993): 413.

Cormack, D.H. *Ham's Histology*. 9th ed. Philadelphia: J.B. Lippincott, 1987, Chapter 15.

Dickman, S. East Germany: Science in the disservice of the state. (Article on steroid abuse in communist East Germany.) *Science* 254 (October 4, 1991): 26–27.

Endo, M. Calcium release from the sarcoplasmic reticulum. *Physiological Reviews* 57 (1977): 71.

Foley, A. Tennis elbow. *American Family Physician* (August 1993): 281.

Fong, P., et al. Increased activity of calcium leak channels in myotubes of Duchenne human muscular dystrophy x mouse origin. *Science* 250 (November 2, 1990): 673–676.

Franklin, D. Steroids heft heart risks in iron pumpers. *Science News* 126 (July 1984): 38.

Goldspink, G. The brains behind the brawn. (An article on why muscles enlarge from weight training.) *New Scientist* (August 1, 1992): 28–32.

Greenberg, J. Exercise: A matter of life and death. *Science News* 126 (September 1984): 138–141.

Hirsch, A., and F. Munnings. Intermittent claudication. *The Physician and Sportsmedicine* 21 (June 1993): 125–138.

Hoberman, J., and C. Yesalis. The history of synthetic testosterone. *Scientific American* (February 1995): 76–81.

Huddart, H., and S. Hunt. *Visceral Muscle*. New York: Halsted Press, 1975.

Huston, C. Ruptured achilles tendon. *American Journal of Nursing* (December 1994): 37.

Huxley, H.E. The mechanism of muscular contraction. *Scientific American* 213 (December 1985): 18–27.

Junqueira, L.C., et al. *Basic Histology*. 6th ed. San Mateo, California: Appleton and Lange, 1989, Chapter 10.

Moore, E. Coupling of the Na^+/Ca^{2+} exchanger, Na^+/K^+ pump and sarcoplasmic reticulum in smooth muscle. *Nature* 365 (October 14, 1993): 657.

Chapter 10: *Muscle Tissue*

Rosse, C., and D.K. Clawson. *The Musculoskeletal System in Health and Disease.* New York: Harper and Row, 1980.

Somlyo, A.P., and A.V. Somlyo. Smooth muscle structure and function. *The Heart and Cardiovascular System.* 2nd ed. H.A. Fozzard, et al. (Editors). New York: Raven Press Ltd., 1992, Chapter 48.

Taylor, E. Molecular muscle. *Science* 261 (July 2, 1993): 35–36.

Wilson, F.C. *The Musculoskeletal System: Basic Processes and Disorders.* 2nd ed. Philadelphia: Lippincott, 1983.

ANSWERS TO TEXTBOOK QUESTIONS

Answers for multiple-choice and matching questions 1–9 are located in Appendix B of the textbook.

Short Answer and Essay Questions

10. The functions are *contractility*—the ability to shorten forcefully; *excitability*—the ability to receive and respond to a stimulus; *extensibility*—the ability to be stretched; and *elasticity*—the ability to return to normal length after being stretched.

11. (a) Tendon, aponeurosis, and direct attachments are alternate ways in which skeletal muscles attach to the skeleton. A tendon is a rope-like cord of fibrous tissue, and an aponeurosis is a broad, flat sheath. In a fleshy attachment, the attaching strands of connective tissue are so short that the muscle fascicles themselves appear to reach the bone. (b) The less-movable attachment of a muscle to the skeleton is its origin, whereas the more movable attachment is its insertion. The insertion is pulled toward the origin.

12. Basically, the myosin heads near the ends of the thick filaments grip the thin filaments and pivot inward, thereby pulling adjacent Z discs together (p. 248 and Figure 10.6). The student's drawing should resemble those in Figure 10.7 on p. 251.

13. *Red slow-twitch fibers:* thin, red, many mitochondria, abundant capillary supply. *White fast-twitch fibers:* thick, white, contain glycogen granules, few mitochondria, supplied by relatively few capillaries. *Intermediate fast-twitch fibers:* intermediate thickness, many mitochondria, and an abundant capillary supply.

14. Cardiac muscle is more resistant to fatigue than is skeletal muscle. The anatomical basis of this is that cardiac fibers contain more mitochondria. If cardiac muscle were to tire easily, routine exercise would exhaust the heart and cause death.

15. Intercalated discs, complex junctions between cardiac muscle cells, consist of desmosomes, desmosome-like fasciae adherens, and gap junctions. The first two of these act to hold the cells together, while the gap junctions let ions pass between the cardiac cells (the ions stimulate contraction).

16. Her list read: "From smallest to largest: 1. *Myofilaments:* rods made of protein; contain actin or myosin; contribute to sarcomeres. 2. *Myofibril:* a long row of sarcomeres that are lined up back to back within the cytoplasm of a muscle cell. 3. *Fiber:* a skeletal muscle cell. 4. *Fascicle:* a bundle of muscle fibers." (Table 10.2 on p. 255)

17. The sarcoplasmic reticulum stores calcium ions. When it releases these ions into the cytoplasm, they act as triggers for the sliding filament mechanism of muscle contraction.
18. The sarcolemma is the plasmalemma of a muscle cell, and the sarcoplasm is the cytoplasm of a muscle cell.
19. Titin, a giant spring-like protein, runs from the end of each thick filament to a Z disc (see Figure 10.4). It holds the thick filament in place, and it contributes to muscle elasticity and resists overextension of striated muscle.

Critical Reasoning and Clinical Applications Questions

1. Regular exercise leads to increased muscle strength by causing muscle cells to hypertrophy or increase in size. The number of myofilaments per cell also increases. Satellite cells may fuse together to form new muscle fibers.
2. A *strain* is pulling and tearing a muscle (p. 261), while a *sprain* is tearing a joint ligament.
3. Since red and intermediate fibers are resistant to fatigue, ducks can maintain prolonged flight. Incidentally, this explains why chicken breast is white meat, and duck breast is dark meat.
4. Myoblasts are the embryonic muscle-forming cells, which fuse together and form new muscle fibers. They also fuse into existing fibers.
5. The textbook says that muscle infections are rare because muscles have a rich blood supply. This brings body-defense cells to the muscles so quickly that most infectious microorganisms are destroyed before multiplying. (Muscles also have a relatively deep location, so they encounter fewer surface microbes than do the superficial skin and respiratory tubes.)
6. RICE stands for Rest, Ice, Compression, Elevation.

SUPPLEMENTAL STUDENT MATERIALS TO HUMAN ANATOMY, THIRD EDITION
Chapter 10: Muscle Tissue

To the Student

Chapter 10 provides the opportunity to learn about muscle tissue. One of the four major types of body tissues, muscle tissue constitutes nearly half of the body's mass. Because of contraction of muscle tissues, you move in countless ways, blood moves through vessels, air enters and exits lungs, and food moves along the digestive tract. Chapter 10 builds the foundation for your future study of myology, the skeletal muscles of your body, the heart and circulation, and the many internal organs that have muscle tissue in their walls.

Step 1: Characterize muscle tissue.

☐ Explain why a muscle cell is a muscle cell.

☐ List and describe four functional properties distinguishing muscle tissue from other tissues.

☐ Using the following characteristics, design a chart for the comparison of skeletal, cardiac, and smooth muscle tissue:

- Location in body
- Cell shape
- Cell appearance
- Type of contraction
- Connective tissue components
- Presence of striations
- Presence of gap junctions
- Presence of neuromuscular junctions

Step 2: Understand the basic features of a skeletal muscle.

☐ List the levels of organization in a muscle going from a whole muscle to a myofilament.

☐ List and explain the connective tissue components of skeletal muscle.

☐ Explain the vascular nature of skeletal muscle.

☐ Describe innervation of skeletal muscle.

☐ Distinguish between the origin and insertion of muscle in several ways.

☐ Distinguish between a tendon and aponeurosis.

Step 3: Understand microscopic and functional anatomy of skeletal muscle.

☐ Describe the shape of a skeletal muscle cell, and explain why it is multinucleated.

☐ Define a *myofibril*.

☐ Draw a myofibril and show the sarcomeres and myofilaments responsible for striations.

☐ Define a *sarcomere*.

☐ Draw a sarcomere and label the following functional units: actin, myosin, titin, Z disc, and M line.

- ☐ Explain the sliding filament theory of muscle contraction.
- ☐ Explain how myofilaments determine the striation pattern in skeletal and cardiac muscle fibers.
- ☐ Describe the functional feature of elasticity of skeletal muscle and how overextension is prevented.
- ☐ Describe the role of the sarcoplasmic reticulum and T tubules in the skeletal muscle fiber.
- ☐ Distinguish between three types of skeletal muscle fibers: red slow-twitch, white fast-twitch, and intermediate fast-twitch.

Step 4: Understand cardiac muscle.
- ☐ Describe the shape of a cardiac muscle cell.
- ☐ Distinguish between a cardiac muscle fiber and cardiac muscle cell.
- ☐ Describe microscopic anatomical features.
- ☐ Distinguish between intercalated discs and striations.
- ☐ List three types of cell junctions characteristic of cardiac muscle.
- ☐ Give a brief explanation of a heartbeat.

Step 5: Understand smooth muscle.
- ☐ Describe the shape of a smooth muscle fiber.
- ☐ List characteristics of smooth muscle.
- ☐ Explain fiber arrangement, type of innervation, and contractility.

Step 6: Explain muscle tissue throughout life.
- ☐ Describe the embryonic origin of muscle tissue.
- ☐ Indicate the degree of regeneration for each type of muscle tissue.
- ☐ Explain why men have more muscle mass than women.
- ☐ Compare muscles of old age and young age in several ways.

CHAPTER 11
Muscles of the Body

LECTURE AND DEMONSTRATION
Student Objectives
1. Explain the three types of lever systems in which muscles participate, and indicate the arrangement of elements (effort, fulcrum, and load) in each.
2. Name some muscles whose fascicles have the following arrangements: parallel, convergent, pinnate, circular.
3. Describe the functions of prime movers (agonists), antagonists, synergists, and fixators.
4. List the criteria used in naming muscles.
5. Organize the body's muscles into four functional groups based on their developmental origins.
6. Name and identify the muscles described in Tables 11.1–11.17. State the origin, insertion, and action of each.

Suggested Lecture Outline
I. Lever Systems: Bone-Muscle Relationships (pp. 266–268, Figs. 11.1 and 11.2)

II. Arrangement of Fascicles in Muscles (p. 268, Fig. 11.3)

III. Interactions of Skeletal Muscles in the Body (pp. 268–270)

IV. Naming the Skeletal Muscles (p. 270)

V. A Development-Based Organization of the Muscles (pp. 270–272, Fig. 11.4)

VI. Major Skeletal Muscles of the Body (pp. 272–331, Fig. 11.5)

   A. Muscles of Facial Expression (pp. 276–277, Fig. 11.6)

   B. Muscles of Mastication and Tongue Movement (pp. 278–279, Fig. 11.7)

   C. Muscles of the Anterior Neck and Throat: Swallowing (pp. 280–282, Fig. 11.8)

   D. Muscles of the Neck and Vertebral Column: Head Movements and Trunk Extension (pp. 283–286, Fig. 11.9)

   E. Deep Muscles of the Thorax: Breathing (pp. 287–288, Fig. 11.10)

   F. Muscles of the Abdominal Wall: Trunk Movements and Compression of Abdominal Viscera (pp. 289–291, Fig. 11.11)

118 Instructor's Guide for Human Anatomy

VI. Major Skeletal Muscles of the Body *(continued)*

    G. Muscles of the Pelvic Floor and Perineum: Support of Abdominopelvic Organs (pp. 292–293, Fig. 11.12)

    H. Superficial Muscles of the Anterior and Posterior Thorax: Movements of the Scapula (pp. 294–296, Fig. 11.13)

    I. Muscles Crossing the Shoulder Joint: Movements of the Arm (Humerus) (pp. 297–299, Fig. 11.14)

    J. Muscles Crossing the Elbow Joint: Flexion and Extension of the Forearm (p. 300, Fig. 11.14)

    K. Muscles of the Forearm: Movements of the Wrist, Hand, and Fingers (pp. 301–306, Figs. 11.15 and 11.16)

    L. Summary of Actions of Muscles Acting on the Arm, Forearm, and Hand (pp. 307–308, Fig. 11.17)

    M. Intrinsic Muscles of the Hand: Fine Movements of the Fingers (pp. 309–311, Fig. 11.18)

    N. Muscles Crossing the Hip and Knee Joints: Movements of the Thigh and Leg (pp. 312–318, Figs. 11.19 and 11.20)

    O. Muscles of the Leg: Movements of the Ankle and Toes (pp. 319–325, Figs. 11.21–11.23)

    P. Summary of Actions of Muscles Acting on the Thigh, Leg, and Foot (pp. 326–328, Fig. 11.24)

    Q. Intrinsic Muscles of the Foot: Toe Movement and Foot Support (pp. 329–331, Fig. 11.25)

Lecture Hints

1. Define *myology*.
2. Using Figure 11.1, explore leverage and bone-muscle relationships.
3. Distinguish between first-class, second-class, and third-class levers.
4. Review the definition of *fascicle* and describe possible arrangement patterns of fascicles. Refer to Figure 11.3.
5. Stress that muscles work in groups to accomplish a specific function, such as flexion.
6. Distinguish between functional groups: prime movers (agonists), antagonists, synergists, and fixators.
7. List and explain the criteria for naming muscles.
8. Stress that the name of a muscle conveys much information about it.
9. Explore an overview of muscles that groups them according to embryonic origin and general function.
10. Review body movements, using Figures 9.5 and 9.6.
11. List the names of the principal skeletal muscles you want your students to learn.
12. Define *origin* and *insertion* and relate them to each muscle.
13. Describe the action of each muscle.
14. Stress the relationship of origin and insertion to the action.
15. Instruct students to act out actions.

Chapter 11: *Muscles of the Body*   119

16. Instruct students that the proper way to study muscles initially is not through memorization, but an understanding of origin, insertion, and action.

Classroom Discussion Topics and Activities

1. If a human cadaver is unavailable, obtain a preserved animal such as a cat or a fetal pig and exhibit the major muscle groups.
2. Obtain a three-dimensional model or a wall chart to show the major human muscle groups.
3. Use implements such as scissors, a wheelbarrow, and forceps to illustrate the three types of lever systems.
4. Select a muscular volunteer or invite a bodybuilder to class, and use him or her to show the main groups of muscles bulging through the skin. (For more on the surface anatomy of muscles, see textbook Chapter 26.)
5. Have students perform various movements and confirm the muscles that are responsible for these movements by feeling particular muscles bulge and tighten beneath their skin.
6. Ask students to bring in photographs of athletes, weight lifters, or other muscular individuals and label evident muscles. Make a scrapbook for storage and easy student use. Plan to use same photos later to label evident blood vessels.
7. Obtain a copy of *The Illustrations from the Works of Andreas Vesalius of Brussels*, with annotations and discussions. Instruct students to compare and contrast these muscle and skeletal drawings of the sixteenth century with their text books.
8. Display a skeleton for quick review of sites of origins and insertions.
9. Mimic a muscle and its actions by attaching the ends of a scarf to appropriate bony locations and moving the skeletal end of insertion.
10. Discuss what happens if a prime mover muscle such as the pectoralis major is surgically removed. How will the actions provided by that muscle be replaced?
11. Injections are often made directly into a muscle. Ask students to discuss the advantages and disadvantages of intramuscular injections compared to other methods of administering injections (intravenous, subdermal, subcutaneous, and intraperitoneal).
12. Discuss why is it necessary for pregnant women to strengthen their "pelvic floor."
13. Discuss the properties possessed by bones that allow them to act as effective levers.
14. Call out an action and ask students to respond with the name of a muscle responsible for that action.
15. Provide the name of a muscle and ask students to identify antagonists or synergists.

Clinical Questions

1. A receiver for the Dallas Cowboys "pulled" his hamstrings. What specific muscles could be affected, and what would the effect be?

   Answer: The hamstring muscles are the biceps femoris, semitendinosus, and semimembranosus on the dorsum of the thigh. They flex the leg at the knee and help extend the thigh at the hip. Injury to these muscles interferes with these movements.

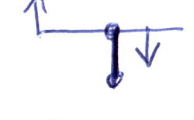

2. Malcolm was bending over to pick up a heavy box when he was startled by a mouse. He experienced severe pain in his back with muscle spasms, and it hurt most when he straightened up (extended his spine). What muscles could have been affected?

   Answer: Malcolm probably pulled his erector spinae muscles, since these muscles readily go into painful spasms when the back is injured during lifting.

3. Micki went to her childbirth class, in which the instructor spoke of the importance of strengthening the muscles of the pelvic floor. What are these muscles?

   Answer: The levator ani and coccygeus form the pelvic diaphragm in the pelvic floor. Some muscles of the urogenital diaphragm might also be included (sphincter urethrae and transverse perineal muscles). Strengthening these muscles makes them less likely to be torn by the passage of the baby's head during delivery.

4. An elderly woman with osteoarthritis of her left hip joint entered the hospital to have total hip-joint replacement surgery (prosthesis implantation). After the surgery, her left thigh had to be maintained in adduction to prevent dislocation of the prosthesis during healing. Physical therapy was prescribed to prevent atrophy of the gluteal muscles during this healing period. Name the gluteal muscles and describe the action of each that was being prevented while the hip was adducted.

   Answer: Gluteus maximus, gluteus medius, and gluteus minimus. The gluteus maximus is a major extensor and lateral rotator of the thigh at the hip, and the other two gluteal muscles normally function to abduct and medially rotate the thigh.

ART RESOURCES
Transparency List

Figure 11.1	Lever systems.
Figure 11.2	Classes of lever systems.
Figure 11.3	The different arrangements of fascicles in various muscles.
Figure 11.5	Superficial muscles of the body.
Figure 11.6	Muscles of the scalp, face, and neck lateral view.
Figure 11.7	Muscles promoting mastication and tongue movements.
Figure 11.8	Muscles of the anterior neck and throat that promote swallowing.
Figure 11.9	Muscles of the neck and vertebral column causing movements of the head and trunk.
Figure 11.10	Muscles of quiet respiration.
Figure 11.11	Muscles of the abdominal wall.
Figure 11.12	Muscles of the pelvic floor and perineum.
Figure 11.13	Superficial muscles of the anterior and posterior thorax and shoulder acting on the scapula and arm.
Figure 11.14	Muscles crossing the shoulder and elbow joint which cause movements of the arm and forearm, respectively.

Chapter 11: *Muscles of the Body* 121

Figure 11.15   Muscles of the anterior fascial compartment of the forearm acting on the wrists and fingers.

Figure 11.16   Muscles of the posterior fascial compartment of the forearm acting on the wrists and fingers.

Figure 11.18   Hand muscles ventral views of right hand.

Figure 11.19   Anterior and medial muscles promoting movements of the thigh and leg.

Figure 11.20   Posterior muscles of the right hip and thigh.

Figure 11.21   Muscles of the anterior compartment of the right leg.

Figure 11.22   Muscles of the lateral compartment of the right leg.

Figure 11.23   Muscles of the posterior compartment of the right leg.

Figure 11.25   Muscles of the right foot, plantar aspect.

Teaching with Art

Figure 11.14   Muscles crossing the shoulder and elbow joint: (a) Superficial muscles of anterior thorax, shoulder, and arm; (b) triceps brachii muscle; (c) biceps brachii muscle; (d) brachialis muscle.

Textbook p. 219; transparencies; Digital Archive CD-ROM.

Checklist of Key Points in the Figure

- Remind students that the term *arm* refers to the upper arm.
- Review the concepts of superficial and deep with respect to the muscles in this figure.
- Comment on the trade-offs between flexibility and instability in the configuration of the shoulder joint.
- Discuss the origin and insertion of each muscle in the figure.
- Describe the action of each muscle in the figure.
- Stress the relationship between the origin and insertion of the muscles in the figure to specific actions, such as anterior origins to flexion.
- Identify the rotator cuff muscles.
- Focus on the biceps brachii as the prime mover and triceps brachii as the antagonist in forearm flexion.
- Focus on the triceps brachii as the prime mover and the biceps brachii as the antagonist in forearm extension.

Common Conceptual Difficulties Interpreting the Art

- Explain the complex nature of the interactions of shoulder muscles.
- Remind students that muscles usually work in groups, not individually, to accomplish a particular movement.
- Explain how muscles return to their relaxed length following contraction.

Art Exercise

Provide copies of Figure 8.2, The scapula, and Figure 8.3, Humerus of the right arm. Referring to Figure 11.4, begin by asking students to identify the origins and insertions of the muscles that form the rotator cuff. Ask students to mark the origin and insertion points on the skeletal diagrams. Use red to denote the muscle origins and blue to denote the insertion points.

Critical Reasoning

Looking at the colored diagrams produced in the art exercise, ask students to identify the muscle of the rotator cuff group that is primarily responsible for the medial rotation of the arm. Ask them to explain their answers.

Answer: The subscapularis is primarily responsible for medial rotation of the arm because of its insertion on the anteriorly positioned lesser tubercle of the humerus.

SUPPLEMENTAL COURSE MATERIALS
Library Research Topics

1. Since skeletal muscle cells do not regenerate well, what methods of treatment are available if a major group of muscles is lost or paralyzed? What is the status of skeletal-muscle transplants?

2. What are the most appropriate modes of therapy for pulled hamstring or groin muscles?

3. What effect does old age have on skeletal muscle? What research is under way concerning this topic?

4. Olympic athletes use scientific training methods to improve their physical performance. Find out what some of these methods are, and if you are an athlete, try to employ them to better your performance.

5. What are the effects of injuries to the major muscle groups in the limbs?

Audiovisual Aids/Computer Software

See Preface of the Instructor's Guide for Key to Audiovisual Distributors

Videotapes

1. *The Guides to Dissection Series* (TFI, C, VHS). Excellent series of 42 programs demonstrating the dissection of all major areas of the human body. Also available as a 16-mm film.

2. *Muscles of the Anterior Forearm* (TFI, 14 min., C, VHS)

3. *The Palmar Hand, Part II: Intrinsic Muscles* (TFI, 15 min., C, VHS)

4. *Muscles of Mastication and Infratemporal Fossa* (TFI, 15 min., C, VHS)

5. *Movement at Joints of the Body* (FHS, 40 min.). Looks at movements at synovial joints and actions of muscles.

6. *Anabolic Steroids: Quest for Superman* (HRM, 31 min., 1991). Covers the pros and cons of using anabolic steroids.

7. *The Anatomy and Physiology Video Series: The Muscular System* (NIMCO, 25 min.). Discusses the anatomy and physiology of the muscular system and some specific muscles.

8. *Body Atlas Series: Muscle and Bone* (NCHCA, 30 min., 1994). Modern imaging techniques used to study muscle and bone.
9. *Bones and Muscles* (FHS, 15 min., 1990). An in-depth look at bones and muscles and their interactions.
10. *The Human Body: Muscular System* (WARD, 15 min., 1993). A detailed look at the muscular system.
11. *The Human Body Series: Muscles* (NIMCO, 28 min., 1993). Discusses muscle tissue and how different types of muscles work.
12. *The Living Body: Muscle Power* (FHS, 27 min., 1990). Study of muscle at the microscopic level.
13. *Moving Parts* (FHS, 27 min., 1990). Demonstrates how the cerebellum coordinates muscle activity, proprioceptors, and the role of joints.
14. *Muscular System at Work: The Inner Athlete* (FHS, 25 min.). Discusses roles played by muscle and skin.
15. *The New Living Body: Muscles* (FHS, 20 min., 1997). An in-depth look from gross structure to detailed microstructure.
16. *Major Skeletal Muscles and Their Actions* (TF, 1988). Describes and demonstrates the actions of the major skeletal muscles using a live model.
17. *Human Musculature* (BC, 23 min., 1993)

Computer Software

1. *Muscular System* (PLP, CH-182005 Apple; CH-182006, IBM)
2. *The Human Systems: Series 2* (PLP, CH-920009, Apple)
3. *A.D.A.M. Interactive Physiology CD-ROM: Muscular System* (ADAM). Discusses muscle physiology; interactive.
4. *Biochemistry of Muscle* (CDL). Covers neuromuscular junctions and sarcomeres.
5. *Body on Disc: Muscles and Bones* (NCHCA, 1996). A detailed look at muscular and skeletal systems.
6. *Muscle Tutorial* (STI, Mac only). Muscle microanatomy and physiology.
7. *Interactive Physiology: Muscular System* (ADAM/BC, 1996, Mac/Win)

Slides

1. *Muscular System and Its Functions* (EI, SS-0355)
2. *Histology of the Skeletomuscular System* (CVB, 20 slides)
3. *Muscle Contraction Set* (CBSC, 20 slides)

Suggested Readings

Basmajian, J.V. *Grant's Method of Anatomy*. 11th ed. Baltimore: Williams and Wilkins, 1989.

Dolan, P., et al. Passive tissues help the back muscles to generate extensor moments during lifting. *Journal of Biomechanics* 27 (1994): 1077–1085.

Foley, A. Tennis elbow. *American Family Physician* (August 1993): 281.

Hildebrand, M. The mechanics of horse legs. *American Scientist* 75 (November-December 1987): 594–601.

Hinson, M.M. *Kinesiology.* 2nd. ed. Dubuque, IA: W.C. Brown, 1981.

Huston, C., Ruptured achilles tendon. *American Journal of Nursing* (December 1994): 37.

Keeding, C., et al. Quadriceps strains and contusions. *The Physician and Sportsmedicine* 23 (January 1995): 59–64.

Koeslag, P, and J. Koeslag. The mechanics of bi-articular muscles. *South African Journal of Science* 81 (February 1993): 73.

McMinn, R., and R. Hutchings, et al. *Color Atlas of Human Anatomy.* 3rd ed. Chicago: Year Book Medical Publishers, 1993.

Moore, K.L. *Clinically Oriented Anatomy.* 34th ed. Philadelphia: Lippincott Williams and Wilkins, 1999.

Romanes, G.J. *Cunningham's Textbook of Anatomy.* 12th ed. Oxford, New York: Oxford University Press, 1981.

Rosse C., et al. *Textbook of Anatomy.* 5th ed. Philadelphia: Lippincott-Raven, 1997.

Veggeberg, S. Beyond steroids. *New Scientist* 149 (1996): 28–31.

Williams, P.L., et al. *Gray's Anatomy.* 38th ed. New York: Churchill Livingstone, 1995.

Woodburne, R.T. *Essentials of Human Anatomy.* 7th ed. New York: Oxford University Press, 1983.

ANSWERS TO TEXTBOOK QUESTIONS

Answers for multiple-choice and matching questions 1–11 are located in Appendix B of the textbook.

Short Answer and Essay Questions

12. See Figure 11.2, p. 267, to obtain the characteristics of the lever systems. First-class levers may operate at a mechanical advantage, and second-class levers always do. Third-class levers always operate at a mechanical disadvantage.

13. (a) Rectus abdominis, external oblique, internal oblique, transversus abdominis. (b) The fascicles of adjacent muscle sheets are arranged at cross-directions to each other. (c) Rectus abdominis. (d) Diaphragm.

14. Flexion (pectoralis major and deltoid), extension (latissimus dorsi and deltoid), abduction (deltoid), adduction (pectoralis major and latissimus dorsi), medial rotation (subscapularis), lateral rotation (infraspinatus and teres minor). (Table 11.12 on p. 307)

15. (a) Extensor carpi radialis longus and brevis. (b) Flexor digitorum profundus. (c) Opponens pollicis and opponens digiti minimi.

16. (a) Piriformis, obturator externus, obturator internus, gemellus muscles, quadratus femoris and adductor magnus, adductor longus, adductor brevis, pectineus. (b) Gluteus maximus is the most powerful extensor of the thigh at the hip; gluteus medius and gluteus minimus adduct the thigh at the hip.

17. The dorsal muscles of the leg must propel the entire weight of the body as they flex the plantar muscle of the foot during walking. The ventral leg muscles need only lift (dorsiflex) the foot to prevent it from dragging on the ground during the foreswing of walking.

18. (a) A fascia compartment is a group of functionally related muscles that are enclosed in a layer of fascia. For example, the fibularis muscles occupy the lateral compartment of the leg, which is set off by walls of fascia from an anterior and posterior muscle compartment. (See Figures 11.24 and 11.17.) (b) A retinaculum is a band-like thickening of deep fascia in the wrist or ankle region. Retinacula prevent the tendons of the many muscles running to the hand and wrist from jumping outward when tensed. (Table 11.11, p. 301)

19. (a) abductor pollicis brevis, flexor pollicis brevis, opponens pollicis, adductor pollicis (any two: p. 309). (b) extensor carpi radialis longus, extensor carpi radialis brevis, extensor digitorum, extensor carpi ulnaris, supinator, abductor pollicis longus, extensor pollicis brevis, extensor pollicis longus, extensor indicis (any two: pp. 304–305). (c) flexor pollicis longus, flexor digitorum profundus, pronator quadratus (any two: pp. 301–303). (d) biceps brachii, brachialis, brachioradialis (any two: p. 300). (e) masseter, temporalis, medial pterygoid, lateral pterygoid, buccinator (any two: p 278). (f) flexor hallucis brevis, adductor hallucis, flexor digiti minimi brevis (any two: pp. 329–330). (g) gastrocnemius, soleus, plantaris, flexor digitorum longus, flexor hallucis longus, tibialis posterior (any two: pp. 322–323). (h) adductor magnus, adductor longus, adductor brevis, pectineus, gracilis (any two: pp. 312–313). (i) biceps femoris, semitendinosus, semimembranosus (any two: p. 318).

20. (a) extrinsic eye muscles, tongue muscles, and pharyngeal arch (branchiomeric) muscles. (b) muscles of facial expression, chewing muscles, suprahyoid muscles, pharyngeal constrictors, sternocleidomastoid, and trapezius. (c) superior, middle, and inferior pharyngeal constrictors.

Critical Reasoning and Clinical Applications Questions

1. Trapezius and latissimus dorsi.
2. Levator ani and the muscles of the urogenital diaphragm (especially sphincter urethrae).
3. The main flexors of the forearm are the biceps brachii and the brachialis muscles. The biceps brachii cannot flex the forearm without also working to supinate it (see p. 300). Therefore, if you pick up a load with a pronated hand that must remain pronated, the biceps cannot be called into action and the task is more difficult.
4. The adductor muscles, probably adductor longus.

SUPPLEMENTAL STUDENT MATERIALS TO HUMAN ANATOMY, THIRD EDITION

Chapter 11: The Muscular System

To the Student

In previous chapters, you learned about the skeleton, joints, movements, and muscle tissues. Now it is time to study the skeletal muscles of the body. Chapter 11 explores the bone–muscle relationships and is a culmination of things learned in Chapters 7–10. Movements are determined by muscle attachments to bone, lever systems, arrangement of fascicles, and skeletal muscle group interactions. Many muscles are listed in the Muscle Gallery Tables, and your instructor will tell you which individual muscles you must learn. Keep in mind that muscles act in groups to perform specific functions, such as flexion or extension, and rarely, if ever, act individually. For simplicity, you will examine individual muscles, learning their origins, insertions, actions, and possibly the innervations of each. The proper way to study muscles initially is not through memorization, but a thorough understanding of origin, insertion, and action. If needed, review movements covered in Chapter 9.

Step 1: Describe lever systems and their relationships to bone and muscle.
- [ ] Define *lever*.
- [ ] Distinguish between effort, fulcrum, and load.
- [ ] Explain the conceptual relationship of leverage to bone, joints, and muscle.
- [ ] Describe first-class, second-class, and third-class levers.
- [ ] Explain why most lever systems in the body are third-class.

Step 2: Summarize the different arrangements of fascicles in muscles.
- [ ] Describe the parallel pattern of arrangement and name an example.
- [ ] Describe convergent pattern of arrangement and name an example.
- [ ] Describe pennate (unipennate, bipennate, and multipennate) patterns of arrangement and name examples.
- [ ] Describe the circular pattern of arrangement and name an example.

Step 3: Summarize skeletal muscle group interactions in the body.
- [ ] Define and give an example of a *prime mover* (*agonist*).
- [ ] Define and give an example of an *antagonist*.
- [ ] Define and give an example of a *synergist*.
- [ ] Define and give an example of a *fixator*.

Step 4: Understand the naming of skeletal muscles.
- [ ] List criteria for the naming of skeletal muscles.
- [ ] Give an example of a muscle that fits each criterion listed.

Step 5: Organize the body's muscles into functional groups based on developmental origins.

- ☐ Distinguish between myotomes and somitomeres.
- ☐ Explain the developmental-based scheme for the development of musculature of the visceral organs.
- ☐ Describe the developmental-based scheme for the development of pharyngeal arch muscles.
- ☐ Describe the developmental-based scheme for the development of axial muscles.
- ☐ Explain the developmental-based scheme for the development of limb muscles.

Step 6: Focus on specific skeletal muscles and respective groups described in Muscle Gallery 11.1–11.17 as assigned by your instructor.

- ☐ List criteria for determining the origin and insertion of a muscle.
- ☐ Make sure you understand all the body movements detailed in Figures 9.5 and 9.6.
- ☐ Describe the action of each assigned muscle and explain the action based on the origin and insertion of the muscle.
- ☐ Design flash cards for assigned muscles, including muscle shape, location, attachments, actions, and innervation.

CHAPTER **12**

Fundamentals of the Nervous System and Nervous Tissue

LECTURE AND DEMONSTRATION
Student Objectives

1. List the main functions of the nervous system.
2. Explain the structural and functional divisions of the nervous system.
3. Define *neuron,* describe its structural components, and relate each structure to its functional role.
4. Describe the fine structure of a synapse.
5. In simple terms, explain how electrical signals are generated and propagated along neurons.
6. Classify neurons both structurally and functionally.
7. List the six types of supporting cells in nervous tissue, and distinguish them by shape and function.
8. Describe the structure of myelin sheaths.
9. Define *nerve* and describe the structural components of nerves.
10. Define *reflex,* and list the basic components of a reflex arc. Distinguish monosynaptic reflexes from polysynaptic reflexes.
11. Sketch a reflex arc consisting of a sensory neuron, an interneuron, and motor neuron, and show how these neurons relate to the basic organization of the nervous system.
12. Distinguish gray matter from white matter in the central nervous system.
13. Consider how multiple sclerosis relates to myelin and axon function.
14. Describe the development of the nervous system in the embryo.

Suggested Lecture Outline

I. Basic Divisions of the Nervous System (pp. 336–338, Figs. 12.1 and 12.2)

II. Nervous Tissue (pp. 338–348)

  A. The Neuron (pp. 338–345, Figs. 12.4–12.12)

    1. The Cell Body

    2. Neuron Processes

    3. Synapses

II. Nervous Tissue *(continued)*

    4. The Signals Carried by Neurons

    5. Classification of Neurons

  B. Supporting Cells (pp. 345–348, Figs. 12.13–12.16)

    1. Supporting Cells in the CNS

    2. Supporting Cells in the PNS

    3. Myelin Sheaths

III. Nerves (pp. 348–350, Figs. 12.2 and 12.17)

IV. Basic Neuronal Organization of the Nervous System (pp. 350–353, Figs. 12.18–12.19)

  A. Reflex Arcs (p. 351, Fig. 12.18)

  B. Simplified Design of the Nervous System (pp. 351–353, Fig. 12.19)

V. Disorders of the Nervous System (pp. 353–354)

VI. Nervous Tissue Throughout Life (pp. 354–356, Fig. 12.19)

Lecture Hints

1. Using the Figure 12.1 transparency, emphasize the simplified basic functions of the nervous system.
2. Distinguish between the CNS and the PNS structurally.
3. Distinguish between afferent (sensory) and efferent (motor) divisions functionally.
4. Summarize the types of sensory and motor information carried by the nervous system using the Figure 12.3 transparency.
5. Describe nervous tissue.
6. Define *neuron*, including structural features. Refer to Figure 12.4.
7. Relate each structural feature of the neuron to its functional role.
8. Describe a synapse, including structural and functional details. Refer to Figure 12.8.
9. Explain how electric signals are generated and propagated along neurons. Refer to Figure 12.9.
10. Using Figures 12.10–12.13, classify neurons both structurally and functionally.
11. Distinguish the six types of supporting cells based on structural and functional characteristics.
12. Describe the structure and function of myelin sheaths.
13. Define *nerve* and describe the structural details.
14. Distinguish between nerve, nerve fiber, and neuron.
15. Summarize the basic neuronal organization of the nervous system.
16. Define *reflex* and list the basic features of a reflex arc.

Chapter 12: *Fundamentals of the Nervous System and Nervous Tissue*   131

17. Distinguish between monosynaptic reflexes and polysynaptic reflexes.
18. Draw and discuss a reflex arc, relating component neurons to the basic structure of the nervous system.
19. Distinguish between gray matter and white matter in the CNS.
20. Discuss symptoms of multiple sclerosis, the most common cause of neural disability in young adults.
21. Explain the embryological development of nervous tissue.

Classroom Discussion Topics and Activities

1. Obtain a slide projector and microscope slides of neurons, supporting cells, and peripheral nerves to illustrate the histology of nervous tissue.
2. Demonstrate nervous tissue stained by a variety of procedures (Golgi method versus basic Nissl stains versus stains that demonstrate neurofibrils). Discuss the strengths and weaknesses of each stain for studying the structure of neurons.
3. Obtain three-dimensional models of motor and sensory neurons to illustrate their similarities and differences.
4. To illustrate proprioception, have the students place their hands at their sides and then, without allowing them to look, have them visualize where the backs of their hands are.
5. Select a student to help in the demonstration of reflexes, such as the patellar, plantar, and abdominal reflexes.
6. Ask students to compare and contrast the regenerative capacities of the two tissues that regenerate most poorly (nervous tissue and cardiac muscle) with those of the tissues that regenerate most effectively (epithelium and bone).
7. Ask students why supporting cells divide and regenerate better than neurons.
8. Point out that the chemical acetylcholine has long been recognized as a neurotransmitter. Ask students why has it been so difficult to identify other neurotransmitters.
9. Ask students to identify structures in the adult body, other than the sensory neurons, derived from the neural crest.
10. Instruct students to list some human activities that are reflexive, some subconscious behaviors that involve higher levels of neural integration, and some behaviors that involve conscious thought.

Clinical Questions

1. Zoe was bitten on the leg by a mad dog that was foaming at the mouth. She was unaware of the dangers of rabies and never sought treatment. What symptoms did she develop from this disease?

    Answer: When the rabies viruses in the dog's saliva entered the bite wound, the virus was transported through Zoe's peripheral nerve axons to her spinal cord and brain. It led to inflammation of the brain, madness, and death.

2. Mr. Kelly staggered home after a "rough night" at the local pub. While attempting to navigate the stairs, he passed out cold and lay (all night) with his right armpit straddling the staircase

banister. When he awoke the next morning, he had a severe headache, but what bothered him more was that he had no sensation in his right upper limb, which seemed to be paralyzed. Explain.

Answer: Continuous pressure interrupts blood circulation (along with oxygen and nutrients) to the neuronal processes. As a result, the transmission of impulses through the nerves was inhibited temporarily.

ART RESOURCES
Transparency List

Figure 12.2	Basic divisions of the nervous system: The CNS and the PNS.
Figure 12.3	Types of sensory and motor information carried by the nervous system.
Figure 12.4	Structure of a typical large neuron (a motor neuron).
Figure 12.7	Some important types of synapses.
Figure 12.9	A segment of an axon, illustrating the generation and propagation of an action potential (nerve impulse).
Figure 12.10	Neurons classified by structure.
Figure 12.11	Neurons classified by function, as sensory neurons, motor neurons, and interneurons.
Figure 12.13	Supporting cells of nervous tissue.
Figure 12.14	Myelin sheaths in the PNS and CNS.
Figure 12.15	Schwann cells on myelinated and unmyelinated axons in the PNS.
Figure 12.17	Structure of a nerve.
Figure 12.19	Simplified diagram of the human nervous system, based on the locations of sensory neurons, motor neurons, and interneurons.

Teaching with Art

Figure 12.11 Neurons classified by function, as sensory neurons, motor neurons, and interneurons.

Textbook p. 344; transparencies; Digital Archive CD-ROM.

Checklist of Key Points in the Figure

- Review the principal structural features of a neuron. (Also display Figure 12.4.)
- Explain that the figure depicts three simplified unipolar neurons. Mention that the nervous system also contains multipolar and bipolar neurons. (Compare Figure 12.10.)
- Differentiate between the roles of sensory neurons, motor neurons, and interneurons.
- Review the structure of a synapse (also see Figure 12.8); point out the synapse locations in the figure (in receptors and effectors; within the gray matter).
- Identify the locations in the body of some typical sensory receptors.
- Identify some typical effector organs in the body.

Chapter 12: *Fundamentals of the Nervous System and Nervous Tissue*   **133**

Common Conceptual Difficulties Interpreting the Art

- Differentiate the CNS from the PNS portions of this figure for students.
- Explain why action potentials only travel from dendrite to axon in a unipolar neuron. (Also display Figure 12.9 to show the mechanism of an action potential.)
- Characterize the sensory integration role of interneurons in the CNS. (Also see Figure 12.12 to depict the structural variety of interneurons. Also display Figure 12.19 to highlight the presence of interneurons in the brain.)
- Describe the structure and function of a ganglion.

Art Exercise

1. Provide unlabeled copies of Figure 12.11. Instruct students to color code each type of neuron represented. Students should label all parts of each neuron, and indicate the direction of impulse transmission with arrows, especially at a synapse.

2. Provide students with unlabeled copies of the left side of Figure 12.18b, a simple stretch reflex, and instruct students to color code the neurons of the reflex arc. Label all neuronal parts and indicate the direction traveled by the nerve impulse.

3. Ask students to apply the concepts of Figure 12.18b to their own bodies by identifying (a) the site of receptor stimulation, (b) the type of reflex, (c) the name of the specific effector, and (d) the type of action produced in response to the stimulus.

    Answers: (a) the patellar ligament, (b) stretch (somatic) reflex, (c) the quadriceps femoris group of muscles, and (d) extension of the knee.

Critical Reasoning

Ask students to study Figure 12.19. Trace the circuit of interneurons, starting from the body of the interneuron in the simple reflex arc at the left, extending upward through the brain, and returning back to the synapse of the interneuron and motor neuron. Explain that this circuit signifies that the brain somehow modifies the action of the reflex arc. Ask the following question: "Can you think of an example of how it benefits you to be able to voluntarily modify the action of some reflex arcs?"

Answer: You are modifying the action of a reflex arc whenever you voluntarily control the reaction to a painful stimulus. For example, when you receive a hypodermic injection at your doctor's office, you voluntarily overcome (or strongly suppress) your reflex to flinch and pull away from the needle stick.

SUPPLEMENTAL COURSE MATERIALS
Library Research Topics

1. Scientists have recently begun to appreciate the fact that many small neurons within the gray matter of the central nervous system have dendrites but no axon, or they have very short "axons" that conduct graded potentials rather than action potentials. How can a neuron communicate without carrying an impulse?

2. What are the most recent advances in the quest to stimulate effective regeneration of the CNS, to aid accident victims who have had their spinal cords severed?

3. Explore the ultrastructure of dendrites, axons, and synapses. Can the detailed ultrastructure of a synapse reveal whether it is excitatory versus inhibitory in function?
4. Research the mechanism and functions of axonal transport, and relate them to the known functions of the cytoskeleton.
5. What chemical factors signal the development of the central nervous system?

Audiovisual Aids/Computer Software

See Preface of the Instructor's Guide for Key to Audiovisual Distributors

Videotapes

1. *Nerves at Work* (FHS, QB-831, 26 min., C, VHS/BETA). Program explores nerve signals, impulse transmission, and reflex activities. Also available in 16-mm film.
2. *Decision* (FHS, QB-832, 26 min., C, VHS/BETA). Program shows how the brain organizes input and output, and how circuits of nerve cells operate. Also available in 16-mm film.
3. *The Anatomy and Physiology Video Series: The Nervous System* (NIMCO, 27 min.). Discusses the parts of the nervous system and their functions.
4. *Animated Neuroscience and the Action of Nicotine, Cocaine, and Marijuana in the Brain* (FHS, 24 min.). Covers nerve cell communication and nerve impulse conduction.
5. *The Brain* (FHS, 23 min.). Includes transmission of nerve impulses and mechanisms of chemical transmitters.
6. *Brain and Nervous System* (FHS, 25 min.). Includes electrical impulses.
7. *The Human Body: Nervous System* (COR, 14 min., 1993). Covers all aspects of the nervous system.
8. *The Human Body Series: The Biological Basis of Thinking* (NIMCO, 28 min., 1993). Covers the chemical and neural processes of brain activity.
9. *The Human Body Series: Nerves and Nerve Cells* (NIMCO, 28 min., 1993). Demonstrates the structure and functioning of nerve cells.
10. *The Human Nervous System* (SVE, 12 min.). Includes functions of neurons.
11. *The Living Body: Decision* (FHS, 28 min., 1990). Demonstrates mechanisms of circuits and individual nerve cells and describes brain coordination of function.
12. *The Living Body: Nerves at Work* (FHS, 27 min., 1990). Covers nerve signal transmission and reflex signals.
13. *The Nature of the Nerve Impulse* (FHS, 15 min., 1988). Discusses the nerve impulse.

Computer Software

1. *The Nervous System: Our Information Network* (CA, MLC 5131, Apple)
2. *Dynamics of the Human Nervous System* (EI, C-3050, Apple/IBM)
3. *Nervous System* (PLP, CH-381079, Apple 64K)
4. *Body Language: Study of Human Anatomy, Nervous System* (PLP, CH-182013, Apple; CH-182014, IBM)
5. *The Human Systems: Series 2* (PLP, CH-920009, Apple)

6. *A.D.A.M. Interactive Physiology CD-ROM: The Nervous System I* (ADAM). Describes neurons and the action potential.

7. *A.D.A.M. Interactive Physiology CD-ROM: The Nervous System II* (ADAM, 1999). Describes the neuron, synapse potentials, and neurotransmitters.

8. *A Primer of Brain Anatomy and Function* (DGI, 1997). Describes the structure and function of nervous system cells as well as electrochemical signaling, including conduction and neurotransmission.

Slides

1. *Histology of the Nervous System* (EI, #613, Slides). Various staining techniques used to show cell bodies, myelin sheaths, neurons, and glial cells.

2. *Nervous System and Its Function* (EI, SS-0350F, Filmstrips or Slides). Reviews neural transmission, brain areas, and spinal cord.

3. *The Reflex Arc* (NTA, #70, Microviewer)

Suggested Readings

Allstetter, B. Cheating brain death. (An article on preventing damage from strokes.) *Discover* (August 1991): 24.

Altman, J. The intricate wiring that lets us move. (An article on the basal nuclei.) *New Scientist* (March 10, 1990): 60–63.

Barr, M.L., and J. Kiernan. *The Human Nervous System: An Anatomical Viewpoint*. 5th ed. Philadelphia: Lippincott, 1988.

Begley, S. Gray matters. (An article about how men and women's brains differ.) *Newsweek* (March 27, 1995): 48–54.

Botto, L.D., et al. Neural-tube defects. *New England Journal of Medicine* 341 (November 11, 1999): 1509–1519.

Bower, B. Human brain reveals the anatomy of pain. *Science News* 139 (March 16, 1991): 167.

Brodal, A. *Neurological Anatomy in Relation to Clinical Medicine*. 3rd ed. New York: Oxford University Press, 1981.

Brodal, P. *The Central Nervous System: Structure and Function*. 2nd ed. New York: Oxford University Press, 1998.

Cowan, W.M. The development of the brain. *Scientific American* 241 (September 1979): 106–117.

Davidoff, J., and D. Concar. Brain cells made for seeing. *New Scientist* (April 10, 1993): 32–36.

Dobkin, B. Playing for time. (An article on amyotrophic lateral sclerosis.) *Discover* (April 1991): 36–37.

Fackelmann, K. Mice show Alzheimer brain plaques. *Science News* 147 (February 11, 1995): 84.

Ferry, G. Parkinson's: A suitable case for treatment? *New Scientist* (December 3, 1994): 36–40.

Fisher, L.J., and F.H. Gage. Grafting in the mammalian central nervous system. *Physiology Review* 73 (July 1993): 583–616.

Gershon, E.S., and R.O. Rieder. Major disorders of mind and brain. *Scientific American* 267 (September 1992): 126–133.

Gibbons, A. New maps of the human brain. *Science* 249 (July 13, 1990): 122–123.

Gibbons, A. The brain as "sexual organ." *Science* 253 (August 30, 1991): 956–959.

Gluhbegovic, N., and T.H. Williams. *The Human Brain: A Photographic Guide*. New York: Harper and Row, 1980.

Golden, J., and G. Chernoff. Multiple sites of anterior neural tube closure in humans: Evidence from anterior neural tube defects (anencephaly*). Pediatrics* 95 (April 1995): 506–510.

Kaas, J. The functional organization of the somatosensory cortex in primates. *Annals of Anatomy* 175 (1993): 509–518.

Kandel, E.R., J. Schwartz, and T. Jessell. *Principles of Neural Science*. 4th ed. New York: McGraw-Hill, Health Professions Division, 2000.

Klawans, H.L. *Toscanini's Fumble and Other Tales of Clinical Neurology*. Chicago: Contemporary Books, 1988.

Koshland, D.E., Jr. The dimensions of the brain. *Science* 285 (October 9, 1992): 199.

LeDoux, J. Emotion, memory and the brain. (An article on the amygdala.) *Scientific American* (June 1994): 50–57.

LeMay, M. Functional and anatomical asymmetries of the human brain. *European Journal of Neurology* 6 (January 1999): 79–85.

LeVay, S., and D. Hamer. Evidence for a biological influence in male homosexuality. *Scientific American* (May 1994): 44.

Lewis, R. Gateway to the brain. (An article on the blood-brain barrier.*) BioScience* 44 (March 1994): 133–137.

McDonald, J.W. Repairing the damaged spinal cord. *Scientific American* 281 (September 1999): 64–73.

Mischkin, M., and T. Appenzeller. The anatomy of memory. *Scientific American* 256 (June 1987): 80–89.

Montgomery, G. The mind in motion. *Discover* 10 (March 1989): 58–68.

Parent, André. *Carpenter's Human Neuroanatomy*. 9th ed. Baltimore: Williams and Wilkins, 1996.

Paulin, M. The role of the cerebellum in motor control and perception. *Brain, Behavior, and Evolution* 41 (1993): 39–50.

Petersen, S.E., et al. Positron emission tomographic studies of the cortical anatomy of single-word processing. *Nature* 331 (February 18, 1988): 585–582 (also see pp. 560–562).

Raichle, M. Visualizing the mind. (An article on PET and functional MRI techniques.) *Scientific American* 270 (April 1994): 58–64.

Roberts, L. A call to action on a human brain project. *Science* 282 (June 28, 1991): 1794.

Romeo, J.H. The critical minutes after spinal cord injury. *RN* (April 1988): 61–67.

Romero-Sierra, C. *Neuroanatomy: A Conceptual Approach*. New York: Churchill Livingstone, 1986.

Roush, W. Protein studies try to puzzle out Alzheimer's tangles. *Science* 267 (February 10, 1995): 793–794.

Schreeve, J. The brain that misplaced its body. (An article on the gnostic area of the cortex.) *Discover* (May 1995): 82–91.

Scientific American. Special Issue: Mind and Brain. Various articles and authors. September 1992.

Seligmann, J., and J. McCormick. Saving spina bifida babies. *Newsweek* (November 15, 1982): 110.

Sperry, R. Some effects of disconnecting the cerebral hemispheres. *Science* 217 (1982): 1223.

Squire, L., and S. Zola-Morgan. The medial temporal lobe memory system. *Science* 253 (September 20, 1991): 1380–1386.

Thompson, C. Paralysis lost. *New Scientist* 150 (1996): 26–27.

Thompson, F.F. *The Brain: An Introduction to Neuroscience.* New York: W.H. Freeman and Co., 1985.

Williams, P.L., et al. *Gray's Anatomy.* 38th ed. New York: Churchill Livingstone, 1995.

Zivin, J., and D. Choi. Stroke therapy. *Scientific American* (July 1991): 56–63.

ANSWERS TO TEXTBOOK QUESTIONS

Answers for multiple-choice and matching questions 1–10 are located in Appendix B of the textbook.

Short Answer and Essay Questions

11. Proprioception is sensing the degree of stretch in the muscles, tendons, and joint capsules.

12. Proprioception, as it relates to muscles, *senses* muscle stretch. The skeletal muscles innervated are in the outer, *somatic,* part of the body and are widespread (*general* innervation): thus, *general somatic sensory.*

13. An interneuron can be the middle neuron in a reflex arc (between a sensory neuron and a motor neuron); but more broadly, an interneuron is any neuron that is confined entirely within the central nervous system.

14. Gray matter, which occupies the central region of the spinal cord and brain, is where neuron cell bodies are clustered. More specifically, it consists of neuron cell bodies, dendrites, and short unmyelinated axons. White matter, which lies external to the central gray matter, consists of axons running between different parts of the CNS. Its white color reflects the color of the myelin around many of its axons.

15. The nucleus of a neuron is spherical and appears clear (has little condensed chromatin) with a distinctive central nucleolus. It resembles an owl's eye.

16. The answer is Neuron b, with its tremendous complexity of dendrites. As explained in the legend to Figure 12.12 on p. 345, neurons with the most complex pattern of dendrites receive the most axon terminals.

17. A neuron is a nerve cell, a nerve fiber is a long axon, and a nerve is a collection of nerve fibers in the PNS.

18. If the axons are severed in the PNS, sprouting axonal endings can grow peripherally along solid bands formed by the surviving Schwann cells and eventually reinnervate the peripheral structures. In the CNS, by contrast, the neuroglia never forms bands to guide the regrowing axons, and the neuroglia even hinders such axons by secreting growth-inhibiting chemicals.

19. The drawing should show a sensory neuron, interneuron, and motor neuron, as they relate to the dorsal root, spinal cord, ventral root, and spinal nerve. The reflex would not function if

the cells in the sensory ganglion (sensory neurons) were destroyed, because that would break the chain of neurons in the arc.

20. An axon is a neuronal process that carries impulses (action potentials) away from the cell body, whereas a dendrite is a process that carries signals (graded potentials) toward the cell body.

Critical Reasoning and Clinical Applications Questions

1. The peripheral process could be called an axon because (1) it conducts an action potential, and (2) its fine structure is identical to that of a true axon. The peripheral process could be called a dendrite because it conducts signals toward the cell body of the neuron.

2. A glioma is a tumor that originates from the glial cells, so an oligodendroglioma is a tumor derived from oligodendrocytes.

3. Blood began reflowing through the blood vessels in the arm as soon as the vessels were rejoined to the vessels of the body trunk. In the nerves of the severed arm, by contrast, all the axons degenerated, and reinnervation occurred only after sprouting axons grew back into the limb structures.

4. In multiple sclerosis, the myelin sheaths around motor (and sensory) axons gradually disappear, and the conduction of motor (and sensory) nerve impulses slows and ceases. Thus, Rochelle lost motor control of her muscles.

SUPPLEMENTAL STUDENT MATERIALS TO HUMAN ANATOMY, THIRD EDITION

Chapter 12: Fundamentals of the Nervous System and Nervous Tissue

To the Student

It is important to understand an overview of the human nervous system before focusing on the functional anatomy of the nervous tissue, especially neurons. Without a complete understanding of sensory input, integration, and motor output, basic principles of neural function are elusive. The nervous system shares important functions with the endocrine system; you will explore the endocrine system in detail in a later chapter. The nervous system is the master controller of the other systems and enables you to respond to internal and external environmental information.

Step 1: Explain the basic organization of the nervous system.

☐ List functions of the nervous system.

☐ Distinguish between afferent input and efferent output.

☐ Define *integration*.

☐ Define *CNS*.

☐ Define *PNS*.

☐ Explain the following types of sensory and motor information carried by the nervous system:
- Somatic sensory
- Visceral sensory
- Somatic motor
- Visceral motor
- Branchial motor

Step 2: Describe nervous tissue.

☐ Define *neuron*, and list its structural features.

☐ Relate each structural feature of a neuron to its functional role.

☐ Define and describe a *synapse*.

☐ Explain the generation and propagation of electrical signals along neurons.

☐ Classify neurons structurally.

☐ Classify neurons functionally.

☐ Name six types of supporting cells and describe them by shape and function.

☐ Describe the structure of myelin sheaths.

Step 3: Explain nerves and the basic neuronal organization of the nervous system.

☐ Define *nerve*.

☐ Describe basic components of nerves.

☐ Define *reflex*, distinguishing between monosynaptic and polysynaptic reflexes.

☐ Draw a reflex arc, including its basic features: sensory neuron, interneuron, and motor neuron.

- ☐ Explain how the reflex arc relates to the basic organization of the nervous system.
- ☐ Distinguish between gray matter and white matter in the CNS.

Step 4: Understand the development and disorders of nervous tissue.
- ☐ Describe the symptoms of multiple sclerosis.
- ☐ Describe the embryological development of nervous tissue.

CHAPTER 13
The Central Nervous System

LECTURE AND DEMONSTRATION
Student Objectives

1. Describe the development of the five embryonic divisions of the brain.
2. Name the major parts of the adult brain.
3. Name and describe the location of the ventricles of the brain.
4. List the major lobes, fissures, and functional areas of the cerebral cortex.
5. Name three classes of fiber tracts in the white matter of the cerebrum.
6. Describe the form and function of the basal nuclei (basal ganglia).
7. Name the divisions of the diencephalon and their functions.
8. Identify the three basic subdivisions of the brain stem and list the major nuclei in each.
9. Describe the structure and function of the cerebellum.
10. Describe the locations and functions of the reticular formation and the limbic system.
11. Explain how meninges, cerebrospinal fluid, and the blood-brain barrier protect the CNS.
12. Explain the formation of cerebrospinal fluid, and describe its pattern of circulation.
13. Describe the gross structure of the spinal cord, including the arrangement of its gray matter and white matter.
14. List the largest tracts in the spinal cord, and explain their positions in the major neuronal pathways to and from the brain.
15. Describe the signs and symptoms of concussions, brain contusions, strokes, and Alzheimer's disease.
16. Explain the effects of severe injuries to the spinal cord.
17. Describe these congenital disorders: anencephaly, cerebral palsy, and spina bifida.
18. Explain the effects of aging on brain structure.

Suggested Lecture Outline

I. The Brain (pp. 360–391, Fig. 13.1)

   A. Embryonic Development of the Brain (pp. 360–361, Figs. 13.2 and 13.3)

   B. Basic Parts and Organization of the Brain (p. 362, Figs. 13.4 and 13.5)

   C. Ventricles of the Brain (p. 363, Fig. 13.6)

I. THE BRAIN *(continued)*

    D. The Cerebral Hemispheres (pp. 363–374, Figs. 13.7–13.14)

        1. Cerebral Cortex

        2. Cerebral White Matter

        3. Basal Nuclei (Basal Ganglia)

    E. The Diencephalon (pp. 374–379, Figs. 13.15–13.19)

        1. The Thalamus

        2. The Hypothalamus

        3. The Epithalamus

    F. The Brain Stem (pp. 379–382, Figs. 13.15 and 13.20–13.21)

        1. The Midbrain

        2. The Pons

        3. The Medulla Oblongata

    G. The Cerebellum (pp. 382–385, Fig. 13.22)

        1. Cerebellar Peduncles

    H. Functional Brain Systems (pp. 385–388, Figs. 13.23 and 13.24)

        1. The Limbic System

        2. The Reticular Formation

    I. Protection of the Brain (pp. 388–391, Figs. 13.25–13.27)

        1. Meninges

        2. Cerebrospinal Fluid

        3. Blood-Brain Barrier

II. *The Spinal Cord (pp. 391–401, Figs. 13.29 and 13.30)*

    A. Gray Matter of the Spinal Cord and Spinal Roots (p. 395, Fig. 13.31)

    B. White Matter of the Spinal Cord (pp. 395–397, Fig. 13.32)

    C. Sensory and Motor Pathways (pp. 397–401, Figs. 13.33 and 13.34)

        1. Ascending (Sensory) Pathways

        2. Descending (Motor) Pathways

III. *Disorders of the Central Nervous System (pp. 401–403)*

    A. Brain Dysfunction (pp. 401–403, Fig. 13.35)

        1. Traumatic Brain Injuries

        2. Degenerative Brain Diseases

    B. Spinal Cord Damage (p. 403)

IV. *The Central Nervous System Throughout Life (pp. 403–404)*

Chapter 13: *The Central Nervous System* 143

Lecture Hints

1. Introduce the central nervous system, stressing the fantastic complexity and myriad of functions.
2. Describe the consistency and weight of the brain.
3. Define the unique CNS directional terms *rostral* and *caudal*.
4. Draw a diagram relating the five secondary brain vesicles to adult brain structures. Figure 13.2 provides an excellent basic comparison of embryonic and adult features.
5. List basic parts of the brain: cerebral hemispheres, diencephalon, brain stem (midbrain, pons, medulla), and cerebellum, referring to Figure 13.4.
6. Describe the organization of the white matter and gray matter, especially contrasting the brain stem to the cerebrum and cerebellum. Refer to Figure 13.5.
7. Caution students not to confuse *brain nuclei* with *nuclei of cells*.
8. Aid students to visualize spatial relationships of basic brain parts initially by identifying the specific locations of each of the ventricles. Refer to Figure 13.6.
9. Discuss surface anatomy of the cerebral hemispheres, including fissures, gyri, sulci, and lobes. Point out the deeply located insula. Refer to Figure 13.7.
10. Using Figure 13.8, describe the basic regions of the cerebrum evident in a frontal section.
11. Explain to students why the cerebral cortex is the "conscious mind."
12. Describe basic features of the gray matter of the cerebral cortex, including components, thickness, approximate surface area, and approximate total mass of the brain.
13. Relate the structural (Brodmann) areas of the cerebral cortex to the functional areas using Figures 13.10 and 13.11, and define *homunculus*.
14. Caution students not to confuse motor and sensory *areas* with motor and sensory *neurons*.
15. Distinguish between a precentral gyrus and postcentral gyrus. Refer to Figures 13.7 and 13.11.
16. Define *somatotopy* and give an example of it in both the brain and spinal cord.
17. List and discuss specific functions of four cortical motor areas in the frontal lobe, explaining contralateral projections.
18. Stress that the *left* and *right* primary motor cortexes control muscles on the *right* and *left* sides of the body, respectively.
19. List and discuss specific functions of six cortical sensory areas in the parietal, occipital, and temporal lobes, explaining spatial discrimination and dorsal/ventral streams (higher-order visual processing). Refer to Figure 13.15.
20. List and discuss specific functions of three cortical association areas, defining cognition and describing the location of language areas around the lateral sulcus of the left cerebral cortex.
21. Summarize right and left cerebral hemisphere functions: The left side is specialized for languages and math skills, and the right side is more concerned with visual-spatial and creative abilities.
22. Distinguish between the types of white matter fibers in the cerebrum: commissural, projection, and association. Refer to Figure 13.13.
23. List and give basic functions of the basal nuclei of the cerebrum. Refer to Figure 13.14.

24. List and describe the three paired structures composing the diencephalon, including their functions. Refer to Figures 13.16–13.20.
25. List the three regions of the brain stem, going from rostral to caudal, including the anatomical details and functions of each. Refer to Figures 13.19–13.21.
26. List and describe the anatomical features of the cerebellum, including its functions. Refer to Figure 13.22.
27. Distinguish between the limbic system and the reticular formation. Refer to Figures 13.23 and 13.24.
28. Describe four ways the CNS is protected.
29. Distinguish between the three meninges: dura mater, arachnoid mater, and pia mater. Refer to Figures 13.25 and 13.26.
30. Using Figure 13.27, describe functions of the cerebrospinal fluid, including its origin and circulation pattern.
31. Discuss the importance of the blood-brain barrier, explaining why it is effective.
32. Using Figure 13.29, describe the gross anatomy of the spinal cord and its nerve roots, including the location, superior and inferior boundaries, meninges, enlargements, conus medullaris, and cauda equina.
33. Contrast the spinal dura sheath with the cranial dura mater, pointing out significant differences.
34. Explain the clinical procedure of lumbar puncture, commenting on relative safety and diversity of uses.
35. Describe the gray matter of the spinal cord. Refer to Figure 13.31.
36. Distinguish between dorsal sensory roots and ventral motor roots of spinal nerves and emphasize that roots are in the PNS, not CNS.
37. Describe the white matter of the spinal cord, distinguishing between the ascending fibers, descending fibers, and commissural fibers. Refer to Figure 13.32.
38. Compare and contrast sensory pathways and motor pathways, using Figures 13.33 and 13.34.
39. Describe symptoms and causes of brain dysfunction: concussion, contusion, stroke, and Alzheimer's disease.
40. Discuss spinal cord damage: paralysis, paresthesia, paraplegia, and quadriplegia.
41. Comment on birth defects and birth disorders involving the brain: anencephaly, spina bifida, and cerebral palsy.

Classroom Discussion Topics and Activities

1. Display a three-dimensional model of a human brain and compare it to a real human brain and/or a dissected sheep brain.
2. Display a three-dimensional model of a spinal cord, both in longitudinal section and in cross section, to illustrate its features.
3. Display stained, thin, cross sections of a brain (or thicker sections sliced with a knife) to illustrate the differences between gray and white matter and to show the internal parts of the brain.

4. Demonstrate a three-dimensional model or cast of the ventricles of the brain. Ask students how they think a cast of the ventricles was obtained.

5. Using a real human brain specimen or a model, instruct students to sketch a lateral view of the brain and to label the cerebral hemisphere, lobes of the cerebrum, precentral gyrus, postcentral gyrus, central sulcus, lateral sulcus, transverse fissure, cerebellum, pons, and medulla oblongata.

6. Display a sheep brain with the cranium and meninges still intact.

7. When discussing the inferior colliculus, make an unexpected large noise (such as banging a yardstick against the table). When the students jump reflexively and look up, tell them that their reflex was mediated by the inferior colliculus.

8. Discuss the difference between encephalitis and meningitis.

9. Discuss why prefrontal lobotomies (cutting the fiber tracts to the prefrontal lobes) have been used in psychotherapy along with electrical shock. Ask students how and why these techniques have been used. Ask why lobotomies are now in disfavor.

10. Since a right-handed person's left cerebral hemisphere appears to dominate many cerebral functions, ask what could be done to increase the use of the right hemisphere.

11. Mention that anencephalic children always die soon after birth. There is currently a desire among some medical groups to transplant the organs of these children to help others. Discuss the pros and cons of this type of organ transplantation.

12. Discuss the actions/effects of opiates, antidepressants, and anesthetics or the biology of drug addiction.

13. Discuss the role of the hypothalamus and the medulla in controlling homeostasis, a topic that will be important later in the course.

14. Assign *A Closer Look: Sex-Related Differences in Brain Structure*, on p. 373 of the textbook, as required reading for classroom discussion.

Clinical Questions

1. Describe the cause of hydrocephalus, and explain why this condition is much more serious in adults than in newborns.

   Answer: Hydrocephalus refers to a blockage of the normal circulation and drainage of cerebrospinal fluid throughout the ventricles and meninges. If allowed to accumulate, the fluid will exert excessive pressure on the brain. In newborns, the fontanels and sutures allow the skull to enlarge, while in adults, the cranial bones are fused and no expansion is possible. Thus, the danger of crushing the brain is greatest in adults.

2. Six-year-old Jeremy is confined to a wheelchair. He frequently drools, and his limbs hang limply in angular positions. His diagnosis is cerebral palsy. Name several possible causes of cerebral palsy.

   Answer: Cerebral palsy may be due to a lack of oxygen at birth; a viral infection; or excessive smoking, radiation exposure, drug intake, or alcohol consumption by the mother. Cerebral palsy is a disability of the motor regions of the brain, in which the voluntary muscles are poorly controlled or paralyzed.

3. Lucy is suffering from right-sided paralysis and sensory loss. She cannot speak at all. Cerebral angiography and a CT scan have shown no cerebral vascular defects, but the CT scan did reveal a mass wedged between the left thalamus and basal nuclei. Using your knowledge of anatomy, explain Lucy's symptoms in terms of the specific lesion site.

   Answer: The mass, located in the left half of the brain, will affect the right side of the body due to the crossing over of sensory and motor pathways. The mass indicates damage to the fibers of the internal capsule, which carry both motor and sensory signals to and from the cerebral cortex. Thus, Lucy has both motor and sensory disorders.

4. A victim of a motorcycle accident fractured vertebra T12, and there was concern that the spinal cord was crushed at the level of this vertebra. At what spinal cord segment was the damage expected? Choose from the following and explain your choice: (a) between C4 and C8, and the ability to move the arms was tested; (b) at C1, and the respiratory movements of the diaphragm were tested; (c) spinal cord level L3; (d) there could be no deficits because the cord always ends above T12; and (e) the functions of all the cranial nerves were tested.

   Answer: The correct choice is (c), the injury was at spinal cord level L3. Recall that the spinal cord levels are several segments superior to vertebral levels (L3 corresponds to T12).

5. Harold, a 70-year-old man, walks up and down the street in front of his house daily. Initially, he has trouble getting going; but once started, he walks quickly and in a mechanical fashion. Although he says hello to those he passes, he never smiles and has been considered generally unpleasant for this reason. His hands tremble when he is not voluntarily moving them. What is Harold's problem?

   Answer: Harold has Parkinson's disease, a depression of the "starter motor" function of the basal nuclei (see p. 000 in the textbook).

ART RESOURCES
Transparency List

Figure 13.4   Parts of the brain.

Figure 13.5   Arrangement of gray and white matter in the CNS.

Figure 13.6   The ventricles of the brain.

Figure 13.7   Lobes and fissures of the cerebral hemispheres.

Figure 13.8   Internal structure of the forebrain.

Figure 13.10 Functional and structural areas of the cerebral cortex.

Figure 13.11 Body maps in the primary motor cortex and somatosensory cortex of the cerebrum.

Figure 13.12 The ventral stream and dorsal stream for processing visual information in the posterior part of the cerebral cortex.

Figure 13.13 Types of fiber tracts in the white matter of the cerebral hemispheres.

Figure 13.14 Basal nuclei.

Figure 13.15 Brain sectioned in the midsagittal plane.

Figure 13.16 The diencephalon.

Figure 13.17 The thalamus and its relationship to the cerebral cortex.

Figure 13.18 Nuclei of the hypothalamus.

Figure 13.19 Ventral view of the brain.

Figure 13.20 Brain stem and diencephalon.

Figure 13.21 Cross sections through the brain stem.

Figure 13.22 Cerebellum.

Figure 13.23 The limbic system.

Figure 13.24 The reticular formation.

Figure 13.25 Meninges around the brain.

Figure 13.26 Partitions of dura mater in the cranial cavity.

Figure 13.27 The sites of formation and circulation pattern of cerebrospinal fluid.

Figure 13.29 Gross structure of the spinal cord.

Figure 13.30 Anatomy of the spinal cord.

Figure 13.31 General organization of the gray matter of the spinal cord.

Figure 13.32 Major fiber tracts in the white matter of the spinal cord.

Figure 13.33 Major ascending pathways for the general somatic senses.

Figure 13.34 Descending motor pathways, by which the brain influences movements.

Teaching with Art

Figure 13.27 Sites of formation and circulation pattern of cerebrospinal fluid.

Textbook p. 392; transparencies; Digital Archive CD-ROM.

Checklist of Key Points in the Figure

- Review the principal functions of cerebrospinal fluid (CSF).
- Describe CSF's watery consistency and mention its rate of formation—about 500 ml per day.
- Point out that there is only between 100 to 160 ml (about 1/2 cup) of CSF in a healthy adult.
- Contrast the rate of CSF formation with the average CSF volume to reinforce the concept of CSF circulation.
- Point to the locations of the choroid plexuses—part (a)—and describe the functional relationship between the ependymal cells and the highly vascular pia mater—part (b).
- Emphasize the continuity between the ventricles, subarachnoid space, and central canal, which allows circulation of CSF.
- Display Figure 13.6 ("transparent" three-dimensional views of the brain) to demonstrate the continuity and extent of the ventricles.
- Describe the typical pattern of circulation of CSF from its point of origin to its return to the venous blood.

Common Conceptual Difficulties Interpreting the Art

- Point out that a venous sinus is a specialized blood vessel (vein).
- Describe the function of ependymal cells; comment on the ciliated ependymal epithelium lining the ventricles.
- Describe how CSF differs from blood.
- Describe the structural differences in the capillaries of the choroid plexuses that enable them to form the blood-brain barrier.
- Remind students that CSF obtained from a lumbar puncture can provide clinical information about an injury, infection, or disease of the CNS. (Refer to Figure 13.29.)

Art Exercise

1. Referring to Figure 13.27, instruct students to design a flow diagram tracing the pathway of CSF from its formation site in the third ventricle to its ultimate return to the circulatory system.
2. Provide unlabeled copies of Figure 13.27 and instruct students to label the CSF pathway using the flow diagram devised in 1.
3. Using an unlabeled copy of Figure 13.25, ask students to trace CSF movement in this enlarged view of the meninges around the brain.

Critical Reasoning

The production and circulation of CSF is a continuous process. If CSF accumulates in ventricles or the subarachnoid space due to a blockage, excessive pressure is exerted on the brain, a condition called hydrocephalus. Refer students to Figure 13.28 and ask, "Why do you think the skull of an infant with hydrocephalus distorts so noticeably?"

Answer: An infant lacks fused cranial sutures, and the skull expands.

SUPPLEMENTAL COURSE MATERIALS
Library Research Topics

1. What techniques are currently used to locate and treat tumors of the brain?
2. How has the human brain changed in size and shape over the millions of years of evolution? Explore the evolution of the human brain, especially of the cerebral cortex.
3. What drugs are used to enhance memory? Where and how do they work?
4. What kinds of experiments have been used to study the limbic system? What research has been done on determining whether some habitual criminals have defects in this system?
5. Some research indicates humans experience circadian rhythms. How are these rhythms coordinated, and do we really have them? Do they occur in other animals?
6. What are the new techniques, PET and functional MRI, revealing about the functional organization of the cerebral cortex?
7. Research whether there is a link between maternal vitamin deficiency (for example, of folic acid) and neural tube defects in newborns.

Audiovisual Aids/Computer Software

See Preface of the Instructor's Guide for Key to Audiovisual Distributors

Videotapes

1. *The Addicted Brain* (FHS, QB-1363, 26 min., C, VHS/BETA). Documentary explores drug use and its effect on the brain.
2. *The Anatomical Basis of the Brain Function Series* (TFI, C, 1988). Twenty titles, ranging from 14 to 23 minutes, presenting virtually every aspect of the neuroanatomy of the human brain.
3. *Alzheimer's: The Tangled Mind* (FHS, 23 min., 1997). Covers the symptoms, treatment, and prognosis of Alzheimer's disease.
4. *Anatomy of The Human Brain* (FHS, 34 min., 1998). Dissection of a normal human brain.
5. *The Body Atlas Series: The Brain* (NCHCA/NIMCO, 30 min., 1994). A study of the brain.
6. *The Brain.* 2nd ed. (ACPB, three videos, 4 hr., 31 min., 1997). All aspects of the brain covered by 32 teaching modules.
7. *The Brain (A Video Workbook)* (EBEC, 50 min.). Intensive study of brain physiology.
8. *The Brain: Our Universe Within Set* (CBSC, three videos, 1 hr. each). Functional MRI and PET scans of living brains, including computer animation.
9. *The Brain: The Ultimate Puzzle* (SVE, two videos, 18 min. each). Detailed discussion of brain development and disorders.
10. *Brain Cancer: From Diagnosis to Treatment* (FHS, 30 min., 1998). Covers brain cancer types, diagnosis, treatments, and prognosis.
11. *Brain and Nervous System: Your Information Superhighway* (FHS, 25 min.). Covers parts of the brain and their functions, including protection of the brain.
12. *The Development of the Human Brain* (CBSC, 40 min.). Follows human brain development from conception through age 8.
13. *Fear and Anxiety* (FHS, 56 min., 1998). Covers anxiety disorders and fear.
14. *Fetal Alcohol Syndrome: Life Sentence* (FHS, 24 min.). Describes the effect of alcohol on the fetal brain and the lifetime effects.
15. *The Human Body Series: The Brain* (NIMCO, 28 min., 1993). Covers the development of the brain, its parts, and their functions.
16. *The Human Body Series: Reflexes and Conscious Movement* (NIMCO, 28 min., 1993). Examines the range of reflexive and controlled, conscious, and unconscious movements of the body.
17. *The Human Body Series: Sleep* (NIMCO, 28 min., 1993). Describes activities in the brain during sleep.
18. *The Human Brain In Situ* (FHS, 19 min., 1993). Uses museum pieces in a basic anatomical examination of the brain and its connections.
19. *In Control: Our Brain and Nervous System* (SVE, 24 min.). Describes functions of parts of the brain.
20. *Inside Information: The Brain and How It Works* (FHS, 58 min., 1992). A study of brain structure and function.

21. *Is Your Brain Really Necessary?* (FHS/NIMCO, 50 min., 1992). Examines three patients with different brain problems.
22. *The Living Body: Decisions* (FHS, 28 min., 1990). Demonstrates how the brain coordinates functions in order to make lifesaving conditions.
23. *The Living Body: Moving Parts* (FHS, 27 min., 1990). Includes coordination of muscle activity by the brain.
24. *The Living Body: Our Talented Brain* (FHS, 28 min., 1990). Describes brain structure.
25. *Memory* (FHS, 56 min.). An in-depth look at data storage and retrieval in the brain.
26. *Memory: Fabric of the Mind* (FHS, 28 min., 1988). Describes memory.
27. *Men, Women, and the Brain* (FHS, 56 min., 1988). Examines differences between the male and female brain.
38. *The Mind's I* (FHS, 58 min.). Demonstrates how brain parts coordinate to make an individual.
39. *Mysteries of the Mind* (NIMCO, 58 min.). Discusses manic-depression, obsessive-compulsive disorder, alcoholism, and other mood disorders, including neurochemical and genetic components.
30. *The Nature of Memory* (FHS, 26 min., 1990). Examines the physical and chemical aspects of memory.
31. *The Neuroanatomy Series* (TF, 1988). A comprehensive review of nervous system structure.
32. *The New Living Body: The Brain* (FHS, 20 min., 1995). Topics include brain structure and function, motor and sensory neurons, and simple reflex arcs.
33. *Parkinson's Disease* (FHS, 19 min., 1990). An in-depth view of the causes, symptoms, treatments, and prognosis of Parkinson's disease.
34. *Pathology Examples in the Human Brain* (FHS, 28 min., 1998). Describes pathologies of various brain disorders.
35. *The Seven Ages of the Brain* (FHS, 58 min.). Demonstrates the basic development and aging of the brain.
36. *The Sexual Brain* (FHS/NIMCO, 28 min.). Displays gender-based differences in brain structure and function.
37. *Teaching Modules: The Brain* (32 teaching modules on three cassettes) (NIMCO, 4 hr., 31 min., 1997). Examines brain structure, physiology, and disorders.

Computer Software

1. *The Human Brain: Neurons* (PLP, R-51003, Apple). Explores neuron structures, types of neurons, potentials, and neurotransmitters.
2. *Body Language, Study of Human Anatomy, Nervous System* (PLP, CH-182013, Apple; CH-182014, IBM)
3. *The Human Brain* (PLP, CH-510003, Apple)
4. *A Primer of Brain Anatomy and Function* (DGI, 1997). Describes the structure and function of nervous system cells, as well as electrochemical signaling including conduction and neurotransmission.
5. *The Anatomy Project: Neuroanatomy I—The Forebrain* (NIMCO, 1998)

6. *The Anatomy Project: Neuroanatomy II—The Midbrain and Hindbrain* (NIMCO, 1998)
7. *The Brain* (NIMCO). Demonstrates brain anatomy and function.
8. *Brain Anatomy: Neural Function* (CDI). An interactive study of brain anatomy and physiology, including conduction and synaptic transmission.

Slides

1. *The Central Nervous System* (NTA, #69, Microviewer)
2. *Spinal Cord, Nerves, and Reflexes* (PHM)
3. *Exploring the Brain: The Newest Frontier, Parts 1–5* (HRM)

Suggested Readings

Allstetter, B. Cheating brain death. (An article on preventing damage from strokes.) *Discover* (August 1991): 24.

Altman, J. The intricate wiring that lets us move. (An article on the basal nuclei.) *New Scientist* (March 10, 1990): 60–63.

Barr, M.L., and J. Kiernan. *The Human Nervous System: An Anatomical Viewpoint.* 5th ed. Philadelphia: Lippincott, 1988.

Begley, S. Gray matters. (An article about how men and women's brains differ.) *Newsweek* (March 27, 1995): 48–54.

Botto, L.D., et al. Neural-tube defects. *New England Journal of Medicine* 341 (November 11, 1999): 1509–1519.

Bower, B. Human brain reveals the anatomy of pain. *Science News* 139 (March 16, 1991): 167.

Brodal, A. *Neurological Anatomy in Relation to Clinical Medicine.* 3rd ed. New York: Oxford University Press, 1981.

Brodal, P. *The Central Nervous System: Structure and Function.* 2nd ed. New York: Oxford University Press, 1998.

Cowan, W.M. The development of the brain. *Scientific American* 241 (September 1979): 106–117.

Davidoff, J., and D. Concar. Brain cells made for seeing. *New Scientist* (April 10, 1993): 32–36.

Dobkin, B. Playing for time. (An article on amyotrophic lateral sclerosis.) *Discover* (April 1991): 36–37.

Fackelmann, K. Mice show Alzheimer brain plaques. *Science News* 147 (February 11, 1995): 84.

Ferry, G. Parkinson's: A suitable case for treatment? *New Scientist* (December 3, 1994): 36–40.

Fisher, L.J., and F.H. Gage. Grafting in the mammalian central nervous system. *Physiology Review* 73 (July 1993): 583–616.

Gershon, E.S., and R.O. Rieder. Major disorders of mind and brain. *Scientific American* 267 (September 1992): 126–133.

Gibbons, A. New maps of the human brain. *Science* 249 (July 13, 1990): 122–123.

Gibbons, A. The brain as "sexual organ." *Science* 253 (August 30, 1991): 956–959.

Gluhbegovic, N., and T.H. Williams. *The Human Brain: A Photographic Guide.* New York: Harper and Row, 1980.

Golden, J., and G. Chernoff. Multiple sites of anterior neural tube closure in humans: Evidence from anterior neural tube defects (anencephaly). *Pediatrics* 95 (April 1995): 506–510.

Kaas, J. The functional organization of the somatosensory cortex in primates. *Annals of Anatomy* 175 (1993): 509–518.

Kandel, E.R., J. Schwartz, and T. Jessell. *Principles of Neural Science*. 4th ed. New York: McGraw-Hill, Health Professions Division, 2000.

Klawans, H.L. *Toscanini's Fumble and Other Tales of Clinical Neurology*. Chicago: Contemporary Books, 1988.

Koshland, D.E., Jr. The dimensions of the brain. *Science* 285 (October 9, 1992): 199.

LeDoux, J. Emotion, memory and the brain. (An article on the amygdala.) *Scientific American* (June 1994): 50–57.

LeMay, M. Functional and anatomical asymmetries of the human brain. *European Journal of Neurology* 6 (January 1999): 79–85.

LeVay, S., and D. Hamer. Evidence for a Biological Influence in Male Homosexuality. *Scientific American* (May 1994): 44.

Lewis, R. Gateway to the brain. (An article on the blood-brain barrier.) *BioScience* 44 (March 1994): 133–137.

McDonald, J.W. Repairing the damaged spinal cord. *Scientific American* 281 (September 1999): 64–73.

Mischkin, M., and T. Appenzeller. The anatomy of memory. *Scientific American* 256 (June 1987): 80–89.

Montgomery, G. The mind in motion. *Discover* 10 (March 1989): 58–68.

Parent, André. *Carpenter's Human Neuroanatomy*. 9th ed. Baltimore: Williams and Wilkins, 1996.

Paulin, M. The role of the cerebellum in motor control and perception. *Brain, Behavior, and Evolution* 41 (1993): 39–50.

Petersen, S.E., et al. Positron emission tomographic studies of the cortical anatomy of single word processing. *Nature* 331 (February 18, 1988): 585–587 (also see pp. 560–562).

Raichle, M. Visualizing the mind. (An article on PET and functional MRI techniques.) *Scientific American* 270 (April 1994): 58–64.

Roberts, L. A call to action on a human brain project. *Science* 282 (June 28, 1991): 1794.

Romeo, J.H. The critical minutes after spinal cord injury. *RN* (April 1988): 61–67.

Romero-Sierra, C. *Neuroanatomy: A Conceptual Approach*. New York: Churchill Livingstone, 1986.

Roush, W. Protein studies try to puzzle out Alzheimer's tangles. *Science* 267 (February 10, 1995): 793–794.

Schreeve, J. The brain that misplaced its body. (An article on the gnostic area of the cortex.) *Discover* (May 1995): 82–91.

Scientific American. Special Issue: Mind and Brain. Various articles and authors. September 1992.

Seligmann, J., and J. McCormick. Saving spina bifida babies. *Newsweek* (November 15, 1982): 110.

Sperry, R. Some effects of disconnecting the cerebral hemispheres. *Science* 217 (1982): 1223.

Squire, L., and S. Zola-Morgan. The medial temporal lobe memory system. *Science* 253 (September 20, 1991): 1380–1386.

Thompson, C. Paralysis lost. *New Scientist* 150 (1996): 26–27.

Thompson, F.F. *The Brain: An Introduction to Neuroscience*. New York: W.H. Freeman and Co., 1985.

Williams, P.L., et al. *Gray's Anatomy*. 38th ed. New York: Churchill Livingstone, 1995.

Zivin, J., and D. Choi. Stroke therapy. *Scientific American* (July 1991): 56–63.

ANSWERS TO TEXTBOOK QUESTIONS

Answers for multiple-choice and matching questions 1–5 are located in Appendix B of the textbook.

Short Answer and Essay Questions

6. See Figure 13.2 on p. 361 for a diagram of the embryonic brain vesicles and their adult derivatives.

7. (a) The drawing will roughly resemble those in Figures 13.7a and 13.11a. (b) Right. (c) *Primary motor cortex*: voluntary (skilled) movements; *premotor cortex*: controls complex movements in three-dimensional space; *somatosensory association area*: perception (understanding) of the general somatic senses being felt; *primary visual area*: conscious awareness of what is being viewed; *prefrontal cortex*: complex learning abilities (cognition) and higher thought functions, perseverance, mood; *Broca's area*: speech production.

8. (a) The basal nuclei are important in starting and stopping the voluntary movements that are ordered by the primary motor cortex of the cerebrum. They also regulate the intensity of these movements, control repetitive tasks, and estimate the passage of time. (b) Globus pallidus and putamen. (c) Caudate.

9. The cerebellar cortex receives sensory information on current body movements, then compares this information to an image of how the body should be moving (as sent by the primary motor cerebral cortex). In this way, the cerebellum carries out a dialogue with the motor cerebral cortex on how to coordinate our skilled and voluntary movements. The cerebellum also communicates with various nuclei in the brain stem (red nucleus, reticular formation) to smooth our coarse and subconscious movements.

10. (a) The medial aspect of each cerebral hemisphere and in part of the diencephalon. (b) Septal nuclei, cingulate gyrus, hippocampal formation, part of the amygdala, fornix, anterior nucleus of the thalamus, and the hypothalamus. (c) The limbic system acts as our "emotional" brain and forms factual and emotional memories.

11. (a) The reticular formation extends through the central core of the brain stem (medulla, pons, and midbrain). (b) RAS means reticular activating system, which is our arousal mechanism. It maintains the cerebral cortex in a conscious, alert state.

12. (a) The CNS is protected by (1) the bony cranium and vertebrae; (2) meninges; (3) cerebrospinal fluid; (4) blood-brain barrier. (b) Cerebrospinal fluid is formed by choroid plexuses and drained by arachnoid villi. See Figure 13.27 on p. 392 for the circulatory pathway.

13. (a) The medulla/spinal cord junction is in the foramen magnum superiorly, and the tip of the conus medullaris is at the level of vertebrae L1–L2 inferiorly. (b) In a spinal tap, the needle enters the vertebral canal inferior to L2, whereas the spinal cord (conus medullaris) terminates superior to this.

14. (a) Fasciculus cuneatus and fasciculus gracilis. (b) The spinocerebellar tracts. (p. 000 and Table 13.2)

15. (a) The cell bodies of the first-order neurons of the spinothalamic pathway are located in the dorsal root ganglia, for these first neurons are the sensory neurons. The cell bodies of the third-order neurons are located in the thalamus. (b) The pyramidal-tract pathway extends from the motor cerebral cortex to the spinal gray matter and then continues via short interneurons to spinal motor neurons. For more detail, see Figure 13.34 on p. 399.

16. There is a decline in brain weight and volume with aging.

17. Somatotopy, literally "body mapping," means that specific regions of the CNS carry or process information involving specific regions of the body. The sensory homunculus on the primary somatosensory cortex is an example of somatotopy in the brain. The organization of axons according to body region within the ascending tracts of the spinal white matter is an example of somatotopy in the spinal cord.

18. The layers are the skin of the scalp, periosteum, bone of the skull, dura mater (periosteal and meningeal layers), subdural space, arachnoid mater, subarachnoid space, pia mater, brain.

19. (a) differences in size and organization of some tiny nuclei in the hypothalamus. (b) women have a longer left temporal lobe and visual cortex. (c) differences in the shape of the corpus callosum. (d) in men alone, the gray matter is thicker in the right cerebral cortex than in the left. (e) in the spinal cord, certain clusters of motor neurons that control erection are larger in men than in women.

20. See Figures 13.30b and 13.32 on pp. 394 and 396.

21. Periaqueductal gray matter is around the cerebral aqueduct, deep in the midbrain. Whereas its ventral part contains the cell bodies of motor neurons to the eye muscles, the rest signals many of the physical responses to terror.

22. For the locations of these streams in the parietal and temporal lobes, see Figure 13.12. The dorsal stream locates what we see in space ("where"), and the ventral stream recognizes what we see ("what").

Critical Reasoning and Clinical Applications Questions

1. Both Kim and L'Shawn are correct. Although the basic structural design of the CNS is "gray matter internally/white matter externally," there is a tendency in the brain for collections of gray to migrate externally into the white during development. The most extreme examples of this are the outer gray cortex of the cerebrum and cerebellum.

2. Answer (c) is correct. The postcentral gyrus is the primary somatosensory cortex, so stimulating it gives a conscious sensation of being touched somewhere on the body surface. Evidently, the surgeon stimulated the hand area of Ralph's somatosensory homunculus.

3. "A shunt would be put in": In most cases of spina bifida, the medulla is compressed in the foramen magnum, so cerebrospinal fluid accumulates in the ventricles and threatens to cause

hydrocephaly. To allow the CSF to drain, a permanent plastic tube is inserted from the ventricles to a large vein in the base of the neck. "Weak in the ankles": There was some damage to the caudal part of the infant's spinal cord, affecting the motor nerves that innervate the leg muscles.

4. The prefrontal cortex—involved with intelligence and social skills—was damaged.

5. In a quadriplegic (paralysis and paresthesia in all four limbs), the injury to the spinal cord is in the cervical region. In a paraplegic (paralysis and paresthesia in the lower limbs only), the injury to the spinal cord is inferior to the T1 segment.

6. A blow that causes unconsciousness twists the brain stem, depressing the activity of the reticular formation (i.e., the reticular activating system) postcentral gyri.

SUPPLEMENTAL STUDENT MATERIALS TO HUMAN ANATOMY, THIRD EDITION
Chapter 13: The Central Nervous System

To the Student

This chapter most likely will be one of the most challenging and intriguing ones you will deal with in your study of human anatomy. Much is known about the structure and function of the brain and spinal cord. But, so much is unknown that many scientists consider the brain a last frontier in the study of neuroanatomy. It is amazing that the most highly organized structure known to man does not understand itself. Only the future will answer questions about memory, senility, and mental illness. Approach your study with a clear understanding of the overall organization of the nervous system and the details and concepts presented to you in Chapter 13 will be easier to understand.

Step 1: Describe the embryological development, basic parts, organization, and protection of the brain.

☐ Summarize basic functions of the brain and describe its consistency and weight.

☐ Define *rostral* and *caudal*.

☐ Draw a diagram with labels representing the primary brain vesicles of the neural tube dividing into secondary brain vesicles followed by differentiation into adult structures. Refer to Figure 13.2 for help.

Step 2: Describe the basic parts and organization of the brain.

☐ Devise a quick reference vocabulary list of all the bold terms and key terms, adding to it as your study progresses.

☐ Classify the brain parts according to the system used by your textbook.

☐ Explain the organization of the white matter and gray matter of the brain stem and compare it to that of the matter in the cerebrum and cerebellum.

☐ Explain the ventricles of the brain as adult neural canal regions, including specific locations.

☐ Describe the gross anatomy of the cerebral hemispheres, including sulci, gyri, fissures, and lobes.

☐ Identify specific functions of the cerebral cortex as well as structural (Brodmann) areas.

☐ List three functional areas of the cerebral cortex.

☐ Identify specific functional areas for (1) recognizing objects, (2) spatial relationships, and (3) language.

☐ Define *somatotopy* and give examples, including "homunculus."

☐ Describe pyramidal tracts.

☐ Distinguish left cerebral hemisphere specialization from right hemisphere specialization.

☐ Distinguish between commissural tracts, association tracts, and projection tracts in the white matter.

☐ Distinguish between the caudate, lentiform, and amygdala basal nuclei of gray matter.

- ☐ Name the three parts of the diencephalon and describe the basic function, location, and any associated structural details for each part.
- ☐ Name the three parts of the brain stem and describe the basic function, location and any associated structural details for each part.
- ☐ Describe the structure and function of the cerebellum.
- ☐ Explain the functional brain systems: limbic system and reticular formation.

Step 3: Describe the protective structures associated with the brain.
- ☐ Name four structures that protect the brain.
- ☐ Describe the three meninges, including the dural extensions.
- ☐ Describe cerebrospinal fluid (CSF), including formation and circulation pattern.
- ☐ Describe the blood-brain barrier.

Step 4: Describe the spinal cord.
- ☐ Describe the gross anatomy of the spinal cord, including location, enlargements, and conus medullaris.
- ☐ Summarize functions of the spinal cord.
- ☐ Describe the meningeal coverings of the spinal cord and indicate the differences from cranial meninges.
- ☐ Distinguish between the epidural space, subdural space, and subarachnoid space.
- ☐ Distinguish between dorsal sensory roots and ventral motor roots.
- ☐ Describe the organization of the white matter of the spinal cord.
- ☐ Distinguish between ascending tracts (sensory pathways) and descending tracts (motor pathways) of the spinal cord.

CHAPTER 14
The Peripheral Nervous System

LECTURE AND DEMONSTRATION
Student Objectives

1. Define *peripheral nervous system,* and list its basic divisions.
2. Classify sensory receptors according to body location, stimulus detected, and structure.
3. Describe the motor innervation of skeletal muscle fibers at neuromuscular junctions.
4. Describe the innervation of visceral muscle and glands.
5. Name the 12 pairs of cranial nerves, and describe the structures innervated by each.
6. Describe the location of a spinal nerve, and distinguish spinal roots from rami.
7. Describe the somatic innervation of the neck, trunk, and limbs.
8. Define a *nerve plexus*. Name the four main plexuses by ventral rami, and the body region innervated by each. Describe the major nerves originating from each plexus.
9. Define *dermatomes* and explain Hilton's law of the innervation of joints.
10. Explain the causes and symptoms of shingles, migraine headaches, and myasthenia gravis.
11. Relate the development of the PNS to the basic segmental pattern of the human body.

Suggested Lecture Outline

I. *Peripheral Sensory Receptors (pp. 411–416, Table 14.1)*

   A. Classification by Location

   B. Classification by Stimulus Detected

   C. Classification by Structure (pp. 413–416, Figs. 14.3 and 14.4)

      1. Free Dendritic Endings

      2. Encapsulated Dendritic Endings

II. *Peripheral Motor Endings (pp. 416–418)*

   A. Innervation of Skeletal Muscle (pp. 416–417, Figs. 14.2–14.6)

   B. Innervation of Visceral Muscle and Glands (pp. 417–418)

III. *Cranial Nerves (pp. 419–420, Fig. 14.7 and Table 14.3)*

   A. The Olfactory Nerves

   B. The Optic Nerves

   C. The Oculomotor Nerves

III. CRANIAL NERVES *(continued)*

    D. The Trochlear Nerves

    E. The Trigeminal Nerves

    F. The Abducens Nerves

    G. The Facial Nerves

    H. The Vestibulocochlear Nerves

    I. The Glossopharyngeal Nerves

    J. The Vagus Nerves

    K. The Accessory Nerves

    L. The Hypoglossal Nerves

IV. *Spinal Nerves (pp. 426–437, Figs. 14.8–14.14)*

    A. Innervation of the Back (p. 428, Fig. 14.9b)

    B. Innervation of the Anterior Thoracic and Abdominal Wall (p. 428, Figs. 14.8–14.9b)

    C. Introduction to Nerve Plexuses (p. 428, Fig. 14.8)

    D. The Cervical Plexus and Innervation of the Neck (pp. 428–429, Fig. 14.10 and Table 14.4)

    E. The Brachial Plexus and Innervation of the Upper Limb (pp. 429–432, Fig. 14.11 and Table 14.5)

    F. The Lumbar Plexus and Innervation of the Lower Limb (p. 432, Fig. 14.12 and Table 14.6)

    G. The Sacral Plexus and Innervation of the Lower Limb (pp. 432–435, Figs. 14.13 and 14.7)

    H. Innervation of Joints of the Body (p. 435)

    I. Innervation of the Skin: Dermatomes (pp. 435–437, Fig. 14.14)

V. *Disorders of the Peripheral Nervous System (p. 437)*

VI. *The Peripheral Nervous System Throughout Life (p. 437)*

Lecture Hints

1. Review the overall organization of the nervous system and make sure students understand how information flows through the system, including the difference between nerve and tract, and nucleus and ganglion.

2. Define *peripheral nervous system* and describe its basic functional organization. Refer to Figure 14.1.

3. Using Figure 14.2, describe the basic structural components of the PNS.

4. Explain peripheral sensory receptors.

5. Using Table 14.1, classify peripheral sensory receptors according to location, to type of stimulus detected, and according to structure.

6. Explain peripheral motor endings.

7. Describe the motor innervation of skeletal muscle fibers at neuromuscular junctions. Refer to Figures 14.2, 14.5, and 14.6.

8. Describe the innervation of visceral muscle and glands.

9. List the 12 cranial nerves in a rostral-to-caudal sequence, including their Roman numeral designations, and describe the structures innervated by each.

10. Provide students with a favorite mnemonic to aid in learning the cranial nerves. An adaptation of the old classic is "On Old Olympus's Towering Top, A Fat, Vain German Viewed A Hop." (Of course, you may or may not have to explain the meaning of "hop.")

11. Point out the unique nature of the highly branched olfactory nerves (I).

12. Explain the difference between a tract and nerve, using optic nerves (II) as examples.

13. Point out the rostral-to-caudal ventral attachments, with the exception of the trochlear nerves (IV).

14. Using skull transparencies from Chapter 6, identify/review each of the cranial nerve passageways.

15. Classify each of the cranial nerves as sensory, motor, or mixed.

16. Identify the cranial nerves with parasympathetic fibers.

17. Caution students not to confuse "branchial" and "brachial."

18. Caution students that the names of the cranial nerves in Table 14.2 are not listed rostral to caudal.

19. Describe the location of spinal nerves and distinguish roots from rami. Refer to Figures 14.8 and 14.9.

20. Describe the somatic innervation of the neck, trunk, and limbs.

21. Define *nerve plexus* and name four major nerve plexuses formed by ventral rami, indicating the body region innervated by each.

22. For each plexus, (a) identify the specific spinal nerve ventral rami forming it, (b) name the major nerves originating from it, and (c) indicate structures served by the major nerves. Refer to Figures 14.10–14.13 and Tables 14.4–14.7.

23. Define dermatomes and explain Hilton's law of the innervation of joints. Refer to Figure 14.14.

24. Discuss disorders of the peripheral nervous system: shingles (herpes zoster), migraine headaches, and myasthenia gravis.

25. Discuss the embryological development of the PNS, relating it to the basic segmental pattern of the human body.

Classroom Discussion Topics and Activities

1. Using a skull and pipe cleaner, demonstrate the openings through which the cranial nerves pass.

2. Using a preserved sheep brain with the cranial nerves intact, demonstrate where these nerves attach to the brain.

3. Demonstrate the distribution of the spinal nerves using a three-dimensional model of the peripheral nervous system.

4. Invite a police officer to class and discuss motor and sensory dysfunction caused by alcohol and field sobriety tests.

5. Discuss why the injection of Novocain, or other anesthetics used by dentists, into just one point in the lower jaw can anesthetize one entire side of the jaw and tongue.

6. Ask students how seat belts for both the front and back seat prevent serious neurological damage in auto accidents. How can the use of lap belts without shoulder belts cause severe damage?

7. Ask students what neural damage can result from some overly enthusiastic parents swinging their infants around by the hands.

8. Discuss why pregnant women often experience numbness in their fingers and toes.

9. Ask students of what benefit is knowledge of dermatomes to a physician. (Some benefits were mentioned in the textbook, but there are more.)

Clinical Questions

1. While working in the emergency room, you receive two patients who were in an auto collision. One is dead on arrival, having sustained a transection of the spinal cord at the level of C2. The other patient suffered a similar injury but at the level of C6 and is still alive. Explain briefly, in terms of the origin and function of the phrenic nerves, why one injury was fatal and the other was not.

   Answer: Cell bodies of the motor neurons whose axons contribute to the phrenic nerves lie in the C3–C5 segments of the spinal cord. Transection of the cord above this level—at C2 in the first victim of the auto accident—cuts the axons from the respiratory centers in the brain stem that signal these motor neurons, thereby inactivating them and halting the respiratory movements of the diaphragm. This leads to death. Transection of the cord inferior to the C3–C5 does not interrupt this respiratory nervous pathway, so the phrenic nerves are still functional, and ventilation remains normal.

2. Rodney sustained a leg injury in a bowling accident and had to use crutches. Unfortunately, he did not take the time to learn how to use them properly. After 2 weeks of use, he noticed his fingers were becoming numb. Shortly after this, the entire upper limbs were getting weaker and tingling. What could be his problem?

   Answer: Simply speaking, he is probably compressing the brachial plexus, thus affecting the sensory and motor innervation of the upper limbs.

3. George, a 40-year-old man, inexplicably began to experience a sharp, stabbing pain in the skin of the left half of his face that began whenever his skin was touched. He described it as the most agonizing pain he had ever experienced and dreaded every attack. What could be his condition?

   Answer: George probably has tic douloureux. This mysterious condition is thought to result from compression of the trigeminal nerve or its main branches within the foramina from which they exit the skull. This compression might arise from an enlarged blood vessel near the nerve, or from a normal shrinkage of the brain with age that pulls the trigeminal tightly against the margins of the cranial foramina (see pp. 374 and 304 in the textbook).

4. Dominic, a minor-league baseball player, was struck on the left side of his face with a fast pitch while batting. His zygomatic arch was crushed, and the left ramus of his mandible was

broken. Following the incident and reconstructive surgery, he noticed that his left lower eyelid was still drooping, and the corner of his mouth sagged. What nerve had been damaged?

Answer: He suffered damage to the left facial nerve, which caused paralysis to the muscles of facial expression.

ART RESOURCES
Transparency List

Figure 14.1	Functional organization of the PNS.
Figure 14.2	Basic anatomical scheme of the PNS in the region of a spinal nerve.
Figure 14.4	Structure of the proprioceptors.
Figure 14.5	The neuromuscular junction.
Figure 14.6	Motor units.
Figure 14.7	The 12 pairs of cranial nerves.
Figure 14.8	Spinal nerves, posterior view.
Figure 14.9	Roots and branches of the spinal nerves in the thorax.
Figure 14.10	The cervical plexus.
Figure 14.11	The brachial plexus.
Figure 14.12	The lumbar plexus.
Figure 14.13	The sacral plexus.
Table 14.2	Olfactory nerves and optic nerves.
Table 14.2	Oculomotor nerves and trochlear nerves.
Table 14.2	Trigeminal nerves.
Table 14.2	Abducens nerves.
Table 14.2	Facial nerves.
Table 14.2	Vestibulocochlear nerves and glossopharyngeal nerves.
Table 14.2	Vagus nerves.
Table 14.2	Accessory nerves and hypoglossal nerves.

Teaching with Art

Figure 14.7 The 12 pairs of cranial nerves.

Table 14.3 The cranial nerves.

Textbook p. 418; transparencies; Digital Archive CD-ROM.

Checklist of Key Points in the Figure

- Differentiate between the cranial nerves and the spinal nerves.
- Emphasize that cranial nerves are part of the PNS, not the CNS.
- Point out that the cranial nerves are numbered using Roman numerals I–XII, in a rostral-to-caudal order of attachment.

- Note that almost all cranial nerves attach to the ventral side of the brain, pointing out the trochlear nerves as exceptions.
- Note that all cranial nerves serve the structures of the head and neck except for the vagus nerve (X), and describe the structures innervated by each.
- Explain the unique anatomical features of the first two pairs of cranial nerves—the olfactory nerve (I) and the optic nerve (II).
- Display Table 14.3, and for each cranial nerve, describe the sensory function, motor function, or mixed function.
- Note the cranial nerves that have parasympathetic fibers and briefly explain the significance.

Common Conceptual Difficulties Interpreting the Art
- Distinguish between the forebrain and the brain stem when noting attachments. Refer to Figures 13.2 and 13.19.
- Distinguish between a tract and nerve, including the optic chiasma in the discussion.
- Explain that each cranial nerve passes through specific skull openings, describing the origin and course of fibers. Refer to Table 14.3.

Art Exercises
1. Provide students with unlabeled copies of Figure 14.7 with instructions to color and label the 12 pairs of cranial nerves. Encourage students to devise a mnemonic to aid in learning the cranial nerves.
2. Provide students with unlabeled copies of Figure 7.4, Inferior aspect of the skull. Instruct students to label the foramina responsible for the passage of cranial nerves, along with the name and number of the nerve that passes through each opening.

Critical Reasoning
1. Sensory receptors are classified according to their location in the body or the location of the stimuli to which they respond. Ask students to identify the type of sensory receptor (exteroceptors, interoceptors, proprioceptors, or none) associated with each of the 12 cranial nerves.

    Answer:
    I   *Olfactory—exteroceptors*
    II *Optic—exteroceptors*
    III *Oculomotor—proprioceptors*
    IV *Trochlear—proprioceptors*
    V   *Trigeminal—exteroceptors and proprioceptors*
    VI *Abducens—proprioceptors*
    VII *Facial—interoceptors, proprioceptors, and exteroceptors (bit of skin on ear)*
    VIII *Vestibulocochlear—exteroceptors*
    IX *Glossopharyngeal—interoceptors, proprioceptors, and exteroceptors (bit of skin on ear)*
    X   *Vagus—interoceptors, proprioceptors (laryngeal muscles), and exteroceptors (bit of skin on ear)*
    XI *Accessory—none*
    XII *Hypoglossal—none*

2. Why may certain smells trigger strong emotions?

   Answer: The olfactory cortex is part of a brain area called the rhinencephalon, and the rhinencephalon connects to the limbic system, which is known as the "emotional brain." Some fibers of the olfactory nerve terminate at the limbic system. Thus, when a smell is associated with a particularly strong emotional memory, the same smell experienced again may evoke a similar emotional response or, at least, the recollection of the original response.

SUPPLEMENTAL COURSE MATERIALS
Library Research Topics

1. How does acupuncture relate to the distribution of spinal nerves?
2. Will all victims of polio be rendered paralyzed? What different forms are there?
3. How has microsurgery been used to reconnect severed peripheral nerves?
4. What are the standard tests by which clinicians evaluate the functions of the 12 cranial nerves?
5. Some people who have lost a limb experience a phenomenon called phantom limb pain. What is the basis of this phenomenon, and what methods are available to treat it?

Audiovisual Aids/Computer Software

See Preface of the Instructor's Guide for Key to Audiovisual Distributors

Videotapes

1. *The Anatomy and Physiology Series: The Nervous System* (NIMCO, 27 min.). Topics include nerve interaction, the brain and its parts, cranial nerves, and the ANS.
2. *Brain and Nervous System: Your Information Superhighway* (FHS, 25 min.). Covers parts of the brain and spinal cord, including protection of these areas.
3. *The Human Body Series: Reflexes and Conscious Movement* (NIMCO, 28 min., 1993). Examines the range of reflexive and controlled, conscious and unconscious movements of the body, including how nerve impulses originate and work.
4. *The Human Nervous System* (SVE, 12 min.). Includes the functions of neurons.
5. *The Living Body: Nerves at Work* (FHS, 27 min., 1990). Examines nerve and reflex signals and includes how they are transmitted.
6. *Multiple Sclerosis* (FHS, 26 min.). A thorough discussion of multiple sclerosis.
7. *Spinal Cord and Its Relations* (TF, 13 min.). Covers the structure of the spinal cord and spinal nerves.
8. *Spinal Cord and Spinal Nerves* (BC). Live-action video study of the spinal cord and the spinal nerves.

Computer Software

1. *The Anatomy Project; Neuroanatomy 3: The Spinal Cord, Meninges and Blood Supply* (NIMCO). An interactive study of the spinal cord, spinal nerves, meninges, and blood supply.
2. *A Primer of Brain Anatomy and Function* (DGI, 1997). Describes the structure and function of nervous system cells, as well as electrochemical signaling including conduction and neurotransmission.

3. *McInn's Interactive Clinical Anatomy CD-ROM* (DGI, 1996). Includes a complete three-dimensional human body showing dermatomes.

Slides

1. *Touch, Taste, and Smell* (EI, SS-0345F, Filmstrip or Slides). Current theories on neural receptors.
2. *Histology of the Nervous System* (CVB, 20 slides). Displays components of cells of the nervous system.
3. *The Nervous System and Its Functions* (CVB, 20 slides). Covers neural transmission, major brain areas, and the spinal cord.

Suggested Readings

Amato, I. In search of the human touch. *Science* 258 (November 27, 1992): 1436–1437.

Banks, R. The motor innervation of mammalian muscle spindles. *Progress in Neurobiology* 43 (1994): 323–362.

Barr, M.L., and J. Kiernan. *The Human Nervous System: An Anatomical Viewpoint.* 4th ed. Philadelphia: Harper and Row, 1983.

Klawans, H.L. *Toscanini's Fumble and Other Tales of Clinical Neurology.* Chicago: Contemporary Books, 1988.

Lopate, G., and A. Pestronk. Autoimmune myasthenia gravis. *Hospital Practice* (January 15, 1993): 109.

Moore, K.L. *Clinically Oriented Anatomy.* 34th ed. Philadelphia: Lippincott Williams and Wilkins, 1999.

Romanes, G.J. *Cunningham's Textbook of Anatomy.* 12th ed. Oxford, New York: Oxford University Press, 1981.

Sheperd, G.M. *Neurobiology.* 2nd ed. New York: Oxford University Press, 1987.

Stone, R. Post-polio syndrome: Remembrance of viruses past. *Science* 264 (May 13, 1994): 909.

Tardif, G. Nerve injuries. *The Physician and Sportsmedicine* 23 (April 1995): 61

Williams, P.L., et al. *Gray's Anatomy.* 38th ed. New York: Churchill Livingstone, 1995.

Willis, W.D., and R.G. Grossman. *Medical Neurobiology.* 3rd ed. St Louis: C.V. Mosby, 1981.

ANSWERS TO TEXTBOOK QUESTIONS

Answers for multiple-choice and matching questions 1–10 are located in Appendix B of the textbook.

Short Answer and Essay Questions

11. The capsules consist of connective tissue (connective tissue proper).
12. A motor unit is a single somatic motor neuron plus all the skeletal muscle fibers that the neuron innervates.
13. (1) Each axon terminal lies in a trough-like depression of the postsynaptic membrane (sarcolemma), and such a depression does not characterize neuron-to-neuron synapses.
    (2) A basal lamina occupies the synaptic cleft.

14. (a) Spinal nerves form from dorsal and ventral roots that unite at the dorsal root ganglion in the intervertebral foramen to form the spinal nerve. Spinal nerves contain both sensory and motor fibers. (b) These roots are outside the spinal cord, so they are in the PNS. (c) Major branches of each spinal nerve are the ventral and dorsal rami, which supply the somatic region of the body. The ventral rami and their branches supply the lateral and anterior body regions (including limbs), and the dorsal rami supply the dorsal body region (the back).

15. (a) A plexus is a branching, interlacing network of nerves. The nerve plexuses considered in this chapter (cervical, brachial, lumbar, and sacral) are formed by interconnecting branches from ventral rami. (b) *Cervical plexus,* C1–C4, innervates the neck, diaphragm, and other structures (see Table 14.4 on p. 429); *brachial plexus*, C5–T1, innervates the upper limb and other structures (see Table 14.5 on p. 431); *lumbar plexus*, L1–L4, innervates the anterior thigh, some of the abdominal wall, and other structures (see Table 14.6 on p. 433); *sacral plexus*, L4–S4, innervates the perineum and most of the lower limb except the anterior thigh (see Table 14.7 on p. 435).

16. The upper trunk of the brachial plexus forms from the junction of the C5 and C6 rami, the middle trunk is at C7, and the lower trunk forms from C8 and T1. (See Figure 14.11.)

17. Muscles that cross the hip joint include the rectus femoris, obturator externus, and gluteal muscles. Therefore, this joint is innervated by the femoral nerve, obturator nerve, and a gluteal nerve (superior gluteal nerve). (See Table 11.14.)

18. Abdul is correct: The facial nerve got its name because it crosses the face to innervate *muscles* of facial expression. The trigeminal nerve, not the facial nerve, innervates the skin of the face.

19. The correct answer is (c) just superior to S1. Except in the neck, every spinal nerve exits through the intervertebral foramen directly *inferior* to its correspondingly numbered vertebra. Nerve L5, therefore, exits just inferior to vertebra L5 or just superior to S1.

20. Because the spinal cord usually ends between vertebrae L1 and L2, the highest roots in the cauda equina must belong to L2. Thus, the cauda equina contains the roots of L2, L3, L4, L5, S1, S2, S3, S4, S5, and Co. That is ten nerves per side, multiplied by two sides (right and left), multiplied by two roots per nerve (dorsal and ventral). That comes to 40 roots. (See Figure 14.8.)

Critical Reasoning and Clinical Applications Questions

1. He had stretched the brachial plexus, damaging and tearing its nerves.

2. The right hypoglossal nerve. Muscles waste away when denervated like this.

3. The correct answer is (a) a few dorsal (sensory) roots in the cauda equina. All the other choices would have produced motor disorders as well as sensory disorders and are, therefore, impossible in this case.

4. He cannot dorsiflex his foot and will experience footdrop, because the deep fibular nerve to the anterior compartment extensors is functionless. (See Table 14.7.) Furthermore, he cannot evert his foot, because the superficial fibular nerve to the fibular muscles is functionless.

5. (1) Median nerve (Chapter 8). (2) See Related Clinical Terms, under Nerve Injuries. (3) If an axon grows back at 1 cm per week, and the hand is 17-cm long, recovery will take about 4 months.

SUPPLEMENTAL STUDENT MATERIALS TO HUMAN ANATOMY, THIRD EDITION

Chapter 14: The Peripheral Nervous System

To the Student

Chapter 14 introduces you to the peripheral nervous system and its sensory and motor connections that enable you to interact with the outside environment. Without these structures that lie outside of the CNS, you would have no links to the real world. Material covered includes peripheral sensory receptors, peripheral motor endings, cranial nerves, and spinal nerves. Chapter 14 focuses on somatic functions, and the following chapter addresses the visceral nervous system. It is important to review any material that is unclear and to ask questions if you do not grasp a concept.

Step 1: Understand the PNS and peripheral sensory receptors.

☐ Define *peripheral nervous system* and draw a flowchart representing the functional organization of the PNS.

☐ Distinguish between efferent (motor) and afferent (sensory) divisions.

☐ Distinguish between somatic and visceral.

☐ Distinguish between branchial and brachial.

☐ Classify peripheral sensory receptors by location in the body or the location of the stimuli to which they respond.

☐ Classify peripheral sensory receptors by the kind of stimuli to which they respond.

☐ Classify peripheral sensory receptors by structure.

Step 2: Understand peripheral motor endings and activation of skeletal muscles, visceral muscles, and glands.

☐ Describe a neuromuscular junction.

☐ Explain innervation of a skeletal muscle.

☐ Explain innervation of visceral (smooth) muscle and glands.

Step 3: Understand cranial nerves.

☐ List the 12 cranial nerves, including their Roman numeral designations.

☐ Distinguish between rostral and caudal.

☐ Identify structures innervated by each cranial nerve.

☐ Describe the origin and course followed by each nerve, including skull foramina.

☐ Explain the classification of cranial nerves as sensory, motor, or mixed.

☐ Identify the types of sensory receptors (exteroceptors, interoceptors, proprioceptors, or none) associated with each cranial nerve.

Step 4: Understand spinal nerves.

☐ Distinguish between cranial nerves and spinal nerves.

☐ Describe the location of spinal nerves.

- ☐ Distinguish between roots and rami.
- ☐ Identify the cauda equina.
- ☐ Describe the somatic innervation of the neck, trunk, and limbs.
- ☐ Define *nerve plexus*.
- ☐ Name four main plexuses formed by ventral rami, including body regions innervated.
- ☐ Name major nerves originating from each plexus, including structures innervated.
- ☐ Define *dermatomes*.
- ☐ Explain Hilton's law of the innervation of joints.

CHAPTER 15
The Autonomic Nervous System and Visceral Sensory Neurons

LECTURE AND DEMONSTRATION
Student Objectives

1. Define the *autonomic nervous system* (ANS), and explain its relationship to the peripheral nervous system as a whole.
2. Compare autonomic neurons to somatic motor neurons.
3. Describe the basic differences between the parasympathetic and sympathetic divisions of the autonomic nervous system.
4. Describe the anatomy of the parasympathetic division, and explain how it relates to the brain, cranial nerves, and sacral spinal cord.
5. Describe the anatomy of the sympathetic division, and explain how it relates to the spinal cord and spinal nerves.
6. Explain the sympathetic function of the adrenal medulla.
7. Explain how various regions of the CNS help to regulate the autonomic nervous system.
8. Describe the role and location of visceral sensory neurons relative to autonomic neurons.
9. Explain the concept of referred pain.
10. Explain how spinal and peripheral reflexes regulate some functions of visceral organs.
11. Briefly describe some diseases of the autonomic nervous system.
12. Describe the embryonic development of the autonomic nervous system.
13. List some effects of aging on autonomic functions.

Suggested Lecture Outline

I. Introduction to the Autonomic Nervous System (pp. 444–447, Fig. 15.1)

   A. Comparison of the Autonomic and Somatic Motor Systems (pp. 444–445, Fig. 15.2)

   B. Divisions of the Autonomic Nervous System (pp. 445–447, Fig. 15.3–15.4)

II. The Parasympathetic Division (pp. 447–452, Figs. 15.5–15.6)

   A. Cranial Outflow (pp. 448–449)

   1. Outflow via the Oculomotor Nerve (III)

   2. Outflow via the Facial Nerve (VII)

II. The Parasympathetic Division *(continued)*

    3. Outflow via the Glossopharyngeal Nerve (IX)

    4. Outflow via the Vagus Nerve (X)

  B. Sacral Outflow (pp. 449–451)

III. The Sympathetic Division (pp. 452–457, Figs. 15.6–15.14)

  A. Basic Organization (p. 452, Fig. 15.7)

    1. Sympathetic Trunk Ganglia

    2. Prevertebral Ganglia

  B. Sympathetic Pathways (pp. 452–456, Figs. 15.9–15.13)

    1. Sympathetic Pathways to the Body Periphery

    2. Sympathetic Pathways to the Head

    3. Sympathetic Pathways to the Thoracic Organs

    4. Sympathetic Pathways to the Abdominal Organs

    5. Sympathetic Pathways to the Pelvic Organs

  C. The Role of the Adrenal Medulla in the Sympathetic Division (pp. 456–457, Fig. 15.14)

IV. Central Control of the Autonomic Nervous System (pp. 457–458)

  A. Control by the Brain Stem and Spinal Cord

  B. Control by the Hypothalamus and Amygdala

  C. Control by the Cerebral Cortex

V. Visceral Sensory Neurons (p. 458, Fig. 15.15)

VI. Visceral Reflexes (p. 459)

VII. Disorders of the Autonomic Nervous System (pp. 459–460)

VIII. The Autonomic Nervous System Throughout Life (p. 460, Fig. 15.16)

Lecture Hints

1. Encourage students to continue to use the Study Partner CD-ROM, A.D.A.M.® Interactive Anatomy, and the resources available on the web site *The Anatomy and Physiology Place*.

2. Define *autonomic nervous system,* and stress its position in the nervous system hierarchy. Refer to Figure 15.1.

3. Explain why "*and Visceral Sensory Neurons*" is part of the chapter title.

4. Distinguish between the *general visceral motor* division of the PNS and the *general somatic motor* and *branchial* divisions.

5. Compare the autonomic and somatic motor systems. Refer to Figure 15.2.

6. Distinguish between preganglionic and postganglionic neurons, including locations of cell bodies and myelination.

Chapter 15: *The Autonomic Nervous System and Visceral Sensory Neurons* 173

7. Point out that the autonomic ganglia are motor ganglia and clearly different from sensory ganglia of dorsal roots.
8. Summarize the basic structural similarities of the *sympathetic* and *parasympathetic* divisions of the ANS. Refer to Figure 15.3.
9. Summarize the basic functional differences of the sympathetic and parasympathetic divisions of the ANS. Refer to Figure 15.3.
10. Stress sympathetic effects on visceral organs as "fight, flight, or fright" and parasympathetic effects as "resting and digesting."
11. Explain the basic anatomical differences between the sympathetic and parasympathetic systems, including thoracolumbar and craniosacral outflow, length of fibers, branching of axons, and locations of ganglia. Refer to Figure 15.4.
12. To explain the main biochemical difference between the two divisions, clearly differentiate between adrenergic and cholinergic fibers.
13. Name the cranial nerves containing the cranial outflow of the parasympathetic division, indicating the part of the head, thorax, or abdomen served by each. Refer to Figure 15.5.
14. Stress the parasympathetic role of the vagus nerve (X), due to its vast distribution to the viscera of the thorax and abdomen; explain intramural ganglia; name several associated plexuses; and discuss the functional significance of the vagus nerve. Refer to Figures 15.5 and 15.6.
15. Describe the sacral part of the parasympathetic outflow, including the pelvic splanchnic nerves and plexus.
16. Explain the basic anatomical organization of the sympathetic system, including why it is more complex than the parasympathetic system, and location of preganglionic cell bodies. Refer to Figure 15.7.
17. Point out the lack of parasympathetic innervation to the arrector pili, sweat glands, and the smooth muscle of peripheral blood vessels.
18. Name and explain sympathetic trunk ganglia and prevertebral ganglia, including spinal nerve connections to the sympathetic trunk. Refer to Figure 15.8.
19. Review the basic two-neuron pathway and then explain sympathetic pathways to the different body regions: the body periphery, the head, thoracic organs, abdominal organs, and pelvic organs. Refer to Figures 15.9–15.13.
20. Define *white* and *gray rami communicantes* (singular: ramus communicans) and explain why parasympathetic fibers do not innervate blood vessels of the skin and skeletal muscles.
21. Explain how the adrenal medulla functions as a major organ of the sympathetic system, describe its structure, and explain the meaning of "surge of adrenaline."
22. Name the parts of the brain stem and spinal cord that influence visceral motor functions, indicating a function for each part.
23. Stress that the focus of the chapter is *general visceral motor* (ANS), but *general visceral sensory* (PNS) continuously monitors visceral organ activity to maintain optimal performance of visceral functions.
24. Distinguish between and define *visceral pain* and *referred pain*.

25. Discuss visceral reflexes, giving several examples.
26. Discuss disorders of the autonomic nervous system: Raynaud's disease, hypertension, mass reflex reaction, aschalasia of the cardia, and congenital megacolon.
27. Explain the embryonic origin of preganglionic and postganglionic neurons.
28. Name a few age-related conditions that reflect decreased efficiency of the ANS.

Classroom Discussion Topics and Activities

1. Without announcing your intentions, walk quietly into the lecture room, set down your notes, and yell very loudly to scare the students. Ask students to list all organs affected by the fright and what the organ response was. (If you are too bashful to scream in class, simply blow a very shrill whistle to elicit a startle response.)
2. Interact with students to prepare a list of visceral organs. Ask students to surmise the effects of sympathetic and parasympathetic stimulation on each organ. Help the students deduce these effects logically (sympathetic = fight, fright, or flight; parasympathetic = resting and digesting). Ask students to compare their results with Table 15.2 in their textbooks.
3. Ask students to illustrate the sympathetic pathway from the spinal cord to the heart using a simple line drawing, including labels for neurons and ganglia.
4. Ask students to illustrate the parasympathetic pathway to the heart with a simple drawing, including labels for neurons, cranial nerve involvement, and ganglia.
5. Bring a string of white beads to class as a model of the sympathetic trunk.
6. Demonstrate a preserved cat dissected to illustrate the sympathetic trunk, celiac ganglion, some splanchnic nerves, and the vagus nerve.
7. Demonstrate a model of a spinal cord that is cut in cross section in the thoracic or lumbar region. Point out the lateral gray columns (sympathetic cell bodies) of the gray matter, and if present on the model, the gray and white rami communicantes.
8. Set up a live, exposed frog heart or turtle heart to illustrate the effects of acetylcholine and epinephrine.
9. Lie detector machines have been used for decades. In light of autonomic functions, discuss how such machines work. In light of autonomic functions, why do they sometimes give false answers? How could someone fool a lie detector machine?
10. At certain times, when people are very excited or scared, their bowels and/or urinary sphincters lose control. Ask students why this occurs in terms of the role of the autonomic nervous system.
11. Ask students why most people feel very tired after they eat a big meal.
12. When someone is punched in the "solar plexus," he or she may lose consciousness. What autonomic structure is the "solar plexus"?

Clinical Questions

1. How are hypertension and the ANS related?

   Answer: The ANS is involved in nearly every process that goes on in the body. Since it controls the rate and force of the heartbeat and the constriction action of smooth muscles in the blood vessels, it is not surprising that hypertension and the ANS are related. Overstimulation of the sympathetic response, caused by long-term stress, can keep the arterioles constricted and the heart rate and blood pressure elevated excessively. Drugs that block the release of neurotransmitters from adrenergic nerve endings can be used in treatment.

2. Jed, a rather obese couch potato, likes to eat a very large meal in the evening. After the meal, his wife asks him to help clean the dishes, but Jed explains that he is "too tired" and promptly goes to sleep. What seems to be his problem?

Answer: The parasympathetic division is involved in the activation of the digestive viscera and the conservation of body energy. Following a meal, this system promotes digestive activity and lowers the heart rate and respiratory rate. The sympathetic division is only minimally active at this time. Therefore, the person will feel "very sleepy." If the person is overweight, he probably should not overexert himself. However, doing the dishes would not be hazardous to his health.

3. Amy, a high-strung teenager, was suddenly startled by a loud bang that sounded like a gunshot. Her heartbeat accelerated rapidly. When she realized that the noise was only a car backfiring, she felt greatly relieved but her heart kept beating heavily for half an hour. Why does it take a long time to calm down after we are scared?

Answer: Sympathetic innervation is widespread throughout the body, and since large amounts of epinephrine from the adrenal medulla pour into the blood, it will take time for the hormone to be broken down throughout the body. (Later, in their physiology class, the students will also learn that both epinephrine and norepinephrine are inactivated very slowly, prolonging their effects.)

4. Ms. Johnson, who has been paralyzed from the neck down since an automobile accident 4 years ago, lives in a nursing home. One night on evening rounds, her nurse discovered her in a fetal position, her body drenched with sweat. She was incontinent of feces and urine, and her blood pressure was dangerously high. After a while, she was stabilized. What had happened to Ms. Johnson?

Answer: She had experienced a mass reflex reaction, perhaps because her bladder had overfilled with urine. The mass reflex reaction is a life-threatening condition involving extensive activation of both somatic motor and autonomic output from the spinal cord. The high blood pressure that results from a massive sympathetic activation may precipitate a stroke. The exact mechanism is unknown.

5. Susan was attracted to Ryan, one of her classmates, because he looked intriguingly "different." When he looked at her, she saw that one of his pupils was larger than the other one, and the skin was redder on one side of his face. She looked up these traits in a medical encyclopedia and learned that Ryan's exotic features simply reflected a mild pathological condition. What was Ryan's condition?

Answer: Ryan has Horner's syndrome, reflecting damage to the cervical part of a sympathetic trunk in the inferior region of the neck. (See the chapter's Related Clinical Terms on p. 461 in the textbook.)

ART RESOURCES

Transparency List

Figure 15.1   General visceral motor system and general visceral sensory system.

Figure 15.2   Automatic and somatic motor nervous systems.

Figure 15.3   Overview of the sympathetic and parasympathetic division of the ANS, issuing from the brain and spinal cord.

Figure 15.4   Some basic differences between the sympathetic and parasympathetic divisions.

Figure 15.5   Parasympathetic division of the ANS.

Figure 15.6   The vagus nerve, autonomic nerve plexuses, and autonomic ganglia.

Figure 15.7   Sympathetic division of the ANS.

Figure 15.8   The sympathetic trunks and trunk ganglia in the thorax.

Figure 15.9   Sympathetic pathways to the body periphery.

Figure 15.10 Sympathetic pathways to the head.

Figure 15.11 Sympathetic pathways to the thoracic viscera.

Figure 15.12 Sympathetic pathways to the abdominal viscera.

Figure 15.13 Sympathetic pathways to the pelvic viscera.

Figure 15.14 The adrenal medulla.

Teaching with Art

Figure 15.7   Sympathetic division of the ANS.

Textbook p. 453; transparencies; Digital Archive CD-ROM.

Checklist of Key Points in the Figure

- Define *sympathetic division* and explain why it is more complex than the *parasympathetic division*.
- Differentiate between preganglionic and postganglionic neurons, indicating locations of cell bodies and defining *thoracolumbar outflow*.
- Describe and define *sympathetic trunk* (chain).
- Distinguish between paravertebral ganglia and prevertebral ganglia, including specific names and locations of each.
- Explain the difference between white and gray rami communicantes.
- Indicate several specific plexuses, also explaining the significance of splanchnic nerves.
- Present an overview of the basic two-neuron sympathetic pathway, explaining variations of the pathway to various body regions: the body periphery, the head, thorax, abdomen, and pelvis.

Common Conceptual Difficulties Interpreting the Art

- Review the concepts of ganglion, plexus, and splanchnic nerve.
- Explain that there are two sympathetic trunks (chains), each one lateral to the vertebral column and attached to spinal nerves.

- Note that the number of sympathetic trunk ganglia is not identical to the number of spinal nerves because some adjacent ganglia fuse during development, mostly evident in the cervical region.
- Indicate locations of ganglia as sites of synapses.
- Mention the lack of parasympathetic innervation to the body periphery: blood vessels, sweat glands, and arrector pili.
- Explain why gray rami occur on all the sympathetic trunk ganglia and white rami occur only in the region of thoracolumbar outflow.

Art Exercises

1. a. Provide unlabeled copies of Figure 15.7 and instruct students to color code and label the paravertebral ganglia, including the three cervical ganglia, as well as the four prevertebral ganglia.

   b. Provide labeled copies of Figure 7.13, The vertebral column, and instruct students to identify and color code the specific locations of the sympathetic ganglia as described in their textbooks on p. 452.

2. Provide unlabelled copies of Figure 15.7 and instruct students to color code and label parts of a sympathetic pathway to any one (or more) of the following: eye, heart, stomach, adrenal gland, and/or urinary bladder.

3. Provide unlabeled copies of Figures 15.9–15.13 and instruct students to color code and label parts of the sympathetic pathways to various body regions: periphery of the body, the head, thoracic organs, abdominal organs, and pelvic organs.

Critical Reasoning

Ask students to study Figure 15.7 to perform the following exercise. For each of the following sympathetic pathways, indicate whether the synapse between preganglionic and postganglionic neurons occurs in trunk ganglia, prevertebral ganglia, or in both:

   a. Pathway to the head structures (eye and various glands)

   b. Pathway to the thoracic viscera (e.g., heart, lungs)

   c. Pathway to abdominal viscera (e.g., stomach, small intestine)

   d. Pathway to pelvic viscera (e.g., bladder, large intestine)

Answers: (a) trunk ganglia, (b) trunk ganglia, (c) prevertebral ganglia, and (d) both.

SUPPLEMENTAL COURSE MATERIALS
Library Research Topics

1. Do other groups of vertebrates (fish, amphibians, reptiles, and lower mammals) have an autonomic nervous system? If so, is it more or less advanced than ours?

2. The autonomic nervous system regulates peristalsis of the alimentary canal. If the ganglia and nerve fibers that control this activity were damaged, what would happen? What bacterial toxins or types of trauma could cause this?

3. Ulcers seem to occur in people who have high blood pressure. What are the causes of ulcers, and what treatments are available?

4. Research the manipulation of autonomic functions through the use of drugs, such as alpha-blockers and beta-blockers.

Audiovisual Aids/Computer Software

See Preface of the Instructor's Guide for Key to Audiovisual Distributors

Videotapes

1. *The Anatomy and Physiology Series: The Nervous System* (NIMCO, 27 min.). Topics include nerve interaction, the brain and its parts, cranial nerves, and the ANS.
2. *Brain and Nervous System: Your Information Superhighway* (FHS, 25 min.). Explores the brain, its parts and their functions, and the ANS and its functions.
3. *Exploring Your Brain: Fear and Anxiety* (FHS, 56 min.). Examines how the brain handles fear and anxiety.
4. *The Human Body Series: The Autonomic Nervous System* (NIMCO, 28 min., 1993). Studies the ANS and its functions.
5. *The Human Nervous System* (SVE, 13 min.). Covers the functioning of the ANS.
6. *The New Living Body: The Brain* (FHS, 20 min., 1995). Examines all aspects of the brain, including the ANS.
7. *The Human Body Series: Pain* (NIMCO, 28 min., 1993). Describes the nature of the sensation of pain.
8. *The Living Body: Our Talented Brain* (FHS, 28 min., 1990). Examines brain structure and function, including the use of memory.
9. *Memory: Fabric of the Mind* (FHS, 28 min., 1988). Describes memory.
10. *Mysteries of the Senses Set* (CBSC, five programs, 60 min. each). A Nova set exploring the different special and general senses.
11. *The Nature of Memory* (FHS, 26 min., 1990). Examines the physical and chemical aspects of memory.
12. *The Nervous System.* 3rd ed. (EBEC, 17 min.). Discusses how the nervous system controls and integrates specific body activities.

Computer Software

1. *Body Language: Nervous System* (PLP). Covers the anatomy of the nervous system.
2. *Explorations in Human Anatomy and Physiology* (Ward's Mac/Win)
3. *The Human Brain* (IM, Mac/Win)

Slides

1. *The Autonomic Nervous System* (PHM)

Suggested Readings

Barr, M.L., and J. Kiernan. *The Human Nervous System: An Anatomical Viewpoint.* 4th ed. Philadelphia: Harper and Row, 1983, Chapter 24.

Bower, B. Human brain reveals the anatomy of pain. *Science News* 139 (1991): 167.

Brodal, A. *Neurological Anatomy in Relation to Clinical Medicine*. 3rd ed. New York: Oxford University Press, 1981, pp. 698–782.

Cahill, L. Beta-adrenergic activation and memory for emotional events. *Nature* 371 (October 20, 1994): 702.

Decara, L.V. Learning in the autonomic nervous system. *Scientific American* 222 (January 1970): 30–39.

Fackelmann, K. Gutsy genetics. (An article on Hirschsprung's disease.) *Science News* 144 (September 11, 1993): 174–175.

Kalin, N. The neurobiology of fear. *Scientific American* (May 1993).

Melzack, R. The tragedy of needless pain. *Scientific American* (February 1990).

Parker, T., et al. The innervation of the mammalian adrenal gland. *Journal of Anatomy* 183 (1993): 265–278.

Romero-Sierra, C. *Neuroanatomy: A Conceptual Approach*. New York: Churchill Livingstone, 1986, Chapter 20.

Williams, P.L., et al. *Gray's Anatomy*. 38th ed. New York: Churchill Livingstone, 1995.

ANSWERS TO TEXTBOOK QUESTIONS

Answers for multiple-choice and matching questions 1–8 are located in Appendix B of the textbook.

Short Answer and Essay Questions

9. No. As it was originally defined, the autonomic nervous system is strictly motor in nature, the general visceral motor division of the peripheral nervous system. (However, some modern authorities do now include the visceral sensory neurons as part of the ANS.)

10. (a) The rami communicantes attach to the proximal part of the ventral ramus, directly lateral to the spinal nerve. Gray rami are medial to white rami. (White rami consist of myelinated preganglionic fibers; gray rami consist of unmyelinated postganglionic fibers.) (b) Gray rami communicantes consist of postganglionic sympathetic axons, and postganglionic axons are unmyelinated. Bundles of unmyelinated axons have a gray color.

11. Sympathetic impulses signal (1) sweat glands to secrete sweat; (2) eye pupils to dilate; (3) cells of the adrenal medulla to secrete their excitatory hormones into the blood; (4) the heart to pump faster and more forcefully; (5) air tubes in the lungs to dilate; (6) blood vessels supplying skeletal muscles to dilate; (7) blood vessels of the digestive viscera to constrict; (8) salivary glands to stop secreting saliva (i.e., inhibit the secretion of digestive glands). (See Table 15.2 on p. 451.)

12. Parasympathetic activity can reverse effects 2, 4, 5, and 8 in the previous answer.

13. Destruction of the ciliary ganglia would cause an inability to constrict the pupil (which would remain wide open) and an inability to focus the eye for near vision. Destruction of the sphenopalatine ganglia would make it impossible to cry, and interfere with the ability of the mucous glands in the nose to produce mucus. Destruction of the submandibular ganglia would stop secretion of saliva from two large salivary glands, the submandibular and the

sublingual (although the largest salivary gland, the parotid, would still function normally). None of the above symptoms is really life threatening, so the death ray is a failure.

14. The long vagus nerves leave the cranial region and carry preganglionic parasympathetic fibers to the thoracic and abdominal organs.

15. Elderly people often complain of constipation and dry eyes, and they may faint if they stand up too fast.

16. (a) postganglionic sympathetic. (b) postganglionic parasympathetic. (c) postganglionic parasympathetic. (See Figures 15.5 and 15.7; intramural ganglia are defined on p. 449)

17. (a) Cell bodies of preganglionic neurons are in the upper thoracic spinal cord; axons run in thoracic ventral roots, spinal nerves, and ventral rami; to white rami communicantes; ascend in sympathetic trunk to synapse in superior cervical ganglion; postganglionic axons run on head arteries to reach the submandibular gland (p. 454 and Figure 15.7). (b) Cell bodies of preganglionic neurons are in the thoracic and lumbar spinal cord; axons run in thoracic ventral roots, spinal nerves, and ventral rami; to white rami communicantes; descend in sympathetic trunk; synapse there or pass through and synapse in inferior hypogastric ganglia; postganglionic axons run through hypogastric plexus to bladder (p. 456 and Figure 15.7). (c) See the pathway in Figure 15.9 on p. 455. (d) Cell bodies of preganglionic neurons are in the lower thoracic spinal cord; axons run in thoracic ventral roots, spinal nerves, and ventral rami; to white rami communicantes; pass through sympathetic chain ganglia without synapsing and run in thoracic splanchnic nerves; pass through celiac plexus; reach adrenal medulla; synapse with adrenal medulla cells, which are modified postganglionic neurons (see p. 457 and Figure 15.14). (e) Preganglionic cell bodies in upper thoracic cord; axons in thoracic ventral roots, spinal nerves, white rami. Some ascend in nearest trunk ganglia, with postganglionic axon running through cardiac plexus to heart. Other preganglionic axons ascend in sympathetic trunk to synapse in a cervical ganglion, with postganglionic axon descending through cardiac plexus to heart. (f) Preganglionic cell bodies in inferior half of thoracolumbar spinal cord; axons run in thoracic ventral roots, spinal nerves, white rami, through trunk ganglion to splanchnic nerve to synapse in the celiac prevertebral ganglion. From there, postganglionic axons run to stomach. (Figure 15.7)

18. (a) preganglionic cell bodies are in midbrain; axons run in oculomotor nerve; synapse in ciliary ganglion in orbit; postganglionic axons run to eye (p. 448 and Figure 15.5). (b) preganglionic cell bodies in sacral spinal cord; axons run in ventral roots, spinal nerves, ventral rami, and pelvic splanchnic nerves; through inferior hypogastric plexus; synapse with postganglionic neurons in the intramural ganglia in the bladder wall (p. 449 and Figure 15.5). (c) preganglionic cell bodies are in medulla oblongata; axons run in vagus nerve (into abdomen and through inferior mesenteric plexus); synapse with postganglionic neurons in intramural ganglia in intestinal wall (p. 449 and Figure 15.5).

19. The vagus descends through the neck, goes onto the esophagus, and follows that tube inferiorly onto the stomach. From there, it sends branches through the celiac and superior mesenteric plexuses to various abdominal organs (e.g., intestines, liver, pancreas). For more information, see Figure 15.5.

20. Distal half of the large intestine plus pelvic organs.

Critical Reasoning and Clinical Applications Questions

1. The infant probably has congenital megacolon (Hirschsprung's disease). In this condition, the parasympathetic innervation of the distal region of the large intestine has failed to develop normally. Feces are not propelled through, and accumulate in the bowel.

2. The superior central region of the abdomen, directly superficial to the infrasternal angle. This is the 'stomach' area of the referred pain map in the figure.

3. Visceral pain exhibits an unusual feature: One often feels no pain when a visceral organ (lining of the large intestine) is torn. However, the true skin around the anus is innervated by *somatic* sensory fibers, which do transmit pain.

4. Yes, pain from the kidney is referred to the thighs, as well as to the lower abdomen. (See Figure 15.15 on page 459.)

5. Raynaud's disease, a sympathetic-vasoconstrictive disorder.

SUPPLEMENTAL STUDENT MATERIALS TO HUMAN ANATOMY, THIRD EDITION

Chapter 15: The Autonomic Nervous System and Visceral Sensory Neurons

To the Student

A study of the autonomic nervous system enables you to understand actions the body performs without conscious thought. You involuntarily experience countless smooth muscle and cardiac muscle contractions and gland secretions that provide a stable internal environment for you. Some of the important visceral functions under the regulation of the ANS are maintenance of heart rate and blood pressure, digestion, and urination. Anatomically, the ANS is described as a motor (efferent) pathway made up of two neurons, and Chapter 15 does focus on the general visceral motor functions. But, you must also realize that the general visceral sensory system constantly monitors these activities. Otherwise, how would you know you had a tummy ache? It is necessary to thoroughly review the peripheral nervous system hierarchy, as represented in Figure 15.1, to ensure a complete and factual understanding of the autonomic nervous system.

Step 1: Understand the relationship of the autonomic nervous system to the body's nervous system as a whole.

- [ ] Define the *autonomic nervous system* (ANS).
- [ ] Explain the relationship of the ANS to the PNS and the CNS.
- [ ] Summarize functions of the ANS, including the influence of the general visceral senses.

Step 2: Compare the autonomic nervous system to the somatic motor system.

- [ ] Distinguish effectors of the ANS from the effectors of the rest of the motor (efferent) division.
- [ ] Compare the number of neurons in a somatic (or branchial) motor pathway to the number of neurons in an autonomic motor pathway, including location of cell bodies.
- [ ] Distinguish between preganglionic and postganglionic neurons.

Step 3: Describe the autonomic nervous system.

- [ ] Name the two divisions of the ANS.
- [ ] Outline the basic functional differences between the sympathetic and parasympathetic divisions of the ANS.
- [ ] Give examples of "fight, flight, or fright" responses experienced by your body.
- [ ] Name examples of "resting and digesting" responses experienced by your body.
- [ ] Describe three major anatomical differences between the sympathetic and parasympathetic divisions.
- [ ] Describe major biochemical differences between the sympathetic and parasympathetic neurotransmitters.
- [ ] Study textbook Table 15.1 for a summary of major anatomical and physiological differences between the sympathetic and parasympathetic divisions.

Step 4: Explain the outflow of the parasympathetic division of the ANS.
- ☐ Describe how the parasympathetic division relates to the brain and define *cranial outflow*.
- ☐ Name the cranial nerves that support parasympathetic fibers.
- ☐ Describe the precise locations of the preganglionic and postganglionic neurons for each of the following cranial nerves:
  - Outflow via the oculomotor nerve (III)
  - Outflow via the facial nerve (VII)
  - Outflow via the glossopharyngeal nerve (IX)
  - Outflow via the vagus nerve (X)
- ☐ Explain how the parasympathetic division relates to the sacral spinal cord and describe sacral outflow.

Step 5: Explain the sympathetic division of the ANS.
- ☐ Describe the anatomy of the sympathetic division.
- ☐ Describe why the sympathetic division is more complex than the parasympathetic division.
- ☐ Distinguish between trunk ganglia and paravertebral ganglia, including examples of each.
- ☐ Explain how the sympathetic division relates to the spinal cord and spinal nerves.
- ☐ Describe and draw simple diagrams representing sympathetic innervation to the following body regions:
  - Periphery of the body
  - The head
  - Thoracic viscera
  - Abdominal viscera
  - Pelvic viscera
- ☐ Explain the role of the adrenal medulla in the sympathetic division.

Step 6: Understand the central nervous system control of the ANS.
- ☐ Using Chapter 13, The Central Nervous System, review structures of the brain and spinal cord, as needed.
- ☐ Explain the role played by the brain stem and spinal cord, including reticular formation and spinal visceral reflexes.
- ☐ Explain the role played by the hypothalamus as the main *integration center*.
- ☐ Discuss the amygdala in terms of fear-related behavior.
- ☐ Explain the role of the cerebral cortex and conscious control over some autonomic functions.

Step 7: Explain the relationship of visceral sensory neurons and visceral reflexes to the ANS.

☐ Define *visceral sensory neurons*.

☐ Explain the role played by visceral sensory neurons, including examples of visceral information provided. Refer to Figure 15.1.

☐ Describe the concept of referred pain.

☐ Explain how spinal and peripheral reflexes regulate some functions of visceral organs.

Step 8: Understand the ANS throughout life.

☐ Distinguish between the embryonic origin of postganglionic neurons and the embryonic origin of postganglionic neurons.

☐ List examples of age-related problems that are associated with the declining efficiency of the ANS.

☐ Briefly describe some disorders of the ANS, such as Raynaud's disease and hypertension.

CHAPTER 16
The Special Senses

LECTURE AND DEMONSTRATION
Student Objectives

1. Describe the receptors for taste and smell. Describe the paths by which sensory information from these receptors travels to the brain.
2. Describe the anatomy and function of the accessory structures of the eye, the eye tunics, the lens, and the humors of the eye.
3. Explain the structure of the retina and the photoreceptors.
4. Explain how light is focused for close vision.
5. Trace the pathway of nerve impulses from the retina to the cerebral cortex.
6. Describe the embryonic development of the eye.
7. List the basic structures of the outer and middle ear and their corresponding functions.
8. Name the parts of the bony and membranous labyrinths in the inner ear.
9. Describe the receptors for hearing and equilibrium.
10. Describe the pathways taken by auditory and equilibrium information through the brain.
11. Compare and contrast the embryonic derivations of the outer, middle, and inner ears.
12. List the causes and symptoms of motion sickness, Meniere's Syndrome, and deafness.
13. Describe changes in the special senses that occur with aging.

Suggested Lecture Outline

I. The Chemical Senses: Taste and Smell (pp. 466–470)

    A. Taste (Gustation) (pp. 466–468, Figs. 16.1 and 16.2)

        1. Taste Buds

        2. Taste Sensations and the Gustatory Pathway

    B. Smell (Olfaction) (pp. 468–470, Fig. 16.3)

    C. Disorders of the Chemical Senses (p. 470)

    D. Embryonic Development of the Special Senses (p. 470, Fig. 21.18)

II. The Eye and Vision (pp. 470–486)

    A. Accessory Structures of the Eye (pp. 470–474, Figs. 16.4 and 16.6)

        1. Eyebrows

        2. Eyelids

II. The Eye and Vision *(continued)*

    3. Conjunctiva

    4. Lacrimal Apparatus

    5. Extrinsic Eye Muscles

  B. Anatomy of the Eyeball (pp. 474–480, Figs. 16.7–16.13)

    1. The Fibrous Tunic

    2. The Vascular Tunic

    3. The Sensory Tunic (Retina)

    4. Internal Chambers and Fluids

    5. The Lens

  C. The Eye as an Optical Device (pp. 480–481, Fig. 16.14)

  D. Visual Pathways (pp. 481–484, Fig. 16.15)

    1. Visual Pathway to the Cerebral Cortex

    2. Visual Pathways to Other Parts of the Brain

  E. Disorders of the Eye and Vision (pp. 484–485)

  F. Embryonic Development of the Eye (pp. 485–486, Fig. 16.16)

III. The Ear: Hearing and Equilibrium (p. 486)

  A. The Outer (External) Ear (p. 486, Fig. 16.17)

  B. The Middle Ear (pp. 486–489, Figs. 16.17–16.19)

  C. The Inner (Internal) Ear (pp. 489–494, Figs. 16.17 and 16.18, 16.20–16.24)

    1. The Vestibule

    2. The Semicircular Canals

    3. The Cochlea

  D. Equilibrium and Auditory Pathways (pp. 494–495, Fig. 16.25)

  E. Disorders of Equilibrium and Hearing (p. 495)

    1. Motion Sickness

    2. Meniere's Syndrome

    3. Deafness

  F. Embryonic Development of the Ear (p. 496, Fig. 16.26)

IV. The Special Senses Throughout Life (pp. 496–497)

Lecture Hints

1. Define *taste*, and describe taste bud histology using Figure 16.1.

2. Point out the importance of smell (and other sensations) on the perception of taste.

3. Name four basic taste sensations and point out tongue regions where they are best sensed.

4. Explain that substances must be dissolved in saliva to activate the sense of taste.

5. Name the cranial nerves that support taste and describe the *gustatory pathway*. Refer to Figure 16.2.
6. Define *smell*, and describe olfactory epithelium. Refer to Figure 16.3.
7. Describe the olfactory nerve (I), how smell is relayed to the brain, and where in the brain the input is analyzed.
8. Explain embryonic development of the olfactory epithelium and taste buds.
9. Describe disorders of the chemical senses: anosmia and uncinate fits.
10. Define *vision*, and explain that the eye is a receptor for light impulses as well as an energy transducer because the eye converts light energy into the electrical energy of an action potential.
11. Describe the location of the eye, as well as locations and functions of the accessory structures associated with the eye: eyebrows, eyelids, conjunctiva, lacrimal apparatus, and extrinsic eye muscles. Refer to Figures 16.4–16.6.
12. Describe the anatomical and functional features of the three *tunics* of the eye. Refer to Figures 16.7–16.10.
13. Distinguish between *rod cells* and *cone cells*, explaining functions. Refer to Figure 16.11.
14. Describe the internal chambers of the eye and the fluids contained in these chambers.
15. Describe the structure and function of the lens, including a clinical application: cataract.
16. Using Figure 16.14, describe how light is focused on the retina and refer to this chapter's *A Closer Look* for a discussion of focusing disorders of the eye.
17. Explain that the ear is a receptor for sound impulses as well as an energy transducer because the ear converts sound energy into the electrical energy of an action potential.
18. Describe the features of the external ear that accommodate the gathering of sound waves and transmission of sound waves to the middle ear. Refer to Figure 16.17.
19. Describe the bony location of the middle ear and explain the function of the associated structures, the pharyngotympanic tube and ossicles. Refer to Figures 16.17–16.19.
20. Describe the structure of the inner ear, clearly distinguishing between the bony labyrinth and the membranous labyrinth. Refer to Figure 16.20.
21. Describe the membranous labyrinth in terms of functions: equilibrium and hearing.
22. Distinguish between perilymph and endolymph.
23. Distinguish between static equilibrium and linear acceleration.
24. Explain how the maculae and otoliths contribute to the sense of static equilibrium. Refer to Figure 16.21.
25. Explain the events occurring in the cochlea that participate in the mechanism of hearing. Refer to Figure 16.24.
26. Summarize the pathway to the *lower* brain centers, traveled by impulses generated by equilibrium receptors.
27. Summarize a simplified pathway to the primary auditory cortex, traveled by impulses generated by hearing receptors. Refer to Figure 16.25.
28. Describe the embryonic origins of the inner ear, the middle ear, and the outer ear.

29. Summarize some of the symptoms and causes of disorders of equilibrium and hearing: motion sickness, Meniere's syndrome, and deafness.
30. Summarize the changes that occur with aging in the special senses.

Classroom Discussion Topics and Activities

1. Display a three-dimensional model of an eye and ear to illustrate the anatomy of each.
2. Use an onion, orange, and apple to test the interaction between taste, smell, and sight. Cut pieces in similar sizes and shapes, and provide water between samplings. First, ask two student volunteers to taste and smell each item normally. Second, cover their eyes and have them taste each item and identify the item. Third, instruct them, with eyes still covered, to pinch shut their noses, then taste and identify. Ask the class to explain the results.
3. Spray cologne with a strong scent into the air and ask students to indicate when they first smell it by raising their hands. Instruct students to time the presence of the cologne until it is no longer detectable. This is a jumping-off point for a discussion on adaptation of the sensory apparatus (receptors).
4. To demonstrate that rods do not distinguish color, lower or turn off the lights in the classroom and ask students to identify variously colored papers.
5. Dissect a preserved cow (or sheep) eye to illustrate its anatomical structure and the nature of its tissues and fluids. Be sure to point out the very fragile retina and demonstrate its single point of attachment, the optic disc.
6. Obtain a skull to illustrate the bony structures associated with our senses. Also, review the openings through which pass the special sensory nerves (olfactory, optic, vestibulocochlear, facial, glossopharyngeal, and vagus).
7. Demonstrate a set of ear ossicles to illustrate how tiny they really are.
8. Have one student twirl like a dancer, another run straight forward from a standing position, and another stand still with a tilted head, to demonstrate angular acceleration and linear acceleration (the two aspects of dynamic equilibrium) and static equilibrium.
9. Display Ishihara's color plates and permit students to test themselves for evidence of color blindness, and/or display an eye chart so students can assess their visual acuity.
10. Display examples of optical illusions and ask students to explain them.
11. To demonstrate that substances must be dissolved in saliva to taste them, ask students to dry the tongue surface with a paper towel before dropping a few grains of sugar or salt on the tongue surface.
12. Provide a jumbled list of various eye and ear structures and ask students to arrange the structures in the order that light or sound signals travel through these receptors.
13. Most people with sinus infections cannot smell, and their ability to taste is much diminished. Ask students why.
14. Amplified rock and roll music has long been implicated in auditory deafness. Ask students for suggestions to help alleviate this problem in teenagers.
15. Fish and plant-eating mammals (such as horses) have eyes on the sides of their heads. Ask students why this is useful to these animals.

16. Certain types of sunglasses can cause more harm than good. Ask students what is wrong with these inexpensive sunglasses.
17. One's ears "ring" after prolonged loud noise stops. Ask students what causes ringing in the ears.

Clinical Questions

1. During an ophthalmoscopic examination, Mr. James was found to have bilateral papilledema. Further investigation indicated that this condition resulted from a rapidly growing intracranial tumor. First, define *papilledema*. Then, explain its presence in terms of Mr. James' diagnosis.

   Answer: As mentioned in this chapter's Related Clinical Terms, papilledema is a protrusion of the optic disc into the eyeball, and it is caused by any condition that raises the intracranial pressure (the tumor, in this case).

2. Brenda, a 6-year-old girl, told the clinic physician that her "ear lump" hurt and that she kept "getting dizzy and falling down." As she told her story, she pointed to her mastoid process. An otoscopic examination of the external auditory canal revealed a red, swollen, eardrum, and her throat was inflamed. Her condition was described as mastoiditis with secondary labyrinthitis (inflammation of the labyrinth). Describe the most likely route of infection in Brenda's case. Also explain the cause of her dizziness and falling.

   Answer: Most ear infections start as throat infections that spread through the pharyngotympanic tube into the middle ear. Brenda's infections had spread farther, through the mastoid antrum behind the middle ear to the mastoid air cells. It had also spread medially to infect the inner ear, and the pressure of inflammatory fluids in the inner ear disrupted the balance receptors, making Brenda dizzy and prone to falling.

3. A 60-year-old woman is experiencing vertigo. She ignores the symptoms at first, but now her attacks are accompanied by severe nausea, and following each attack she hears a crackling in her ears. What do you think her problem is, and what is its suspected cause?

   Answer: She probably has Meniere's syndrome. It affects both the balance receptors in the semicircular ducts and the hearing receptors in the cochlear ducts. The cause is uncertain, but it probably results from an excessive production of endolymph, whose pressure distorts the membranous labyrinth.

4. Mariam, a 75-year-old grandmother, complained that her vision was becoming obscured. Upon examination by an ophthalmologist, she was told she had cataracts. What are they and how are they treated?

   Answer: A cataract is a clouding of the lens that causes the world to appear distorted, as if looking through frosted glass. Some cataracts are congenital, but most are related to the age-related hardening and thickening of the lens or are a secondary consequence of diabetes mellitus. The direct cause is probably inadequate delivery of nutrients to the deeper lens fibers, followed by an unfolding of the crystalline proteins in these fibers. Fortunately, the offending lens can be removed surgically and an artificial lens implanted.

5. After trauma to the head during an automobile accident, a man has anosmia. Define *anosmia*. Why is this condition fairly common after head injuries?

   Answer: Anosmia means loss of the sense of smell. As trauma to the head shakes the brain, it can pull and tear the delicate filaments of the olfactory nerve where they pass through the cribriform plate of the ethmoid bone.

ART RESOURCES
Transparency List

Figure 16.1	Taste buds.
Figure 16.2	The gustatory pathway from the taste buds on the tongue to the gustatory area of the cerebral cortex.
Figure 16.3	Olfactory receptors.
Figure 16.4	Surface anatomy of the right eye.
Figure 16.5	Accessory structures of the eye.
Figure 16.6	Extrinsic muscles of the eye.
Figure 16.7	Medial view of the lateral half of the right eye.
Figure 16.8	Structures in the anterior region of the eye.
Figure 16.9	Posterior view of the anterior half of the eye.
Figure 16.10	Microscopic anatomy of the retina.
Figure 16.11	Three photoreceptors (rod cells and cone cells) in the retina.
Figure 16.14	The eye as an optical device.
Figure 16.15	Visual pathway to the brain, and visual fields of the eyes.
Figure 16.17	Structure of the ear.
Figure 16.18	Superior view of ear structures in the floor of the cranial cavity of the skull.
Figure 16.19	The three ossicles in the right middle ear.
Figure 16.20	Membranous labyrinth in the bony labyrinth of the inner ear.
Figure 16.21	Anatomy and function of the maculae in the inner ear.
Figure 16.22	Structure and function of a crista ampullaris in the inner ear.
Figure 16.23	Anatomy of the cochlea.
Figure 16.24	Role of the cochlea in hearing.
Figure 16.25	The auditory pathway, from spiral organ of Corti to the primary auditory cortex in the temporal lobe.

Teaching with Art

Figure 16.15 Visual pathway to the brain, and visual fields of the eyes.

Textbook p. 484; transparencies; Digital Archive CD-ROM.

Checklist of Key Points in the Figure

- Describe the formation of optic nerves as a bundle of axons of ganglia cells of the retina. (Refer to Figure 16.16 for the embryology of the eye.)
- Clearly distinguish between the optic nerve, optic chiasma, and optic tract.
- Explain decussation of axons from the medial half of each eye.
- Clearly differentiate between ipsilateral and contralateral fibers.
- Point out how overlapping fields of vision permit depth perception.
- Point out the termination point of impulses in the the visual cortex in the occipital lobe.

Common Conceptual Difficulties Interpreting the Art

- Describe the beginning of the visual pathway in the retina, pointing out that light traveled through the retina and in the reverse neuron sequence to get to the rod and cone cells.
- Explain stereoscopic vision and monocular vision, relating these visual fields to colored parts of the figure.
- Discuss the significance of the optic chiasma, decussation, and depth perception.
- Clarify the difference between perception and sensation.
- Explain why some visual information goes to the midbrain and diencephalon.
- Explain the role of the lateral geniculate nucleus of the thalamus.
- Explain the role of the occipital cerebral cortex.

Art Exercise

Provide students with unlabeled copies of Figure 16.15. Instruct students to trace the visual pathway to the brain from the right eye and left eye, using color-coded fibers and to label each part of the pathway from the retina to the visual cortex.

Critical Reasoning

Instruct students to look at Figure 16.15 and answer the following questions:

1. If the optic chiasma is cut longitudinally, what is the effect on vision?

    Answer: Peripheral vision is lost in both eyes, leaving only "tunnel vision."

2. If the left visual cortex (or any area beyond the optic chiasma, such as the optic tract or thalamus) is damaged, what is the effect on vision?

    Answer: Blindness occurs throughout the right half of the visual field.

3. If the left eye or left optic nerve is destroyed, what is the effect on vision?

    Answer: True depth perception is eliminated and peripheral vision on the left side is lost.

4. If an optic tract is cut, what is the effect on vision?

    Answer: Both eyes will be partially blind: one eye loses the medial field of vision and the other eye loses the lateral field of vision.

SUPPLEMENTAL COURSE MATERIALS
Library Research Topics

1. How successful are cochlear implants? What surgical techniques are used?
2. Some permanently deaf people have been helped by means of computers and electrical probes connected to certain areas of the brain. How is this possible, and what is the current research in this area?
3. Contact lenses have been used for decades to correct vision problems. What is the status of contact lens implants, and why do many ophthalmologists hesitate to prescribe them?
4. How effective is the technique of reshaping the cornea with lasers as a means of correcting focusing disorders (farsightedness or nearsightedness)?
5. If hearts, lungs, livers, and kidneys can be transplanted, why not eyes? What would be some technical difficulties?
6. What are the present treatments for otitis media, and are they really effective?

Audiovisual Aids/Computer Software

See Preface of the Instructor's Guide for Key to Audiovisual Distributors

Videotapes

1. *Eyes and Ears* (FHS, QB-823, 26 min., C, VHS/BETA). Fascinating camera action used to show the functions of the eye and ear. Also available in 16-mm film.
2. *Anatomy of the Human Eye Series* (TFI, C, 1987). A series of seven videotapes (or 16-mm films), ranging from 13 to 19 minutes, explaining the gross anatomy of the human eye.
3. *Optics of the Human Eye Series* (TFI, C, 1987). A series of four videotapes (or 16-mm films), each 10 minutes long, that illustrates basic optics relating to the eye.
4. *Dissection and Anatomy of the Beef Eye* (CBS, 49-2300, VHS)
5. *The Anatomy and Physiology Series: The Special Senses* (NIMCO, 28 min.). Covers general and special senses with emphasis on special senses.
6. *The Body Atlas Series: Now Hear This* (HCHCA/NIMCO, 30 min., 1994). Explores hearing and equilibrium.
7. *The Body Atlas Series: Taste and Smell* (HCACA/NIMCO, 30 min., 1994). Explores the senses of taste and smell and their interactions.
8. *The Body Atlas Series: Visual Reality* (HCACA/NIMCO, 30 min., 1994). Discusses all aspects of vision.
9. *Eye Dissection and Anatomy* (IM, 16 min., 1989). Explores the anatomy of the eye through dissection.
10. *The Eye and the Ear* (IM, 29 min., 1990). Discusses the anatomy and physiology of the eye and ear.
11. *The Five Senses* (FHS, 28 min., 1993). Studies each of the five senses.
12. *Hearing* (FHS, 28 min., 1993). Explores the anatomy and physiology of the ear.

13. *The Human Body Series: The Senses of Smell and Taste* (FHS/NIMCO, 28 min., 1993). Explores the senses of smell and taste and how they interact.
14. *The Human Body Series: Balance* (NIMCO, 28 min., 1993). Covers balance and the role of the inner ear.
15. *Inside Information: The Brain and How It Works* (FHS, 58 min.). Examines the functioning of the brain, including the recognition of sounds, visual images, smells, etc.
16. *The Living Body: Eyes and Ears* (FHS, 28 min., 1990). Demonstrates how the eye and ear work.
17. *Nova Series: Mystery of the Senses* (CBSC/TVC, five videos, 60 min. each). Examines each of the special senses.
18. *The Senses* (FHS, 20 min., 1995). Studies each of the special senses.
19. *Smell and Taste* (FHS/NIMCO, 30 min., 1993). Explores smell and taste; discusses the connections between the sense of smell and Alzheimer's disease.
20. *The Sound of Silence* (FHS, 26 min., 1990). Studies vision and hearing.
21. *What Smells?* (FHS, 60 min., 1992). Studies the sense of smell.
22. *Where Am I?* (FHS, 26 min., 1990). Explores body awareness in space, proprioception.
23. *Balance (Human Body Live Action Video Series)* (CAP, 28 min., 1993)

Computer Software
1. *Dynamics of the Human Eye* (EI, C-3060, Apple or IBM)
2. *Dynamics of the Human Ear* (EI, C-3061, Apple or IBM)
3. *Dynamics of the Human Senses of Touch, Taste, and Smell* (EI, C-3063, Apple or IBM)
4. *The Eye* (QUE, COM4210A, Apple)
5. *The Anatomy Project: The Ear* (NIMCO). Interactive CD-ROM explores the ear.
6. *The Anatomy Project: The Eye* (NIMCO). Interactive CD-ROM explores the eye.
7. *Dynamics of the Human Senses of Touch, Taste, and Smell* (EI). Explores touch, taste, and smell.
8. *Human Vision* (CDL/SKBL/SVE/VWSP). Explores the inner workings of the human eye.
9. *Senses* (CBSC). Examines the general and special senses.
10. *Senses: Physiology of Human Perception* (PLP). Examines the senses.
11. *Senses: Physiology Study Unit* (EI). Examines the senses.

Slides
1. *Touch, Taste, and Smell* (EI, SS-0345F, Filmstrip or Slides). Current theories on neural receptors.
2. *Histology of the Sensory System* (EI, 614, Slides). Shows structural and functional correlations of a variety of sensory organs, including the eye and the ear.
3. *Eyes and Their Function* (EI, SS-0870F, Filmstrip or Slides). Functional description of the eyeball and accessory structures.
4. *Ears and Their Function* (EI, SS-0330F, Filmstrip or Slides). Studies the middle and inner ear.

Suggested Readings

Abu-Mostafa, Y.S., and D. Psaltis. Optical neural computers. *Scientific American* 256 (March 1987): 88–96.

Barinaga, M. How the nose knows. *Science* (April 12, 1991): 209–210.

Brooks, A. Middle ear infections in children. *Science News* 146 (November 19, 1994): 332–333.

Craig, Owen. Eye implant promises "reversible" surgery. *New Scientist* (June 1, 1991): 23.

Discover. Special Issue: The Mystery of Sense. Articles on all the special senses, by various authors. June 1993.

Durrant, J.D., and J.H. Lovrinic. *Basics of Hearing Science*. Baltimore: Williams and Wilkins, 1988.

Fackelmann, K. Light at the end of the tunnel: Visionary research probes the genesis of glaucoma. *Science News* 143 (June 12, 1993): 376–377.

Farbman, A. The cellular basis of olfaction. *Endeavour,* New Series 18 (1994): 2–8.

Fawcett, D.W. *A Textbook of Histology*. 12th ed. New York: Chapman & Hall, 1994, Chapters 34 and 35.

Gibbons, B. The intimate sense. *National Geographic* 170 (September 1986): 324–360.

Glickstein, M. The discovery of the visual cortex. *Scientific American* 295 (September 1988): 118–127.

Greenberg, J. Early hearing loss and brain development. *Science News* 131 (March 1987): 149.

Hess, B.J., and D.E. Angelaki. Inertial vestibular coding of motion: Concepts and evidence. *Current Opinion in Neurobiology* 7 (December 1997): 860–866.

Holley, M., and B. Kachar. Hi-fi cells at the heart of the ear. *New Scientist* (March 27, 1993): 27–30.

Holloway, M. Seeing the cells that see. *Scientific American* 272 (January 1995): 27.

Koretz, J.F., and G.H. Handelman. How the human eye focuses. *Scientific American* 259 (July 1988): 92–99.

Loeb, G.E. The functional replacement of the ear. *Scientific American* 252 (February 1985): 104–111.

McLaughlin, S., and R. Margolskee. The sense of taste. *American Scientist* 82 (November-December 1994): 538–545.

Mestel, R. Hearing pictures, seeing sounds. (An article on cochlear implants.) *New Scientist* (June 4, 1994): 20–23.

O'Day, D. Management of cataract in adults. *American Family Physician* (May 1, 1993): 1421.

Parker, D.D. The vestibular apparatus. *Scientific American* 243 (November 1980): 98–111.

Pollen, D.A. Cortical areas in visual awareness. *Nature* 377 (September 28, 1995): 293–295.

Roberts, A. Systems of life: The eye and vision: 3. *Nursing Times* 89 (September 8–14, 1993): 51–54.

Schnapf, J.L., and D.A. Gaylor. How photoreceptor cells respond to light. *Scientific American* 256 (April 1987): 40–47.

Seligmann, J., et al. A light for poor eyes: Correcting nearsightedness with a new "cool" laser. *Newsweek* (June 17, 1991): 61.

Sininger, Y.S., K.J. Doyle, and J.K. Moore. The case for early identification of hearing loss in children. Auditory system development, experimental auditory deprivation, and development of speech perception and hearing. *Pediatric Clinics of North America* 46 (February 1999): 1–14.

Weiss, P.L. Eye diving. *Science News* 138 (September 15, 1990): 170–172.

White, T.W., and R. Bruzzone. Intercellular communication in the eye: Clarifying the need for connexon diversity. *Brain Research Reviews* 32 (April 1, 2000): 130–137.

Wilson, B., et al. Better speech recognition with cochlear implants. *Nature* 352 (July 18, 1991): 236.

Zatorre, R., et al. Functional localization and lateralization of human olfactory cortex. *Nature* 360 (November 26, 1992): 339–340.

ANSWERS TO TEXTBOOK QUESTIONS

Answers for multiple-choice and matching questions 1–12 are located in Appendix B of the textbook.

Short Answer and Essay Questions

13. The student is clearly correct, as the "traditional" five senses (vision, hearing, smell, touch, and taste) do not even acknowledge the existence of balance (equilibrium), an important sense. As listed in Figure 12.2 on p. 337, our many senses include touch, pain, pressure, vibration, temperature, proprioception, vision, smell, hearing, equilibrium, and sensing chemical changes and irritation in viscera, nausea, hunger, and smell.

14. (a) The olfactory epithelium, containing the olfactory receptors, lies in the superior part of the nasal cavity, on the superior nasal concha and the superior part of the nasal septum. (b) It seems that each receptor cell has just one kind of membrane receptor, but it can bind to several different types of odor molecules that share the same kind of region to which the receptor can bind.

15. The fovea centralis, a part of the retina in the precise posterior pole of the eye, contains only cone cells (no rod cells) and provides detailed color vision.

16. The receptor cells for taste and smell are replaced throughout life. The receptor cells for vision, hearing, and balance are not effectively replaced.

17. (a) The retinas form from the forebrain as paired lateral outgrowths called optic vesicles, which indent to form double-layered optic cups. The external layer of each cup forms the pigmented layer of the retina, and the internal layer forms the neural layer of the retina. (See Figure 16.16.) (b) The middle ear cavity forms from the lateral region of the first pharyngeal pouch. (See Figure 16.26.)

18. With age, the lens loses its crystal clarity and becomes discolored. It becomes less able to round up for accommodation, leading to presbyopia. Atrophy of the spiral organ of Corti reduces hearing acuity, especially to high-pitched sounds.

19. Auditory pathway: hair cells in the inner ear, to the cochlear nerve (VIII), to cochlear nuclei in the medulla, to the superior olivary nucleus or inferior colliculus (some fibers only), to the

medial geniculate nucleus in the thalamus, to the primary auditory cerebral cortex in the temporal lobe. (See Figure 16.25.)

20. Both the inferior oblique and superior rectus muscles elevate the eye. However, the inferior oblique tends to turn the eye laterally, while the superior rectus turns it medially.

21. (a) A semicircular canal is a tube-shaped *space* carved in the petrous temporal bone, whereas a semicircular duct is a membrane-walled duct that lies within the semicircular canal. The semicircular canal is part of the bony labyrinth, and the semicircular duct is part of the membranous labyrinth. Similarly, the cochlea is the curved space that holds the membranous cochlear duct. (b) (1) semicircular ducts and (2) utricle/saccule (for balance); (3) cochlear duct (for hearing).

22. The sphincter of the pupil, innervated by parasympathetic fibers in the oculomotor nerve, decreases pupil size. The dilator of the pupil, innervated by sympathetic fibers from the superior cervical trunk ganglion, increases pupil size. (See Chapter 15.)

Critical Reasoning and Clinical Applications Questions

1. Enrique probably has otitis externa, an infection of the external auditory canal that can result from swimming in water that contains bacteria (see Related Clinical Terms on p. 497). He probably does not have otitis media, which generally arises from a sore throat, and he does not need ear tubes (which relieve pressure from infection in the middle ear cavity).

2. The children probably had conjunctivitis, caused by bacteria or viruses, which is highly contagious. (p. 485)

3. High intraocular pressure generally indicates the patient has glaucoma.

4. The left optic tract carries all the visual information from the right half of the visual field. Thus, Lionel cannot see the right half of visual space. (See Figure 16.15a.)

5. The babies had retinopathy of prematurity (p. 485: Disorders section). They received oxygen after birth, which caused retinal vessels to grow, rupture and detach the retina, leading to blindness.

6. The condition is tinnitus (see Related Clinical Terms on p. 497). Other treatments are masking the "noise" with soothing sounds and biofeedback.

SUPPLEMENTAL STUDENT MATERIALS TO HUMAN ANATOMY, THIRD EDITION
Chapter 16: The Special Senses

To the Student

The special senses explored in this chapter are the chemical senses of taste and smell, vision in the eye, and hearing and equilibrium in the ear. These senses have specific receptor cells that differ from the receptors of the general senses and are not like the dendritic endings of sensory neurons. The receptors for taste, smell, hearing, and equilibrium are specialized sensory epithelium that interfaces with the nervous system and the environment. Photoreceptors in the eye are considered neurons, but they also closely resemble epithelial cells.

This chapter summarizes basic functional anatomy of the special senses and explains the basic concepts of sensory processing for taste, smell, vision, hearing, and equilibrium.

Step 1: Understand the chemical senses: taste and smell.

- ☐ Describe the receptors for taste and outline the gustatory pathway.
- ☐ Distinguish between sensation and perception.
- ☐ Identify the taste sensations and the general location of the corresponding taste buds on the tongue.
- ☐ Describe the receptors for smell and outline the pathway that the smell sensory information travels to the brain.
- ☐ Distinguish between olfactory tract and olfactory nerve.

Step 2: Understand the eye and vision.

- ☐ Describe the structure and function of the accessory structures of the eye: eyebrows, eyelids, conjunctiva, lacrimal apparatus, and extrinsic eye muscles.
- ☐ List the three tunics of the eyeball, describing the parts and functions of each.
- ☐ Describe the structure and function of the lens.
- ☐ Describe the structure and function of the internal chambers and fluids (humors) of the eyeball.
- ☐ Explain the structure of the retina and the photoreceptors.
- ☐ Distinguish between the rod cells and the cone cells.
- ☐ Explain how light is focused for close vision.
- ☐ Trace the pathway of visual information from the retina to the cerebral cortex.
- ☐ Label a card with each of the structures in the visual pathway and practice placing the cards in the correct sequence.
- ☐ Define *decussation*.
- ☐ Distinguish between optic nerve, optic tract, and optic chiasma.
- ☐ Describe stereoscopic vision.
- ☐ Explain the visual fields of the eyes.

Step 3: Understand the ear: hearing and equilibrium.
- ☐ List the basic structures of the outer ear, middle ear, and inner ear, and their corresponding functions.
- ☐ Name the parts of the bony labyrinth in the inner ear.
- ☐ Name the parts of the membranous labyrinth and corresponding functions in the inner ear.
- ☐ Describe the receptors for hearing.
- ☐ Describe the receptors for equilibrium.
- ☐ Describe how the equilibrium pathway transmits information on the position and movements of the head.
- ☐ Discuss how the auditory pathway transmits auditory information from the cochlear receptors to the cerebral cortex.

CHAPTER 17
Blood

LECTURE AND DEMONSTRATION
Student Objectives

1. Distinguish the circulatory system from the cardiovascular system.
2. Name the basic components of blood, and define *hematocrit*.
3. List some of the molecules in blood plasma.
4. Explain the technique for making a blood smear.
5. Describe the special structural features and functions of erythrocytes.
6. List the five classes of leukocytes, along with the structural characteristics and functions of each.
7. Describe the structure of platelets and their role in blood clotting.
8. Distinguish red bone marrow from yellow bone marrow.
9. Describe the basic histologic structure of red bone marrow.
10. Define *hematopoiesis* and *hematopoietic stem cell.*
11. Explain the differentiation of the various types of blood cells.
12. Name some common disorders of erythrocytes, leukocytes, and platelets.
13. Describe the embryonic origin of blood cells. List four different organs that form blood cells in the fetus.
14. Name some blood disorders that become more common as the body ages.

Suggested Lecture Outline

I. Overview: Composition of Blood (p. 504, Fig. 17.1)

II. Blood Plasma (pp. 504–505)

III. Formed Elements (pp. 505–511, Fig. 17.2)

    A. Erythrocytes (pp. 505–506, Fig. 17.3)

    B. Leukocytes (pp. 506–510, Figs. 17.4–17.6)

        1. Granulocytes

        2. Agranulocytes

    C. Platelets (pp. 510–511, Fig. 17.7)

IV. Blood Cell Formation (pp. 512–515)

    A. Bone Marrow as the Site of Hematopoiesis (pp. 512–513, Fig. 17.8)

    B. Cell Lines in Blood Cell Formation (pp. 513–515, Fig. 17.9)

        1. Genesis of Erythrocytes

        2. Formation of Leukocytes and Platelets

V. Blood Disorders (pp. 515–516)

    A. Erythrocytes

    B. Leukocytes

    C. Platelets

VI. The Blood Throughout Life (pp. 516–517)

Lecture Hints

1. Distinguish between the circulatory system and the cardiovascular system.
2. Explain that the blood inside the blood vessels, together with interstitial fluid within the tissues and lymph contained in the lymph vessels, constitute the internal environment of the body.
3. Remind students that blood is a specialized connective tissue with a fluid matrix (plasma).
4. Summarize the functions of blood.
5. Present a very brief overview of blood circulation: heart, arteries, capillaries, and veins.
6. Describe the composition of blood and clearly distinguish between formed elements and plasma. Refer to Figure 17.1.
7. Define *hematocrit*, including effects of gender and altitude.
8. Describe the physical nature of blood plasma, including a summary of its components and how it differs from interstitial fluid.
9. Name the plasma proteins, including organs of origin, and functions.
10. Distinguish between plasma and serum.
11. Identify the formed elements (blood cells), describing some unique features, distinguishing between RBCs and WBCs, and including their percentages in blood.
12. Describe how blood smears are prepared for microscopic viewing, pointing out their clinical significance.
13. Describe the size, shape, and structural features of erythrocytes, and comment on the significance of hemoglobin. Refer to Figure 17.3.
14. Describe the structure and function of leukocytes, including diapedesis.
15. Classify five types of leukocytes based on the presence or absence of cytoplasmic granules, explaining that this classification is visually convenient but artificial because of modern developmental evidence.
16. Cite the mnemonic "Never Let Monkeys Eat Bananas" to aid students in learning the names of the leukocytes as well as appreciating the abundance of leukocytes. Refer to Figure 17.4.

17. Compare and contrast the structure and function of granulocytes with agranulocytes, including specific types of each.
18. Review phagocytosis and refer students to Chapter 2, if needed.
19. Identify the most important cells of the immune system: lymphocytes, and compare the killing functions of T cells and B cells. Refer to Figure 17.6.
20. Distinguish between antibodies and antigens.
21. Define *lysis* and explain the difference between apoptosis and phagocytosis.
22. Describe the structure of platelets, how they differ from other blood cells, and their role in the clotting of blood.
23. Distinguish between thrombus and embolus.
24. Distinguish between red bone marrow and yellow bone marrow, including histologic features.
25. Explain hematopoiesis and the hematopoietic stem cell.
26. Using Figure 17.9, describe the differentiation of blood cells, indicating the cells that are located in the bone marrow and the cells that are in circulating blood.
27. Discuss leukemia, incorporating the special feature *A Closer Look: Bone Marrow and Cord-blood Transplants* from the textbook.
28. Describe the embryonic origin of blood cells and name four hematopoietic fetal organs.
29. Name some blood disorders that become more common with age.

Classroom Discussion Topics and Activities

1. Use models and charts to exhibit blood cells.
2. a. It is possible to have the students make their own blood smears and do WBC counts on their own blood. Strictly enforce safety procedures for proper care and handling of blood and lab materials if you attempt this in class. All that is needed are glass slides, coverslips, a bottle of blood stain, methyl alcohol, microscopes, and sterile needles to prick fingertips. Closely follow safety guidelines for handling and disposing of blood and lab materials. Autoclaving is necessary to ensure sterility.
   b. Provide blood-typing sera for typing students' blood. Strictly follow safety guidelines.
   c. Collect student data about WBC counts and blood types and compare data to expected frequencies.
3. Demonstrate a sample of centrifuged animal blood so students can examine the consistency, texture, and color of plasma. Use pH paper to determine the blood's acidity or alkalinity. This is an excellent lead-in to a discussion about the composition and importance of plasma.
4. Use a magnet and iron filings to model the attraction between antibodies and antigens.
5. Use a lock and several keys (only one of which fits the lock) to demonstrate the specificity of antigens and antibodies.
6. Discuss the fears and facts associated with blood donation, blood transfusions, and AIDS.
7. Discuss the problems associated with injecting illegal drugs intravenously. What diseases are commonly spread in this manner?
8. Discuss the procedure of autologous transfusion.

9. Students are interested in discussion of anemias, leukemias, and hemophilia. Explain how classification schemes are used in the naming of anemias and leukemias.
10. Discuss the various uses of donated blood, e.g., for packed red cells, platelets, and serum.
11. Discuss blood groups. Explain the many varieties, role of antigens and antibodies, donor and recipient compatibilities and incompatibilities, genetics of ABO and Rh inheritance, and importance of blood analysis in forensics or inheritance disputes.
12. Levels of cholesterol, triglycerides, and fatty acids in the blood are important indicators of possible heart attack or stroke. Ask students to explain the connection of these indicators to health problems.

Clinical Questions

1. A complete blood count and a differential WBC count have been ordered for Mrs. Ulevich. What information is obtained from the differential count that the total count cannot provide?

   Answer: The differential count determines the relative proportions of the individual types of leukocytes (a valuable diagnostic tool). For example, elevated neutrophils indicate bacterial infections, and elevated eosinophils may indicate the patient is suffering from an allergy or parasitic worms. The complete blood count will only reveal the total number of leukocytes, which will allow one to recognize only that there is a systemic infection—without revealing any specifics about the type of infection.

2. List three blood tests that might be ordered if anemia is suspected and one test that would be done if infectious mononucleosis were suspected.

   Answer: The tests for anemia are hematocrit, complete blood count, and microscopic study of the erythrocytes. A test for infectious mononucleosis is a differential WBC count (in which large lymphocytes that resemble monocytes are sought).

3. A bone marrow biopsy is ordered for two patients—one a small child and the other an adult. The specimen is taken from the tibia of the child but from the iliac bone of the adult. Explain why different sites are used for marrow samples in children versus adults.

   Answer: In adults, red marrow—the marrow that actively produces blood cells—occurs chiefly in the bones of the axial skeleton and limb girdles (e.g., iliac bone), but not in the tibia. In children, red marrow occurs throughout the skeleton.

4. A man of Greek ancestry goes to his doctor with the following symptoms. He is very tired all the time and has difficulty catching his breath after even mild exercise. His doctor orders the following tests: complete blood count, hematocrit, and differential WBC count. The tests show small, pale, immature erythrocytes; fragile erythrocytes; and around 2 million erythrocytes per cubic millimeter. What is the tentative diagnosis?

   Answer: The diagnosis is thalassemia. It can be treated with a blood transfusion.

ART RESOURCES
Transparency List

Figure 17.1   The separation of whole blood into its major components.

Figure 17.3   An erythrocyte in cross sectional and in superior view.

Figure 17.5   Relative percentages of the different types of leukocytes.

Figure 17.6   Function of a cytotoxic T lymphocyte and a B lymphocyte.

Figure 17.9   Stages of differentiation of blood cells in the bone marrow.

Teaching with Art

Figure 17.6   Functions of a cytotoxic T lymphocyte (a) and a B lymphocyte (b).

Textbook p. 509; transparencies; Digital Archive CD-ROM.

Checklist of Key Points in the Figure

- Discuss the role of lymphocytes in the body's immune system.
- Distinguish between T cells and B cells.
- Describe the direct role of antigen attack by the T cell and the indirect role of antigen attack by the B cell.
- Give examples of target cells attacked by T cells and B cells.
- Define *apoptosis*, and distinguish apoptosis from phagocytosis.

Common Conceptual Difficulties Interpreting the Art

- Emphasize that the events depicted occur in infected tissue, not in the blood.
- Point out that the macrophage in the figure is not a transformed B lymphocyte.
- Clearly distinguish between an antigen and an antibody.
- Stress that although agranulocytes (lymphocytes and monocytes) resemble each other structurally, they are distinct functionally, and thus, they are different cell types.
- Explain what "B" and "T" stand for in T lymphocytes and B lymphocytes.

Art Exercises

1. Provide students with unlabeled diagrams of Figure 17.6 and instruct them to color and label the following:
   a. Color and label the antigen and antibody representations in both (a) and (b) parts of the figure.
   b. Label the sites of apoptosis and phagocytosis.
2. Instruct students to make a table that compares the similarities and differences (structural and functional) between B and T lymphocytes.

Critical Reasoning

Ask the students the following questions about the Figure 17.6:

1. Identify the class of specific target cells represented in Stage 2 of part (a).
   Answer: Eukaryotic cells, such as a human cells introduced in transplants.
2. Identify the class of specific target cells represented in Stage 3 of part (b).
   Answer: Bacterial cells.
3. Lymphocytes represent 20 to 45 percent of all leukocytes in the blood, yet lymphocytes do not function in the blood. Where is the activity in the figure occurring?
   Answer: Lymphocytes function in the connective tissues, especially lymphoid connective tissues.

4. Where did the macrophage in the figure come from?

   Answer: A macrophage is a phagocytic monocyte and uses the blood stream to reach connective tissues, like all leukocytes.

SUPPLEMENTAL COURSE MATERIALS
Library Research Topics

1. Research the blood disorders associated with the use of intravenous street drugs.
2. Research information about clinical uses of recombinant erythropoietin, colony-stimulating factors, and tissue plasminogen activator.
3. How close is medical science to developing an effective blood substitute (artificial blood)?
4. Research the history of blood transfusions since World War II.
5. Is allergy related to our body's ability to fight parasitic worms? (See *Scientific American*, September 1993, p. 117, and *Discover*, September 1993, p. 54.)
6. Research the effects of sickle-cell disease, as well as the revolutionary drug for its treatment, hydroxyurea.

Audiovisual Aids/Computer Software

See Preface of the Instructor's Guide for Key to Audiovisual Distributors

Videotapes

1. *The Living Body: Life Under Pressure* (FHS, VHS, or BETA). This program follows the journey of blood cells around the circulatory system to demonstrate the oxygen- and waste-transporting functions of blood.
2. *Blood* (PLP, CH-460755, VHS). A thorough and up-to-date look at the cellular functions of blood.
3. *The Human Body: What Can Go Wrong?—Circulatory System* (PLP, CH- 140501, VHS)
4. *Blood: River of Life, Mirror of Health* (EI, 600-2365V, VHS)
5. *Circulation* (EI, 475-2354V, VHS). In three parts: blood, the heart, and lymphatics.
6. *The Anatomy and Physiology Series: The Cardiovascular System* (NIMCO, 29 min.). Covers blood cells, clotting, blood pressure, and techniques for the study of blood.
7. *Blood* (IM, 22 min., 1995). Examines components, functions, and diseases of blood.
8. *Blood* (PLP, 33 min., 1990). Covers blood cells, functions, and clotting.
9. *Blood Cell Counting: Identification and Grouping* (CVB, 30 min.). Demonstrates drawing, typing, and testing of blood.
10. *Blood is Life* (FHS, 45 min., 1995). An in-depth study of blood.
11. *The Body Atlas Series: The Human Pump* (Nimco/NHCA, 30 min., 1994). Covers blood and the heart.
12. *Circulation* (FHS, 15 min.). Covers blood components and the functions of red and white blood cells.
13. *Circulation* (IM, 20 min., 1994). Details how the heart and components of the blood work.

14. *Circulation: A River of Life* (IM, 30 min., 1997). Demonstrates transport of nutrients to and waste products from the cells by blood.
15. *Circulatory System: The Plasma Pipeline* (FHS, 25 min.). Covers the functions of the formed elements of the blood.
16. *The Human Body Series: The Blood—The Body's Freight Carrier* (NIMCO, 28 min., 1993). Covers the function of blood as a transport mechanism.
17. *The New Living Body: Blood* (FHS, 20 min., 1995). Describes blood and circulation, using the story of a sickle-cell sufferer.
18. *Pumping Life: The Heart and Circulatory System* (SVE, 22 min.). Examines the functions of the formed elements of the blood and the circulatory system, including WBC phagocytosis.
19. *Blood—River of Life, Mirror of Health* (HRM, 60 min., 1990)
20. *The Cardiovascular System* (HCA, 29 min.)
21. *Human Cardiovascular System: The Blood Vessels* (BC, 25 min., 1995)
22. *Leukemia* (FHS, 19 min., 1995)
23. *The Lymphatic and Reticuloendothelial Systems* (HCA, 25 min.)
24. *New Directions in Blood Transfusions* (FHS, 20 min., 1995)
25. *Our Nation's Blood Supply: The Next Threshold for Safe Blood* (FHS, 22 min., 1995)
26. *William Harvey and the Circulation of Blood* (FHS, 29 min., 1995)

Computer Software
1. *Blood and Immunity* (IM, Mac/Win, 1996)
2. *Blood and Immunity* (Queue/CBS/NS, Mac/Win, 1997)
3. *Interactive Physiology: Cardiovascular System* (ADAM/BC, Mac/Win, 1995)
4. *The Living Body* (Queue, Win)
5. *Circulation and Respiration* (Queue, Apple/IBM)
6. *Dynamics of the Human Circulatory System* (EI)

Slides
1. *Visual Approach to Histology: Blood and Bone Marrow* (FAD, 19 Slides)
2. *Hematology* (EI, 99 Slides)

Suggested Readings

Atkinson, M.A., and N.K. Maclearen. The search for man made blood. *Scientific American* (February 1998).

Beardsley, T. Stem cells come of age. *Scientific American* 281 (July 1999): 30–31.

Brown, B. *Hematology: Principles and Procedures.* 6th ed. Philadelphia: Lea & Febiger, 1993.

Coller, B.S. Platelets and thrombolytic therapy. *New England Journal of Medicine* 322 (January 4, 1990): 33–42.

Cormack, D.H. *Essential Histology.* Philadelphia: J.B. Lippincott, 1993.

Fackelmann, K. Drug wards off sickle-cell attacks. *Science News* 147 (February 4, 1995): 68.

Fawcett, D.W. *A Textbook of Histology*. 12th ed. New York: Chapman & Hall, 1994, Chapter 4.

Gold, D. The stem cell. *Scientific American* 265 (December 1991): 86–93.

Junqueira, L.C., et al. *Basic Histology*. 9th ed. Stamford, Conn.: Appleton and Lange, 1998.

Kaushansky, K. Thrombopoietin. *New England Journal of Medicine* 339 (September 10, 1998): 746–754.

Lee, G. R., et al. *Wintrobe's Clinical Hematology*. 10th ed. Baltimore: Williams and Wilkins, 1999.

McKenzie, S.B. *Textbook of Hematology*. 2nd ed. Baltimore: Williams and Wilkins, 1996.

Nossal, G.J. Life, death and the immune system. *Scientific American* 269 (September 1993): 52–62.

Pedersen, R.A. Embryonic stem cells for medicine. *Scientific American* 280 (April 1999): 68–73.

Platt, W.R. *Color Atlas and Textbook of Hematology*. 2nd ed. Philadelphia: J.B. Lippincott, 1979.

Radetsky, P. Of parasites and pollen. *Discover* 14 (September 1993): 54–62.

Radetsky, P. The mother of all blood cells. *Discover* 16 (March 1995): 86–93.

Samuels-Reid, J. Common problems in sickle cell disease. *American Family Physician* (May 1, 1994): 1477–1486.

Zucker, M.B. The functioning of blood platelets. *Scientific American* 242 (June 1980): 86.

ANSWERS TO TEXTBOOK QUESTIONS

Answers to multiple-choice and matching questions 1–7 are located in Appendix B of the textbook.

Short Answer and Essay Questions

8. The buffy coat in a hematocrit tube consists of white blood cells and platelets.

9. (a) Red marrow is actively manufacturing blood cells, whereas yellow marrow is dormant. (b) Yellow marrow occupies the long bones of the adult limbs (except in the proximal epiphyses of the humerus and femur).

10. (a) Proerythroblasts accumulate iron and give rise to erythroblasts, then normoblasts, stages in which hemoglobin is accumulating. Then, the nucleus and organelles are ejected, and the reticulocyte stage is reached. (b) Reticulocytes are released into the circulation.

11. Platelets are disc-shaped fragments of cytoplasm that are enclosed by a plasma membrane; they contain secretory granules. Platelets adhere to the edges of tears in blood vessels, plugging small tears. They also help initiate clotting and become trapped in the network of fibrin strands that forms when clotting is complete. Then, the platelets contract, pulling on the fibrin network and drawing the torn edges of the vessel back together.

12. These structurally undifferentiated cell types look almost identical. They differ functionally, however, in that the stem cell can produce any type of blood cell, whereas a committed cell can give rise to only one kind of blood cell (e.g., eosinophil, neutrophil, erythrocyte, basophil, or monocyte).

13. The cytoplasm of megakaryocytes fragments to produce platelets.

14. The granulocytes Tina was seeing actually have single nuclei, but each nucleus has several lobes. Sometimes the connections between these lobes are not evident in blood smears, so a granulocyte may appear to have two nuclei.

15. (a) The circulatory system consists of the lymphatic vessels and the cardiovascular system (blood vessels and heart). Thus, the circulatory system and cardiovascular system are not exactly the same (p. 504). (b) The differential WBC count is just a part of a complete blood count. In a complete blood count, a sample of blood is taken, and the hematocrit, hemoglobin content, and overall concentrations of red and white cells and platelets are measured; a differential WBC count follows, in which the percentages of the different classes of leukocytes are counted on a blood smear.

16. Both people are correct about polymorphonuclear cells. The name can be used either for neutrophils or for all granulocytes.

17. The first function of platelets is to plug tears in the walls of blood vessels. Then, they help initiate clotting. Finally, they retract the clot to close the tear.

18. No. T and B cells are structurally identical under the microscope.

19. An eosinophil contains larger, pink-staining granules, in contrast to the purple-staining granules of the basophil. Eosinophils have a two-lobed nucleus shaped like a telephone receiver, whereas the basophil nucleus is U- or S-shaped. Basophils mediate the late stages of allergic inflammation, whereas eosinophils *stop* this allergic response (among other functions).

20. Ready availability, safety from infection, long-term storage, reduced risk of rejection (see *A Closer Look* on p. 516).

Critical Reasoning and Clinical Applications Questions

1. Janie's cancerous leukocytes are immature or abnormal and are incapable of defending against infection in the usual way. Furthermore, the nonfunctional cancer cells become so abundant in the bone marrow that they crowd out the healthy lines of leukocyte-forming cells.

2. Since an erythrocyte is about 8 micrometers wide, the neuron cell body was about 80 micrometers wide.

3. Blood eosinophil levels increase when one has parasitic worms, and the daughters' eosinophil counts were about 10 times greater than normal. The daughters must have gotten tapeworms from the dog, which picked up the worms from infected sheep.

4. Polycythemia is an abnormally high amount of erythrocytes in the blood, and this would naturally be associated with a high hematocrit (percent of blood volume occupied by erythrocytes). The reticulocyte count is well above normal as well, indicating that erythrocyte levels are high because the bone marrow has accelerated the rate at which it produces these cells and/or releases them into the blood. (p. 515)

5. Blood stem cells and committed cells are among the most rapidly dividing cells in the body. Therefore, chemotherapy drugs destroy many healthy stem cells, the short-lived blood cells are not replaced, and concentrations of blood cells in the circulation can drop to life-threatening levels.

SUPPLEMENTAL STUDENT MATERIALS TO HUMAN ANATOMY, THIRD EDITION
Chapter 17: Blood

To the Student

Blood is the fluid of the circulatory system and plays many vital interactive roles within the body. Blood interacts with the respiratory system in the delivery of oxygen to cells and removal of waste from tissues of the body. Nutritive interactions result in the transport of food molecules from the small intestine to the liver and, ultimately, to the cells of the body. Blood carries metabolic wastes and excess water to the kidneys, resulting in urine production and excretory interaction. Regulatory interaction involves the transport of hormones from the site of production to target tissues. Other functions involve the regulation of body heat and protection against foreign invaders, such as microbes and toxins. Blood keeps you in contact with your external environment. Blood is essential for survival, and any region of the body deprived of blood dies in minutes. Obviously, it is important for you to understand the nature of blood because with every succeeding topic you study in anatomy, blood is featured and is a focal point in some way.

Step 1: Distinguish the circulatory system from the cardiovascular system.
☐ Define *circulatory system*, including functions of blood.
☐ Define *cardiovascular system*.
☐ Define *lymphatic system*.

Step 2: Describe the composition of blood, including functions of its components.
☐ Define and describe *plasma*.
☐ Distinguish between plasma and serum.
☐ Define *hematocrit*.
☐ List the formed elements of blood.
☐ Describe the structure, function, and life span of erythrocytes.
☐ Summarize the role of hemoglobin in the blood.
☐ Discuss the function of leukocytes.
☐ Distinguish between granulocytes and agranulocytes, listing examples of each.
☐ Describe similarities and differences between lymphocytes and monocytes.
☐ Distinguish between antigen and antibody.
☐ Distinguish between T cells and B cells, describing how they attack cells.
☐ Define *apoptosis*.
☐ Define *macrophage* and describe phagocytosis.
☐ Define *platelet* and describe its functions.
☐ Distinguish between thrombus and embolus.

Step 3: Explain blood cell formation.
☐ Define *hematopoiesis* and describe bone marrow as a site of blood cell formation.

- ☐ Distinguish between yellow bone marrow and red bone marrow both structurally and functionally.
- ☐ Define *blood stem cell*.
- ☐ Describe the formation of red blood cells.
- ☐ Describe the formation of white blood cells and platelets.

Step 4: Describe common blood disorders and blood embryologic development.
- ☐ Name and describe symptoms of blood disorders, such as anemia, polycythemia, sickle-cell disease, and leukemia.
- ☐ Name four hematopoietic organs in the fetus.

CHAPTER 18
The Heart

LECTURE AND DEMONSTRATION
Student Objectives

1. Define the *pulmonary* and *systemic circuits.*
2. Describe the orientation, location, and surface anatomy of the heart in the thorax.
3. Describe the layers of the pericardium and the tissue layers of the heart wall.
4. List the important structural features of each heart chamber: right and left atria, and right and left ventricles.
5. Describe the path of a drop of blood through the four chambers of the heart and the systemic and pulmonary circuits.
6. Name the heart valves, and describe their locations and functions. Indicate where on the chest wall each of the valves is heard.
7. Describe the fibrous skeleton of the heart, and explain its functions.
8. Name the components of the conducting system of the heart, and describe the conduction pathway.
9. Describe the locations of the coronary arteries and cardiac veins on the heart surface.
10. Define *coronary artery disease, heart failure,* and *atrial* and *ventricular fibrillation*.
11. Explain how the heart develops, and describe some congenital heart defects.
12. List some effects of aging on the heart.

Suggested Lecture Outline

I. Location and Orientation Within the Thorax (pp. 522–524, Figs. 18.1 and 18.2)

II. Structure of the Heart (pp. 524–528)

    A. Coverings (p. 524, Fig. 18.3)

    B. Layers of the Heart Wall (pp. 524–525, Figs. 18.3–18.4)

    C. Heart Chambers (pp. 525–528, Figs. 18.5–18.6)

        1. Right Atrium

        2. Right Ventricle

        3. Left Atrium

        4. Left Ventricle

III. Pathway of Blood Through the Heart (pp. 528–529, Figs. 18.1 and 18.5c)

IV. Heart Valves (pp. 529–532)
    A. Valve Structure (p. 529, Fig. 18.8)
    B. Valve Function (p. 529, Figs. 18.9 and 18.10)
    C. Heart Sounds (pp. 530–532, Fig. 18.11)

V. Fibrous Skeleton (p. 532, Fig. 18.8a)

VI. Conducting System and Innervation (pp. 532–534)
    A. Conducting System (pp. 532–533, Fig. 18.12)
    B. Innervation (pp. 533–534, Fig. 18.13)

VII. Blood Supply to the Heart (pp. 534–535, Fig. 18.14a)

VIII. Disorders of the Heart (pp. 535–537)
    A. Coronary Artery Disease
    B. Heart Failure
    C. Disorders of the Conduction System

IX. The Heart Throughout Life (pp. 537–539)
    A. Development of the Heart (pp. 537–538, Figs. 18.15–18.17)
    B. The Heart in Adulthood and Old Age (p. 539)

Lecture Hints

1. Define and describe the *pulmonary* and *systemic circuits*. Refer to Figure 18.1.
2. Stress the two-pump concept and that arteries carry blood *away* from the heart and veins carry blood *toward* the heart. Refer to Figure 18.1.
3. Identify the four chambers of the heart and relate each chamber to the pulmonary and systemic circuits.
4. Describe the location and orientation of the heart within the mediastinum. Refer to Figure 18.2.
5. Describe the structural coverings of the heart, distinguishing between the pericardial sac, parietal pericardium, and visceral pericardium. Refer to Figure 18.3.
6. Going from external to internal, describe the layers of the heart wall. Refer to Figure 18.4.
7. Explain how the heart may be viewed as an enlarged blood vessel, relating wall layers to tunics of blood vessels.
8. Name the four chambers of the heart and describe each chamber anatomically. Refer to Figure 18.5.
9. Describe the pathway followed by a drop of blood through the heart, incorporating pulmonary and systemic circuits. Refer to Figs. 18.1 and 18.5.
10. Define *heartbeat* and clearly distinguish between systole and diastole.

11. Name the valves of the heart and describe the structure of each. Refer to Figures 18.9 and 18.10.

12. Stress that the only function of the valves of the heart is to ensure the one-way conduction of blood.

13. Describe the sounds of the heart and indicate the location on the heart surface where each valve is best heard. Refer to Figure 18.11.

14. Describe the location of the fibrous skeleton of the heart and discuss its functions. Refer to Figure 18.8a.

15. Explain the conducting system of the heart, pointing out the heart's inherent ability to contract without extrinsic innervation. Refer to Figure 18.12.

16. Distinguish between the SA node and the AV node, tracing the elements of the conduction system from the pacemaker to the termination point.

17. Describe the autonomic innervation of the heart muscle, indicating effects of parasympathetic and sympathetic fibers.

18. Describe coronary circulation, blood supply to and from the heart muscle itself, naming the major vessels and structures involved. Refer to Figure 18.14.

19. Explain one or more diseases of the heart: coronary heart disease, heart failure, or conduction system disorders. This is an excellent time to incorporate this chapter's *A Closer Look: Treating Heart Disease*, from the textbook.

20. Discuss the embryologic development of the heart and, using Figure 18.16, show the relationship of embryological structures to adult structures.

21. Describe age-related changes in the heart.

Classroom Discussion Topics and Activities

1. Use a model of a human torso, or a dissected rat or cat, to show the position of the heart in the chest cavity.

2. Use a model of a human heart to show the structure of the heart.

3. Demonstrate a dissected fresh cow or sheep heart obtained from a butcher to show gross anatomy of the heart. This is an excellent way to demonstrate the thin and delicate nature of valves and other internal structures.

4. To show that the long axis of the human heart is not located simply in the midsagittal plane of the body like the heart of other animals, do the following demonstration: Orient a sharpened pencil vertically in front of you with the point down, then rotate the point 45 degrees (halfway) anteriorly and 45 degrees (halfway) to the left. The point represents the heart's apex, and you will have angled the heart into its proper position.

5. Show a video of a beating heart, ideally with heart sounds. Stress that while the right side of the heart is a pulmonary pump and the left side is a systemic pump, both atria contract at the same time and both ventricles contract at the same time.

6. Although the left side of the heart generates more pressure than the right side, approximately the same volume of blood is ejected from each side per beat. Ask students to think about what would happen if this were not the case. Follow up with a discussion of congestive heart failure.

7. Provide stethoscopes and instruct students to identify the first and second "lub-dup" heart sounds produced by the individual valves. Define *auscultation*.

8. Relate the functioning of the heart to the functioning of a water pump. Include problems associated with low blood pressure going into the heart and high blood pressure leaving the heart. Use a simple pump apparatus to demonstrate the work (pumping action) of the heart.

9. Discuss the significance of the heart's pacemaker, including the use and roles of artificial pacemakers.

10. Discuss the steps in recovery from a heart attack.

11. Discuss the role of cardiac muscle in ejecting blood from the ventricles as opposed to ejecting blood from the atria.

12. Explore the topic of heart transplants and ask students why transplanted hearts are not often reinnervated.

Clinical Questions

1. Eleanor, an older woman, complains of shortness of breath and intermittent fainting spells. Her doctor runs various tests and finds that her AV node is not functioning properly. What is the suggested treatment?

   Answer: The suggested treatment is surgery to implant an artificial pacemaker.

2. Linda, a 14-year-old girl undergoing a physical examination before being admitted to summer camp, was found to have a loud heart murmur at the second intercostal space on the left side of the sternum. The murmur creates a swishing sound with no high-pitched whistle. What, exactly, is producing the murmur?

   Answer: Incompetence (not stenosis) of the pulmonary semilunar valve. Incompetent valves produce swishing sounds, and the pulmonary semilunar valve is heard at the superior left corner of the heart as indicated in this question.

3. Clark, age 7, was rushed to the emergency room and found to be in right heart failure. He was found to have a congenital pulmonary stenosis, which had not been detected at birth and had grown worse during the boy's childhood. Although it was now weakening, the muscular wall of Clark's right ventricle was found to be thicker than that of his left ventricle, the opposite of the normal condition. Can you explain the thickened wall of the right ventricle?

   Answer: With a stenotic (narrowed) pulmonary semilunar valve, the right ventricle had been forced to contract harder to pump blood into the pulmonary trunk. Thus, over the years, the musculature in this ventricle grew stronger and hypertrophied. Finally, it became exhausted from the effort of pumping blood through a progressively narrowing valve, causing Clark's heart failure.

4. A 48-year-old man enters the hospital complaining of chest pain. His history includes chain smoking, a high-stress job, a diet heavy in saturated fats, lack of exercise, and high blood pressure. Although he is not suffering from a heart attack, his doctor explains to him that a heart attack is quite possible. What did the chest pain indicate? Why is the man a prime candidate for a heart attack? (Note: It might be best to have the students read *A Closer Look* in the next chapter of the textbook, p. 574, before answering this question.)

Answer: His symptoms indicate angina pectoris, a transient ischemia attack from severe narrowing (or spasms) of his coronary arteries. A narrowed coronary artery is likely to become fully occluded, causing the heart muscle to die from oxygen deprivation—a full-blown heart attack.

ART RESOURCES
Transparency List

Figure 18.1   The route by which the heart pumps blood around the pulmonary and systemic circuits.

Figure 18.2   Location of the heart in the thorax.

Figure 18.3   Layers constituting the pericardium and heart wall.

Figure 18.4   The circular and spiral arrangement of cardiac muscle bundles in the myocardium of the heart.

Figure 18.5   Gross anatomy of the heart.

Figure 18.7   Anatomical differences between the right and left ventricles.

Figure 18.8   Structure and location of the heart valves.

Figure 18.9   Function of the atrioventricular valves.

Figure 18.10 Function of the semilunar valves.

Figure 18.12 The conducting system of the heart.

Figure 18.13 Autonomic innervation of the heart.

Figure 18.14 Coronary blood vessels.

Figure 18.17 Congenital heart defects.

Teaching with Art

Figure 18.5   Gross anatomy of the heart: (a) Anterior view; (b) Anterior view emphasizing right atrium; (c) Frontal section showing the interior chambers and valves; (d) Inferior view.

Textbook p. 526; transparencies; Digital Archive CD-ROM.

Checklist of Key Points in the Figure

- Describe the surface anatomy of the heart.
- Distinguish between atria and ventricles.
- Indicate the important structural features of each chamber.
- Point out that the view in part (c) is a frontal section specially cut to show the valves as well as the chambers.
- Identify the valves.
- Identify the great vessels associated with the heart.
- Identify the layers of the heart wall.

Common Conceptual Difficulties Interpreting the Art

- Explain that the pericardial sac surrounding the heart has been removed.
- Clarify the difference between atrium and auricle.
- Stress that an artery carries blood away from the heart and veins carry blood toward the heart.
- Explain that it is a visual convention to depict red-colored vessels carrying oxygen-rich blood and blue-colored vessels carrying oxygen-poor blood.
- Distinguish between the pulmonary circulation and systemic circulation. (Show Figure 18.1 to reinforce the distinction.)

Art Exercises

1. Provide unlabeled copies of the (c) part of Figure 18.5. Instruct students to draw a representation of systemic and pulmonary circulation, including the flow of blood through the heart and labels of chambers, valves, and great vessels. Ask students to color oxygen-rich vessels red and oxygen-poor vessels blue.
2. Instruct students to sketch the adult heart and associated vessels. Referring to Figure 18.16, Stages in heart development, in their textbook, color and label the adult regions derived from each embryonic heart chamber: (a) sinus venosus, (b) embryonic atrium, (c) embryonic ventricle, (d) bulbus cordis.

Note: An additional exercise involving the conduction system also is suggested.

Critical Reasoning

Instruct students to look at the atrioventricular valves in part (c) of Figure 18.5 and ask them to explain the role of the AV valves when the ventricles contract (ventricular systole). After an explanation of the one-way flow of blood, ask the question, "What is the exact role of the papillary muscles during contraction of the ventricles?"

Answer: Papillary muscles contract along with the rest of the ventricle, pulling the chordae tendineae and anchoring the valve to prevent eversion of the AV valves into the atria. Papillary muscles do not act to open AV valves.

SUPPLEMENTAL COURSE MATERIALS
Library Research Topics

1. Research the alternatives to coronary bypass operations. (This also applies to material covered in Chapter 19 of the textbook: pp. 574–575.)
2. Research the effects of smoking on the heart and heart function.
3. Research the criteria used for heart transplants and their success rate.
4. Research the status of artificial hearts and their problems.
5. Research the effects of exercise on heart function.
6. Research the various types of heart block and their significance and treatment.
7. Research the procedures and types of artificial valves currently used in valve-replacement surgery.

Audiovisual Aids/Computer Software

See Preface of the Instructor's Guide for Key to Audiovisual Distributors

Videotapes

1. *The Living Body: Two Hearts That Beat As One* (FHS, VHS, or BETA). Describes the structure and functioning of the heart. It analyzes the basic components of the heart muscle, valves, and pacemaker, and shows how each one contributes to the demands of daily life.
2. *Your Body* (PLP, DH-140202, VHS)
3. *Circulation—Blood; the Heart; Arteries and Veins; Lymphatics* (EI, 475-2354V)
4. *Arteries: Highways of the Body* (*Human Body Live Action Video Series*) (CAP, 28 min., 1993)
5. *Circulation* (FHS, 15 min.)
6. *Coronary Heart Disease* (PYR, 38 min., 1990)
7. *The Heart* (*Human Body Live Action Video Series*) (CAP, 28 min., 1993)
8. *Heart and Circulation Media Module* (CAP, 11 min., 1994)
9. *The Heart as Circulatory Pump* (*Human Body Live Action Video Series*) (CAP, 28 min., 1993)
10. *Human Biology* (FHS, 58 min.)
11. *The Human Body: Circulatory System* (Ward's, 15 min.)
12. *The Human Body: Work of the Heart* (Ward's, 21 min.)
13. *The Human Cardiovascular System; The Heart* (BC, 22 min., 1995)
14. *The Mammalian Heart* (AIMS, 15 min.)
15. *Sheep Heart* (Ward's, 15 min.)
16. *Veins: The Way to the Heart* (*Human Body Live Action Video Series*) (CAP, 28 min., 1993)
17. *Work of the Heart.* 2nd ed. (EBE)

Computer Software

1. *The Heart* (QUE, Apple II, 64K). A tutorial introducing the structure and function of the human heart.
2. *The Heart Stimulator* (PLP, Apple). Uses high-resolution color graphics and animation to depict blood flowing through the heart as it beats. It is a student interactive program.
3. *Your Heart* (EI, Apple, IBM, 1984). A self-paced tutorial program featuring crisp, colorful high-resolution graphics. Introduces and reviews the basic structures of the heart chambers and the flow of blood through them.
4. *Cardiac Muscle Mechanics* (QUE, COM4204B, IBM)
5. *Cardiovascular System* (PLP, CH-182011, Apple, CH-182012, IBM). A two-part program that covers the basic anatomy of the heart and blood vessels.
6. *Cardiovascular System* (IM, Mac/Win, 1997)
7. *Cardiovascular System—Biology Explorer Series* (CL/NG, Mac/Win)
8. *Circulation of the Blood* (IM, Mac/Win)
9. *Heart: The Engine* (Queue, Win)
10. *Interactive Physiology: Cardiovascular System* (ADAM/BC, Mac/Win, 1995)

11. *The Living Body* (Queue, Win)

12. *The Total Heart* (MC, Win, 1993)

Suggested Readings

Abe, Y., et al. Present status of the total artificial heart at the University of Tokyo. *Artificial Organs* 23 (March 1999): 221–228.

Bloom, J.M. Prevention of sudden death in patients with coronary artery disease. *New England Journal of Medicine* 342 (April 27, 2000): 1291–1292.

Bove, L. Now! Surgery for heart failure. *RN* (May 1995): 26–30.

Cowley, G. Bypassing the surgeon. (An article on a new way to strengthen a weakened heart.) *Newsweek* (May 11, 1992): 64.

Fabius, D. Solving the mystery of heart murmurs. *Nursing* 94 (July 1994): 39–44.

Henein, M.Y., and D.G. Gibson. Normal long axis function. *Heart* 81 (February 1999): 111–113.

Hennekens, C.H. Aspirin in the treatment and prevention of cardiovascular disease. *Annual Review Public Health* 18 (1997): 37–49.

Hicks, S. Standing guard against silent ischemia. *Nursing* 94 (January 1994): 34–39.

Lee, J., and L. Manning. Heart attacks. *New Scientist* (June 12, 1993): Inside Science 1–4.

Marshall, E. Artificial heart: The beat goes on. *Science* 253 (August 2, 1991): 500–502.

Miller, M. Effect of lifestyle changes on coronary heart disease. *JAMA* 282 (July 14, 1999): 130; discussion 131–132.

Moore, K.L. *Clinically Oriented Anatomy.* 34th ed. Philadelphia: Lippincott Williams and Wilkins, 1999.

Pantano, J. *Living With Angina.* New York: Harper Collins, 1990.

Renlund, D. Cardiac transplantation: 2. Life with a new heart. *Hospital Practice* (December 15, 1994): 69–79.

Romanes, G.J. *Cunningham's Textbook of Anatomy.* 12th ed. Oxford, New York: Oxford University Press, 1981.

Shamsham, F., and J. Mitchell. Essentials of the diagnosis of heart failure. *American Family Physician* 61 (March 1, 2000): 1319–1328.

Toro, T. Portable pump keeps the rhythm of the heart. *New Scientist* (June 22, 1991): 26.

Williams, P.L., et al. *Gray's Anatomy.* 38th ed. New York: Churchill Livingstone, 1995.

ANSWERS TO TEXTBOOK QUESTIONS

Answers for multiple-choice and matching questions 1–11 are located in Appendix B of the textbook.

Short Answer and Essay Questions

12. The key concept is that the right ventricle pumps blood to the lungs (pulmonary circuit), and the left ventricle pumps blood throughout the body (systemic circuit). One may also add that

the right atrium receives blood returning from the systemic circuit, and the left atrium receives blood returning from the pulmonary circuit.

13. The heart lies in the mediastinum, posterior to the sternum and costal cartilages, and rests on the superior surface of the diaphragm. Its four corner points, as projected onto the anterior thoracic wall, are indicated in Figure 18.2a.

14. Left atrium to left ventricle to systemic circuit to right atrium to right ventricle to pulmonary circuit to left atrium (and the cycle repeats).

15. (a) From the sinoatrial node through atrial musculature to atrioventricular (AV) node, through AV bundle and its bundle branches, through Purkinje fibers through ventricular musculature. (b) No, it consists of cardiac muscle cells. (c) The conducting system initiates each heartbeat, sets the basic rate of the heartbeat, and ensures that the heart chambers contract in the proper sequence. (See Figure 18.12.)

16. Blockage of the circumflex branch affects the left atrium and the posterior part of the left ventricle.

17. See Figure 18.14.

18. See Figure 18.12. The fibrous skeleton should be shown in the coronary sulcus between the atria and the ventricles.

19. The right ventricle dominates the heart's anterior surface (Figure 18.5a).

20. (a) from sinus venosus: posterior, smooth-walled part of the right atrium; coronary sinus; sinoatrial node. (b) from embryonic atrium: anterior, ridged parts of the right and left atria. (c) from embryonic ventricle: left ventricle. (d) from embryonic bulbus cordis: right ventricle, pulmonary trunk, and the first part of the aorta.

Critical Reasoning and Clinical Applications Questions

1. (1) Mixing of oxygenated with deoxygenated blood: ventricular septal defect and tetralogy of Fallot; (2) Increased workload for ventricles: coarctation of the aorta, pulmonary stenosis, tetralogy of Fallot; (3) Both: tetralogy of Fallot.

2. A myocardial infarction, or heart attack, is death of cardiac muscle in the heart through ischemia, resulting from prolonged blockage of a coronary artery. The most common cause of such blockage is a blood clot lodging in an atherosclerotic coronary artery. Mrs. Hamad's heart rhythm was disrupted because her heart attack killed some muscle of the heart's conducting system.

3. (a) All sounds of the aortic semilunar valve are best heard near the superior right corner of the heart on the anterior thoracic wall: second intercostal space at the right sternal margin. (b) All sounds of the mitral valve are best heard at the apex point of the heart: fifth left intercostal space in line with the middle of the clavicle. (See Figure 18.11.)

4. Cardiac tamponade is the condition in which excess fluid in the pericardial cavity compresses the heart; therefore, the heart cannot expand during diastole and cannot propel blood effectively. In the man's case, excess blood has leaked into the pericardial cavity from the heart itself, through a puncture in the heart wall caused by the knife. With the heart unable to pump blood effectively, the drainage of blood from the great veins of the head to the heart is slowed considerably, and blue, deoxygenated, venous blood accumulates in the face and

brain. The man's cardiac tamponade will be treated by draining the excess blood from the pericardial cavity (and by surgically closing the hole in his heart wall).

5. Bacteria or fungus in the bloodstream causes endocarditis, an infection of the endocardium. Drug addicts may develop endocarditis by injecting themselves with infected needles.

6. *Stenosis* of a heart valve is when the valve has a narrowed opening, as when its cusps are fused or stiffened. An incompetent valve, by contrast, is one that fails to close tightly. Both lead to abnormal heart sounds. (See Clinical Applications: Valve Disorders p. 532.)

SUPPLEMENTAL STUDENT MATERIALS TO HUMAN ANATOMY, THIRD EDITION
Chapter 18: The Heart

To the Student

Place your hand over your heart. As you feel the beat of this muscular organ, think about what it does to sustain life for you. It is the force behind pumping blood to the lungs to pick up oxygen and the pumping of blood to deliver oxygen and nutrients to your entire body. In 1 year, the heart pumps an estimated 1 million gallons of blood and beats approximately 40 million times. A daily estimate is 2,700 gallons of blood pumped and 100,000 beats! Add the fact that blood is pumped through an estimated 60,000 miles of vessels in your body, and the heart becomes even more phenomenal. The heart has fascinated and intrigued man for centuries and still today is linked with human emotions. The resemblance to the popular valentine is unmistakable. Your goal in this chapter is to learn the gross anatomy and functions of the heart and its structures, how blood moves through the heart, and circulation patterns. Don't forget the availability of the *Study Partner CD-ROM, A.D.A.M. Interactive Anatomy*, and *The Anatomy and Physiology Place* web site as additional multimedia resources for study of the heart.

Step 1: Explain the orientation and location of the heart in the human body.
- ☐ Describe the physical characteristics, orientation, and location of the heart in the mediastinum.
- ☐ Distinguish between the apex and base.
- ☐ Name the structure that the heart contacts inferiorly.
- ☐ Define *mediastinum*.

Step 2: Explain systemic, pulmonary, and coronary circuits.
- ☐ Define *artery* and *vein*.
- ☐ Describe the heart as being organized into two pumps.
- ☐ Define and summarize the pathway of *systemic circulation*.
- ☐ Define and summarize the pathway of *pulmonary circulation*.
- ☐ Define and summarize the pathway of *coronary circulation*.

Step 3: Describe the gross anatomy of the heart.
- ☐ Define *pericardium* and distinguish between visceral pericardium, parietal pericardium, and pericardial sac.
- ☐ Name the layers of the heart wall, from external to internal, including tissue components of each layer.
- ☐ Describe the surface anatomy of the heart.
- ☐ Name the four chambers of the heart, and list structural features of each.
- ☐ Draw the heart in an anterior view and cut open, and label as many parts as you can.
- ☐ Distinguish between the following:
  - Atrium and auricle

- Atrium and ventricle
- Pectinate muscle and trabeculae carneae
- Trabeculae carneae and papillary muscle
- Bicuspid valve and tricuspid valve

Step 4: Describe blood flow through the heart, and include valves and heart sounds.

☐ Trace a drop of blood from the right atrium back to the right atrium.

☐ Review pulmonary and systemic pathways.

☐ Define and describe *heartbeat*.

☐ Name the four valves; describe locations, structures, and functions.

☐ Explain the cause of the first and second heart sounds, "lub", and "dup", indicating the location on anterior chest wall for best observations using a stethoscope.

☐ Describe the fibrous skeleton structural support of the AV valves, including functions.

Step 5: Describe the conduction system and explain innervation to the heart.

☐ Discuss the initiation of the heartbeat. (Is innervation needed?)

☐ Distinguish heartbeat from heart rate.

☐ Draw a frontally sectioned heart, and label parts of the conduction system.

☐ List the sequence of events in conduction of an electrical impulse from the SA node to Purkinje fibers, including contraction of chambers.

☐ Name the kind of tissue that composes the conduction system. (Hint: it is *not* nervous.)

☐ Describe the effects on the heart of innervation by parasympathetic and sympathetic fibers.

Step 6: Describe blood supply to and from the heart muscle.

☐ Name the vessels that supply the heart with oxygenated blood.

☐ Name the vessels that drain the heart muscle of deoxygenated blood.

☐ Indicate where venous blood of the heart muscle joins systemic venous blood.

☐ Trace the pathway of a drop of blood from the myocardium back to the myocardium.

Step 7: Examine common disorders of the heart.

☐ Describe conditions, causes, and symptoms of disorders of the heart: coronary artery disease, heart failure, and disorders of the conduction system.

Step 8: Examine embryonic development of the heart, and effects of old age on the heart.

☐ Summarize the stages in heart development evident in week 4 of gestation, naming the four embryonic chambers.

☐ Draw an adult heart and its great vessels, indicating regions derived from each embryonic heart chamber.

☐ Give examples of congenital heart defects.

☐ List several age-related changes that affect the heart.

CHAPTER 19
Blood Vessels

LECTURE AND DEMONSTRATION
Student Objectives

PART 1: GENERAL CHARACTERISTICS OF BLOOD VESSELS

1. Describe the three tunics that form the wall of an artery or vein.
2. Compare and contrast the structure and functions of elastic arteries, muscular arteries, and arterioles.
3. Describe the structure and function of capillaries, sinusoids, and capillary beds, and explain the structural basis of capillary permeability.
4. Compare postcapillary venules to capillaries.
5. Explain how to distinguish a vein from an artery in histological sections.
6. Explain the function of valves in veins.
7. Define *vascular anastomoses*, and explain their functions.
8. Define *vasa vasorum*.

PART 2: BLOOD VESSELS OF THE BODY

1. Name the major vessels of the pulmonary circuit.
2. List the major arteries and veins of the systemic circuit. Describe their locations and the body regions they supply.
3. Describe the structure and special function of the hepatic portal system, and explain the significance of portal-systemic anastomoses.
4. Define *aneurysm, deep vein thrombosis* and *venous disease of the lower limb, microangiopathy of diabetes,* and *arteriovenous malformation*.
5. Trace the cardiovascular circuit in the fetus, and explain how it changes at birth.
6. List some effects of aging on the blood vessels.

Suggested Lecture Outline

PART 1: GENERAL CHARACTERISTICS OF BLOOD VESSELS (pp. 544–551)

I. Structure of Blood Vessel Walls (p. 544, Fig. 19.1)

II. Types of Blood Vessels (pp. 544–551, Figs. 19.1 and 19.2)

A. Arteries (pp. 545–547, Fig. 19.2)

1. Elastic Arteries
2. Muscular Arteries
3. Arterioles

B. Capillaries (pp. 547–550, Figs. 19.3 and 19.4)

1. Capillary Beds
2. Capillary Permeability
3. Sinusoids

C. Veins (p. 550, Fig. 19.5)

D. Vascular Anastomoses (pp. 550–551)

E. Vasa Vasorum (p. 551, Figs. 19.1a and 19.2)

PART 2: BLOOD VESSELS OF THE BODY (pp. 552–573)

I. The Pulmonary Circulation (pp. 552–553, Fig. 19.6)

II. The Systemic Circulation (pp. 553–573)

A. Systemic Arteries (pp. 553–563, Figs. 19.7–19.16)

1. Aorta
2. Arteries of the Head and Neck
3. Arteries of the Upper Limbs
4. Arteries of the Thorax
5. Arteries of the Abdomen
6. Arteries of the Pelvis and Lower Limbs

B. Systemic Veins (pp. 563–573, Figs. 19.17–19.25)

1. Venae Cavae and Their Major Tributaries
2. Veins of the Head and Neck
3. Veins of the Upper Limbs
4. Veins of the Thorax
5. Veins of the Abdomen
6. Veins of the Pelvis and Lower Limbs
7. Portal-Systemic Anastomoses

III. Disorders of the Blood Vessels (pp. 573–576)

IV. The Blood Vessels Throughout Life (pp. 576–578)

A. Fetal Circulation (pp. 576–578, Fig. 19.26)

1. Vessels to and from the Placenta
2. Shunts away from the Pulmonary Circuit

B. Blood Vessels in Adulthood (p. 578)

Lecture Hints

1. Name main types of blood vessels: arteries, capillaries, and veins.
2. Stress that arteries carry blood *away* from the heart and "branch" or "fork."
3. Stress that veins carry blood *toward* the heart and "join" or "serve as tributaries."
4. Describe the structure of the wall of arteries and veins, identifying tunics: tunica intima, tunica media, and tunica externa (formerly tunica adventitia). Refer to Figure 19.1.
5. Explain why the heart may be described as a "large blood vessel."
6. Identify three classes of arteries, describing the structure and function of each type. Refer to Figure 19.2.
7. Define *capillary*, describing size, nature of the capillary wall, and functions.
8. Define *capillary bed*, including structure and function. Refer to Figures 19.3 and 19.4.
9. Distinguish between a metarteriole and thoroughfare channel.
10. Identify examples of poorly vascularized tissues.
11. Examine the anatomical basis of how capillaries deliver and pick up substances, describing their degree of permeability and four routes of capillary permeability. Refer to Figure 19.4.
12. Define *sinusoids*, explaining anatomical features and illustrating their locations in the body, such as the liver, spleen, and bone marrow. Refer to Figure 19.4.
13. Identify different types of veins, including their structure and functions, and clearly distinguish them from arteries.
14. Explain how blood moves through veins and how valves function. Refer to Figure 19.5.
15. Define and describe *vascular anastomoses*.
16. Define *vasa vasorum*. Refer to Figures 19.1 and 19.2.
17. Using Figure 19.6, describe pulmonary circulation, including the names of vessels and heart chambers, where gas exchange occurs, and if vessels are oxygen-rich or oxygen-poor.
18. Review the basics of systemic circulation before describing individual systemic arteries and veins. Refer to Figures 19.7 and 19.25.
19. Point out that vessels in the head and limbs are mostly bilaterally symmetrical, but some vessels on the right side and left side of the body are not always mirror images of each other, and some deep trunk vessels are asymmetrical.
20. Using Figures 19.7–19.16, summarize the major arteries of systemic circulation, pointing out that the circuit begins with the aorta.
21. List the arterial branches of the ascending aorta and the aortic arch.
22. Describe the arterial supply to the head and neck, especially the brain.
23. Describe the arterial supply to the upper limb, thorax, abdomen, pelvis, and lower limb.
24. Using Figure 19.25, summarize the major veins of systemic circulation, pointing out that the circuit ends with the two large venae cavae and the coronary sinus.
25. Explain the important differences in the distributions of arteries and veins.
26. Distinguish a superficial vein from a deep vein.
27. Describe venous tributaries serving the head and neck, especially the brain and dural sinuses.

28. Describe venous tributaries serving the upper limb, thorax, abdomen, pelvis, and lower limb.
29. Using Figures 19.22 and 19.23, explain the hepatic portal system.
30. Define *portal-systemic anastomoses*.
31. Explain how to "trace a drop of blood" from one location in the body to another, beginning and ending in capillaries.
32. Describe disorders of blood vessels, such as aneurysm or deep vein thrombosis of the lower limb.
33. Using Figure 19.26, describe fetal circulation and compare it to newborn (adult) circulation.

Classroom Discussion Topics and Activities

1. Display a model of a human torso, a model of the circulatory vessels, and/or a wall chart to exhibit the major blood vessels of the body.
2. Use a short piece of cloth-wrapped garden hose to show the layers (tunics) of arteries and veins.
3. Use a short piece of soaker hose to illustrate a capillary as the "functional unit" of the circulatory system.
4. Use a handheld pinball machine to illustrate the one-way nature of valves in veins and the heart.
5. Blow up a long balloon to imitate an aneurysm or a varicose vein.
6. Direct the class in solving blood-tracing problems using a flowchart format. Assign several blood-tracing problems, or allow students to make up their own. A few examples include tracing a drop of blood from
    a. The brain to the kidney.
    b. The left foot to the right thumb.
    c. The small intestine to the posterior knee.
    d. The left testis to the spleen.
    e. The myocardium to the liver.
    f. The left thorax to the face.
    g. The placenta back to the placenta.
7. Discuss the significance of a proper diet (low-fat) in maintaining normal blood flow.
8. Discuss why some coronary-bypass surgeries have to be repeated after a few years.
9. Discuss what occurs when an artery loses its elasticity.
10. Ask students to think about answers to the following questions for a class discussion:
    a. What factors or events retard venous return?
    b. Why do water and dissolved solutes leave the bloodstream at the arteriole end of a capillary bed and enter the bloodstream at the venule end of the bed?
    c. Why is the elasticity of the large arteries so important? Or, why is arteriosclerosis such a threat? (Refer to *A Closer Look: Atherosclerosis: Controlling a Silent Killer*.)
11. Project an unlabeled transparency of the vascular system and instruct students to name the vessels as they are indicated.

Clinical Questions

1. Atherosclerosis is a stealthy killer. Describe the disease process, noting the involvement of specific cells and tissue types.

   Answer: See A Closer Look *on p. 574 of the textbook and the articles on atherosclerosis in the Suggested Readings that follow.*

2. A woman in her early 50s appeared at the walk-in clinic complaining of an aching pain in her right leg following a fall. Visual examination revealed that the medial aspect of that leg was red and swollen. A diagnosis of phlebitis was made. What is phlebitis, and what more serious condition may follow if proper healing does not occur?

   Answer: Phlebitis is an inflammation of a vein, accompanied by painful throbbing and redness of the skin over the inflamed vein. If proper healing does not occur, stagnant blood may clot within the vein (this is thrombophlebitis). The danger is that the clot could detach and form an embolus.

3. The day after Spike and Rudy returned from a boxing match, they heard that the boxer who lost suffered a ruptured middle meningeal artery from the knockout blow. Where is this artery located, and what are some likely consequences of its rupture?

   Answer: The middle meningeal artery, a branch of the external carotid and maxillary arteries, runs along the broad internal surfaces of the parietal bone and squamous-temporal bone of the cranium. A rupture of this artery is likely to cause a large hematoma, which exerts pressure on the underlying cerebral cortex of the brain, interfering with the conscious, cortical functions.

4. One way that clinicians check patients for the advanced stages of alcoholism is to look for the caput medusae and hemorrhoids. Explain why these may be symptoms of advanced alcoholism.

   Answer: Both the superficial veins around the navel and the hemorrhoidal veins are anastomoses between portal blood and systemic blood (see the discussion of portal-systemic anastomoses). Chronic alcoholics often have cirrhosis of the liver, which obstructs the flow of portal blood through the liver sinusoids. This blood backs up and overfills the portal-systemic anastomoses around the navel (causing the Medusa head) and overfills the hemorrhoidal veins (causing hemorrhoids).

ART RESOURCES
Transparency List

Figure 19.1   Structure of arteries, veins, and capillaries.

Figure 19.3   Generalized anatomy of a capillary bed, as seen in a mesentery.

Figure 19.4   Structure of capillaries.

Figure 19.5   Valves in veins, and the muscular pump.

Figure 19.6   Pulmonary circulation.

Figure 19.7   Major arteries of the systemic circulation.

Figure 19.8   The great vessels that exit and enter the heart.

Figure 19.9   Arteries of the head, neck, and brain.

Figure 19.10 Arteries of the right upper limb and thorax.

Figure 19.11 Major branches of the abdominal aorta.

Figure 19.12 The celiac trunk and its main branches.

Figure 19.13 Distribution of the superior and inferior mesenteric arteries.

Figure 19.14 Arteries of the right pelvis and lower limb.

Figure 19.15 Internal iliac artery.

Figure 19.16 Flowchart summarizing the main arteries of the systemic circulation.

Figure 19.17 Major veins of the systemic circulation.

Figure 19.19 Venous drainage of the head, neck, and brain.

Figure 19.20 Veins of the right upper limb and thorax wall.

Figure 19.21 Tributaries of the inferior vena cava.

Figure 19.22 The basic scheme of the hepatic portal system and associated vessels.

Figure 19.23 Veins of the hepatic portal system.

Figure 19.24 Veins of the right lower limb and pelvis.

Figure 19.25 Flowchart summarizing the main veins of the systemic circulation.

Figure 19.26 Fetal and newborn circulation compared.

Teaching with Art

Figure 19.26 Fetal and newborn circulation compared.

Textbook p. 577; transparencies; Digital Archive CD-ROM.

Checklist of Key Points in the Figure

- Explain that major vessels are in place by the third month and blood flows in the same direction as the adult.
- Describe the placenta as the organ of transport between the fetus and the mother, functioning as the fetal respiratory organ.
- Explain that fetal lungs and liver receive very little blood.
- Define *umbilical cord*, stressing there are two umbilical arteries and one umbilical vein.
- Define a *shunt*.
- Describe the location and function of the ductus venosus, foramen ovale, and ductus arteriosus.

Common Conceptual Difficulties Interpreting the Art

- Stress that an umbilical artery carries blood away from the fetal heart and an umbilical vein carries blood to the fetal heart. It is the fetal heart that is the point of reference, not the maternal heart.
- Describe the mixing of oxygenated and deoxygenated blood.
- Explain why shunts are necessary in the fetal heart.
- Point out that the prenatal circulatory pattern must be able to rapidly convert to the postnatal circulatory pattern.

Art Exercise

Using Figure 19.26, instruct students to design a flowchart that traces a drop of blood from the placenta back to the placenta. Include all shunts and indicate high, moderate, low, and very low regions of blood oxygenation.

Critical Reasoning

Looking at Figure 19.26, ask students to identify the adult ("newborn") structures derived from the following fetal structures *and* to describe their locations in the adult using additional figures from the textbook:

a. Umbilical vein

b. Umbilical arteries

c. Ductus venosus

d. Foramen ovale

e. Ductus arteriosus

Answer:

a. *The* ligamentum teres *("round ligament"), the remnant of the umbilical vein, is contained in the anterior margin of the falciform ligament of the liver. Refer to Figure 22.20.*

b. *The umbilical arteries become the* medial umbilical ligaments *in the anterior abdominal wall inferior to the navel. Refer to Figure 19.26.*

c. *The* ligamentum venosum *on the liver's inferior surface is the fetal remnant of the ductus venosus. Refer to Figure 22.21.*

d. *The* fossa ovalis *is the fetal remnant of the foramen ovale and appears as a depression in the interatrial septum. Refer to Figure 18.5b.*

e. *Postnatally, the ductus arteriosus becomes the* ligamentum arteriosum, *a fibrous interconnection between the pulmonary trunk and aortic arch. Refer to Figure 18.5a.*

SUPPLEMENTAL COURSE MATERIALS
Library Research Topics

1. Research the congenital defects of the circulation that result from differences between the fetal and adult circulations.

2. Research the most recent hypotheses on how various types of molecules traverse the walls of capillaries.

3. Research the risk factors implicated in atherosclerosis and what can be done to minimize the risk.

4. Research the various theories of what causes atherosclerosis in arteries. Concentrate on theories other than the response-to-injury theory given in the textbook.

Audiovisual Aids/Computer Software

See Preface of the Instructor's Guide for Key to Audiovisual Distributors

Slides

1. *Arteries, Veins, and Lymphatics* (PHM)

Videotapes

1. *Your Body, Part 2: Your Circulatory System* (PLP, CH-140202, VHS)
2. *The Human Body: What Can Go Wrong?—Circulatory System* (PLP, CH-140501, VHS)

Computer Software

1. *Disk X: The Human Body, Part 1* (QUE, COM4239A, Apple; COM4239M, Macintosh; COM4239B, IBM)
2. *Body Language: Study of Anatomy and Physiology—Cardiovascular System* (PLP, CH-182011, Apple; CH-182012, IBM)

Suggested Readings

Angier, N. Storming the wall. (Article on the blood-brain barrier.) *Discover* (May 1990): 66–72.

Baim, D. New devices for coronary revascularization. *Hospital Practice* (October 15, 1993): 41–52.

Beattie, S. Coronary artery bypass surgery: The second time around. *American Journal of Nursing* (August 1993): 42–45.

Donald, D.E., and J.T. Shepard. Autonomic regulation of the peripheral circulation. *Annual Review of Physiology* 42 (1980): 419.

Gore, R.W., and P.F. McDonagh. Fluid exchange across single capillaries. *Annual Review of Physiology* 42 (1980): 337.

Hazzard, W.R. Atherosclerosis: Why women live longer than men. *Geriatrics* 40 (January 1985): 1042.

Hickey, A. Catching deep vein thrombosis in time. *Nursing* 94 (October 1994): 34–41.

Johansen, K. Aneurysms. *Scientific American* 247 (July 1982): 110.

Levine, G., et al. Cholesterol reduction in cardiovascular disease. *The New England Journal of Medicine* (February 23, 1995): 512–521.

McGuigan, J., and J. Beard. Sound probe peers inside the arteries. *New Scientist* (June 16, 1990): 35.

Moore, K.L. *Clinically Oriented Anatomy.* 3rd ed. Baltimore: Williams and Wilkins, 1992.

Robbins, S.L., and V. Kumar. *Basic Pathology.* 4th ed. Philadelphia: W.B. Saunders, 1987, pp. 285–295.

Romanes, G.J. *Cunningham's Textbook of Anatomy.* 11th ed. London: Oxford University Press, 1972, pp. 837–941.

Ross, R. The pathogenesis of atherosclerosis—An update. *New England Journal of Medicine* 314 (1986): 488–500.

Ross, R. The pathogenesis of atherosclerosis—A perspective for the 1990s. *Nature* 362 (April 29, 1993): 801–809.

Rubin, E., and J. Farber. *Essential Pathology*. Philadelphia: J.B. Lippincott, 1990, pp. 255–264.

Sandler, R. Abdominal aortic aneurysm. *American Journal of Nursing* (January 1995): 38.

Silberner, J. One-cell origin for atherosclerosis? *Science News* 130 (November 15, 1986): 310.

Steinberg, D., et al. Beyond cholesterol. Modifications of low-density lipoprotein that increase its atherogenicity. *New England Journal of Medicine* 320 (1989): 915–924.

Wenger, N. Coronary heart disease in women: A "new" problem. *Hospital Practice* (November 15, 1992): 59.

Williams, P.L., et al. *Gray's Anatomy*. 37th ed. New York: Churchill Livingstone, 1989, pp. 661–821.

Wood, J.E. The venous system. *Scientific American* 218 (January 1968): 86–96.

ANSWERS TO TEXTBOOK QUESTIONS

Answers for multiple-choice and matching questions 1–13 are located in Appendix B of the textbook.

Short Answer and Essay Questions

14. (a) There are four paths by which molecules pass into and out of capillaries (Figure 19.4): (1) through the clefts between the endothelial cells; (2) through the pores of fenestrated capillaries; (3) by diffusing directly through the endothelial cell membranes; and (4) through cytoplasmic vesicles (caveolae) that invaginate from the plasma membrane and migrate across the endothelial cells. Most of the exchange of small molecules seems to occur through route #1. (b) Brain capillaries of the blood-brain barrier lack pores, caveolae, and intercellular clefts.

15. *Elastic arteries* are the large, thick-walled arteries close to the heart. These arteries contain many layers of elastin in their walls, especially in the tunica media. This large amount of elastin enables the arteries to withstand large pressure fluctuations by expanding when the heart contracts, forcing blood into them, and recoiling as blood flows forward into the circulation during heart relaxation. The tunica media of elastic arteries contains substantial amounts of smooth muscle, but these vessels are not as active in vasoconstriction as are the muscular arteries.

    Muscular arteries are medium- and smaller-sized arteries farther along the circulatory pathway that carry blood to specific body organs. Their tunica media contains proportionately more smooth muscle and less elastic tissue than that of elastic arteries. They are most active in vasoconstriction, although the elastin in their walls continues to dampen the pulsatile force produced by the heartbeat.

    Arterioles are the smallest of the arterial vessels, feeding directly into the capillary beds. Larger arterioles exhibit all three tunics, with tunica media being the thickest of these. The walls of the smaller arterioles are little more than smooth muscle cells that coil around the endothelium of the tunica intima. When arterioles constrict, the tissues served are largely bypassed. When the arterioles dilate, blood flow into the local capillaries increases dramatically.

16. (a) The examples given in the chapter are the small intestine and the synovial membranes of synovial joints. (b) A sinusoid is a wide, twisty, leaky capillary.

17. (a) The venous blood in the legs has to travel the farthest distance to return to the heart, all "uphill" against gravity. Thus, the drainage of this blood may be slowed or halted, especially in people who stand still for long periods. Pooling of blood in the veins of the lower limb puts backpressure on the valves and walls of these veins so that the valves may fail and the walls may stretch. This is varicose veins. (b) Valves prevent backflow of blood, and they direct the flow of venous blood to the heart. In the neck, gravity directs venous blood in the proper direction anyway, so few valves are necessary—unlike in the lower limbs.

18. The sketch of the arterial circle (of Willis) should resemble that in Figure 19.9c.

19. (a) The two tributaries of the hepatic portal vein are the superior mesenteric vein and the splenic vein. (b) The function of the hepatic portal circulation is to deliver blood laden with nutrients from the stomach and intestine to the liver, where the nutrients are processed.

20. The azygos vein ascends along the right surface, or the center, of the bodies of the thoracic vertebrae. It drains most systemic blood from the thorax region of the body.

21. These are the superior left, superior right, inferior left, and inferior right pulmonary veins.

22. Both are fetal vessels. Ductus venosus lies on the caudal surface of the liver and shunts some of the blood from the umbilical vein around the liver. Ductus arteriosus lies near the heart, connecting the pulmonary trunk to the arch of the aorta, and shunting blood into the systemic circulation so as not to overload the pulmonary vessels in the nonfunctional lungs.

Critical Reasoning and Clinical Applications Questions

1. Bacteria from infections in the danger triangle of the face can enter the facial vein, which communicates with the ophthalmic vein, which drains into the cavernous sinus, which is continuous with all other dural sinuses. Thus, infections may spread widely throughout the dural sinuses in the skull.

2. Closing a patent foramen ovale is much more difficult and dangerous because it requires opening the heart—and open heart surgery is always difficult, especially in a small child.

3. As evident in the figure, there are no major arteries in the *center* of the distal forearm, so Sam should survive.

4. The aneurysm was a balloon widening or outpocketing of a brain artery with weak walls that was compressing nearby nervous structures and in danger of bursting. The surgeons removed the aneurysm and replaced this arterial segment with a strong tube that will not burst.

SUPPLEMENTAL STUDENT MATERIALS TO HUMAN ANATOMY, THIRD EDITION
Chapter 19: Blood Vessels

To the Student

The main blood vessels are the arteries, veins, and capillaries. They are dynamic structures that accomplish the delivery of blood throughout your body. There are two basic circuits that comprise the vascular system: pulmonary circulation and systemic circulation. The pulmonary circuit carries blood to the lungs for gas exchange, oxygen is picked up, and carbon dioxide is removed. The systemic circuit delivers oxygenated blood to the tissues of the body in exchange for carbon dioxide. As you study the vascular system, keep in mind many of the arteries and veins are named the same and run side by side. Arteries always carry blood away from the heart, and veins always carry blood toward the heart. Regardless of type, vessels carrying oxygen-rich blood are colored red, and vessels carrying oxygen-poor blood are colored blue. First, learn the general characteristics of blood vessels. Second, practice numerous blood-tracing problems to truly understand the "circuit" of blood circulation.

Step 1: Describe the general characteristics of blood vessels.
- ☐ Name the main types of vessels, describing the directional flow of blood within each type.
- ☐ Describe the structure and function of three types of arteries and name a body location for each.
- ☐ Clearly distinguish between capillaries and sinusoids, naming body locations for each.
- ☐ Explain the structural basis of capillary permeability.
- ☐ Describe four routes involved in capillary permeability.
- ☐ Define *shunt*.
- ☐ Distinguish between a metarteriole and thoroughfare channel.
- ☐ Define *precapillary sphincter* and describe its function.
- ☐ Compare postcapillary venules to capillaries.
- ☐ Name the tunics of a blood vessel.
- ☐ Explain how to histologically distinguish a vein from an artery, including comments on lumina and tunics.
- ☐ Explain the function of valves in veins, and describe them on varicose veins.
- ☐ Define *vascular anastomoses*, explain their functions, and identify body locations.
- ☐ Define *vasa vasorum*, explain their functions, and name a couple of their locations.

Step 2: Review the heart and the great vessels.
- ☐ Identify the major vessels associated with the heart.
- ☐ Review how blood moves through the heart.

Step 3: Describe pulmonary circulation.
- ☐ Name the major vessels of the pulmonary circuit.

- ☐ Trace a drop of blood in the pulmonary trunk back to the left atrium.
- ☐ Explain why pulmonary arteries are colored blue and pulmonary veins are colored red in Figure 19.6 in your textbook.

Step 4: Describe systemic circulation.
- ☐ List the major arteries that branch off directly from the aorta and name the part of the body they supply.
- ☐ List the major veins that serve as tributaries for the superior and inferior venae cavae, naming the parts of the body that they drain.
- ☐ Describe the special function of the hepatic portal system, and explain the significance of the portal-systemic anastomoses.
- ☐ Diagram the pathway of the hepatic portal system using a flowchart format.
- ☐ Name each part of the body drained by a vessel of the hepatic portal system.
- ☐ Explain what makes a portal system extremely unique and answer the question, "Does the human body have other portal systems, and if so where?"
- ☐ Trace a drop of blood from the kidney to the spleen.
- ☐ Trace a drop of blood from the descending colon to the right hand.
- ☐ Formulate several blood-tracing problems and check your answers with your professor.

Step 5: Describe fetal circulation.
- ☐ Define *placenta*.
- ☐ Name fetal vessels that carry blood to and from the placenta and describe the concentration of oxygen contained in them.
- ☐ Define *shunt*.
- ☐ Explain how the ductus venosus, ductus arteriosus, and foramen ovale function as fetal circulatory shunts.
- ☐ Describe what happens to the ductus arteriosus and foramen ovale at birth.
- ☐ Identify the adult structures derived from the ductus venosus, ductus arteriosus, foramen ovale, umbilical arteries, and umbilical vein.
- ☐ Trace a drop of fetal blood from the placenta back to the placenta, including shunts. Indicate regions of oxygen concentration (high, moderate, low, and very low) along the pathway.

CHAPTER 20
The Lymphatic and Immune Systems

LECTURE AND DEMONSTRATION
Student Objectives

1. Describe the structure and distribution of lymphatic vessels.
2. Explain how lymph forms and the mechanisms by which it is transported.
3. List and explain the important functions of the lymphatic vessels.
4. Describe how lymph nodes function as lymphatic organs.
5. Describe the function, recirculation, and activation of lymphocytes.
6. Relate the structure of lymphoid tissue to its infection-fighting function.
7. Describe the locations, histological structure, and immune functions of the following lymphoid organs: lymph nodes, spleen, thymus, tonsils, lymphoid follicles in the intestine, and appendix.
8. Describe the basic characteristics of chylothorax, lymphangitis, mononucleosis, Hodgkin's disease, and non-Hodgkin's lymphoma.
9. Outline the development of the lymphatic vessels and lymphoid organs.

Suggested Lecture Outline

I. **The Lymphatic System (pp. 584–589)**
   A. Lymph Capillaries (p. 585, Fig. 20.2)
   B. Lymphatic Collecting Vessels (pp. 585–586)
   C. Lymph Nodes (pp. 586–587, Figs. 20.3 and 20.4)
   D. Lymph Trunks (pp. 587–589, Fig. 20.3)
   E. Lymph Ducts (p. 589, Figs. 20.3 and 20.5)

II. **The Immune System (pp. 589–598, Figs. 19.5 and 19.6)**
   A. Lymphocytes and Other Cells of the Immune System (pp. 589–593)
      1. Activation of Lymphocytes (pp. 589–593, Fig. 20.6)
   B. Lymphoid Tissue (pp. 593–595, Fig. 20.7)
   C. Lymphoid Organs (pp. 595–598, Figs. 20.8–20.12)
      1. Lymph Nodes
      2. Spleen

II. THE IMMUNE SYSTEM *(continued)*

    3. Thymus

    4. Tonsils

    5. Aggregated Lymphoid Follicles and the Appendix

III. Disorders of the Lymphatic and Immune Systems (pp. 598–599)

IV. The Lymphatic and Immune Systems Throughout Life (pp. 599–600)

Lecture Hints

1. Define and distinguish between the *lymphatic system* and the *immune system*.
2. Distinguish between blood, lymph, and interstitial fluid.
3. Distinguish between lymph vessels and blood vessels, particularly veins and capillaries.
4. Name and describe the vessels of the lymphatic system, including their structure and distribution. Refer to Figure 20.1.
5. Describe important functions of the lymph vessels.
6. Explain the formation of lymph and how it is transported.
7. Describe lymph capillaries in detail, explaining their structure, permeability, and minivalves. Refer to Figure 20.2.
8. Identify areas of the body that lack lymph capillaries, particularly the central nervous system, and remind students how the CNS deals with excess tissue fluid.
9. Describe the location and function of *lacteals*.
10. Describe the location of lymph collecting vessels with respect to blood vessels, and also describe basic structural differences between lymph and blood vessels.
11. Explain the various mechanisms that support the movement of lymph within lymph vessels.
12. Describe the consequences of blocked or sporadic and slow movement of lymph, i.e., edema.
13. Using Figure 20.3, present an overview of lymph node locations along lymph trunks and ducts pathways.
14. Describe how lymph nodes function as lymphatic organs, including movement of lymph through a node. Refer to Figure 20.4.
15. Summarize the lymph drainage patterns, naming major trunks and ducts and stressing locations where lymph ducts empty into major veins. Refer to Figure 20.5.
16. Discuss the body's immune system, explaining the central functions of the key defense cells, the lymphocytes.
17. Remind students that the body's first line of defense is the skin and mucous membranes, performing nonspecific resistance to disease.
18. Name the major components of the body's specific line of defense to disease, the immune system, beginning at the cellular level and progressing to the organ level.
19. Review conceptual distinctions between antigens and antibodies.
20. Review briefly the basics of inflammatory response, explaining this is a beneficial, essential defense mechanism (although sometimes painful). Refer to Chapter 4, if necessary.

21. Describe functions of lymphocytes and review distinctions between B cells and T cells, referring students to Chapter 17, if necessary.

22. Explain how B cells and T cells attack antigens, using the analogy of sending weapons (in the case of antibody-mediated [humoral] immunity and indirect antigen attack) as opposed to sending troops (in the case of cell-mediated immunity and direct antigen attack) to fight infection, respectively.

23. Point out that although immunity represents specific responses to antibodies, the system does not work perfectly all the time.

24. Explain the basis for the formation of vaccines.

25. Define *recirculation of lymphocytes*, explaining its significance.

26. Using the flowchart representation in Figure 20.6, describe lymphocyte activation, including origin, immunocompetence, and antigen challenge.

27. Distinguish between effector lymphocytes and memory lymphocytes.

28. Describe lymphoid tissue, including structure, function, and locations. Refer to Figure 20.7.

29. Caution students not to confuse the terms *lymphoid nodule* and *lymph node*.

30. List lymphoid organs within the body.

31. Relate the structure of a lymph node to its infection-fighting function. Refer to Figure 20.7b.

32. Describe the gross anatomy of the spleen. Refer to Figure 20.9.

33. Describe the two main blood-cleansing functions of the spleen, distinguishing between red pulp and white pulp. Refer to Figure 20.9.

34. Using Figure 20.10, describe the location, structure, and functions of the thymus, and explain how the thymus differs from other lymphoid organs.

35. Explain how the *blood-thymus barrier* is analogous to the *blood-brain barrier*.

36. Describe the normal changes that occur in the thymus from infancy to old age.

37. Name and identify locations of the various tonsils, describing their infection-fighting function. Refer to Figure 20.11.

38. Explain aggregated lymphoid nodules and the appendix as parts of MALT, including their infection-fighting functions.

39. Note that the more current terminology for "Peyer's patch" is aggregated lymphoid nodule.

40. Use the chapter feature *A Closer Look: AIDS: The Modern-Day Plague* to emphasize the significance of disorders of the body's immune system, and provide up-to-date information on a serious health threat.

41. Discuss one or more of the following disorders of the lymphatic system and immune system: chylothorax, lymphangitis, mononucleosis, Hodgkin's disease, and non-Hodgkin's lymphoma.

42. Describe the effects of aging on the body's lymphatic and immune systems, pointing out that contrary to popular belief, a newborn does have an active immune system, and the atrophied thymus of the elderly continues to produce T cells.

Classroom Discussion Topics and Activities

1. Use a model and chart of the human torso to demonstrate lymphatic organs.
2. Demonstrate lymphatic organs using a dissected cat or rat.
3. Use a soaker hose to emphasize the leakiness of lymph capillaries.
4. Use a handheld pinball machine to show the one-way nature of valves in lymph vessels.
5. Ask students why a body region develops edema after the lymphatics are removed from that area, possibly using the example of severe edema in the upper limb of a woman recovering from a radical mastectomy.
6. Use a visual aid that shows a person with elephantiasis to illustrate the edema that results from obstruction of the lymphatic vessels.
7. Survey the class to determine how many students have had their palatine tonsils removed. Explain that in the 1950s, tonsillectomy was a routine operation, and almost 100% of the children in North America had their tonsils taken out. In the 1960s, this operation was recognized to be largely unnecessary, so your current survey should indicate that only a minority of students have had a tonsillectomy. (The textbook authors' surveys indicated a 50% rate among their own students in 1980, less than 20% in 1991, and less than 5% in 1995.)
8. Assign *A Closer Look: AIDS: The Modern-Day Plague* as required reading. Instruct students to look up newspaper and popular magazine articles that concern the social, medical, and economic problems surrounding AIDS for class discussion and/or reports.
9. Discuss why a physician checks for swollen lymph nodes in the neck when examining a patient who shows symptoms of ventilatory disorder.
10. Discuss the ramifications of removing the spleen.
11. Discuss the ramifications of removing tonsils.
12. Discuss the role of the thymus in the body's immune response, including newborns and the elderly. What is the immune status of a person born without a thymus?
13. Discuss the pros and cons surrounding laws that require universal immunization of American children against diseases such as tuberculosis, smallpox, measles, and mumps.
14. Discuss the rationale for the demise of the Martian invaders in H.G. Wells' *The War of the Worlds*. That book was written in the 1890s; is its ending still valid today, or do more recent scientific findings make the ending nonsensical?
15. Discuss allergy, explaining it is an abnormally vigorous immune response to an otherwise harmless antigen. Ask students to explain allergic symptoms and the role of T cells in some responses.

Clinical Questions

1. What is the consequence of obstruction of the lymphatic vessels of a body region?
   Answer: Obstruction of the lymphatic vessels results in severe, localized edema.
2. How does the lymphatic system both help and hinder the spread of cancer through the body?
   Answer: Cancer cells can easily enter the "leaky" lymphatic capillaries and, therefore, can travel in the lymph stream through the body. Lymph nodes, located along the lymph collecting vessels, filter and help destroy the cancer cells.

3. A pregnant woman complains to her doctor that her ankles and feet stay swollen all the time. She is very worried about this. As her doctor, what would you tell her?

    Answer: She has edema, an accumulation of excess tissue fluid in the extracellular spaces of the areolar connective tissues of her lower limbs. This is caused by her pregnancy and the fact that the enlarged womb is pressing on the lymphatic vessels in the pelvis (which drain the lower limb). (It also results from the fact that blood volume increases during pregnancy; this increases the hydrostatic pressure at capillaries, resulting in the formation of more tissue fluid.) She should be monitored for edema until she delivers, but it should clear up at the end of pregnancy.

4. A woman has a modified radical mastectomy with removal of the axillary lymph nodes on her left side. What can she expect to happen to her left arm and why?

    Answer: The large lymph vessels draining the upper limb are inevitably removed along with the axillary nodes. Therefore, she can expect chronic edema in the left upper limb, although lymph drainage will eventually be reestablished by regrowth of the vessels.

5. A man involved in a traffic accident is rushed to the emergency room of a hospital with severe internal bleeding. Examination reveals that his spleen has ruptured. What is the treatment of choice and the prognosis?

    Answer: Surgical removal of the spleen, with tying off of the splenic vessels, is indicated. If the splenectomy is performed quickly enough to avoid massive loss of blood through internal bleeding, the prognosis is very good—because most functions of the spleen will be taken over by macrophages in the liver and bone marrow.

6. Why do the elderly tend to develop cancer more frequently than younger people?

    Answer: One reason is that, as one ages, the efficiency of the immune system declines. T cells become less effective at killing cancer cells.

7. James, a 36-year-old engineer, appeared at the clinic in an extremely debilitated condition. He had purple-brown lesions on his skin and a persistent cough. A physical examination revealed swollen lymph nodes. Laboratory tests revealed a low lymphocyte count. Information taken during the personal history revealed that James was upwardly mobile economically and homosexual in sexual preference. The skin lesions proved to be evidence of Kaposi's sarcoma. What is James' problem, and what is his outlook?

    Answer: James is suffering from AIDS. To date, it is 100% fatal.

8. Children born without a thymus must be kept in a germfree environment if they are to survive. Explain why this is necessary.

    Answer: If the thymus fails to develop, the T cells will not form. If there are no T cells to recognize foreign antigens, there is no resistance to disease. Furthermore, there will be no helper T cells—and since helper T cells are necessary to activate B cells, there will be no active B lymphocytes either.

ART RESOURCES

Transparency List

Figure 20.1   Simplified scheme of the lymphatic vessels.

Figure 20.2   Location and structure of lymph capillaries.

Figure 20.3 Overview of the lymph nodes and lymph trunks and ducts.

Figure 20.4 Structure of a lymph node.

Figure 20.5 The lymphatic trunks and ducts in relation to surrounding structures.

Figure 20.7 Lymphoid tissues.

Figure 20.8 Lymphoid organs.

Figure 20.9 Structure of the spleen.

Teaching with Art

Figure 20.7a Structure of a lymph node.

Figure 20.7b Lymphoid tissues (lymphoid tissue in a lymph node).

Textbook p. 594; transparencies; Digitial Archive CD-ROM.

Checklist of Key Points in the Figure

- Remind students of the general distribution of lymph nodes in the body, including the locations of the largest ones and what it means to have a "swollen gland" (also see Figure 20.03).
- Indicate basic anatomical features of a lymph node such as the capsule, trabeculae, and hilus.
- Identify two sets of lymph vessels attached to the node, indicating the direction of lymph flow.
- Using Figure 20.4, emphasize the percolation and filtration of lymph through the lymph sinuses, and the presence of macrophages on the internal framework of the sinuses.
- Using Figure 20.7b, emphasize the lymphoid nodules, the tadpole-shaped masses of lymphoid tissue, as the sites of antigen challenge and where B cells and T cells are activated.
- Define and distinguish between a lymph node's *cortex* and *medulla*, using the tadpole analogy.

Common Conceptual Difficulties Interpreting the Art

- Explain that lymph nodes have two functions, filtrating lymph as well as being sites of antigen challenge.
- Caution students not to confuse lymph vessels with blood vessels. Explain the difference between a lymph capillary and a blood capillary and the difference between a lymph vessel and vein.
- Distinguish between lymph *node* and lymph *nodule*.
- Explain germinal center.

Art Exercises

1. Using a copy of Figure 20.4, instruct students to trace a drop of lymph through a lymph node, labeling passageway structures beginning with an afferent vessel and ending with an efferent vessel. Additional labels of lymph node anatomy may be included.

    (Sequence students should follow: afferent lymph vessel → subcapsular sinuses → cortical sinuses → medullary sinuses → efferent lymph vessel.)

2. Using a copy of Figure 20.7b, instruct students to color code locations of sinuses, cortex, medulla, T cells, B cells, macrophages, and dendritic cells.

Critical Reasoning

Ask students to explain what happens to the foreign materials in lymph that enter a lymph node.

Answer: Foreign materials are phagocytized by macrophages or are attacked by lymphocytes in an immune response.

SUPPLEMENTAL COURSE MATERIALS
Library Research Topics

1. Chronic fatigue syndrome, in which people suffer extreme fatigue and flu-like symptoms for years, has recently received much media attention. Research this condition and evaluate the evidence that it is an immune-deficiency disease.

2. Research the differences between lymph nodes swollen due to infection and those swollen due to cancer.

3. Research the changes that appear in the thymus with age, and relate these changes to the body's immune response.

4. Research the difficulties involved in organ-transplant surgeries. How is the drug cyclosporine used?

5. Research the possible side effects of vaccines.

Audiovisual Aids/Computer Software

See Preface of the Instructor's Guide for Key to Audiovisual Distributors

Slides

1. *Visual Approach To Histology: Lymphatic System* (FAD, 18 Slides)

2. *The Immune Response* (EI, Slides, or Filmstrips). High-quality artwork provides a detailed look at antibody formation and antigen-antibody interactions. Explores the lymphatic system and passive and active immunity.

3. *Mounting Immune Responses* (EI, 98 Slides). Defines the general nature of immune response and diagrams the lymphatic system's role in it, using graphics as well as color photomicrographs. Various influences on the immune response and dose tolerance are studied in detail.

4. *Immunologic Deficiency States* (EI, 51 Slides). Explores and explains infantile hypogammaglobulinemia, defects in the inflammatory response that lead to immune deficiency, defects in stem cells, defects in T cells, defects in B cells, defective synthesis of immunoglobulins, alterations in the fate of immunoglobulins, and evaluation of an immunologic defect. An effective combination of clear, precise artwork; medical photomicrographs; and unadorned concise narrative.

Videotapes

1. *AIDS: A Biological Perspective* (FHS, 30 min.)

2. *Allergy and Immunotherapy* (FHS, 26 min., 1990)

3. *Basic Immunology* (IM, 37 min., 1994)

4. *Cell Wars: How the Immune System Works* (FHS, 26 min., 1990)
5. *Defend and Repair* (*Body Atlas Series*) (HCA, 30 min., 1994)
6. *Defense Mechanisms* (*Human Body Live Action Video Series*) (CAP, 28 min., 1993)
7. *External and Internal Defenses* (*Human Body Live Action Video Series*) (CAP, 28 min., 1993)
8. *The Human Immune System: The Fighting Edge* (FHS, 44 min.)
9. *The Immune System* (*Human Body Live Action Video Series*) (CAP, 28 min., 1993)
10. *Our Immune System* (FHS, 23 min.)
11. *Stress and the Immune Function* (FHS, 26 min., 1990)

CD-ROMs

1. *Blood and Immunity* (CAP/NS/CBS, Mac/Win, 1997)
2. *Explorations in Human Anatomy and Physiology* (Ward's, Mac/Win)
3. *Immune System* (Queue, Mac/Win)

Suggested Readings

Alberts, B., et al. *Molecular Biology of the Cell*. 3rd ed. New York: Garland, 1994, Chapter 23.

Bolognesi, D.P., and M.D. Cooper. Immunodeficiency. *Current Opinions in Immunology* 7 (August 1995): 433–435.

Chambers, W.H., and C.S. Brissette-Storkus. Hanging in the balance: Natural killer cell recognition of target cells. *Chemistry and Biology* 2 (July 1995): 429–435.

Clinical and Experimental Immunology: Primary Immunodeficiency Diseases. Report of a WHO scientific group. 109 Supplement 1 (August 1997): 1–28.

Cohen, I.R. The cognitive principle challenges clonal selection. *Immunology Today* 13 (November 1992): 441–444.

Cohen, J. International AIDS conference: Basic research comes to the fore as clinical results lag. *Science* 265 (August 19, 1994): 1028–1029.

Dixon, F. Current understanding of autoimmune disease. *Hospital Practice* (February 15, 1995): 11–12.

Duke, R.C., et al. Cell suicide in health and disease. *Scientific American* 275 (December 1996): 80–87.

Fackelmann, K. Staying alive: Scientists study people who outwit the AIDS virus. *Science News* 147 (March 18, 1995): 172–174.

Fawcett, D.W. *A Textbook of Histology*. 12th ed. New York: Chapman & Hall, 1994, Chapters 13–16.

Fields, B. AIDS: Time to turn to basic science. *Nature* 369 (May 12, 1994): 95–96.

Fischl, M. Combination antiretroviral therapy for HIV infection. *Hospital Practice* (January 15, 1994): 43.

Forsdyke, D.R. The origins of the clonal selection theory of immunity as a case study for evaluation in science. *FASEB Journal* 9 (February 1995): 164–166.

Hanninen, A., and L.C. Harrison. Gamma delta T cells as mediators of mucosal tolerance: The autoimmune diabetes model. *Immunology Review* 173 (February 2000): 109–119.

Jacobsen, K., and D.G. Osmond. Microenvironmental organization and stromal cell associations of B lymphocyte precursor cells in mouse bone marrow. *European Journal of Immunology* 28 (November 1990): 2395-2404.

Jacobsen, K., et al. Early B-lymphocyte precursor cells in mouse bone marrow: Subosteal localization of B220+ cells during postirradiation regeneration. *Experimental Hematology* 18 (May 1990): 304-310.

James, S.P. The gastrointestinal mucosal immune system. *Digestive Diseases* 11 (1993): 146-156.

Junqueira, L.C., et al. *Basic Histology*. 9th ed. Stamford, Conn.: Appleton and Lange, 1998.

Kos, F.J., and E.G. Engleman. Immune regulation: A critical link between NK cells and CTLs. *Immunology Today* 17 (April 1996): 174-176.

Kuper, B., and S. Failla. Shedding new light on lupus. *American Journal of Nursing* (November 1994): 26-32.

Laissue, J.A., et al. The intestinal immune system and its relation to disease. *Digestive Diseases* 11 (July-October 1993): 298-312.

Mayerson, H.S. The lymphatic system. *Scientific American* 208 (June 1963): 80-90.

Marx, J. Testing of autoimmune therapy begins. *Science* 252 (April 5, 1991): 27-28.

Nossal, G.J. Life, death and the immune system. *Scientific American* 269 (September 1993): 52-62.

Pabst, R., and I. Gehrke. Is the bronchus-associated lymphoid tissue (BALT) an integral structure of the lung in normal mammals, including humans? *American Journal of Respiratory Cell and Molecular Biology* 3 (August 1990): 131-135.

Paul, W. Reexamining AIDS research priorities. *Science* 267 (February 3, 1995): 633-636.

Rennie, J. The body against itself. *Scientific American* 263 (December 1990): 106-115.

Richardson, S. The race against AIDS. *Discover* (May 1995): 28-32.

Schmitt D. Immune response of the skin. *Clinical Reviews in Allergy and Immunology* 13 (Fall 1995): 177-188.

Scientific American. Special Issue: The Immune System. Various articles and authors. September 1993.

Seroogy, C.M., and C.G. Fathman. The application of gene therapy in autoimmune diseases. *Gene Therapy* 7 (January 2000): 9-13.

Shute, N. Allergy epidemic. *U.S. News and World Report* 128 (May 8, 2000): 46-53.

Sprent, J., and D. Tough. Lymphocyte life-span and memory. *Science* 265 (September 2, 1994): 1395-1400.

Steinman, L. Autoimmune disease. *Scientific American* 269 (September 1993): 106-114.

Stingl G. The skin: Initiation and target site of immune responses. *Recent Results Cancer Res* 128 (1993): 45-57.

Szuromi, P. Dendritic cells as HIV-1 reservoirs. *Science* 257 (July 17, 1992): 305. (Also see the article by Cameron, et al., on p. 383 of the same issue.)

Thorbecke, G.J., et al. Biology of germinal centers in lymphoid tissue. *FASEB Journal* 8 (August 1994): 832-840.

Travis, J. AIDS update 1996. *Science News* 149 (March 23, 1996): 184-185.

Waldmann, T.A. T-cell receptors for cytokines: Targets for immunotherapy of leukemia/lymphoma. *Annals of Oncology* 11, Supplement 1 (2000): 101–106.

Weintraub, L. Splenectomy: Who, when, and why? *Hospital Practice* (June 15, 1994): 27–34.

Weissman, I.L., and M.D. Cooper. How the immune system develops. *Scientific American* 269 (September 1993): 64–71.

Whitman, M. Preventing lymphedema, an unwelcome sequel to breast cancer. *Nursing* 93 (December 1993): 36–39.

Virella, G. Antigenicity and immune recognition. *Immunology Series* 50 (1990): 53–76.

von Boehmer, H., and P. Kisielow. How the immune system learns about self. *Scientific American* 265 (October 1991): 74–81.

Yang, K., et al. Do germinal centers have a role in the generation of lymphomas? *Current Topics in Microbiology and Immunology* 246 (1999): 53–60, discussion 61–62.

Young, L.H., et al. How lymphocytes kill. *Annual Review of Medicine* 41 (1990): 45–54.

Zanetti, M. Antigenized antibodies. *Nature* 355 (January 30, 1992): 476–477.

ANSWERS TO TEXTBOOK QUESTIONS

Answers for multiple-choice and matching questions 1–11 are located in Appendix B of the textbook.

Short Answer and Essay Questions

12. Lymph nodes cleanse antigens from the lymph, whereas the spleen cleanses antigens from the blood.

13. The lymphatic vessel has more bulges ("string of pearls" appearance), more valves than a vein, and thinner walls than any blood vessel.

14. The thoracic duct originates at the cisterna chyli on the bodies of lumbar vertebrae L1 and L2, and ascends along the thoracic vertebral bodies. In the superior thorax, it turns to the left and empties into the venous circulation in the root of the neck—at the junction of the left internal jugular and left subclavian veins. For the locations of the lymph trunks, see Figure 20.3.

15. (1) Lymph vessels return excess tissue fluid to the blood. (Slightly more tissue fluid is produced by blood capillaries than returns directly to them.) (2) Lymph vessels return leaked proteins to the blood. (Plasma proteins slowly but continually leak from the blood capillaries and must be returned in order to maintain normal circulatory dynamics.) (3) Lymph vessels carry absorbed fats from the intestine to the blood. (These lipids are absorbed into intestinal lymph capillaries called lacteals.)

16. The axillary nodes, inguinal nodes, and cervical nodes are superficially located and easily palpated. (See the legend to Figure 20.3.)

17. Cytotoxic T cells directly destroy antigen-bearing cells by spearing their membranes (or by signaling apoptosis). B cells, by contrast, act more indirectly by becoming plasma cells that secrete antibodies, which mark foreign antigens and cells for destruction. B cells and antibodies are best at fighting bacteria and bacterial toxins, but T cells can only destroy eukaryotic cells.

18. Germaine is correct. Lymph begins as tissue fluid, which is a filtrate of the blood; then the lymph vessels carry lymph back to the bloodstream by draining into the great veins at the root of the neck.

19. She is correct. The white pulp consists of true lymphoid tissue, and lymphoid nodules are characteristic features of lymphoid tissue.

20. She is mistaken. Although the thymus atrophies with age and becomes impregnated with fat, it continues to produce T cells throughout adulthood.

Critical Reasoning and Clinical Applications Questions

1. Her swollen "glands" are inflamed cervical lymph nodes. Bacteria have spread from lymph vessels that drain the region of the cut in her face and have lodged in the lymph nodes of the neck, infecting these nodes.

2. The immediate danger of a ruptured spleen is death through internal bleeding, as large quantities of blood leak from the spleen into the peritoneal cavity.

3. In portal hypertension, the flow of blood through liver sinusoids is impeded, and venous blood backs up through the veins of the portal system, including the splenic vein. With this backup, large amounts of blood accumulate in the spleen, enlarging it. (Recall that splenic sinusoids are leaky, so blood can leak out of them into the substance of the spleen.) Notice that this particular question has nothing to do with infection or the immune function of the spleen.

4. (a) The mastectomy removed lymph nodes and lymph vessels from the armpit, preventing drainage of lymph from the upper limb. (b) Lymphatic vessels usually regenerate well, so she will probably have relief from these symptoms in weeks or months.

5. Traci has an infection of the hand, bacteria easily enter the lymph capillaries of the hand, and movements of her arm would move infected lymph up toward the neck and into her general circulation (right lymph duct and great veins of the neck). Thus, keeping her arm motionless will minimize the chance of spreading infection throughout the body. Incidentally, the red streaks visible through her skin may be evidence of lymphangitis.

6. Simi had splenomegaly, because only an enlarged spleen can be felt protruding anterior to the costal margin. Microorganisms from all three of her blood infections had been filtered by the spleen and were infecting that organ, causing its enlargement.

SUPPLEMENTAL STUDENT MATERIALS TO HUMAN ANATOMY, THIRD EDITION

Chapter 20: The Lymphatic and Immune Systems

To the Student

Your eyes itch; your nose is runny; you break out in hives, and hives itch, too. What happened to your otherwise feeling of perfect comfort? Your body initiated a vigorous immune response to a specific foreign molecule, usually a protein, to which you are allergic. Daily your body is subjected to cuts, scrapes, bumps, bruises, burns, bites, stings, and a multitude of disease-causing microorganisms such as bacteria and viruses; any one of these has significant potential to cause harm to your body. Usually you stay healthy because of the tremendous effort of the all-important lymphatic and immune systems.

Lymphatic vessels collect tissue (interstitial) fluid, which is called lymph once it enters the lymphatic vessels. Specialized white blood cells traveling in blood and lymph provide protection to tissues and clean up tissue debris, such as dead cells. And, interestingly, an additional function of the lymphatic system aids in the absorption of fats. Whether or not your career goal involves the health profession, this chapter is of paramount importance to you because it explains how disease organisms travel throughout the body and how your body mounts an attack to contain and eradicate these organisms.

Step 1: Perceive clearly and fully the structure and function of the lymphatic vessels and lymph.

- ☐ Describe the structure and distribution of lymphatic vessels.
- ☐ Define *lymph*, explaining the formation process and its contents.
- ☐ Describe lymph, comparing and contrasting it to both interstitial fluid and blood.
- ☐ Identify each type of lymphatic vessel, indicating important functions and specialized structural features.
- ☐ Define *lacteal*, explaining its location and function.
- ☐ Explain why it is possible for disease-causing organisms and cancer cells to gain easy access to the lymphatic stream.
- ☐ Describe the structural features of lymph collecting vessels, explaining how to distinguish a lymph vessel and blood vessel if you observe them side-by-side.
- ☐ Describe the mechanics of lymph flow, including how flow is maintained.
- ☐ Identify two main lymph ducts, and explain the drainage pathway of each.
- ☐ Describe the entire course of the thoracic duct.
- ☐ Trace a drop of lymph from its point of formation to its return to the bloodstream.

Step 2: Understand the structure and function of lymph nodes.

- ☐ Identify primary locations of lymph nodes in the body.
- ☐ Explain how lymph nodes function as lymphatic organs.
- ☐ Diagram a simple flowchart of the pathway of lymph into, through, and out of a lymph node.

- ☐ Define and distinguish between the anatomical terms *afferent* and *efferent*, *hilus*, and *sinus* and *sinusoid*.

Step 3: Understand the structure and function of lymphocytes in the immune system.

- ☐ Define and describe *lymphocytes*.
- ☐ Distinguish between T cells and B cells, explaining how each attacks antigens.
- ☐ Explain the recirculation of lymphocytes, including its function.
- ☐ Explain the three stages in the activation of lymphocytes: origination, development of immunocompetence, and antigen challenge.
- ☐ Distinguish between effector lymphocytes and memory lymphocytes.
- ☐ Explain the important difference between natural killer cells and cytotoxic T cells.
- ☐ Explain why helper T cells can be called "managers of the immune system."

Step 4: Understand the structure and function of lymphoid tissues.

- ☐ Identify the type of tissue that makes up lymphoid tissue.
- ☐ Summarize the basic characteristics of lymphoid tissues, including their locations.
- ☐ Relate the structure of lymphoid tissue to its infection-fighting function.
- ☐ Define *MALT*.
- ☐ Relate the structure of a lymphoid nodule to its immune function.
- ☐ Distinguish between a lymph node and a lymphoid nodule (follicle).

Step 5: Understand the structure and function of lymphoid organs.

- ☐ List structures classified as lymphoid organs.
- ☐ Describe the anatomical location of each of the listed lymphoid organs.
- ☐ Describe the significant histological features of each of the listed lymphoid organs.
- ☐ Describe the immune functions of each of the listed lymphoid organs.
- ☐ Compare the functions of a lymph node to the functions of the spleen.
- ☐ Distinguish between red pulp and white pulp.
- ☐ Identify lymphoid organs described as parts of MALT.

Step 6: Identify some specific disorders of the lymphatic and immune systems and explain the effects of aging.

- ☐ Read *A Closer Look: AIDS: The Modern-Day Plague* in Chapter 20 of the textbook and summarize the social, medical, and economic implications of the disease.
- ☐ Explain a simple way to identify an enlarged spleen and describe the ramifications of a ruptured spleen.
- ☐ Outline the development of the lymphatic vessels and lymphoid organs.
- ☐ Explain why the effectiveness of the immune system declines with age.

CHAPTER 21
The Respiratory System

LECTURE AND DEMONSTRATION
Student Objectives

1. Identify the respiratory tubes and passageways in order, from the nose to the alveoli in the lungs. Distinguish the structures of the conducting zone from those of the respiratory zone.
2. List and describe several protective mechanisms of the respiratory system.
3. Describe the structure and functions of the larynx.
4. Explain how the walls of the upper respiratory passages differ histologically from those in the lower parts of the respiratory tree.
5. Describe the structure of a lung alveolus and of the respiratory membrane.
6. Describe the gross structure of the lungs and the pleurae.
7. Explain the relative roles of the respiratory muscles and lung elasticity in the act of ventilation.
8. Define *surfactant*, and explain its function in ventilation.
9. Explain how the brain and peripheral chemoreceptors control the ventilation rate.
10. Consider the respiration causes and consequences of asthma, chronic bronchitis, emphysema, lung cancer, pneumonia, tuberculosis, cystic fibrosis, and nosebleeds.
11. Trace the development of the respiratory system in the embryo and fetus.
12. Describe the normal changes that occur in the respiratory system from infancy to old age.

Suggested Lecture Outline

I. *Functional Anatomy of the Respiratory System* (pp. 604–621, Fig. 21.1)

  A. The Nose and the Paranasal Sinuses (pp. 604–608, Figs. 21.1–21.4 and Fig.7.11)

   1. The Nose

   2. The Paranasal Sinuses

  B. The Pharynx (pp. 608–609, Figs. 21.1 and 21.3)

   1. The Nasopharynx

   2. The Oropharynx

   3. The Laryngopharynx

  C. The Larynx (pp. 609–612, Figs. 21.5 and 21.6)

   1. Voice Production

I. FUNCTIONAL ANATOMY OF THE RESPIRATORY SYSTEM *(continued)*

    2. Sphincter Functions of the Larynx

    3. Innervation of the Larynx

  D. The Trachea (p. 612, Fig. 21.7)

  E. The Bronchi and Subdivisions: The Bronchial Tree (pp. 613–614, Figs. 21.8–21.10)

    1. Bronchi in the Conducting Zone

    2. The Respiratory Zone

  F. The Lungs and Pleurae (pp. 615–621, Figs. 21.11–21.14)

    1. The Pleura

    2. Gross Anatomy of the Lungs

    3. Blood Supply and Innervation of the Lungs

II. *Ventilation (pp. 621–626)*

  A. The Mechanism of Ventilation (pp. 621–623, Fig. 21.15)

    1. Inspiration

    2. Expiration

  B. Neural Control of Ventilation (p. 626, Fig. 21.16)

III. *Disorders of the Respiratory System (pp. 623–628, Fig. 21.17)*

  A. Disorders of the Lower Respiratory Structures

    1. Bronchial Asthma

  B. Chronic Obstructive Pulmonary Disease

    1. Pneumonia

    2. Tuberculosis

    3. Cystic Fibrosis

  C. Disorders of the Upper Respiratory Structures

    1. Epistaxis

    2. Epiglottitis

IV. *The Respiratory System Throughout Life (pp. 628–629, Fig. 21.18)*

Lecture Hints

1. Introduce the respiratory system as the first one of four internal organ systems lined by mucosa and possessing openings to the external surface of the body; the other systems with external openings and mucosae are the digestive, urinary, and reproductive systems.

2. Describe the physical requirements of the respiratory system, include its major functions, and list four major processes that occur to collectively accomplish respiration.

3. Define *pulmonary ventilation* (also simply termed "ventilation" or "breathing").

4. Explain the transport of respiratory gases.

Chapter 21: *The Respiratory System*   253

5. Distinguish clearly between external (*systemic*) respiration and internal (*cellular*) respiration. (Refer to basic texts covering general biology, cell biology, or physiology for details of cellular respiration.)

6. Stress a *summary* of the basics of respiration: ventilation (breathing or pulmonary ventilation), external respiration, and internal (cellular/tissue) respiration.

7. Referring to Figure 21.1, identify the respiratory structures in order, from the nose to the alveoli in the lungs.

8. Distinguish between the *upper* respiratory structures and the *lower* respiratory structures, identifying a landmark separation point.

9. Distinguish the structures of the *conducting zone* from the structures of the *respiratory zone*.

10. Describe the bony framework of the nasal cavity. Refer to Figure 21.2, as well as Figure 7.10, if needed.

11. Describe the basic gross anatomy of the upper respiratory tract. Refer to Figure 21.3.

12. Distinguish between olfactory mucosa and respiratory mucosa, including their locations and functions.

13. Distinguish between *mucous* cells and *serous* cells, explaining their location and the significance of their secretions to the respiratory mucosa.

14. Describe the location of nasal conchae, including meatuses.

15. Describe the functions of nasal conchae during inhalation as well as exhalation, stressing turbulence. Refer to Figure 21.3.

16. Using Figure 7.11, review the locations of the paranasal cavities in the skull, and remind students that the paranasal cavities not only open into the nasal cavity, but they also are lined with the same mucosa and perform similar air-processing functions.

17. Comment on the location of the maxillary paranasal sinus opening; explain the significance of the opening not being optimally positioned for easy drainage into the nasal cavity when the head is upright and the unfortunate drainage of the frontal and ethmoidal sinuses into the maxillary sinus as well.

18. Explain the anatomical location of the pharynx using Figure 21.3, indicating functional areas, and describing the structural differences between the three regions of the pharynx, naming tonsils and openings.

19. Explain the passageways and openings between ears, nose, and throat that invading bacteria may travel. (Refer to the Art Exercises for several examples.)

20. Describe the location and cartilaginous framework of the larynx. Refer to Figure 21.5.

21. Explain the mechanics of swallowing that prevent food from entering the larynx, and why humans are the only animals that routinely choke to death.

22. Describe sound production, also naming several structures that contribute to vocal qualities such as pitch, resonance, loudness, and articulation. Refer to Figure 21.6.

23. Define *Valsalva's maneuver*, explaining how closing of the glottis along with abdominal muscle contraction aid in urination, defecation, and childbirth.

24. Explain the innervation of the larynx, describing the route of the recurrent laryngeal nerves.

25. Describe the anatomical structure and function of the trachea, explaining its relationship to the esophagus and the vertebral column, and explain the significance of the C-shaped rings of cartilage and the trachealis muscle. Refer to Figure 21.7.
26. Explain the organization of the several layers (tunics) of the tracheal wall.
27. Using Figure 21.8, point out the bronchi and other lower respiratory passages.
28. Construct a flowchart diagram showing the air pathway from a primary bronchus to the terminal bronchioles, explaining the transition from gross anatomical structures to microscopic anatomical structures and summarizing changes in bronchial wall tissue composition as the conducting tubes become smaller.
29. Construct a flowchart diagram of the structures of the respiratory zone, explaining gas exchange across the respiratory membrane of the alveoli. Refer to Figure 21.9.
30. Describe unique histological features (such as dust cells) of the alveoli, including surfactant production and function in ventilation. Refer to Figure 21.10.
31. Initially introduce the lungs by describing the structure and function of the pleurae.
32. Distinguish clearly between visceral pleura, parietal pleura, pleural fluid, pleural cavity, and the mediastinum. Refer to Figure 21.11.
33. Describe the gross anatomy of the lungs, distinguishing between the right lung and the left lung, and explain the anatomical relationships of organs in the thoracic cavity. Refer to Figures 21.12–21.14.
34. Describe the texture of the lungs, relating to microscopic air tubes, spaces, and stroma.
35. Summarize the blood supply to lung tissue (bronchial arteries and veins), and review pulmonary circulation and innervation by the pulmonary plexus.
36. Define *ventilation*, and distinguish between inhalation and exhalation, describing the roles of respiratory muscles and lung elasticity in ventilation. Refer to Figure 21.15.
37. Identify the brain's most important respiratory center for neural control of ventilation, including the role of central and peripheral chemoreceptors.
38. Identify major upper and lower respiratory disorders covered in the textbook and discuss at least one common disorder (nosebleed) and one serious disorder (lung cancer).
39. Summarize embryological and fetal development of the respiratory system and comment on normal changes that occur with aging.

Classroom Discussion Topics and Activities

1. Demonstrate the respiratory organs using a model of a human torso and/or a model of the respiratory system.
2. Display preserved human respiratory structures.
3. Demonstrate respiratory structures using a dissected cat or rat.
4. Identify a source for fresh lung tissue and, if possible, obtain a fresh thoracic pluck (lungs plus attached trachea and heart). One suggested source of fresh tissue is from a colleague who sacrifices animals for research. A slaughterhouse also is a possible source for a fresh lamb or calf pluck. Make a small incision in the trachea, insert a straw, pinch off the trachea, and blow through the straw to demonstrate the elasticity and inflation of fresh lung tissue.

An alternative to the straw is compressed air and an attached hose. Students are amazed at the difference between preserved tissue and fresh tissue. Fresh lung tissue may be frozen and thawed several times before it "expires."

5. Demonstrate the cohesive effect that exists between the two pleural layers (parietal pleura lining the thoracic wall and visceral pleura covering the lungs) by placing a drop of water on a glass slide and then covering it with a second glass slide. Demonstrate the slides moving easily from side to side and the difficulty pulling them apart directly.

6. Demonstrate the changing pressures in the thorax as the diaphragm contracts and relaxes, using a "model lung." Use a bell jar with balloon "lungs" attached to a glass "Y" tube inserted into a one-hole stopper in the top of the bell jar. Cover the bottom of the jar with flexible elastic sheeting to simulate the diaphragm.

7. Instruct students to relax, close their eyes, and take a few deep breaths. Ask them to focus on breathing and identify the nostril through which air is flowing faster. Refer to *Advances in Understanding* on textbook p. 607 for up-to-date information on the functions of nasal conchae.

8. Compare the vocal cords to guitar strings to explain pitch and intensity of sound. Ask students to explain why men have deeper voices than boys or women.

9. Enter class one day with a toilet seat (which in itself is quite an attention getter!). Put the toilet seat on a table in front of the students, stand an open book upright on the back part of the ring-like seat, lift up the toilet lid and say, "This lid is the epiglottis." Ask the students to identify the laryngeal structures represented by the open book (thyroid cartilage) and the ring-like seat (cricoid cartilage).

10. Demonstrate the locations of the paranasal sinuses using a midsagittal-cut half skull. Tell students to observe their own frontal paranasal sinuses by shining a flashlight on their faces just below the eyebrows while they are looking in a mirror in a darkened room. Maxillary sinuses also are evident by shining light into the oral cavity and closing the mouth around the flashlight.

11. Obtain animal blood from a veterinary science facility. Using rubber tubing, bubble air through the blood to demonstrate the color change that occurs when hemoglobin is well oxygenated.

12. Display visual aids comparing healthy lung tissue and cancerous or emphysematous lung tissue, and discuss with the class how an individual who has never smoked can get lung cancer.

13. Ask students why respiratory infections are more common than infections of most other organ systems.

14. Discuss with students how the pseudostratified ciliated columnar epithelium in the respiratory tract is adapted for its function of filtering air and explore the effects of nicotine from cigarette smoke on the lining of the respiratory tract.

15. Instruct students to prepare an answer for the following question: Why is it desirable (and smart) to practice at high altitudes for a few weeks before an athletic event held in the high mesa of Mexico City?

16. Demonstrate how to perform the Heimlich maneuver to alleviate choking.

17. Invite a health professional to class to demonstrate and discuss artificial respiration (mouth-to-mouth/nose resuscitation). Consider situations when this procedure is more desirable than the Heimlich maneuver.

18. Ask students to explain what fills the space when a lung is removed surgically.

Clinical Questions

1. Why do asthmatic people have difficulty breathing? How does epinephrine provide relief?

   Answer: During an asthma attack, the smooth muscles of the walls of the bronchioles contract, markedly narrowing the air channels. Since this is an exaggerated parasympathetic response, it can be countered by the sympathetic neurotransmitter epinephrine, which stimulates the bronchi to dilate.

2. Yvonne had been suffering through a severe cold and was complaining of a frontal headache and a dull, aching pain at the side of her face. What regions have become sites of secondary infection following respiratory infection of Yvonne's nasal cavity?

   Answer: Following nasal infection, the paranasal sinuses can become infected. Yvonne's frontal and maxillary sinuses were hurting.

3. Mr. Rowel has tuberculosis of the right lung. In an effort to rest his lung and promote recovery, the doctor injects a measured amount of air into the pleural cavity, a procedure called "artificial pneumothorax." How does this rest the lung? Is it permanent? Explain.

   Answer: In artificial pneumothorax, the pressure of the air in the pleural cavity causes the lung to collapse, making it unable to expand and recoil, so its ventilatory movements cease. No longer subjected to the stresses of expansion and contraction, the lung can rest and recover. The pneumothorax is not permanent because air can be drawn out of the pleural cavity with chest tubes, permitting the lung to reinflate and resume its normal function.

4. Alvin, a smoker, sees his doctor because he has a persistent cough and becomes short of breath after very little exertion. He has a barrel chest and a red face, and he explains that it is difficult for him to exhale but not to inhale. What diagnosis will the doctor make?

   Answer: Alvin has the symptoms of emphysema.

5. Mr. Rasputin agitated a bee's nest while making repairs on his roof. As expected, he promptly was stung several times. Since he knew he was allergic to bee stings, he rushed to the hospital. While waiting, he went into a state of shock and had extreme difficulty breathing. Examination showed his larynx to be edematous and a tracheotomy was performed. Why is edema of the larynx likely to obstruct the airway? What is a tracheotomy, and what purpose does it serve? Why will Mr. Rasputin remain in the hospital for a while?

   Answer: The larynx functions to provide an open airway to the trachea and lungs. Edematous swelling of the mucosa of the larynx will close the airway, blocking all air entering the trachea. Tracheotomy is a surgical incision into the trachea through the anterior neck. It allows air to reach the lungs when the larynx is blocked. Mr. Rasputin will have to remain in the hospital until the swelling subsides and the larynx once again becomes patent, for a tracheotomy is only a temporary measure.

ART RESOURCES
Transparency List

Figure 21.1 Organs of the respiratory system.

Figure 21.2 Skeletal framework of the external nose.

Figure 21.3   Basic anatomy of the upper respiratory tract.

Figure 21.5   Anatomy of the larynx.

Figure 21.6   Movements of the vocal cords.

Figure 21.8   Bronchi and other lower respiratory passages.

Figure 21.9   Structures of the respiratory zone.

Figure 21.10 Anatomy of the alveoli and the respiratory membrane.

Figure 21.11 Diagram of the pleurae and pleural cavities.

Figure 21.12 Anatomical relationships of organs in the thoracic cavity.

Figure 21.14 Bronchopulmonary segments.

Figure 21.16 Location of the peripheral chemoreceptors in the carotid and aortic bodies.

Teaching with Art

Figure 21.3   Basic anatomy of the upper respiratory tract.

Textbook p. 606; transparencies; Digital Archive CD-ROM.

Checklist of Key Points in the Figure

- Identify conducting zone structures, distinguishing between upper respiratory structures and lower respiratory structures, explaining their functions, and stressing differences between the pharynx and larynx.
- Distinguish between the external nose and internal nasal cavity.
- Point out precise locations of tonsils forming a ring of protection for the pharynx entrance, reminding students of their immune system function.
- Distinguish between the hard palate and soft palate.
- Discuss the mechanics of preventing food from entering the trachea during swallowing.
- Explain the anatomy of the larynx, and point out the structures that aid in sound production.
- Compare the structure of the trachea to the esophagus.
- Distinguish between respiratory mucosa and olfactory mucosa, explaining that different types of epithelium are located along the respiratory tract.

Common Conceptual Difficulties Interpreting the Art

- Remind students that some respiratory tract openings are very evident, while others are not, such as those of the paranasal sinuses.
- Clearly distinguish between the external nares and internal nares (choanae).
- Clearly distinguish between choanae and fauces.
- Identify each region of the pharynx, explaining where *and how* air and food share a common passageway.
- Continue to reinforce the concept of structures functioning as *organs*.

Art Exercises

Provide students with several unlabeled copies of the figure. Instruct students to do the following exercises:

1. Epithelium Exercise: Color code the regions of different types of epithelium in the respiratory mucosa lining the structures in the figure. Provide students with the names of different types of epithelium and color assignments (or instruct students to identify epithelial types on their own as part of the exercise). Ideally, students will identify the following:

    a. Vestibule of the nasal cavity (lined with skin)—keratinized stratified squamous epithelium of the epidermis

    b. Roof of the nasal cavity (and covering of the superior nasal conchae and the superior part of the nasal septum)—specialized olfactory epithelium (composed of pseudostratified columnar epithelium)

    c. Rest of the nasal cavity—pseudostratified ciliated columnar epithelium

    d. Paranasal sinuses—pseudostratified ciliated columnar epithelium

    e. Nasopharynx—pseudostratified ciliated columnar epithelium

    f. Oropharynx—stratified squamous epithelium

    g. Laryngopharynx—stratified squamous epithelium

    h. Larynx, superior to the vocal folds (true vocal cords)—stratified squamous epithelium

    i. Larynx, inferior to vocal folds—pseudostratified ciliated columnar epithelium

    j. Trachea—pseudostratified ciliated columnar epithelium

2. Openings Exercise: Using an unlabeled copy of the figure, instruct students to identify all openings and passageways that provide a method of communication from the nasal cavity and the pharynx to some other place in the body. Explain to students that some of the openings are obvious, such as the opening of the auditory tube, and others are not obvious, such as those of the paranasal sinuses. Ideally, students will identify the following openings: perforations of the cribriform plate of the ethmoid, all of the paranasal sinuses, the opening of the nasolacrimal duct, internal nares (choanae), external nares (nostrils), the pharyngotympanic tube, fauces, the laryngeal entrance, and the esophageal entrance.

3. Passageway Exercise: Using an unlabeled copy of the figure, instruct students to trace the movement of air from the nostrils to the larynx, labeling the structures air passes through.

Critical Reasoning

1. Instruct students to look at their colored figure of the Epithelium Exercise (1) and determine the direction the cilia propel dusty mucus in the following regions:

    a. Nasopharynx

       Answer: Mucus is propelled downward.

    b. Larynx, inferior to the vocal folds

       Answer: The power stroke of cilia is directed upward, toward the pharynx.

2. Instruct students to look at their labeled figure of the Openings Exercise (2) and to construct a flowchart identifying all possible channels of communication for disease organisms from the nasal cavity to other places in the body.

Answer: *nasal cavity → cranial cavity*

    nasal cavity → paranasal sinuses

    nasal cavity → nasolacrimal duct → orbit

    nasal cavity → pharynx → oral cavity

    nasal cavity → nasopharynx → middle ear

    nasal cavity → pharynx → larynx → (lungs)

    nasal cavity → pharynx → esophagus → (digestive tract)

3. Referring students to the labeled Passageway Exercise (3), ask why it is possible for a feeding tube inserted into a patient's nostril to end up in the stomach.

    Answer: The laryngopharynx is a common passageway for food and air with an opening into the esophagus, and when the patient swallows the tube during insertion, it is directed into the esophagus (not the larynx) and ultimately enters the stomach.

SUPPLEMENTAL COURSE MATERIALS
Library Research Topics

1. Research and list the respiratory diseases caused by inhalation of toxic particles associated with specific occupations such as coal mining and working in an asbestos factory.
2. Research the incidence of cancer in smokers versus nonsmokers, in people working in respiratory-hazard areas versus those working in safe respiratory areas.
3. Research the current status of heart-lung transplants, and the circumstances under which such a transplant is possible.
4. Research the causes, known and supposed, of sudden infant death syndrome.
5. What treatments are used to keep infants with respiratory distress syndrome alive?

Audiovisual Aids/Computer Software

See Preface of the Instructor's Guide for Key to Audiovisual Distributors

Videotapes
1. *The Art of Breathing* (FHS, 29 min., 1995)
2. *Asthma: In Search of Answers* (FHS, 45 min.)
3. *The Body Atlas: Breath of Life* (NIMCO, 30 min., 1994)
4. *Breathing* (*New Living Body Series*) (FHS, 20 min., 1995)
5. *Breath of Life* (*Body Atlas Series*) (CAP/HCA, 30 min., 1994)
6. *The Common Cold* (FHS, 28 min., 1990)
7. *Cystic Fibrosis* (FHS, 26 min., 1990)
8. *Human Biology* (FHS, 38 min.)
9. *The Human Body: Respiratory System* (Ward's, 15 min.)
10. *The Human Body: Respiratory System* (COR, 14 min., 1993)
11. *The Human Body Series: Respiration* (NIMCO, 28 min., 1993)

12. *The Human Respiratory System* (BC, 25 min., 1998)
13. *The Living Body: Breath of Life* (FHS, VHS, or BETA, 26 min., C). Explains why the body needs regular supplies of air and how it gets them. The camera follows the process of breathing through the ultrathin membrane of the lungs into the blood, and considers the control of ventilation.
14. *Lung Action and Function* (Ward's, 8 min.)
15. *Lungs* (Revised) (AIMS, 10 min.)
16. *The New Living Body: Breathing* (FHS, 20 min., 1995)
17. *Outbreak: Diagnosing Respiratory Tract Infection* (FHS, 12 min., 1998)
18. *Respiration* (*Human Body Live Action Video Series*) (CAP, 1993, 29 min.)
19. *Respiration* (FHS, 15 min., 1997)
20. *Respiration* (IM, 30 min., 1997)
21. *The Respiratory System:* (*Anatomy and Physiology Series*) (CAP/HCA, 25 min.)
22. *The Respiratory System* (NIMCO, 25 min.)
23. *Respiratory System: Intake and Exhaust* (FHS, 25 min.)
24. *Tuberculosis: Its Origins and Effects* (FHS, 17 min., 1998)
25. *Up In Smoke: How Smoking Affects Your Health* (GA, 38 min., 1990)

Computer Software
1. *The Anatomy Project: The Respiratory Tract* (NCHCA/NIMCO, 1998)
2. *Body Language: Study of Human Anatomy, Respiratory System* (PLP, CH-182009, Apple; CH-182008, IBM)
3. *Body Systems: Interactive Physical Education* (HCA, 1995, Disk for Mac/Win)
4. *Circulation and Respiration* (Queue, Disk for Apple II/Mac/IBM)
5. *Dynamics of the Human Respiratory System* (EI, Apple II, IBM, 1988). Contains a straightforward, concise text with engaging animated graphics, sound effects, and an interactive quiz to instruct and challenge.
6. *The Human Body, Part I* (CL, Disk for Apple II/Mac/IBM)
7. *The Human Systems: Series 3. The Respiratory, Excretory, and Reproductive Systems* (PLP, CH-140220, Apple)
8. *Interactive Physiology: Respiratory System* (ADAM/BC, 1997, Mac/Win)
9. *The Living Body* (Queue, Mac/Win)
10. *LOGAL Biology Simulations: Respiratory System* (EI)
11. *Respiratory Diseases and Disorders* (PLP, Apple). Covers prevention, symptoms, and treatment of bronchitis, cystic fibrosis, emphysema, tuberculosis, pneumonia, asthma, and shortness of breath.
12. *Respiratory System* (IM, 1997, Mac/Win)
13. *Respiratory System* (*Biology Explorer Series*) (CL/LOG, Mac/Win)
14. *Respiratory System* (FREY/NIMCO, 1996)

Slides

1. *Respiration* (EI, 71 Slides)
2. *Respiratory System and Its Function* (EI, Slides, and Filmstrips). The respiratory tree is viewed macroscopically and microscopically. Augmented with a discussion of respiratory gases and changes in thoracic pressure.
3. *Visual Approach to Histology: Respiratory System* (FAD, 11 Slides)

Suggested Readings

Bartecchi, C., et al. The global tobacco epidemic. *Scientific American* (May 1995): 44.

Beard, J. How lungfuls of liquid can save a tiny life. *New Scientist* (March 19, 1994): 19.

Cormack, D.H. *Ham's Histology*. 9th ed. Philadelphia: J.B. Lippincott, 1987, Chapter 20.

Dwyer, T., et al. The contribution of changes in the prevalence of prone sleeping position to the decline in sudden infant death syndrome in Tasmania. *Journal of the American Medical Association* 273 (March 8, 1995): 783.

Fackelmann, K. Respiratory rescue: Taking aim at allergy's drip and asthma's wheeze. *Science News* 139 (March 2, 1991): 138–139.

Fackelmann, K. Two new wrinkles for cigarette smokers. *Science News* 139 (May 18, 1991): 309.

Fawcett, D.W. *A Textbook of Histology*. 12th ed. New York: Chapman & Hall, 1994, Chapter 29.

Junqueira, L.C., et al. *Basic Histology*. 6th ed. San Mateo, California: Appleton and Lange, 1989, Chapter 17.

Mestel, R. The secret life of the nose. *New Scientist Supplement* (April 17, 1993): 13.

Moore, K.L. *Clinically Oriented Anatomy*. 3rd ed. Baltimore: Williams and Wilkins, 1992.

Palca, J. The promise of a cure. (An article about cystic fibrosis.) *Discover* (June 1994): 77–86.

Palta, M., et al. A population study: Mortality and morbidity after availability of surfactant therapy. *Archives of Pediatrics and Adolescent Medicine* 148 (December 1994): 1295–1301.

Robbins, S.L., and V. Kumar. *Basic Pathology*. 4th ed. Philadelphia: W.B. Saunders, 1987, pp. 446–451.

Roberts, L. Cystic fibrosis corrected in lab. *Science* (September 28, 1990): 1503.

Romanes, G.J. *Cunningham's Textbook of Anatomy*. 11th ed. London: Oxford University Press, 1972, pp. 469–501.

Sarseny, S. Respiratory distress. *RN* (April 1988): 47.

Undem, B. Neural-immunologic interactions in asthma. *Hospital Practice* (February 15, 1994): 59–70.

Waldron, B. Tyranny and cruelty. (An article about asthma.) *Discover* (August 1993): 90–92.

Weiss, R. TB trouble: Tuberculosis is on the rise again. *Science News* 133 (February 1988): 92.

Weiss, R. Cystic fibrosis treatments promising. *Science News* 139 (March 2, 1991): 132.

Williams, P.L., et al. *Gray's Anatomy*. 37th ed. New York: Churchill Livingstone, 1989, pp. 1248–1285.

ANSWERS TO TEXTBOOK QUESTIONS

Answers to multiple-choice and matching questions 1–10 are located in Appendix B of the textbook.

Short Answer and Essay Questions

11. Expired air travels from an alveolus in an alveolar sac, alveolar duct, or respiratory bronchiole to a terminal bronchiole, larger bronchioles, many orders of bronchi, trachea, larynx, pharynx (laryngopharynx, oropharynx, nasopharynx), choanae, nasal cavity, and external nares. The first four of these structures, which have alveoli, are in the respiratory zone (alveolus, alveolar sac, alveolar duct, respiratory bronchiole); all the other, larger structures are in the conducting zone.

12. All these cilia propel sheets of mucus that trap dust from the inhaled air. The beat directions propel the mucus down to the pharynx from upper respiratory passages and up to the pharynx from lower respiratory passages. In both cases, this dusty mucus is swallowed and disposed of through the digestive tract.

13. These elastin fibers are largely responsible for quiet expiration. At the end of inhalation, the recoil of the elastin fibers helps decrease the volume of the lungs and thorax. This raises the pressure within the lungs, and air moves along its pressure gradient out of the lungs (= expiration).

14. (a) The palatine tonsils occupy the fauces. (b) Yes, the lingual tonsil and the superior part of the epiglottis lie near one another on the posterior surface of the tongue. (see Figure 21.3)

15. (a) The *hilus* of the lung is the region of the lung's medial surface through which structures enter and leave the lung. These structures themselves form the *root* of the lung. The main structures of the root are the pulmonary artery, pulmonary veins, and primary bronchus. In essence, the root passes through the hilus. (b) The visceral pleura and the parietal pleura are both serous membranes and are continuous with one another. The visceral pleura covers the lung, whereas the parietal pleura covers the inner surface of the thoracic wall, superior surface of the diaphragm, and lateral surface of the mediastinum. That is, the parietal pleura lines the outer aspect of the pleural cavity. (see Figure 21.14)

16. A *choana* is an internal nostril, an opening between nasal cavity and nasopharynx. A *concha* is mucosa-covered, scroll-shaped bone that projects into the nasal cavity. The *carina* is a mucosa-covered ridge on the last tracheal cartilage that is sensitive to irritation.

17. Men have longer vocal cords, which naturally produce a lower pitch when they vibrate than do the shorter vocal cords of females and boys. The same principle is illustrated by the longer versus shorter strings of a musical harp.

18. The picture should resemble that in Figure 21.12a and should show the following. *Right lung*: upper, middle, and lower lobes; horizontal and oblique fissures. *Left lung*: upper and lower lobes; oblique fissure and cardiac notch.

19. This epithelium has goblet cells that secrete a thin layer of mucus onto the epithelial surface. The mucus traps dust and other small particles from the inhaled air. Many of the epithelial cells are ciliated and the cilia propel the dust-filled mucus sheet to the pharynx for swallowing.

20. Dust cells are macrophages that phagocytize the finest suspended particles in the inhaled air.

Critical Reasoning and Clinical Applications Questions

1. (a) Normally, during swallowing, the soft palate reflects superiorly to seal the nasopharynx and prevent food or drink from entering the nasal cavity. During giggling, however, this sealing mechanism sometimes fails to operate (because giggling demands that air be forced out the nostrils), and swallowed fluids may enter the nasal cavity and then exit through the nostrils. (b) Even though standing on his head, the boy made certain that he swallowed carefully, so that his soft palate did correctly seal the entrance to his nasal cavity. Then, his swallowing muscles directed the milk through his esophagus to the stomach, against gravity.

2. Adjacent bronchopulmonary segments are separated from one another by partitions of dense connective tissue, which no major vessels cross. Therefore, it is possible for a surgeon to dissect adjacent segments away from one another. The only vessels that had to be cauterized were the few main vessels to each bronchopulmonary segment.

3. The child put the safety pin in his mouth and "inhaled" it. Such objects often lodge in the right primary bronchus because it is wider, shorter, and more vertical than the left primary bronchus.

4. (a) The piercing wound let outside air enter the pleural cavity. This air broke the seal of pleural fluid that held the lung to the thoracic wall, allowing the elastic lung to collapse like a deflating balloon. (b) The right and left pleural cavities are completely separated from one another by the mediastinum. Thus, air entering the left pleural cavity will not enter the right pleural cavity.

5. (a) The probable reason that respiration stopped is that damage to the spinal cord at the level of vertebra C2 interrupted the passage of nerve signals from the brain-stem respiratory centers to the motor neurons of the phrenic nerve (C3–C5). (A disrupted pulse rate might suggest damage to cardiac centers in the reticular formation of the medulla—which suggests direct damage to nearby medullary respiratory centers.) (b) The man is cyanotic because he stopped breathing. Cyanosis is a bluing of the skin due to lack of oxygen in the blood and a lack of oxygen going to the tissues of the body.

6. During the surgery, the left recurrent laryngeal nerve (which supplies some laryngeal muscles) had been cut accidentally, probably at the arch of the aorta where it lies close to the ductus arteriosus.

SUPPLEMENTAL STUDENT MATERIALS TO HUMAN ANATOMY, THIRD EDITION
Chapter 21: The Respiratory System

To the Student
The respiratory system is responsible for delivery of air to your lungs where gas exchange occurs that ensures your survival. Within lung tissue, oxygen is picked up by the bloodstream and the waste product, carbon dioxide, is removed from the bloodstream for disposal via the same air tubes. This life-sustaining interaction between the cardiovascular system and the respiratory system provides the oxygen needed by every cell for its survival. If your cells die, tissues die, and ultimately you "suffocate" in a matter of minutes if cells are deprived of oxygen. The use of oxygen by cells for obtaining energy from food molecules such as glucose is termed cellular respiration, and this is a completely different topic from systemic respiration covered in this chapter. Do not confuse the two concepts. This chapter has several key concepts and focal points explaining how the respiratory system interacts with other organ systems in your body, not just the cardiovascular system. Additionally, the mucosal lining of the respiratory system provides an excellent avenue for disease organisms to travel along, and the many openings and passageways of the nasal cavity to other parts of the body provide disease organisms with a ready-made entry to those regions.

Step 1: Describe the functional anatomy of the principal organs of the respiratory system.
- [ ] For each of the following principal organs of the respiratory system, provide a general anatomical description and note any distinctive features: nose, pharynx, larynx, trachea, bronchial tree, alveoli, lungs, and pleurae.
- [ ] Describe the function of each of the listed principal organs of the respiratory system.
- [ ] Distinguish between the structures of the conducting zone and the structures of the respiratory zone.

Step 2: Describe the mucosa of the respiratory tract.
- [ ] Identify the lining of the respiratory tract, name the major type of epithelium associated with the tract, discuss its functions, and define *goblet cells*.
- [ ] Distinguish between respiratory mucosa and olfactory mucosa.

Step 3: Describe the nose and nasal cavity.
- [ ] Describe the bony framework of the nasal cavity, including functions of conchae.
- [ ] Discuss locations and functions of the paranasal sinuses.
- [ ] Define and distinguish between *choanae* and *fauces*.

Step 4: Describe the pharynx, larynx, and trachea.
- [ ] Describe the structure and function of the pharynx, including regions, openings, tonsils, and location.
- [ ] Describe the structure and function of the larynx, including cartilages, sound (voice) production, sphincter functions, and innervation.
- [ ] Explain the mechanics of swallowing and how entry of food into the nasopharynx and larynx is prevented.

- ☐ Relate the sphincter functions of the larynx, i.e., closing of the glottis and abdominal muscle contractions (Valsalva's maneuver), to functions of the urinary, digestive, and reproductive systems.
- ☐ Describe the structure and function of the trachea, including its anatomical relationship to the esophagus and vertebral column, trachealis muscle, and wall tunics.
- ☐ Define *carina* (and be careful not to confuse it with concha or choana).

Step 5: Describe the bronchial tree.
- ☐ Discuss the structure and function of the bronchial tree, beginning with primary bronchi and ending with terminal bronchioles, distinguishing between bronchi in the conducting zone and bronchi in the respiratory zone.
- ☐ Describe the anatomy of the alveoli, and discuss gas exchange, the blood-air barrier, and other significant features.
- ☐ List tissue changes that occur in the bronchial wall as air tubes progressively become smaller and smaller.

Step 6: Describe the lungs and pleurae.
- ☐ Review the difference between serous membrane and mucous membrane.
- ☐ Distinguish between visceral pleura and parietal pleura, pleural cavity, and pleural fluid and draw and label a diagram of these structures in the thoracic cavity.
- ☐ Draw a right lung and a left lung, labeling gross anatomical features.
- ☐ Define *mediastinum* and explain the anatomical relationships of organs in the thoracic cavity.
- ☐ Review pulmonary circulation, and describe blood supply to the lung tissue itself.
- ☐ Name the plexus of innervation to the lungs.

Step 7: Explain the mechanism of ventilation (breathing).
- ☐ Describe the mechanical aspects of inspiration and expiration, summarizing changes in the thoracic volume, the action of the diaphragm, and the action of intercostal muscles.
- ☐ Explain why surface tension of the alveolar fluid does not collapse the microscopic alveoli after each breath. (Hint: Do you remember the role of surfactant?)
- ☐ Explain the neural control of ventilation, including the location of the respiratory center in the brain and the types of monitoring chemoreceptors.

Step 8: Read about the major disorders of the respiratory system covered in your textbook, study in detail disorders assigned by your instructor, and consider changes in the respiratory system throughout life.
- ☐ Read this chapter's *A Closer Look: Lung Cancer: The Facts Behind the Smoke Screen*.
- ☐ Describe the symptoms and causes of bronchial asthma.
- ☐ Describe the symptoms and causes of cystic fibrosis.
- ☐ Explain the significance of a nosebleed from the posterior nasal cavity as opposed to a nosebleed from the anterior part of the nasal cavity.
- ☐ Summarize prenatal, postnatal, and aging changes that occur in the respiratory system.

CHAPTER 22
The Digestive System

LECTURE AND DEMONSTRATION
Student Objectives

1. Describe the overall function of the digestive system, and differentiate the alimentary canal from the accessory digestive organs.
2. List the major processes that occur during digestion.
3. Draw the major subdivisions of the anterior abdominal wall.
4. Explain the location and function of the peritoneum and peritoneal cavity. Define *mesentery*.
5. Describe the four layers of the wall of the alimentary canal.
6. Describe the location, gross and microscopic anatomy, and basic functions of the mouth and teeth, pharynx, esophagus, stomach, small intestine, and large intestine.
7. Describe the gross and microscopic anatomy of the liver, gallbladder, and pancreas.
8. Name the mesenteries associated with the abdominal digestive organs.
9. Describe some abnormalities of the digestive organs.
10. Explain how the digestive organs develop in the embryo, and define the *foregut, midgut,* and *hindgut*.

Suggested Lecture Outline

I. **Overview of the Digestive System (pp. 634–637, Fig. 22.1)**

    A. Digestive Processes (pp. 635–636, Figs. 22.2 and 22.3)

    B. Abdominal Regions and Quadrants (p. 637, Fig. 22.4)

II. **Anatomy of the Digestive System (pp. 637–666)**

    A. The Peritoneal Cavity and Peritoneum (pp. 637–638, Fig. 22.5)

    B. Histology of the Alimentary Canal Wall (pp. 638–640, Fig. 22.6)

        1. The Mucosa

        2. The Submucosa

        3. The Muscularis Externa

        4. The Serosa

        5. Nerve Plexuses

II. ANATOMY OF THE DIGESTIVE SYSTEM *(continued)*

    C. The Mouth and Associated Organs (pp. 640–645, Figs. 22.7–22.12)

        1. The Mouth

        2. The Tongue

        3. The Salivary Glands

        4. The Teeth

    D. The Pharynx (pp. 645–646, Fig. 22.7)

    E. The Esophagus (p. 646, Figs. 22.1 and 22.13)

        1. Gross Anatomy

        2. Microscopic Anatomy

    F. The Stomach (pp. 646–651, Figs. 22.14 and 22.15)

        1. Gross Anatomy

        2. Microscopic Anatomy

    G. The Small Intestine (pp. 652–654, Figs. 22.16–22.17)

        1. Gross Anatomy

        2. Microscopic Anatomy

    H. The Large Intestine (pp. 654–658, Figs. 22.18 and 22.19)

        1. Gross Anatomy

        2. Defecation

        3. Microscopic Anatomy

    I. The Liver (pp. 658–662, Figs. 22.20–22.22)

        1. Gross Anatomy

        2. Microscopic Anatomy

    J. The Gallbladder (p. 662, Figs. 22.16 and 22.21)

    K. The Pancreas (p. 663, Figs. 22.23–22.25)

    L. Mesenteries (pp. 663–666, Fig. 22.26)

III. *Disorders of the Digestive System (pp. 666–667)*

    A. Intestinal Obstruction

    B. Inflammatory Bowel Disease

    C. Viral Hepatitis

    D. Cystic Fibrosis and the Pancreas

IV. *The Digestive System Throughout Life (pp. 667–668)*

    A. Embryonic Development (pp. 667–668, Fig. 22.27)

    B. The Digestive System in Later Life (p. 668)

Lecture Hints

1. Define *alimentary canal* (also called *gastrointestinal tract*), naming its organs and distinguishing it from the accessory digestive organs. Refer to Figure 22.1.
2. Explain why the alimentary canal is shorter in a living person as opposed to the alimentary canal in a cadaver.
3. Discuss the concept that food inside the alimentary canal is technically *outside* the body because the mouth and anus both open to the external environment.
4. Using Figure 22.2, present a schematic summary and discussion of the six essential food-processing activities that occur during digestion: ingestion, propulsion, mechanical digestion, chemical digestion, absorption, and defecation.
5. Define and distinguish between *peristalsis* and *segmentation*. Refer to Figure 22.2.
6. Draw the major subdivisions of the anterior abdominal wall and locate the abdominopelvic organs with reference to anterior abdominal wall regions and quadrants. Refer to Figure 22.4.
7. Relate the digestive organs in the abdominopelvic cavity to the *peritoneum* and *peritoneal cavity*, including a general review of serous membranes and a description of the location and function of the peritoneum.
8. Distinguish between the visceral peritoneum and parietal peritoneum, explaining that the peritoneal cavity is the fluid-filled, slit-like (and potential) space between the two. Refer to Figure 22.5.
9. Define and describe *mesentery*, including functions.
10. Distinguish between retroperitoneal organs and intraperitoneal organs, giving several examples.
11. Describe the basic arrangement of layers of the alimentary canal wall: mucosa, submucosa, muscularis externa, and serosa (visceral peritoneum), or adventitia.
12. Describe the histological, structural, and functional features of the layers of the alimentary canal wall. Refer to Figure 22.6.
13. Identify nerve plexuses, describe innervation of the alimentary canal (including its enteric system), and compare the effects of sympathetic and parasympathetic fibers.
14. Describe the location; histology; gross anatomy; and functions of the mouth, tongue, salivary glands, and teeth. Refer to Figures 22.7–22.11.
15. Point out that tooth enamel is the hardest substance in the body, explain caries, and ask students if they recall the type of joint that exists between a tooth and its socket.
16. Describe the location; gross anatomy; microscopic anatomy; and functions of the pharynx, esophagus, stomach, small intestine, and large intestine. Refer to Figures 22.12–22.19.
17. Review the mechanics of swallowing, reminding students that the tongue is skeletal muscle and the action is voluntary.
18. Explain that the esophagus has an adventitia rather than a serosa.
19. Explain why the stomach does not digest itself.
20. Stress the duodenum as the site where the bile duct and the main pancreatic duct empty their contents.

21. Stress features of the small intestine that increase its surface area, reminding students of the importance of the concept of surface area for processes such as absorption or gas exchange.
22. Emphasize structural modifications in each area of the GI tract that permit optimum digestion and absorption.
23. Describe the location; gross anatomy; microscopic anatomy; and functions of the liver, gallbladder, and pancreas. Refer to Figures 22.20–22.25.
24. Trace the flow of bile through the system of ducts ultimately into the duodenum, explaining the role it plays in the digestive process.
25. Present an overall summary statement about secretions made in various parts of the alimentary canal, the salivary glands, the liver, and pancreas as derivatives from blood plasma, emphasizing the role of the large intestine in reabsorption of water and the consequences of diarrhea.
26. Remind students that the liver receives blood from two sources and review the blood supply to the liver, if needed.
27. List and describe the mesenteries associated with the abdominal digestive organs, explaining why the greater omentum is aptly referred to as a "fatty apron." Refer to Figure 22.26.
28. Caution students that some mesenteries are termed "ligaments" and not to confuse that usage with fibrous ligaments that connect bone to bone.
29. Discuss at least one or more of the disorders of the digestive system: intestinal obstruction, inflammatory bowel disease, viral hepatitis, or the effects of cystic fibrosis on the pancreas.
30. Describe the embryonic development of the digestive system and define *foregut*, *midgut*, and *hindgut*. Refer to Figure 22.27.

Classroom Discussion Topics and Activities

1. Use a dissectible model of a human torso to exhibit the digestive organs.
2. Demonstrate the digestive organs of a dissected cat or rat, or display actual human specimens, if available. Displaying a preserved cat is an excellent way to demonstrate mesenteries, as well. (Students gain a greater appreciation of "gross" in gross anatomy when viewing the greater omentum and realizing they have one, too.)
3. Instruct students to touch the lateral folds of tissue immediately posterior to their lower teeth with their tongue. Ask them to identify the salivary ducts they are touching. *(Answer: Ducts of the submandibular salivary glands.)*
4. Display a human skull to demonstrate different tooth shapes, types, and numbers.
5. Demonstrate the emulsifying action of bile. Mix oil and water together and allow the layers to separate. Add bile salts and shake vigorously, explaining the dispersal of oil into hundreds of tiny fatty spheres because of the action of bile salts.
6. When describing the mechanics of swallowing, instruct students to touch their larynx and feel it rise when they swallow.
7. Obtain gallstones from a surgeon and show them to the class, explaining how they form and why they are very painful.
8. Use a long, not quite fully blown-up balloon to demonstrate peristalsis and provide a stethoscope permitting students to listen to sounds of digestive peristalsis.

9. Use a vacuum-cleaner hose to demonstrate gut rotation in the embryo.
10. Use a thick paperback book, opened 360 degrees so that its pages radiate out from its spine, as a model of a classic liver lobule.
11. Bring a washcloth to class and use its nap to model intestinal villi.
12. To help students remember the important structures on the visceral surface of the liver, point out a large "H" on that surface. The left limb of that H is formed by the liver's fissure, the crossbar of the H by the porta hepatis, and the right limb by the inferior vena cava superiorly and the gallbladder inferiorly. (Reinforcement of the "H" for "hepatic" also prevents careless confusion of terms hepatic and renal.)
13. Survey your class, asking students who have had their wisdom teeth removed to raise their hands. (In the textbook authors' classes, the vast majority had undergone this operation.)
14. Discuss why it is necessary for someone with ulcer-like symptoms to consult a physician rather than just using antacids.
15. Discuss the reasons why elderly people should be checked for colorectal cancer.
16. Ask students why rabbits make "pellets" and people don't. (A haustrum in rabbits is capable of setting up churning action independently of neighboring haustra. The human intestine does not have this capability.)
17. Ask students if survival without a stomach is possible. It is. Note that vitamin B production depends on the secretion of a special polypeptide by the stomach, and B_{12} is needed for maturation of red blood cells, so patients with gastrectomies may develop pernicious anemia.

Clinical Questions

1. Colleen had a growth in her left parotid gland, which her physician feared might be cancerous. Surgery was done to remove the growth, which turned out to be only solidified saliva that had blocked some ducts within the parotid. After the operation, some of the left side of Colleen's face was paralyzed. Why is it difficult to avoid paralyzing the face in this kind of operation?

   Answer: The facial nerve, which innervates the muscles of facial expression, radiates within the substance of the parotid gland. Some branches of this nerve are inevitably cut when surgery is performed on this gland.

2. An attorney with a severe gastric ulcer started complaining of back pain. The physician discovered that the back pain occurred because the pancreas was now damaged. How could a perforating gastric ulcer damage the pancreas?

   Answer: The ulcer perforated through the posterior wall of the stomach, leaking stomach acids and pepsin onto the pancreas. These caustic fluids damaged the pancreas.

3. What is a hiatal hernia? What are its causes and symptoms?

   Answer: A hiatal hernia is a structural abnormality in which the fundus of the stomach protrudes superiorly into the thorax through the esophageal hiatus of the diaphragm. Gastric juices regurgitate superiorly into the esophagus. Symptoms include heartburn, inflammation of the esophagus, or esophageal ulcers.

4. A 53-year-old woman enters the emergency room complaining of severe pain in her left iliac region. She claims previous episodes (but this one is the most painful) and says that the con-

dition is worst when she is constipated and is relieved by defecation. A large tender mass is palpated in the left iliac fossa, and a barium study reveals a large number of diverticula in her descending and sigmoid colon. What are diverticula, and what is believed to promote their formation? Does this woman have diverticulitis or diverticulosis? Explain.

Answer: Diverticula are small herniations of the mucosa through the colon wall, a condition called diverticulosis. They are believed to form when the diet lacks bulk and the volume of residue in the colon is small. The colon narrows and contractions of its circular muscle become more powerful, increasing the pressure on its walls and inducing the herniations. Diverticulitis is a condition in which the diverticula become infected and inflamed. The great severity of her pain suggests that the woman's diverticulosis has developed into diverticulitis.

5. Trish goes to the emergency room with the following symptoms: severe pain in the umbilical region, loss of appetite, nausea, and vomiting. While she is waiting to see a doctor, the pain moves to her lower right abdominal quadrant. What is her probable condition?

Answer: Trish probably has appendicitis, although this condition is notoriously difficult to diagnose without more extensive testing. The treatment for appendicitis is surgical removal of the appendix.

6. The health department closed a restaurant because, for the second time in 3 years, over a dozen customers who ate there developed hepatitis. How did this happen?

Answer: Restaurants occasionally have trouble with hepatitis when an infected employee transmits it to the food, via a fecal route. This occurs when the employee fails to thoroughly clean hands after using the washroom.

ART RESOURCES
Transparency List

Figure 22.1	The alimentary canal and the accessory digestive organs.
Figure 22.2	Schematic summary of digestive processes.
Figure 22.3	Peristalsis and segmentation.
Figure 22.5	The peritoneum and peritoneal cavity.
Figure 22.6	Histological layers of the alimentary canal.
Figure 22.7	Anatomy of the mouth.
Figure 22.10	The extrinsic salivary glands.
Figure 22.11	Human deciduous and permanent teeth.
Figure 22.12	Longitudinal section of a canine tooth within its bony alveolus.
Figure 22.14	Gross anatomy of the stomach.
Figure 22.15	Microscopic anatomy of the stomach.
Figure 22.16	The duodenum of the small intestine, and related organs.
Figure 22.17	The small intestine.
Figure 22.18	Gross anatomy of the large intestine.
Figure 22.21	Visceral surface of the liver (posteroinferior view).
Figure 22.22	Microscopic anatomy of the liver.
Figure 22.26	The mesenteries.

Teaching with Art

Figure 22.21 Visceral surface of the liver (posteroinferior view).

Figure 22.22 Microscopic anatomy of the liver.

Textbook pp. 660–661; transparencies; Digital Archive CD-ROM.

Checklist of Key Points in the Figure

- Identify anatomical features on the visceral surface of the liver using Figure 22.21.
- Discuss and point out the various ducts bile travels through from the liver, to storage in the gallbladder, and finally to the duodenum via the common bile duct.
- Explain that bile in the common bile duct may continue directly to the duodenum or enter the cystic duct of the gallbladder for storage.
- Review the function of bile as an emulsifier of fats, *not* a digestive enzyme.
- Using Figure 22.22, explain how bile drains through a liver lobule, indicating its site of production, bile canaliculi, and bile ducts in the portal triads.
- Correlate the relationship of the bile ducts in the microscopic view with the hepatic ducts at the porta hepatis in the gross view.

Common Conceptual Difficulties Interpreting the Art

- Explain the location of the hepatopancreatic sphincter at the duodenum; it controls the entry of bile into the duodenum. Refer students to Figure 22.16.
- Point out that the cystic duct accommodates the flow of bile into the gallbladder for storage as well as the flow out of the gallbladder on its way to the common bile duct.

Art Exercise

Provide students with unlabeled diagrams of Figures 22.16, 22.21, and 22.22. Instruct students to trace the movement of bile from its point of origin to its entry into the duodenum, including its storage in the gallbladder. Students should label all parts of the pathway. Additionally, a flowchart summarizing the same pathway may be of benefit so that coordination between diagrams is evident.

Critical Reasoning

After your students study the figures, ask them to propose a sequence of events that may evolve if the cystic duct or a bile duct becomes blocked because bile became too concentrated and formed gallstones.

Answer: The first event is severe pain as the gallbladder becomes swollen and inflamed. If the blockage does not work its way to the duodenum, the gallstones must be removed surgically or the gallstones must be reduced in size by a procedure such as lithotripsy to ensure their passage to the duodenum. In some cases, the gallbladder must be removed as well.

SUPPLEMENTAL COURSE MATERIALS
Library Research Topics

1. Research the causes and treatments of ulcers.
2. Research the benefits of fiber in the diet.

3. Research liver transplants in terms of the rationale for the transplant, the procedure, and the prognosis.
4. Research the histological changes in the liver that accompany cirrhosis.

Audiovisual Aids/Computer Software

See Preface of the Instructor's Guide for Key to Audiovisual Distributors

Videotapes

1. *An End to Ulcers: A Journey of Discovery* (FHS, 57 min.)
2. *Anorexia and Bulimia* (FHS, 19 min., 1990)
3. *Cellular Respiration: Energy for Life* (HRM, 28 min., 1994)
4. *Cholesterol Explained* (FHS, 19 min., 1995)
5. *Contemporary Nutrition* (FHS, 60 min., 1995)
6. *Digestion* (FHS, 15 min., 1995)
7. *Digestion* (*New Living Body Series*) (FHS, 20 min., 1995)
8. *Digestive and Fluid Balance* (IM, 30 min., 1997)
9. *The Digestive System* (*Anatomy and Physiology Series*) (CAP/HCA, 29 min.)
10. *The Digestive System.* 2nd ed. (EBE, 19 min.)
11. *The Digestive System: Your Personal Power Plant* (IM, 30 min., 1998)
12. *Eating to Live* (FHS, 30 min., 1990)
13. *The Food Machine* (*Body Atlas Series*) (HCA/IM, 30 min., 1994)
14. *Hepatitis A* (FHS, 18 min.)
15. *Hepatitis B: The Enemy Within* (FHS, 21 min.)
16. *Hepatitis C: The Silent Scourge* (FHS, 23 min.)
17. *The Human Body: Digestive System* (Ward's, 14 min.)
18. *The Human Digestive System* (BC, 33 min., 1998)
19. *The Human Digestive System* (AIMS/Ward's, 18 min.)
20. *The Human Body: Digestive System* (*includes endocrine system*) (Ward's, 30 min.)
21. *The Living Body: Breakdown* (FHS, VHS, or BETA, 20 min., 1990). A family sits down to lunch. As the first morsel is put into the mouth, the camera watches from inside as the molars clamp down and the process of breakdown and transformation occurs. Then it follows the food through the entire alimentary tract, showing how it is digested, how the liver and gallbladder work, and how digestive enzymes and absorption work.
22. *The Living Body: Eating to Live* (FHS, VHS, or BETA). This program looks at appetite and hunger, and, by means of dramatic interior film, shows the actions of a salivary gland, the swallowing reflex, and the powerful churning of the stomach as food is broken down and processed.
23. *The Metabolism: Fluid and Electrolyte Balance* (HCA, 27 min.)
24. *The New Living Body: Digestion* (FHS, 28 min., 1990)
25. *Nutrition and Cancer* (FHS, 21 min.)

26. *Nutrition: Eat and Be Healthy* (MF, 18 min., 1994)
27. *Nutrition for Living* (FHS, 59 min., 1995)
28. *Passage of Food Through the Digestive Tract* (Ward's)
29. *Respiration, Circulation, and Digestion* (NGS)
30. *Turning Food Into Fuel* (*Human Body Live Action Video Series*) (CAP, 28 min.)
31. *Ulcer Wars* (FHS, 50 min., 1997)
32. *Wasting Away: Understanding Anorexia and Bulimia* (GA, 40 min., 1991)

Computer Software

1. *The Anatomy Project: The Abdominal Cavity and Digestive Tube* (NIMCO)
2. *Body Language: Study of Anatomy, Digestive System* (PLP, CH-182015, Apple; CH-182016, IBM). Anatomy tutorial.
3. *Cellular Respiration* (CBS, Mac/Win)
4. *Digestion* (CAP, IBM, 1997)
5. *Dynamics of the Human Digestive System* (EI, Apple II, IBM, 1988). Contains straightforward, concise text with engaging animated graphics, sound effects, and an interactive quiz to instruct and challenge.
6. *Enzyme Investigations* (CL, Mac/Win)
7. *Gastroenterology and Hepatology: The Comprehensive Visual Reference* (MOS)
8. *The Human Digestive System* (IM, Mac/Win, 1997)
9. *The Living Body* (Queue, Win)
10. *Body Systems: Interactive Physical Education* (HCA, Disk for Mac/Win, 1995)
11. *Digestion and Excretion* (Queue, Disk for Apple II/Mac/Win)
12. *The Human Body, Part I* (CL, Disk for Apple II/Mac/Win)
13. *The Human Body, Part II* (HCA, Disk for IBM, 1995)

Slides

1. *Digestive System and its Function* (EI, Slides, or Filmstrips). A tour of the alimentary tract brings the student to consider the basic chemical and morphological phenomena of digestion.
2. *Histology of the Digestive System: Mouth to Esophagus* (EI). Presents a general plan of the digestive tract and covers the structure of the oral cavity and associated structures down to the esophagus-stomach junction.
3. *Histology of the Digestive System: Stomach, Intestine, and Major Glands* (EI). The major regions of the stomach and intestine. The thickness of the various layers, presence or absence of lymphatic tissue, and types and position of glands in each region are emphasized. Pancreas, liver, and gallbladder are also included.
4. *Visual Approach to Histology: Digestive System* (FAD, 48 Slides)

Suggested Readings

Alper, J. Ulcers as an infectious disease. *Science* 260 (April 9, 1993): 159–160.

Blaser, M. The bacteria behind ulcers. *Scientific American* 274 (February 1996): 107.

Cormack, D.H. *Essential Histology*. Philadelphia: J.B. Lippincott, 1993.

Fackelmann, K. Nabbing a gene for colorectal cancer. *Science News* 144 (1993): 388.

Fawcett, D.W. *A Textbook of Histology*. 12th ed. New York: Chapman & Hall, 1994, Chapters 23–28.

Fox, C.H. Periodontal disease: Gumming up the works. *Harvard Health Letter* (June 1992).

Gibbs, W. Gaining on fat. *Scientific American* 275 (August 1996): 88–94.

Johnson, L.R. *Gastrointestinal Physiology*. 5th ed. St. Louis: Mosby, 1996.

Junqueira, L.C., et al. *Basic Histology*. 9th ed. Stamford, Conn.: Appleton & Lange, 1998.

Marchiondo, K. When the Dx is diverticular disease. *RN* (February 1994): 42–46.

Moore, K.L. *Clinically Oriented Anatomy*. 34th ed. Philadelphia: Lippincott Williams and Wilkins, 1999.

Pennisi, E. Gut counts calories even when we do not. (An article on the enteric nervous system.) *Science News* (November 26, 1994): 359.

Robbins, S.L., V. Kumar, and R. Cotran. *Basic Pathology*. 6th ed. Philadelphia: W.B. Saunders, 1997.

Romanes, G.J. *Cunningham's Textbook of Anatomy*. 12th ed. Oxford, New York: Oxford University Press, 1981.

Sherlock, S. Alcoholic liver disease. *The Lancet* (January 28, 1995): 227–229.

Siegel, M.I. Decrease your risk of colorectal cancer. *Newsweek* (November 12, 1990): 12–13 (in Special Advertising Section).

Sigurdsson, T., et al. Evaluating surgical, non-surgical therapy in periodontic patients. *Journal of the American Dental Association* (August 1994): 1080–1087.

Small, E.J. Prostate cancer: Who to screen, and what the results mean. *Geriatrics* 48 (December 1993): 28–30, 35–38.

Spiro, H. Hiatus hernia and reflux esophagitis. *Hospital Practice* (January 15, 1994): 51–66.

Tandler, B. Introduction to mammalian salivary glands. (First article in a whole issue about salivary glands.) *Microscopy Research and Technique* 26 (1993): 1–4.

Thompkins, L., and S. Falkow. The new path to preventing ulcers. *Science* 265 (1995): 1621.

Ugolev, A.M., et al. Spatial organization of digestive and barrier functions of the small intestine (new hypotheses and data). *Physiologist* 35 (1 Suppl) (February 1992): S12–15.

Vines, G. The enemy within. (An article about ulcer as an infection.) *New Scientist* (October 15, 1994): 12–14.

Wagstaff, B. Rectal exam during routine pelvic exam. *Journal of Family Practice* 46 (May 1998): 357.

Watkins, J., et al. Gallstones: Choosing the right therapy despite vague clinical clues. *Geriatrics* (August 1993): 48–54.

Williams, P.L., et al. *Gray's Anatomy*. 38th ed. New York: Churchill Livingstone, 1995.

ANSWERS TO TEXTBOOK QUESTIONS

Answers for multiple-choice and matching questions 1–11 are located in Appendix B of the textbook.

Short Answer and Essay Questions

12. A labeled drawing of the digestive organs can be found on p. 634, Figure 22.1.

13. The four basic layers in the wall of the alimentary canal, from internal to external, are the mucosa, submucosa, muscularis externa (or simply, muscularis), and serosa (or adventitia).

    The *mucosa* consists of a lining epithelium, a lamina propria of areolar connective tissue, and the thin muscularis mucosae. The *lining epithelium* performs many functions related to digestion (e.g., absorption, secretion of mucus). Furthermore, this epithelium is continuous with the ducts and secretory cells of the digestive glands. The *lamina propria* contains capillaries that absorb digested nutrients, as well as gut-associated lymphoid tissue to destroy microorganisms that enter the wall of the alimentary canal from its lumen. The *muscularis mucosae* produce local movements of the mucosa.

    The *submucosa* is a connective tissue. It contains a rich vascular network that sends branches to all other layers of the wall of the alimentary canal. It contains elastic fibers, allowing the digestive tube to return to shape after being expanded with food.

    The *muscularis externa* (or simply, muscularis) consists of (usually) two layers of smooth muscle that are responsible for peristalsis and segmentation.

    The *serosa* is a slippery serous membrane formed of a mesothelium underlain by a thin layer of areolar connective tissue. It allows the mobile alimentary canal to glide smoothly within the peritoneal cavity. The parts of the alimentary canal that are not located in the peritoneal cavity are covered instead by an *adventitia* of connective tissue.

    All these layers develop from splanchnic mesoderm except the lining epithelium of the mucosa, which is from endoderm.

14. (a) Deciduous teeth: 2I, 1C, 2M / 2I, 1C, 2M. Permanent teeth: 2I, 1C, 2P, 3M / 2I, 1C, 2P, 3M. (b) Pulp is a loose connective tissue that fills the hollow center of each tooth (the pulp cavity) and contains the tooth's vessels and nerves.

15. Effects of aging on the digestive system include slowing of peristalsis, lessened production of digestive juices, and declining efficiency of nutrient absorption. The likelihood of developing constipation, bowel cancer, and diverticulosis increases.

16. (a) Rectal valves are in the rectum, whereas anal valves are located more inferiorly, in the anal canal. Although both are transverse folds of mucosa, the anal valves are smaller. See Figure 22.18. (b) The pyloric region (consisting of the pyloric antrum and pyloric canal) lies next to the pylorus (which contains the pyloric sphincter), but they are not the same. See Figure 22.14a. (c) The anal canal is the last part of the digestive tube, whereas the anus is the hole at the end of the anal canal. (d) Intestinal villi (finger-shaped projections of the mucosa) are much larger than intestinal microvilli (tiny projections from the apical membranes of individual absorptive cells). See Figure 22.17 on p. 653. (e) The hepatic portal vein enters the liver, whereas the hepatic veins leave the liver. These distinct veins lie on opposite sides of the liver sinusoids. See Chapter 19. (f) The narrow gastric glands open into the wide gastric pits in the wall of the stomach. See Figure 22.15b.

17. (a) The sketch of the visceral surface of the liver should resemble that in Figure 22.21. (b) The exercise is self-explanatory. The two lobes within the H are the caudate and quadrate. The left lobe is divided from the right lobe at the right limb of the H.

18. The *great length of the small intestine*, the *plicae circulares*, the *villi*, and the abundant *microvilli* on the intestinal absorptive cells all serve to increase the surface area for the absorption of nutrients.

19. (a) The three major vessels in a portal triad are a (1) venule branch of the portal vein, (2) arteriole branch of the hepatic artery, and (3) bile duct. Triads lie at the external corners of the liver lobules. (b) Organelles that are abundant within hepatocytes are (student should list any three of these): (1) rough ER, which makes the blood proteins; (2) smooth ER, which detoxifies and metabolizes many poisons and compounds from the blood, and also helps make bile; (3) Golgi apparatus, which packages secretory products of the ER; and (4) mitochondria, which provide the energy for the many activities carried out by the hepatocyte.

20. The parotid gland is the largest salivary gland, and the sublingual gland underlies the tongue.

21. See Figure 22.16.

22. Foregut/midgut boundary: duodenum where the bile duct enters. Midgut/hindgut boundary: two-thirds of the way along the transverse colon. (pp. 667–668)

Critical Reasoning and Clinical Applications Questions

1. (a) The abdominal regions that overlap the upper right quadrant are the right hypochondriac, epigastric, right lumbar, and umbilical. (b) The abdominal regions that overlap the lower left quadrant are the left iliac, hypogastric (pubic), left lumbar, and umbilical. (Figure 22.4)

2. Appendicitis is dangerous because it can cause the appendix to rupture, allowing feces (with abundant bacteria) to enter the peritoneal cavity and infect the peritoneum. Severe peritonitis is dangerous, difficult to treat, and often lethal.

3. The grandfather, a simple man of few words, said that when he was in his 40s, his gums started getting sore. The gums pulled away from the teeth, and his teeth loosened and fell out.

4. Eroded blood vessels in the wall of the stomach or duodenum could cause severe bleeding into the alimentary canal, resulting in anemia through blood loss. The peptic ulcer could perforate, and the digestive juices that enter the peritoneal cavity could cause peritonitis or destroy Eva's pancreas.

5. An endoscope is a viewing tube containing a lens and a light radiating from its tip.

6. The janitor had *ascites*, resulting from alcohol-induced cirrhosis of the liver. Obstruction of venous flow through the liver raised the blood pressure in the capillaries of the visceral peritoneum of the intestine, causing large quantities of tissue fluid (serous fluid) to leave these capillaries and accumulate in the man's peritoneal cavity.

SUPPLEMENTAL STUDENT MATERIALS TO HUMAN ANATOMY, THIRD EDITION
Chapter 22: The Digestive System

To the Student

The digestive system is responsible for the food-processing activities of ingestion, digestion, absorption, and elimination of feces. Because of the external openings, you will be presented with the unique concept that food "inside" the alimentary canal (the GI tract) is actually "outside" of the body. The structural plan of the alimentary canal includes digestive organs: the mouth, pharynx, esophagus, stomach, small intestine, and large intestine. In addition, it contains several accessory digestive organs: the teeth, tongue, gallbladder, salivary glands, liver, and pancreas. A clear understanding of the peritoneum, peritoneal cavity, and associated mesenteries is essential to your study. The general arrangement, location, gross anatomy, microscopic anatomy, and functions of all the aforementioned structures are part of your study of the digestive system.

Step 1: Describe an overview of the digestive system.
- ☐ Differentiate the alimentary canal from the accessory digestive organs.
- ☐ List and describe specific and essential food-processing activities of the digestive system.
- ☐ Draw a simple diagram distinguishing between peristalsis and segmentation.
- ☐ Identify the anatomical abdominal regions and quadrants, locating the positions of the abdominopelvic organs.

Step 2: Explain the peritoneum and peritoneal cavity.
- ☐ Review the difference between serous membranes and mucous membranes.
- ☐ Define *peritoneum*, distinguishing between visceral peritoneum, parietal peritoneum, and the peritoneal cavity.
- ☐ Define *mesentery*. (Note: Refer to end of this exercise for more details.)
- ☐ Explain the difference between retroperitoneal organs and intraperitoneal organs and give several examples.

Step 3: Describe the alimentary canal.
- ☐ Describe the histology of the alimentary canal wall.
- ☐ Draw a cross section and label the four layers of the alimentary canal wall at the level of the esophagus.
- ☐ Draw a cross section and label the four layers of the alimentary canal wall at the level of the small intestine.
- ☐ Name the visceral nerve plexuses that occur in the wall of the alimentary canal, and list the types of fibers and neurons present.
- ☐ Describe the effects of sympathetic and parasympathetic innervation to the stomach.

Step 4: Describe the mouth (oral cavity) and its associated organs.
- ☐ Describe the gross anatomy of the oral cavity.
- ☐ Identify the type of epithelium that lines the oral cavity.

- ☐ Explain the function of lips and cheeks, also explaining why lips are reddish.
- ☐ Describe the structure and function of the tongue, including papillae and taste buds.
- ☐ Name and identify locations of salivary glands.
- ☐ Describe the structure and function of teeth, distinguish between permanent and deciduous teeth, and identify classification types of teeth.

Step 5: Describe the pharynx, esophagus, and stomach as digestive system organs.
- ☐ Explain the role of the pharynx during swallowing.
- ☐ Describe the location and gross anatomy of the pharynx, including openings.
- ☐ Describe the location, gross structure, and function of the esophagus.
- ☐ Explain how the outer layer of the wall of the esophagus differs from the rest of the digestive tract.
- ☐ Describe the location, gross anatomy, and functions of the stomach.
- ☐ Compare and contrast the microscopic structure of the esophagus and stomach.

Step 6: Describe the small intestine and the large intestine as digestive system organs.
- ☐ Describe the location and functions of the small intestine, identifying its individual segments.
- ☐ Explain why the duodenum is retroperitoneal.
- ☐ Identify major ducts and their contents that empty into the duodenum.
- ☐ Describe the features of the small intestine that increase its surface area.
- ☐ Describe the location and functions of the large intestine, identifying its subdivisions.
- ☐ Describe and identify special anatomical features on the external surface of the colon.
- ☐ Compare the lining of the large intestine to the lining of the small intestine.
- ☐ Describe defecation.

Step 7: Describe the liver, gallbladder, and pancreas as accessory digestive organs.
- ☐ Identify the location and list the functions of the liver.
- ☐ Describe the gross anatomy of the liver, including its lobes, mesenteries, and vessels.
- ☐ Describe classic liver lobules.
- ☐ Outline the flow of blood through the liver. (Reminder: It has two blood supply sources.)
- ☐ Explain the function of hepatocytes.
- ☐ Identify the location, structure, and function of the gallbladder.
- ☐ Trace the movement of bile from its point of secretion all the way to the duodenum.
- ☐ Explain the function of bile.
- ☐ Identify the location, structure, and function of the pancreas.

Step 8: Describe the mesenteries associated with abdominal digestive organs.
- ☐ Name several specific examples of mesenteries, describing their locations and indicating if each example is dorsal or ventral. (Note: Some mesenteries are called "ligaments"; do not confuse terminology with fibrous ligaments that connect bone to bone.)
- ☐ Explain the functions of mesenteries.
- ☐ Refer to Figure 22.5 and apply specific names to the two ventral mesenteries indicated in the diagram.

CHAPTER 23
The Urinary System

LECTURE AND DEMONSTRATION
Student Objectives

1. Describe the location, coverings, and external gross anatomy of the kidney.
2. Describe the internal gross anatomy and the main blood vessels of the kidney.
3. Identify the segments of the uriniferous tubule, and explain their specific roles in forming urine.
4. Describe the structure and functions of the capillaries and arterioles in the kidney.
5. Describe the location, histology, and function of the ureters.
6. Describe the shape, location, histology, and function of the bladder.
7. Describe the structure and function of the urethra of both sexes.
8. Define *micturition*, and explain its neural control.
9. Describe the basic features of urinary tract infections, kidney stones (calculi), and bladder and kidney cancers.
10. Trace the embryonic development of the urinary organs.
11. List several effects of aging on the structure and function of the urinary system.

Suggested Lecture Outline

I. Kidneys (pp. 676–686 Fig. 23.1)

  A. Gross Anatomy (pp. 676–681, Figs. 23.1–23.3)

    1. Location and External Anatomy

    2. Internal Gross Anatomy

    3. Gross Vasculature and Nerve Supply

  B. Microscopic Anatomy of the Kidneys (pp. 681–686, Figs. 23.4–23.10)

    1. Mechanisms of Urine Production

    2. The Nephron

    3. Collecting Tubules

    4. Microscopic Blood Vessels Associated with Uriniferous Tubules

    5. Juxtaglomerular Apparatus

    6. Interstitial Connective Tissue

II. Ureters (pp. 686–687, Figs. 23.1 and 23.11–23.12)
A. Gross Anatomy

B. Microscopic Anatomy

III. Urinary Bladder (pp. 687–689, Figs. 23.13–23.16)

IV. Urethra (pp. 689–691, Fig. 23.15)

V. Micturition (pp. 691–692, Fig. 23.17)

VI. Disorders of the Urinary System (pp. 692–693)
A. Urinary Tract Infections

B. Renal Calculi

C. Cancer of Urinary Organs

VII. The Urinary System Throughout Life (pp. 693–695, Fig. 23.18)

Lecture Hints

1. Using Figure 23.1, describe the location of the kidneys and other organs of the urinary system, and summarize the basic functions of the urinary system.
2. Explain that the kidneys are not only the primary organs for the elimination of metabolic waste, but they are responsible for several important functions as well. List these functions.
3. Point out that the kidneys work with other organs, such as lungs, skin, and digestive organs, to accomplish the overall elimination of waste from the body.
4. Clearly distinguish between ureter and urethra.
5. Describe the gross external anatomy of the kidneys, including their retroperitoneal position, relationship to the vertebral column, and all of their supportive and protective layers. Refer to Figure 23.2.
6. Describe the internal gross anatomy of the kidney, identifying structures of the renal cortex and renal medulla. Refer to Figure 23.3.
7. Explain carefully the difference between the renal hilus, renal pelvis, and renal sinus.
8. Discuss the gross vasculature of the kidney, using Figure 23.3 and Figure 19.11, emphasizing the rich blood supply, and the difference between the terms *interlobar* and *interlobular*.
9. Describe the nerve supply to the kidney.
10. Define and describe the main structural and functional unit of the kidney, the *uriniferous tubule*, noting its two major parts: the nephron and the collecting duct (tubule). Refer to Figures 23.4 and 23.5.
11. Compare and contrast filtrate and urine.
12. Referring to Figure 23.4, trace the path of the filtrate through the long tubular section of the nephron, naming each section and continuing into the collecting tubules.
13. Review briefly the basics of diffusion, osmosis, and active transport before explaining the details of kidney activity.

14. Explain and define the three major interacting mechanisms of urine formation: *filtration*, *reabsorption*, and *secretion*, using a single, generalized uriniferous tubule as represented in Figure 23.6.
15. Using Figure 23.7, explain in detail the microscopic anatomy and function of the renal corpuscle of the nephron.
16. Distinguish between cortical nephrons and juxtamedullary nephrons.
17. Explain the very important role of the collecting tubule in conservation of body fluids, and introduce the role of the antidiuretic hormone. (Refer to Chapter 25, if needed.)
18. Remind students of the concept of surface area and its application to the urinary system, including how much filtrate is generated per minute.
19. Diagram a flowchart representation of the path taken by the filtrate (urine) from the glomerulus to the renal pelvis of the ureter, naming all microscopic and gross tube structures urine passes through.
20. Explain the microscopic blood vessels associated with uriniferous tubules, using Figure 23.8, and provide a complete summary of the microscopic and gross vessels, using Figure 23.9.
21. Remind students that the renal vessels function in maintaining homeostasis.
22. Define and explain the function of the *juxtaglomerular apparatus*. Refer to Figure 23.10.
23. Review the nature of the interstitial connective tissue that surrounds the uriniferous tubules evident in Figure 23.5.
24. Describe the location, gross anatomy, and microscopic anatomy of the ureters. Refer to Figure 23.1 and Figures 23.11 and 23.12.
25. Describe the urinary bladder in the following ways: location, shape, internal and external anatomical features, histology, and function. Refer to Figures 23.13–23.16.
26. Describe the location, structure, and function of the urethra of both sexes using Figure 23.15, reminding students of the mucosal lining.
27. Continue the flowchart diagram (in Lecture Hint 19) of the urine pathway from the renal pelvis to the external urethral meatus.
28. Define *micturition*, and explain its neural control using Figure 23.17.
29. Describe the basic features of one or more disorders of the urinary system: urinary tract infections, renal calculi, urinary bladder cancer, or kidney cancer.
30. Using Figure 23.18, trace the development of the urinary organs in the embryo.
31. Summarize several effects of aging on the structure and function of the urinary system.

Classroom Discussion Topics and Activities

1. Display a model of a dissectible human torso or urinary system model to exhibit the urinary organs.
2. Display preserved human kidney and urinary bladder specimens if possible, or display a dissected cat or rat showing gross urinary structures. Additionally, if available, a sheep kidney corrosion cast specimen illustrates beautifully the rich vascular nature of the kidney.
3. Obtain cow or pig kidneys from the market and demonstrate their structure.

4. Use a funnel and filter paper to demonstrate the filtration process in the renal corpuscle. Represent the relationship between the glomerulus and Bowman's capsule with a head of lettuce in a bowl or a baseball in a baseball glove.

5. Have each student form a pyramid of clay as a model for the empty bladder. Ask them to insert pipe cleaners into each corner of the pyramid to represent the ureters, urethra, and urachus.

6. Students realize kidneys are primary excretory organs, but they forget the other functions. Ask students what problems a dialysis patient may encounter.

7. When discussing filtration and tubular reabsorption, make an analogy to cleaning closets. One effective way to clean out a closet is to remove everything (filtration), and then put back into the closet only what you want to keep (reabsorption). The rest is thrown away.

8. Ask students to deduce why physicians tell a sick person to drink plenty of fluids and why fluid intake and output are so carefully monitored in hospital settings.

9. Discuss how kidney stones are formed and how they can be treated.

10. A "logical" design for kidney function would be to directly and actively remove all the undesirable molecules from the blood, yet the kidney does not operate this way at all. Instead, it forms a blood filtrate, then reabsorbs all the desirable molecules, letting the undesirable molecules exit passively in the urine. Discuss the benefits of such an indirect mechanism of ridding the body of wastes.

11. Both the spleen and kidney "cleanse" the blood. What are some similarities and differences between these two blood-cleansing organs?

12. Ask students to list the basic substances that compose normal urine, and then ask for suggestions of abnormal substances that may be in urine. Include a laboratory copy of a urinalysis report in the discussion and ask students to interpret the findings.

13. Ask students to review gout in Chapter 9, and recall that uric acid crystals are deposited around joints.

14. Assign *A Closer Look: ADPKD: The Most Interesting Disease You've Never Heard Of?* as required reading and instruct students to write a short review of this reading.

Clinical Questions

1. Infants and many elderly people are incontinent. Define *incontinence*.

   Answer: Incontinence is the inability to voluntarily control micturition.

2. Richard, an older man, sees his doctor for severe pain in his lower abdominal or flank area. He also has an elevated temperature and nausea. Exhaustive tests rule out abdominal obstructions and infections. X rays indicate a shadow in his right ureter. Diagnose his problem. Give a suggested treatment and prognosis.

   Answer: The symptoms suggest that a large kidney stone is lodged in the ureter. Treatment would be surgical removal, or ultrasound or shock waves to shatter the calculus. The prognosis is for complete recovery. However, there is a possibility that renal calculi will form again.

3. Eleven-year-old Brian is complaining of a severe sore throat and gets to stay home from school. His pediatrician prescribes a course of broad-spectrum antibiotics, and Brian feels much better within a few days. He stops taking his medicine 5 days earlier than the doctor had told him. Two weeks later, Brian's throat still feels fine, but he experiences dull, bilateral

pain in his lower back and his urine is a smoky brown color. On the basis of Brian's signs and symptoms, diagnose his condition and indicate the relationship (if any) between his present condition and his earlier sore throat.

Answer: Brian is showing the symptoms of a severe kidney infection. The smoky brown color of his urine indicates the presence of blood or bile. Apparently, infectious bacteria have spread from the sore throat, through the blood, to lodge and multiply in both kidneys.

4. Whenever Frank, a young father, changed his infant daughter's diaper, he wiped her from back to front. The child developed a urinary tract infection. Why?

Answer: Frank unknowingly was spreading fecal bacteria anteriorly from the region of the anus to the external urethral orifice. From there, the bacteria spread superiorly through the girl's urinary tract.

ART RESOURCES
Transparency List

Figure 23.1   Organs of the urinary system.
Figure 23.2   Position of the kidneys within the posterior abdominal wall.
Figure 23.3   Internal anatomy of the kidney.
Figure 23.4   The uriniferous tubule.
Figure 23.6   Basic kidney functions: the urine-forming part of the kidney, depicted as a single, generalized uriniferous tubule.
Figure 23.7   Renal corpuscle and the filtration membrane.
Figure 23.8   The vessels around the nephron.
Figure 23.9   Summary of the blood vessels supplying the kidney.
Figure 23.10 Juxtaglomerular apparatus.
Figure 23.15 Structure of the urinary bladder and urethra.
Figure 23.17 Micturition.

Teaching with Art

Figure 23.8   The vessels around the nephron.

Textbook p. 684; transparencies; Digital Archive CD-ROM.

Checklist of Key Points in the Figure

- Explain that both cortical and juxtamedullary nephrons are represented.
- Trace the uriniferous tubule (nephron and collecting duct) through the diagram, reminding students of the role of urine production.
- Stress the association of the kidney with a rich blood supply and comment on how much blood is filtered daily (or by the minute or hourly).
- Review the basics of arterial blood supply and venous blood drainage.
- Trace the blood vessel route, beginning with the interlobular artery and ending with the interlobular vein; name the vessel sequence.

- Explain the blood vessel route from the aorta to the interlobular artery and from the interlobular vein to the inferior vena cava.
- Stress the relationship of the microscopic structures to the gross structures, explaining the cortex and medulla.

Common Conceptual Difficulties Interpreting the Art
- Clearly distinguish between the diagrammatic blood vessels and the diagrammatic uriniferous tubular structures.
- Explain there are *two* beds of capillaries in the kidney, as well as the capillary-like *vasa recta*.
- Relate the diagram to the overall gross structure of the kidney.
- Explain why the blood pressure in the glomerulus is extraordinarily high and results in forcing filtrate into the glomerular capsule.

Art Exercise
Provide each student with two (or more) copies of unlabeled Figure 23.8. Instruct students to identify and color code all the parts of the uriniferous tubule on one copy. Permit them to use the textbook for reference to several chapter diagrams. On the second copy, instruct students to look at Figure 23.9 in their textbooks and identify and label all vessels represented in their copies of Figure 23.8. Request that they color arteries red, veins blue, and capillaries any third color. Additionally, it is possible to instruct students to indicate structures located in the cortex and medulla, as well as to identify locations of filtration, reabsorption, and secretion.

Critical Reasoning
Ask students to recall their study of blood vessels, naming another place in the body where two beds of capillaries are significant, the hepatic portal system. Instruct students to look at Figure 23.8, identify the two beds of capillaries, and explain why the renal system is not a portal system.

Answer: The hepatic portal system involves two beds of capillaries in the venous drainage of the body, whereas the glomerulus is both fed and drained by arterioles, and the peritubular capillaries (and vasa recta) are drained by venules.

SUPPLEMENTAL COURSE MATERIALS
Library Research Topics
1. Research the treatments that are available for kidney stones.
2. Research the complications that can arise from chronic infections of the urinary tracts.
3. Research the process of dialysis.
4. What are the effects of atherosclerosis on the kidney?
5. What causes kidney failure in many people who suffer from diabetes mellitus?

Audiovisual Aids/Computer Software
See Preface of the Instructor's Guide for Key to Audiovisual Distributors

Videotapes
1. *Body Fluids: The Critical Balance, Part 1* (CM, 17 min., 1990)

2. *Digestion and Fluid Balance* (IM, 30 min., 1997)
3. *Human Biology* (FHS, 28 min.)
4. *The Human Body: The Excretory System* (Ward's, 15 min.)
5. *The Human Body: The Excretory System* (with reproductive system) (Ward's, 30 min.)
6. *The Human Body: Excretory System* (COR, 12 min., 1993)
7. *The Human Urinary System* (BC, 23 min., 1999)
8. *The Kidney* (FHS, 15 min., 1997)
9. *Kidney Disease* (FHS, 26 min., 1992)
10. *Liquid Waste and the Kidney* (WARD, 8 min.)
11. *The Living Body: Water!* (FHS, 1990, 28 min.)
12. *The Mammalian Kidney* (EI, VHS, or BETA). Details the anatomy and function of the mammalian kidney as it (1) regulates the excretion of metabolic wastes, (2) controls concentrations of salts, and (3) preserves overall water balance.
13. *The Metabolism: Fluid and Electrolyte Balance* (HCA, 27 min.)
14. *Osmoregulation* (FHS, 10 min.)
15. *Transplant: A Decade of Progress, A Century of Hope* (NIMCO, 21 min.)
16. *The Urinary System* (NIMCO, 28 min.)
17. *The Urinary System (Anatomy and Physiology Series)* (CAP/HCA, 29 min.)

Computer Software

1. *Body Language: Study of Human Anatomy—Urinary System* (PLP, CH-182019, Apple; CH-182018, IBM). Covers the human urinary system from microanatomy to gross anatomy.
2. *Digestion and Excretion* (Queue, Disk for Apple II/Mac/IBM)
3. *Dynamics of the Human Urinary System* (EI, Apple II, IBM, 1988). Combines straightforward, concise text with engaging animated graphics, sound effects, and an interactive quiz to instruct and challenge.
4. *The Human Body, Part I* (CL, Disk for Apple II/Mac/IBM)
5. *The Human Body, Part II* (HCA, Disk for IBM, 1995)
6. *Interactive Physiology: Fluids, Electrolytes, and Acid/Base Balance* (ADAM/BC, Mac/Win, 1999)
7. *Interactive Physiology: Urinary System* (ADAM/BC, Mac/Win, 1997)
8. *The Kidney.* 5th ed. (WBS, 1998)
9. *The Kidney: Structure and Function* (EI, Apple). Studies the relation between renal structure and function via several laboratory investigations. Students are presented with data that they must collect, organize, and interpret.
10. *Kidney Functions* (IM, Mac/Win, 1990)
11. *Principles of Urology CD-ROM* (MOS, Win only, 1998)

Slides

1. *Histology of the Respiratory, Circulatory, and Urinary System* (EI). Emphasizes the histological structure of the lungs, heart, and kidneys and associated ducts, vessels, and tubules. Provides a unifying view of the interactions between these three systems.
2. *Urinary System and its Function* (EI). Human water balance and its control are discussed with a definite functionalist viewpoint.

Suggested Readings

Anderson, R. Prevention and management of acute renal failure. *Hospital Practice* (August 15, 1993): 61.

Beard, J. Hammering kidney stones. *New Scientist* (June 15, 1991): 28.

Blantz, R.C. Filtration, reabsorption and oxygen in the kidney. *Advances in Experimental Medicine and Biology* 361 (1994): 579–584.

Bonvalet, J.P. Aldosterone-sensitive cells in the kidney: New insights. *News in Physiological Sciences* (October 1991).

Breza, J., and P. Navratil. Renal transplantation in adults. *BJU International* 84 (July 1999): 216–223.

Budoff, P.W. UTIs: Causes, recurrence, treatment, and prevention. *Pharmacy Times* (1993).

Cormack, D.H. *Essential Histology*. Philadelphia: J.B. Lippincott, 1993.

Cunningham, N.H., et al. Renal transplantation. *Critical Care Nursing Clinics of North America* 4 (March 1992): 79–88.

Fawcett, D.W. *A Textbook of Histology*. 12th ed. New York: Chapman & Hall, 1994, Chapter 30.

Fisher, R., et al. Quality of life after renal transplantation. *Journal of Clinical Nursing* 7 (November 1998): 553–563.

George, A.L., Jr., and E.G. Neilson. Genetics of kidney disease. *American Journal of Kidney Disease* 35 (4 Suppl 1) (April 2000): S160–169.

Giddens, J. Risks and rewards of kidney transplant. *RN* (June 1993): 56–61.

Hooton, T. A simplified approach to urinary tract infection. *Hospital Practice* (February 15, 1995): 23–30.

Junqueira, L.C., et al. *Basic Histology*. 9th ed. Stamford, Conn.: Appleton & Lange, 1998.

Koeppen, B.M., and B. Stanton. *Renal Physiology*. 2nd ed. St. Louis: Mosby, 1996.

Kupin, W. A practical approach to nephrolithiasis. *Hospital Practice* (March 15, 1995): 57–66.

Moore, K.L. *Clinically Oriented Anatomy*. 34th ed. Philadelphia: Lippincott Williams and Wilkins, 1999.

Peggs, J. Urinary incontinence in the elderly: Pharmacologic therapies. *American Family Physician* (December 1992): 1763.

Pendick, D. New kidney-restoring therapy in sight. *Science News* 142 (November 28, 1992): 372.

Resnick, B. Retraining the bladder after catheterization. *American Journal of Nursing* (November 1993): 46–49.

Robbins, S.L., V. Kumar, and R. Cotran. *Basic Pathology*. 6th ed. Philadelphia: W.B. Saunders, 1997.

Romanes, G.J. *Cunningham's Textbook of Anatomy*. 12th ed. Oxford, New York: Oxford University Press, 1981.

Ross, M., et al. *Histology: A Text and Atlas*. 3rd ed. Baltimore: Williams and Wilkins, 1995.

Scheinman, S.J. New insights into causes and treatments of kidney stones. *Hospital Practice* 35 (Off Ed) (March 15, 2000): 49–50, 53–56, 62–63.

Shankland, S.J., and G. Wolf. Cell cycle regulatory proteins in renal disease: Role in hypertrophy, proliferation, and apoptosis. *American Journal of Renal Physiology* 278 (April 2000): 515–529.

Williams, G.W., and N.P. Mallick. *Color Atlas of Renal Diseases*. 2nd ed. London: Wolfe, 1994.

Williams, P.L., et al. *Gray's Anatomy*. 38th ed. New York: Churchill Livingstone, 1995.

ANSWERS TO TEXTBOOK QUESTIONS

Answers for multiple-choice and matching questions 1–11 are located in Appendix B of the textbook.

Short Answer and Essay Questions

12. The perirenal and pararenal fat layers cushion the kidneys against blows. The associated fascia also helps hold the kidneys in place.

13. The *ureters* lead into the bladder, whereas the *urethra* leads out of the bladder (see Figure 23.1). The *perirenal fat* lies internal to the renal fascia, whereas the *pararenal fat* lies external to the renal fascia (see Figure 23.2). *Interlobar arteries* flow into arcuate arteries, whereas *interlobular arteries* branch off of the arcuate arteries (see Figure 23.3). The *renal sinus* is a space in the medial region of the kidney that contains the *renal pelvis* (expanded first part of the ureter) as well as fat, nerves, and branches of renal blood vessels.

14. From the glomerulus through the filtration membrane into the interior of the glomerular capsule, to the proximal convoluted tubule, to the loop of Henle, to the distal convoluted tubule, to the collecting tubule, (to papillary ducts), into the minor calyx, to the major calyx, to the renal pelvis, through the ureter, to the bladder, to the urethra.

15. (a) The kidneys do not act by directly removing wastes from the blood. Instead, they form a filtrate that contains all the small molecules of blood, and then they reclaim all the beneficial molecules and return them to the blood. This leaves the remaining filtrate (including undesirable wastes) to pass as urine. The reclaiming of the beneficial molecules is called reabsorption. (b) The peritubular capillaries surround the proximal and distal tubules within the cortex of the kidney. They readily absorb solutes and water from the tubule cells. They arise from the efferent arterioles draining the glomeruli.

16. The layers of the filtration membrane are (1) the fenestrated endothelium of the glomerulus capillary; the fenestrations (pores) hold back the blood cells; (2) the basement membrane; this serves as a molecular filter, restricting the passage of all plasma proteins except the smallest; and (3) filtration slits between the foot processes of the podocytes, covered by a slit membrane; these also hold back (filter) proteins.

17. (a) and (b): The *urachus* attaches to the anterior angle of the bladder, the *urethra* attaches to the inferior angle, and the paired *ureters* enter the two posterolateral angles. (c) The trigone is defined by the openings of the two ureters superiorly and the opening of the urethra inferiorly. (Technically, these are called ureteric orifices and the internal urethral orifice.) (See Figure 23.14.)

18. Micturition is the act of emptying the bladder. It is controlled by the micturition center in the pons of the brain, which responds to distension of the bladder wall by signaling a parasympathetic contraction of the bladder's detrusor muscle to squeeze out urine. At the same time, the pons inhibits sympathetic pathways to the bladder (pathways that would otherwise prevent micturition). (See Figure 23.17.)

19. In old age, the kidneys shrink, the nephrons decrease in size and number, and the tubules become less efficient at secretion and reabsorption. By age 70, the rate of filtrate formation is only about half that of middle-aged adults. This slowing is believed to result from impaired renal circulation caused by atherosclerosis. The bladder is shrunken, with less than half the capacity of a young adult. Problems of incontinence or urine retention occur.

20. The ureters pass obliquely through the posterior wall of the bladder, so that they are pressed shut when the bladder fills with urine. This prevents reflux of urine into the ureters and kidneys when the bladder is full. That is, it prevents hydronephrosis, an accumulation of urine within the kidney that exerts crushing pressure on the kidney tissue.

Critical Reasoning and Clinical Applications Questions

1. Drinking lots of fluids leads to abundant dilute urine, which will dilute any carcinogenic poisons in the urine.

2. Cystitis is inflammation (and infection) of the urinary bladder, generally resulting from the spread of fecal bacteria up the urethra. Women contract cystitis more often than men because their urethra is short and its external orifice lies closer to the anal opening.

3. Hattie has a renal calculus, or kidney stone, in her ureter. Predisposing conditions are frequent bacterial infections of the urinary tract, urinary retention, high concentrations of calcium in the blood, and alkaline urine. The woman's pain comes in waves because waves of peristalsis pass along the ureter at intervals. The pain results when the ureter walls close in on the sharp kidney stone during this peristalsis.

4. The pleural cavity lies directly posterior to the superior third of each kidney (and to the superior third of the fat that surrounds the kidney). While removing this fat, the surgeon accidentally cut through the parietal pleura, causing a pneumothorax that collapsed the lung.

5. Kidney stones most commonly lodge in the three narrowest parts of the ureter: (1) at the level of vertebra L2 where the renal pelvis first narrows into the ureter, (2) at the sacroiliac joint in the pelvis, (3) where the ureters enter the bladder.

6. Since the external orifice of the urethra lies directly anterior to the anus, wiping from back to front draws fecal bacteria toward the urethra and leads to urinary tract infections. Spermicide kills the normal resident bacteria and allows pathogenic fecal bacteria to colonize the vagina, from which they spread into the nearby urethra. (See the Disorders section.)

SUPPLEMENTAL STUDENT MATERIALS TO HUMAN ANATOMY, THIRD EDITION
Chapter 23: The Urinary System

To the Student

Perhaps a nice, juicy steak is one of your favorite foods. Why mention food in a chapter titled "The Urinary System"? When your body processes food, metabolic wastes are produced. For example, a steak is meat, meat contains protein, protein is made of amino acids, amino acids contain nitrogen, and nitrogen-containing substances are poison to your cells if they accumulate in your tissues and blood. Kidneys filter organic wastes from the blood and help maintain the purity and chemical constancy of the blood with, of course, the production of urine as a vital excretory result. Thoroughly review all the functions of the kidneys because removal of nitrogenous waste is only one of many important functions. There is an excess of 1 million structural and functional units of the kidney called uriniferous tubules, consisting of nephrons plus collecting tubules. Collectively, in one kidney, uriniferous tubules are an estimated 85 miles long, and filter approximately 1200 ml (about 5 cups) of blood per minute. The number of uriniferous tubules is constant from birth, and new ones do not form in the event of injury or disease—hence, the significance of kidney transplants and artificial kidney machines.

Step 1: Describe the gross structure and function of the kidneys.

- ☐ List all functions accomplished by kidneys during the formation of urine.
- ☐ Identify all organs associated with the transport and storage of urine.
- ☐ Describe the external gross anatomy of kidneys, including location and hili.
- ☐ Name the structures that enter and leave the kidney through the renal hilus.
- ☐ Distinguish between perirenal fat and pararenal fat, commenting on their functions.
- ☐ Distinguish between the renal capsule and renal fascia, commenting on their functions.
- ☐ Describe the internal gross anatomy of the kidney, defining *renal cortex, renal medulla, renal pyramids, renal pelvis, renal sinus,* and *major* and *minor calyces.*
- ☐ Explain the nerve supply to the kidneys.
- ☐ Draw a flowchart representing the vascular pathway through a kidney, beginning with the renal artery and ending with the renal vein. (Hint: Refer to Figure 23.8 and 23.9, if needed.)

Step 2: Describe the microscopic anatomy of the kidneys and urine formation.

- ☐ Identify the main structural and functional unit of the kidney, naming its two major parts, and explain their orientation within the kidney.
- ☐ Define basic kidney functions during urine production: *filtration, reabsorption,* and *secretion.*
- ☐ Name the parts and explain how each part of the uriniferous tubule contributes to urine formation.
- ☐ Identify the part of the filtration barrier that prevents the passage of red blood cells into the capsular space. (Hint: Refer to Figure 23.7c.)
- ☐ Explain how the unique structure of podocytes contributes to filtration.

- ☐ Draw a single, generalized uriniferous tubule, showing its basic relationship to blood vessels and sites of filtration, reabsorption, and secretion. (Hint: Refer to Figure 23.6.)
- ☐ Explain how the kidney acts to conserve water and prevent dehydration.
- ☐ Identify two major categories of nephrons, pointing out their major differences.
- ☐ Describe the association of microscopic blood vessels and the uriniferous tubule, being very observant with the interlobar and interlobular vessels.
- ☐ Name specific beds of capillaries and identify their roles in urine production.
- ☐ Explain the structure and function of the juxtaglomerular apparatus and describe its location with respect to the gross structure of the kidney.
- ☐ Define and describe *renal interstitium*.

Step 3: Describe the gross structure and microscopic structure of the other organs of the urinary system: ureters, urinary bladder, and urethra.

- ☐ Describe the location and function of the ureters.
- ☐ Explain the histological structure of the ureteral (ureteric) wall.
- ☐ Explain how urine moves through the ureter.
- ☐ Describe the location of the urinary bladder, explaining positions and shapes of full and empty urinary bladders.
- ☐ Define *urachus*, indicating its embryonic origin.
- ☐ Define *trigone*, explaining the relationship of openings located there.
- ☐ Describe the histological structure of the urinary bladder, explaining why distensibility is unique for this organ.
- ☐ Describe the location and function of the urethra, including the sphincters.
- ☐ Explain the gross anatomical differences of the urethra between males and females.
- ☐ Explain how urine moves through the urethra.
- ☐ Define *micturition*.

Step 4: Describe disorders of the urinary system and changes that occur with aging.

- ☐ List basic symptoms and features of specific disorders such as urinary tract infections, kidney stones, and cancer of the urinary bladder or kidney.
- ☐ Trace the embryonic origin of the organs of the urinary tract.
- ☐ List several effects of aging on the organs of the urinary tract.

CHAPTER 24
The Reproductive System

LECTURE AND DEMONSTRATION
Student Objectives

1. Describe the location, structure, and function of the testes.
2. Describe the histology of the testes, and outline the events of spermatogenesis.
3. Describe the location, structure, and functions of the accessory organs of the male reproductive system.
4. Describe the structure of the penis, and explain the mechanism of erection.
5. Describe the location, structure, and function of the ovaries.
6. Explain the phases of the ovarian cycle and the stages of oogenesis.
7. Describe the anatomy of the uterine tubes in terms of their function.
8. Explain the location, regions, supportive structures, and layers of the uterus.
9. Outline the three phases of the uterine cycle.
10. Explain the structure of the vagina in terms of its functions.
11. Describe the anatomy of the female external genitalia.
12. Describe the anatomy of the mammary glands, and explain their clinical importance.
13. Describe the processes of implantation and placenta formation.
14. Define a *placental (chorionic) villus*, and explain its functions.
15. List the three phases of labor.
16. Consider various cancers of the reproductive organs, especially prostate cancer and breast cancer.
17. Compare and contrast the prenatal development of the male and female sex organs.
18. Note the anatomical changes that occur during puberty and menopause.

Suggested Lecture Outline

I. The Male Reproductive System (pp. 702–715, Fig. 24.1)

    A. The Scrotum (p. 703, Fig. 24.2)

    B. The Testes (pp. 703–708, Figs. 24.3–24.5)

        1. Gross Anatomy

        2. The Seminiferous Tubules and Spermatogenesis

I. THE MALE REPRODUCTIVE SYSTEM *(continued)*

    C. The Reproductive Duct System in Males (pp. 708–710, Figs. 24.6–24.8)

        1. The Epididymis

        2. The Ductus Deferens

        3. The Spermatic Cord

        4. The Urethra

    D. Accessory Glands (pp. 710–712, Figs. 24.8, 24.9, and 24.1)

        1. The Seminal Vesicles

        2. The Prostate Gland

        3. The Bulbourethral Glands

    E. The Penis (pp. 712–715, Fig. 24.7)

    F. The Male Perineum (p. 715)

II. *The Female Reproductive System (pp. 715–726, Figs. 24.10 and 24.11)*

    A. The Ovaries (pp. 715–718, Figs. 24.11–24.15)

        1. The Ovarian Cycle

        2. Oogenesis

    B. The Uterine Tubes (pp. 718–720, Figs. 24.10 and 24.11)

    C. The Uterus (pp. 720–724, Figs. 24.10b, and 24.16–24.19)

        1. Supports of the Uterus

        2. The Uterine Wall

        3. The Uterine Cycle

    D. The Vagina (p. 724, Figs. 24.10 and 24.20)

    E. The External Genitalia and Female Perineum (pp. 724–725, Figs. 24.20 and 24.21)

    F. The Mammary Glands (pp. 725–726, Fig. 24.22)

III. *Pregnancy and Childbirth (pp. 726–732)*

    A. Pregnancy (pp. 727–729, Figs. 24.23–24.26)

        1. Events Leading to Fertilization

        2. Implantation

        3. Formation of the Placenta

        4. Anatomy of the Placenta

    B. Childbirth (pp. 729–732, Fig. 24.27)

IV. *Disorders of the Reproductive System (pp. 732–734)*

    A. Reproductive System Cancers in Males

        1. Testicular Cancer

        2. Prostate Cancer

B. Reproductive System Cancers in Females

    1. Ovarian Cancer

    2. Endometrial Cancer

    3. Cervical Cancer

    4. Breast Cancer

V. *The Reproductive System Throughout Life (pp. 734–738)*

    A. Embryonic Development of the Sex Organs (pp. 734–737, Figs. 24.28 and 24.29)

    B. Descent of the Gonads (pp. 737–738, Fig. 24.30)

    C. Puberty (p. 738)

    D. Menopause (p. 738)

Lecture Hints

1. Describe basic functions of the male and female reproductive systems.
2. Define *genitalia*, *gonads*, and *gametes*.
3. Introduce the structures of the male reproductive system using Figure 24.1.
4. Describe the gross anatomy of the scrotum, distinguishing between the dartos muscle and the cremaster muscles. Refer to Figure 24.2.
5. Continue stressing word origins. ("Testes" is a wonderfully classical example. Historically, men did not "testify or witness" by placing their hands over their hearts or on the Bible, but by placing their hands elsewhere…. And, women were not permitted to testify at all; wonder why?)
6. Describe the location, gross anatomy, and function of the testes, and include the descent of the testes at this time, if desired. Refer to Figures 24.3 and 24.30.
7. Explain the tunica vaginalis as a serous membrane.
8. Describe the histology of the seminiferous tubules. Refer to Figure 24.4.
9. Describe the events of spermatogenesis, distinguishing between formation of the spermatocytes, meiosis, and spermiogenesis. Refer to Figures 24.4 and 24.5.
10. Explain the function of the sustentacular (Sertoli) cells and the formation of the blood-testis barrier. Refer to Figure 24.4.
11. Describe the location and function of the myoid cells and the interstitial (Leydig) cells. Refer to Figure 24.3b.
12. Discuss the mechanisms that are used to keep testes cool for viable sperm production.
13. Describe the location, structure, and function of the epididymis, ductus deferens, spermatic cord, and urethra. Refer to Figures 24.6–24.8.
14. Distinguish clearly between the ductus deferens and the spermatic cord.
15. Trace the route traveled by sperm cells from the testis to the external urethral orifice, stressing passage through the anterior body wall via the inguinal canal. Refer to Figure 24.1 and Figures 24.7–24.8.
16. Identify the location, structure, and functions of the accessory glands involved in semen production: the seminal vesicles, the prostate, and the bulbourethral glands, indicating where

secretions are added to sperm and functions of the secretions. Refer to Figures 24.1 and Figures 24.8–24.9.

17. Using Figure 24.8, describe the gross anatomy of the penis, including erectile tissues and the mechanism of erection. (It may be of interest to students that the penis of various mammals, such as the raccoon, contains a bone called the baculum or os penis.)
18. Define the male *perineum*.
19. Using Figure 24.10, present an overview of the female internal reproductive organs.
20. Describe the location, structure, and function of the ovaries, including various mesenteries and ligaments of support. Refer to Figures 24.10–24.12.
21. Define *menstrual cycle*, stressing the complexity of hormonal control of ovarian and uterine activities.
22. Discuss the three phases of the ovarian cycle, using Figures 24.13 and 24.19, identifying major characteristics of each phase, and including changes to the endometrium (uterine cycle) at this time, if desired.
23. Explain oogenesis, stressing the female gamete maturity time frame (years, as opposed to weeks for male gamete development). Refer to Figure 24.15.
24. Describe the location, structure, and function of the uterine tubes, including how an ovulated oocyte emters the tube, as well as how it is propelled along the tube. Refer to Figure 24.10.
25. Remind students of the unique relationship of a mucous membrane (the lining of the tube) meeting a serous membrane (visceral peritoneum) at the infundibulum.
26. Describe the location, gross anatomy, and function of the uterus, including supports of the uterus, and the anatomy of the uterine wall. Refer to Figure 24.10 and Figures 24.16–24.18.
27. Describe the changes to the endometrium that occur during the uterine cycle. Refer to Figure 24.19.
28. Point out that although FSH and LH are named for female structures, they have male functions as well.
29. Describe the location, gross anatomy, and functions of the vagina, including the anatomy of the vaginal wall and location of the vaginal fornix. Refer to Figures 24.10 and 24.20.
30. Caution students not to confuse the anatomical location of the cervix of the uterus with the fornix of the vagina.
31. Stress the continuity of the mucosa from the vagina to the infundibulum and the potential for pathogens to enter the peritoneal cavity using this pathway.
32. Describe the anatomy of the external female genitalia and perineum. Refer to Figure 24.20.
33. Describe and distinguish between the mammary glands and the breast. Refer to Figure 24.22.
34. Discuss the events related to pregnancy and childbirth, including the processes leading to fertilization, implantation, and formation and anatomy of the placenta. Refer to Figures 24.23–24.26.
35. Discuss disorders of the reproductive system, emphasizing prostate cancer and breast cancer.
36. Compare and contrast the embryonic development of the male and female internal reproductive organs and external genitalia. Refer to Figures 24.28 and 24.29.
37. Describe the descent of the gonads, comparing the testes and ovaries, and explain that if the

testes do not descend, infertility and a higher incidence of testicular cancer result. Refer to Figure 24.30.

38. Compare anatomical changes that occur during puberty and menopause.

Classroom Discussion Topics and Activities

1. Use a dissectible model of the human torso to exhibit male and female reproductive organs.
2. Demonstrate dissected cats or rats of both sexes. Try to obtain a pregnant female.
3. Use a "pregnant" torso model or chart to illustrate the most desirable positioning of the placenta and the vertex presentation of a fetus.
4. Use a chart showing a pregnant and nonpregnant uterus, sagittal view, pointing out the relationship between the uterus, urinary bladder, and pelvic bone, explaining why a pregnant female frequently has to urinate.
5. If available, show preserved specimens of human embryos and/or fetuses in various stages of development. Include a placenta and attached umbilical cord, if possible.
6. Display preserved human male and female reproductive system specimens, if possible. Students are always surprised at how small an ovary or a never-been-pregnant uterus actually is.
7. Display models showing the process of meiosis in spermatogenesis and oogenesis.
8. Tie a long string around a softball to model the male duct system and the testis. Blow up a balloon and push the softball into the balloon to represent the testis surrounded by the tunica vaginalis. The leather cover of the softball represents the tunica albuginea.
9. Use a doll, a drawstring sack (uterus), and a model of the bony pelvis to illustrate the placement of the fetus for vaginal delivery and the turning movements that allow the baby to move through the pelvis during the delivery. (For more information, see the discussion of the female bony pelvis in Chapter 7.)
10. Discuss the need for mammograms and self-examination for early diagnosis of breast cancers. Discuss the self-examination procedure and distribute a handout showing the correct breast examination procedure. Ask the students if it is possible for males to develop breast cancer. Discuss the current treatments for breast cancer.
11. Discuss the need for self-exams for testicular cancer. Discuss how the procedure is done and distribute handouts showing the correct testicular examination procedure.
12. Discuss the various causes of and treatments for infertility.
13. Discuss similarities and differences between the blood-brain barrier and the blood-testis barrier.
14. Multiple births have always attracted attention. Instruct students to find out the difference between fraternal and identical twins, and to illustrate what events occur by combining information from Chapter 3 with Chapter 24.
15. Draw the human life cycle, incorporating the following concepts: meiosis and mitosis, spermatogenesis and oogenesis, haploid and diploid, fertilization and implantation, and embryo and fetus, as well as differentiation, growth, and time of sexual maturity.

Clinical Questions

1. Blaine and Andrew were best friends who, during their youth, had held similar beliefs about preventing world overpopulation. Both had received vasectomies on the same day in the same clinic, and both regretted it later, after they were married. Blaine's vasectomy proved to be surgically reversible, while Andrew's was not. Explain why many vasectomies lead to permanent sterility.

   Answer: Following some vasectomies (Andrew's), lymphocytes are able to enter the cut-open end of the ductus deferens, reach the testis, attack the sperm, and cause sterility. (The lymphocytes go around the blood-testis barrier that normally keeps lymphocytes away from sperm.) In other vasectomies (Blaine's), lymphocytes do not enter the tied end of the ductus deferens, do not reach the testes, and do not cause sterility; thus Blaine's vasectomy was successfully reversed when the two ends of his ductus were surgically reunited. (A newer explanation is that the sperm may leak out the open end of the ductus deferens after a vasectomy, leading to lymphocyte activation.)

2. A man in an isolated rural area called his physician and said that his 3-year-old son had several openings along the underside of his penis. The father and mother had not noticed this when the child was an infant in diapers, but now that the boy was being toilet trained it was obvious that urine dribbled out the wrong part of the penis. What was the boy's condition, and what is its embryological origin? Is the condition correctable?

   Answer: The boy had hypospadias, a condition in which the right and left urethral folds do not fuse completely, leaving openings along the ventral midline of the penis. It is easy to correct surgically.

3. An alcoholic woman had ascites (a buildup of excess serous fluid in the peritoneal cavity). Her physician inserted a syringe into her vagina and drained out most of this excess fluid. Exactly where was the tip of the syringe needle located?

   Answer: The tip of the needle was in the rectouterine pouch, which lies directly posterior to the posterior vaginal fornix. This is the most inferior point of the peritoneal cavity, so gravity causes the fluid of ascites to accumulate here.

4. Assume that a woman could be an "on-demand" ovulator like a rabbit, in which copulation stimulates the hypothalamus and anterior pituitary to release a surge of LH—and that an oocyte was ovulated on day 26 of the woman's 28-day cycle. Why would a successful pregnancy be unlikely at this time?

   Answer: A successful pregnancy would be unlikely so late in the cycle because progesterone levels would have fallen, depriving the uterine endometrium of hormonal support. The endometrial cells would have begun to die, and menstruation would be about to start. The fertilized egg would not be able to implant in the shedding wall of a menstruating uterus.

5. A 30-year-old woman is admitted to the emergency room. Her husband, who rode in the ambulance with her, said that she had suddenly complained of severe pain in the right iliac region of her abdomen and then had collapsed. Upon examination, she showed signs of internal hemorrhage and her abdominal muscles were rigid. Her menstrual history revealed that she had missed her last menstrual period. A diagnosis of ruptured tubal pregnancy was made, and surgery was scheduled. What is an ectopic tubal pregnancy, and why is it problematic?

Answer: An ectopic pregnancy occurs when the embryo implants in any site other than the uterine endometrium. In a tubal pregnancy, the embryo implants in the thin wall of the uterine tube. This tube is unable to establish a placenta or accommodate growth, and it ruptures. Severe internal bleeding results.

ART RESOURCES
Transparency List

Figure 24.1	Reproductive organs of the male, sagittal view.
Figure 24.2	The scrotum, containing the testis and spermatic cord.
Figure 24.3	Structure of the testis.
Figure 24.4	The seminiferous tubule and spermatogenesis.
Figure 24.5	Spermiogenesis: Transformation of a spermatid into a sperm.
Figure 24.8	Male urethra and the penis.
Figure 24.9	The prostate gland.
Figure 24.10	Female internal reproductive organs.
Figure 24.11	Arteries of the internal female genitalia.
Figure 24.12	Structure of the ovary.
Figure 24.13	Schematic diagram of the ovarian cycle: Development and fate of the ovarian follicles.
Figure 24.15	Oogenesis.
Figure 24.20	The external genitalia (vulva) of the female.
Figure 24.21	Deep structures of the external genitalia and perineum of the female.
Figure 24.22	Structure of a lactating (milk-secreting) mammary gland.
Figure 24.23	Events leading to fertilization: The acrosomal and cortical reactions.
Figure 24.25	Implantation and stages of placenta formation.
Figure 24.27	Stages of labor.
Figure 24.28	Development of the internal reproductive organs in both sexes.
Figure 24.29	Development of the external genitalia in both sexes.
Figure 24.30	Descent of the testes.

Teaching with Art

Figure 24.1 Reproductive organs of the male, sagittal view.

Figure 24.10 Female internal reproductive organs: (a) Posterior view; (b) Midsagittal section.

Textbook pp. 702 and 714; transparencies; Digital Archive CD-ROM.

Checklist of Key Points in the Figure

- In Figure 24.1, describe the location, structure, and function of the testes.
- In Figure 24.1, trace the route traveled by sperm, naming ducts, describing the male accessory organs, describing the structure of the penis, and explaining the formation of semen.

- In Figure 24.10, describe the location, structure, and function of the ovaries.
- In Figure 24.10, trace the movement of an ovulated oocyte to the lumen of the uterus, describing the anatomy of the uterine tube and explaining the location, regions, supportive structures, and layers of the uterus.

Common Conceptual Difficulties Interpreting the Art
- Remind students of the difference between meiosis and mitosis.
- Review the basics of spermatogenesis and oogenesis.
- Explain *how* sperm and oocytes move through their respective ducts.

Art Exercises
Provide students with several unlabeled copies of Figures 24.1 and 24.10.

1. Pathway Exercise:
   a. Instruct students to color code the route traveled by sperm from the testis to the external urethral meatus, naming all structures along the way.
   b. Instruct students to color code the route traveled by an ovulated oocyte from the surface of the ovary to the lumen of the uterus, naming all structures along the way.
   c. Instruct students to color code and trace the path followed by a sperm cell from the testis all the way to the location of possible fertilization, naming all structures along the way.

2. Male and Female Homologies Exercise:

   Review the meaning of the term *homology* with students, referring students to Figure 24.29. Provide this list of the male and female reproductive homologies and instruct students to identify and color code each pair of structures using the provided unlabeled figures:

Male	Female
a. scrotum	labia majora
b. testes	ovaries
c. penis	clitoris
d. spermatic cord	round ligament of uterus

Critical Reasoning

1. Two students expressed opposing views as to whether ejaculation comes directly from the testes or directly from the epididymis. Which one is correct?

   Answer: The latter is correct because the sperm must first spend weeks in the epididymis. (Many students do not realize this.)

2. Two students also expressed opposing views as to whether an ovulated oocyte first is deposited directly into the end of the uterine tube or first is deposited into the peritoneal cavity. Which one is correct?

   Answer: The latter is correct. There is essentially no direct contact between the uterine tube and the ovary. The uterine tube only receives the oocyte due to complex movements of the infundibulum and fimbriae, which generate currents in the peritoneal cavity that carry the oocyte into the uterine tube. (There is evidence that one little fimbria of the uterine tube always attaches to the ovary!)

3. Ask students to answer the question "Are the internal male ducts homologous to those in the female, and why or why not?"

    Answer: The answer is "no" because male ducts develop from the embryonic mesonephric duct and female ducts develop from the embryonic paramesonephric duct.

SUPPLEMENTAL COURSE MATERIALS
Library Research Topics

1. Research procedures involved with artificial insemination, including sperm storage, sperm banks, and sperm bank donors.
2. Research the current treatments for disorders of the prostate gland. What is the mechanism of the new pills that can shrink a hyperplastic prostate?
3. Research the disorders associated with the menstrual cycle.
4. Research how birth control pills work. Evaluate the evidence that the pill increases one's likelihood of developing breast cancer.
5. Research the incidence of and reasons for hysterectomies in the United States, and evaluate whether this operation is overperformed.

Audiovisual Aids/Computer Software

See Preface of the Instructor's Guide for Key to Audiovisual Distributors

Videotapes

1. *Cancer: Working Towards a Cure* (FHS, 21 min., 1995)
2. *Chlamydia: The Hidden Disease* (FHS, 22 min.)
3. *Contemporary Childbirth* (FHS, 19 min., C). New trends in childbirth include a strong emphasis on preparation even before conception.
4. *A Dozen Eggs: Time Lapse Microscopy of Normal Development* (IM, 46 min., 1991)
5. *The Female* (NIMCO, 28 min., 1993)
6. *Genetics and Heredity: The Blueprint of Life* (CBS, 22 min.)
7. *Genital Herpes* (FHS, 18 min.)
8. *Gonorrhea/Chlamydia* (PLP, 7 min., 1991)
9. *Herpes* (PLP, 10 min., 1991)
10. *The Human Body: Reproductive System* (COR, 18 min., 1993)
11. *The Human Body: The Reproductive System* (Ward's, 15 min.)
12. *Human Embryology Series* (ACG, 6-part series)
13. *Human Embryology Series: Reproductive or Sexual Cycles in the Female, Parts I and II* (TFI, VHS, or BETA; 11 min. each)
14. *Human Reproduction: Ovulation to Birth* (IM, 18 min., 1992)
15. *Human Reproductive Biology: Overcoming Infertility* (FHS, 23 min., 1998)
16. *The Human Reproductive Systems* (BC, 32 min., 1999)

17. *Infertility: New Treatments* (FHS, 25 min., 1995)
18. *In the Womb* (*Body Atlas Series*) (CAP/HCA, 30 min., 1994)
19. *The Living Body: Coming Together* (FHS, 28 min., 1990)
20. *The Living Body: Shares in the Future* (FHS, 26 min., 1990)
21. *The Male* (NIMCO, 28 min., 1993)
22. *Meiosis* (HRM, 11 min.)
23. *Meiosis* (HRM, 26 min.)
24. *Meiosis—The Key to Genetic Diversity* (HRM, 26 min., 1991)
25. *The Miracle of Life* (CBS/FSE/NS, 60 min.)
26. *Mitosis and Meiosis* (IM, 24 min., 1994)
27. *One out of Eleven: Women and Breast Cancer* (FHS, 26 min., 1992)
28. *The Placenta and Fetal Membranes* (TFI, 24 min., C, 1988). This program demonstrates the early development of the embryo and its associated membranes, and describes how the placenta develops from a combination of embryonic and maternal tissues. The placental circulation is also discussed.
29. *A Practical Guide to Sexually Transmitted Diseases* (FHS, 23 min.)
30. *Reproduction* (FHS, 15 min., 1997)
31. *Reproduction: Designer Babies* (*New Living Body Series*) (FHS, 20 min., 1995)
32. *Reproduction in Humans* (*Anatomy and Physiology Series*) (CAP/HCA, 27 min.)
33. *Reproduction in Humans* (NIMCO, 27 min.)
34. *Reproductive Systems* (IM, 20 min., 1998)
35. *Safe Sex* (FHS, VHS, or BETA; 28 min.; C). Discusses safe sex, especially in reference to AIDS.
36. *Sex* (*Body Atlas Series*) (CAP/HCA, 30 min., 1994)
37. *The Sexual Brain* (FHS, VHS, or BETA; 28 min.; C). Provides some of the answers that separate cultural and social differences between men and women from physiological ones.
38. *Sexually Transmitted Diseases* (FHS, 19 min., 1990)
39. *Sexually Transmitted Diseases: Causes, Prevention, and Cure* (GA, 55 min., 1990)
40. *Shares in the Future* (FHS, VHS, or BETA; 26 min.; C). Shows the characteristics of sperm and ova and how each contains a partial blueprint for the future offspring. The mechanism of cell division is shown through exceptional microphotography.
41. *STDs and Safer Sex: Your Risk and Responsibility* (BC, 20 min., 1992)
42. *What You Don't Know CAN Kill You: Sexually Transmitted Diseases and AIDS* (GA, 54 min., 1990)
43. *Woman and Man* (FHS, 52 min., 1990)
44. *A Woman's Body* (FHS, 49 min., 1990)

Computer Software

1. *The Anatomy Project: The Reproductive System and Pelvis* (NIMCO, 1998)
2. *Biology Achievement Series, Series II: Reproduction and Development* (QUE, MIC4000A, Apple). Over 10,000 problems, some with graphics.

3. *Body Language: Study of Human Anatomy, Reproductive Systems* (PLP, CH-182019, Apple; CH-182018, IBM)
4. *CD-Atlas of Sexually Transmitted Diseases and AIDS* (DGI, 1997)
5. *Describing Patterns in Reproduction, Growth, and Development* (QUE, MVM4008A, Apple; MVM4008H, IBM)
6. *Dynamics of the Human Reproductive System* (EI, C3055A, Apple; C3055M, IBM, 1988). Combines straightforward, concise text with engaging animated graphics, sound effects, and an interactive quiz to instruct and challenge.
7. *Fundamentals of Genetics and Heredity* (CVB)
8. *The Human Body, Part II* (HCA, Disk for IBM, 1995)
9. *The Human Systems: Series 3* (PLP, CH-140220, Apple)
10. *Introduction to General Biology Series: Disk XI—The Human Body, Part II* (QUE, COM4240A, Apple; COM4240B, IBM)
11. *Meiosis* (NIMCO, 1996)
12. *Reproduction, Growth, and Development* (QUE, INT4158A, Apple; INT4158B, IBM)
13. *Reproductive Systems* (PLP, CH-378013, Apple)

Slides

1. *Reproductive System and its Function* (EI, Slides, and Filmstrip). This graphic depiction of human male and female sexual anatomy introduces a discussion of the hormonally directed physiological changes associated with the reproductive system.
2. *Histology of the Reproductive System* (EI, Slides). Views of the male and female tissues, including sections of the forming gametes within the gonads, ducts of the ovaries and testes, accessory reproductive glands, organs of copulation, and the relationships of tissues within each system.

Suggested Readings

Alexander, N. Future contraceptives. *Scientific American* 273 (September 1995): 136–141.

Aral, S.O., and K. Holmes. Sexually transmitted diseases in the AIDS era. *Scientific American* 264 (February 1991): 62–69.

Avisse, C., et al. The inguinal rings. *Surgical Clinics of North America* 80 (February 2000): 49–69.

Brink, S. Prostate dilemmas. *U.S. News and World Report* 128 (May 22, 2000): 66–81.

Cormack, D.H. *Essential Histology*. Philadelphia: J.B. Lippincott, 1993.

Coustan, D.R. *Human Reproduction: Growth and Development*. Boston: Little, Brown, 1995.

Cowley, G., and D. Iarovici. Rethinking prostate surgery. *Newsweek* (August 5, 1991): 48.

Dest, V., and S. Fisher. Breast cancer: Dreaded diagnosis, complicated care. *RN* (June 1994): 48–54.

Fackelmann, K. Refiguring the odds: What's a woman's real chance of suffering breast cancer? *Science News* 144 (July 31, 1993): 76–77.

Fackelmann, K. Setting odds on extremity defects after chorionic villus sampling. *Science News* 146 (July 9, 1994): 21.

Fawcett, D.W. *A Textbook of Histology*. 12th ed. New York: Chapman & Hall, 1994, Chapters 31–33.

Ferenczy, A. Ultrastructure of the normal menstrual cycle: A review. *Microscopy Research and Technique* 25 (1993): 91–105.

Garnick, M. The dilemmas of prostate cancer. *Scientific American* 270 (April 1994): 72–81.

Gibbons, W. Clueing in on chlamydia. *Science News* 139 (April 20, 1991): 250–252.

Grabowski, C.T. *Human Reproduction and Development*. Philadelphia: W.B. Saunders, 1983.

Greer, J. *Mosby's Color Atlas and Text of Obstetrics and Gynecology*. St. Louis: Mosby, 1999.

Hafez, E.S.E. *Human Reproduction*. 2nd ed. New York: Harper and Row, 1980.

Hayes, D.F., et al. *Atlas of Breast Cancer*. St. Louis: Mosby, 1993.

Hermo, L. Introduction. (In an issue on the structure and function of the epididymis and male efferent ducts.) *Microscopy Research and Technique* 29 (1994): 409.

Hillis, S. PID prevention: Clinical and societal stakes. *Hospital Practice* (April 15, 1994): 121–130.

Hinton, B., and M. Palladino. Epididymal epithelium: Its contribution to the formation of a luminal fluid microenvironment. *Microscopy Research and Technique* 30 (1995): 67–81.

Jones, R.E. *Human Reproduction and Sexual Behavior*. Englewood Cliffs, NJ: Prentice Hall, 1984.

Junqueira, L.C., et al. *Basic Histology*. 9th ed. Stamford, Conn.: Appleton & Lange, 1998.

Kirby, R.S., and T.J. Christmas. *Benign Prostatic Hyperplasia*. 2nd ed. St. Louis: Mosby, 1998.

Kirby, R.S., et al. *Prostate Cancer*. St. Louis: Mosby, 1996.

Kotsuji, F., and T. Tominaga. The role of granulosa and theca cell interactions in ovarian structure and function. *Microscopy Research and Techniques* 27 (1994): 97–107.

Lipshultz, L.I., and S.S. Howards. *Infertility in the Male*. 3rd ed. St. Louis: Mosby, 1997.

Mann, W. Diagnosis and management of epithelial cancer of the ovary. *American Family Physician* (February 15, 1994): 613–618.

Mishell, D.R., et al. *Comprehensive Gynecology*. 3rd ed. St. Louis: Mosby, 1997.

Moore, K.L. *Clinically Oriented Anatomy*. 34th ed. Philadelphia: Lippincott Williams and Wilkins, 1999.

Raspa, R. Complications of vasectomy. *American Family Physician* 48 (November 15, 1993): 1264–1267.

Robbins, S.L., V. Kumar, and R. Cotran. *Basic Pathology*. 6th ed. Philadelphia: W.B. Saunders, 1997.

Romanes, G.J. *Cunningham's Textbook of Anatomy*. 12th ed. Oxford, New York: Oxford University Press, 1981.

Roy, S. Regulation of ovarian follicular development: A review of microscopic studies. *Microscopy Research and Technique* 27 (1994): 83–96.

Ryan, K.J., et al. *Kistner's Gynecology and Women's Health*. 7th ed. St. Louis: Mosby, 1999.

Science. Special Issue: Reproduction: New Developments. 266 (December 2, 1994): 1484–1527.

Shulman, L., and S. Elias. Amniocentesis and chorionic villus sampling. *Western Journal of Medicine* 159 (1993): 260–268.

Westrom, L. Pelvic inflammatory disease. *JAMA* 266 (November 13, 1991): 2612.

Williams, P.L., et al. *Gray's Anatomy*. 38th ed. New York: Churchill Livingstone, 1995.

ANSWERS TO TEXTBOOK QUESTIONS

Answers for multiple-choice and matching questions 1–12 are located in Appendix B of the textbook.

Short Answer and Essay Questions

13. The regions of a sperm cell are the head and tail, with the first part of the tail being the midpiece. The head contains the nucleus and the acrosome. Enzymes in the acrosome digest through the zona pellucida and corona radiata around the oocyte prior to fertilization. The tail is a flagellum whose movements propel the sperm, and the midpiece contains many mitochondria that provide energy to move the tail.

14. (a) Each ductus deferens ascends through the scrotum and inguinal canal to enter the pelvic cavity through the deep inguinal ring. From there, it extends posteriorly along the lateral wall of the true pelvis, arches medially over the ureter, and descends along the posterior wall of the bladder. Its expanded end, the ampulla, then joins with the duct of the seminal vesicle to form the ejaculatory duct. Each ejaculatory duct runs within the prostate gland inferior to the bladder, where it empties into the urethra. (b) An ejaculated sperm is squeezed from the epididymis through the ductus deferens, ejaculatory duct, and urethra to exit the penis and enter the female vagina. From there, the sperm swim through the lumen of the uterus to a uterine tube and fertilize an oocyte in the ampulla of this tube.

15. If fertilization fails to occur in a particular menstrual cycle, the corpus luteum in the ovary degenerates and stops secreting progesterone. Blood-progesterone levels fall, depriving the endometrium of hormonal support. Cells in the functional layer leak lysosomal enzymes (which initiate tissue necrosis) and release prostaglandins (which signal the spinal arteries to constrict spasmodically). Denied oxygen, the endometrial cells die and release still more lysosomal enzymes until the functional layer starts to "self-digest." The spinal arteries then constrict one final time and suddenly open wide. As blood gushes into the weakened capillary beds, these vessels fragment, causing the stratum functionale to slough off. This is menstruation (see Figure 24.19).

16. (a) Please see stages 1–6, as described in the legend of Figure 24.13. (b) Middle of the cycle, around day 14.

17. In a mastectomy, the surgeon must cauterize (1) the lateral thoracic artery, and the cutaneous branches of (2) the internal thoracic artery and (3) the posterior intercostal arteries that supply the breast.

18. The bulbourethral glands (and urethral glands) secrete a mucus into the urethra before ejaculation. This lubricates the urethra and clears it of traces of acidic urine before the ejaculated semen passes through.

19. His cremaster muscles had reflexively pulled his testes superiorly, closer to the warmth of his body.

20. The statement is false. There is no mixing of fetal and maternal blood. Any exchange across the placenta is through the diffusion or transport of molecules from one bloodstream to the other. (See the discussion of the placental barrier on p. 729.)

21. The blood-testis barrier is formed by tight junctions between adjacent sustentacular cells near the base of the epithelium in the seminiferous tubules. This barrier prevents antigen

molecules on the sperm-forming cells and sperm from leaking into the blood vessels that lie directly external to the tubules, for such leakage would induce an autoimmune response against sperm cells (and, consequently, sterility).

22. (a) *Sperm* is the final stage in the sequence of male gamete differentiation, in which a *spermatocyte* is an earlier stage (see Figure 24.4). (b) The *epididymis* is a large, comma-shaped structure superior and lateral to the testis; it contains both the coiled *duct of the epididymis* and the efferent ductules. (c) The *ovarian ligament* is a fibrous band extending medially from the ovary, whereas the *suspensory ligament* is a fold of mesentery extending superiorly and laterally from the ovary (see Figure 24.10). (d) The *vulva* is all the female external genitalia, but the *vestibule* is just the space between the two labia minora. (e) *Spermatogenesis* is the entire process of sperm formation, the transformation of spermatogonia stem cells to complete sperm cells. *Spermiogenesis*, on the other hand, is merely the final stage of spermatogenesis, in which spherical spermatids transform into tadpole-shaped sperm cells.

Critical Reasoning and Clinical Applications Questions

1. The correct answer is (a), a radical mastectomy. Only a radical mastectomy removes the pectoralis major muscle deep to the breast, the most important muscle for doing push-ups. (See p. 734 and Table 11.9 on p. 297.)

2. Most of the volume of the ejaculate is formed by the secretions of the seminal vesicles (60%: p. 710) and prostate gland (33%: p. 711), not by the sperm themselves. Vasectomy "deletes" sperm from the semen, but the other secretions are still present. Therefore, vasectomy has very little effect on the volume of the ejaculate.

3. The man probably has a tumor of the prostate gland, and the enlargement of this gland is constricting his prostatic urethra. In the rectal exam, a physician is feeling the prostate for swelling and lumps.

4. The woman had a prolapsed uterus. The supporting muscles of her pelvic floor had been stretched and torn repeatedly during her multiple deliveries, and they had lost the ability to support the uterus, which sank inferiorly.

SUPPLEMENTAL STUDENT MATERIALS TO HUMAN ANATOMY, THIRD EDITION

Chapter 24: The Reproductive System

To the Student

Up to this point, along with the structure and function, you have studied the embryology, growth, and development of all the systems that make you unique from other organisms. Your study of male and female reproductive systems provides the information you need to understand how you, as a species, physically survive from one generation to the next. In terms of the human life cycle, this is the last topic to explore. The reproductive system includes the study of the phenomenal mechanisms that result in the production of gametes by the testes and ovaries, and the supporting roles of the many male and female organs that ultimately accomplish the overall reproductive goal, production of offspring. The amount of information is vast and decidedly complicated because of the vital roles played by hormones in processes such as the menstrual cycle and pregnancy.

Step 1: Describe the structure and function of the organs of the male reproductive system.

- ☐ Define *sexual reproduction*.
- ☐ Identify the primary sex organs or gonads of the male and comment on their delayed development compared to other organ systems of the human.
- ☐ Describe the scrotum, and explain the associated structures that aid in regulation of temperature for the testes.
- ☐ Define *testis*, identifying its primary functions and structural features, and explain the origin of the word.
- ☐ Explain completely the details of spermatogenesis, using diagrams and time lines, including the formation of spermatocytes, meiosis, and spermiogensis.
- ☐ Explain how meiosis differs from mitosis, and indicate how many functional sperm result from one diploid cell.
- ☐ Distinguish clearly between examples, structure, and function of spermatogenic cells, sustentacular cells, myoid cells, and interstitial cells and identify whether each type of cell identified is haploid or diploid.

Step 2: Describe the reproductive duct system in males.

- ☐ List the individual parts of the system of ducts through which sperm travel from their point of origin in the testis to the external urethral orifice, explaining the location of each part.
- ☐ Explain the location, histology, and functions of the epididymis. (Hint: Remember sperm are stored here for weeks.)
- ☐ Explain *how* sperm move through the ductus (vas) deferens.
- ☐ Describe the anatomical path of the ductus deferens through the pelvic cavity.
- ☐ Describe the location of the spermatic cord, including its components, and clearly distinguish between it and the ductus deferens.

- ☐ Describe the descent of the testes, an embryological event covered near the end of the chapter, explaining how the tunica vaginalis is a peritoneal structure.
- ☐ Identify the location, structure, and function of the male urethra, relating to its three parts.

Step 3: Describe the accessory glands associated with the male reproductive system.
- ☐ Describe the location, structure, and function of the seminal vesicles, including details of the secretion produced.
- ☐ Describe the location, structure, and function of the prostate, including details of the secretion produced.
- ☐ Describe the location, structure, and function of the bulbourethral glands, including details of the secretion produced.

Step 4: Describe the penis and male perineum.
- ☐ Describe the gross anatomy of the penis, explaining its function.
- ☐ Identify the types of erectile tissues, explaining the mechanism of erection and why the erect penis does not buckle or kink during intercourse.
- ☐ Distinguish between erection and ejaculation.
- ☐ Draw the diamond-shaped region of the male perineum, and label the bony landmarks, structures, and openings contained there.

Step 5: Describe the structure and function of the female gonads, including ovum production and associated hormonal events.
- ☐ Identify the primary sex organs or gonads of the female and comment on their delayed development compared to other organ systems of the human.
- ☐ Describe the location, structure, and function of the ovaries, including their supporting mesenteries and ligaments.
- ☐ Define and describe the *menstrual cycle*, summarizing structural and hormonal changes occurring to the ovary.
- ☐ Define and describe the *follicular phase*, *ovulation*, and the *luteal phase* of the ovarian cycle, including the names of hormones and hormonal functions.
- ☐ Distinguish clearly between FSH and LH, listing functions associated with the menstrual cycle. (Hint: Do not forget that although these hormones are named for female structures, they also have male functions.)
- ☐ Explain how the corpus luteum functions as an endocrine gland.
- ☐ Explain completely the details of oogenesis, using flowchart diagrams and time lines, including the formation of oogonia, meiosis, and ova.
- ☐ Identify which cells in the oogenesis flowchart are haploid and which are diploid.
- ☐ Explain how many functional ova result from one diploid cell.
- ☐ Identify the structure from which an oocyte ovulates and the precise space into which it is released.
- ☐ Define *fertilization*.

Step 6: Describe the accessory ducts and organs associated with the female reproductive system.

☐ Describe the location, structure, and function of the uterine tubes, including specific regions and the histology of the tubular wall.

☐ Explain *how* the ovulated oocyte is propelled into the infundibulum from the peritoneal cavity of the pelvis.

☐ Note the characteristics of the uterine tube that aid movement and help sustain the oocyte or possible embryo on its journey to the uterus.

☐ Describe the location, structure, and function of the uterus, including its gross anatomical features and the function of cervical mucus.

☐ Name and describe the uterine supporting ligaments and mesenteries.

☐ Name the tunics of the uterine wall, explaining their functions.

☐ Describe the uterine structural and hormonal changes associated with the menstrual cycle, identifying three phases.

☐ Explain what happens if fertilization and implantation occur, as well as what happens physically if those events do not occur.

☐ Relate and explain the structure of the vagina to its function, including the layers of the vaginal wall.

☐ Distinguish between the fornix of the vagina and the cervix of the uterus.

Step 7: Describe the vulva and female perineum.

☐ List, locate, and describe the structures of the female external genitalia.

☐ Define the term *homologue*, and identify four male and female homologous structures.

☐ Diagram the female perineum as a diamond-shaped region, and label its bony landmarks, openings, and associated structures.

☐ Describe the structure and function of the mammary glands, distinguishing between mammary glands and breasts.

Step 8: Describe the events that occur in the female reproductive tract during pregnancy and childbirth.

☐ Review stages of basic embryology in Chapter 3.

☐ Define *fertilization* and discuss events leading to sperm penetration of an oocyte.

☐ Describe the process of implantation.

☐ Explain the formation of the placenta, including its structure and function.

☐ Explain the three successive stages of labor involved in childbirth.

Step 9: Explore the disorders of the reproductive system and changes that occur with aging.

☐ Read about reproductive system cancers in males: testicular cancer and prostate cancer, and focus on specific details as instructed by your professor.

☐ Read about reproductive cancers in females: ovarian cancer, endometrial cancer, cervical cancer, and breast cancer, and focus on specific details as instructed by your professor.

- ☐ Describe the embryonic development of the sex organs, and explain why the male ducts and female ducts are not homologous.
- ☐ Describe the descent of the gonads, naming termination points.
- ☐ Note the anatomical changes that occur during puberty and menopause.

CHAPTER 25
The Endocrine System

LECTURE AND DEMONSTRATION
Student Objectives

1. List the major endocrine organs, and describe their locations.
2. Describe how hormones are classified chemically.
3. Describe the basic interaction between hormones and their target cells. Describe three mechanisms that control hormone secretion.
4. Name the basic divisions of the pituitary gland.
5. List the cell types in the adenohypophysis, the hormones secreted by each cell, and the basic functions of each hormone.
6. Explain how the hypothalamus controls secretion of adenohypophyseal hormones. Define *releasing factors*, and trace their path through the pituitary gland.
7. Describe the structure of the neurohypophysis and the functions of the hormones it releases.
8. Describe the anatomy of the thyroid gland. Define *TH* and *calcitonin*, and explain how TH is secreted.
9. Describe the anatomy of the parathyroid gland and the function of parathyroid hormone.
10. Name the two divisions of the adrenal gland. Compare and contrast these divisions in terms of their structures and the hormones they secrete.
11. Describe the ultrastructure of a cell that secretes steroid hormones.
12. Describe the endocrine functions of the pancreas, thymus, and gonads.
13. Name a hormone produced by the heart, and define *DNES*.
14. Briefly explain the endocrine functions of the placenta, kidney, and skin.
15. Describe the effects of excessive and inadequate hormonal secretion by the pituitary, thyroid, and adrenal glands; define *diabetes mellitus*.
16. Describe the development of the major endocrine glands.
17. Describe the effects of aging on some endocrine organs.

Suggested Lecture Outline

I. The Endocrine System: An Overview (pp. 744–745)

A. Endocrine Organs (pp. 744–745, Fig. 25.1)

I. THE ENDOCRINE SYSTEM: AN OVERVIEW *(continued)*

    B. Hormones (p. 745, Fig. 25.2)

        1. Classes of Hormones

        2. Basic Hormone Action

        3. Control of Hormone Secretion

II. *The Major Endocrine Organs (pp. 745–753)*

    A. The Pituitary Gland (pp. 745–753, Figs. 25.2–25.7)

        1. The Adenohypophysis

        2. Hypothalamic Control of Hormone Secretion from the Adenohypophysis

        3. The Neurohypophysis

    B. The Thyroid Gland (pp. 753–754, Fig. 25.8)

    C. The Parathyroid Glands (p. 754, Fig. 25.9)

    D. The Adrenal (Suprarenal) Glands (pp. 754–758, Figs. 25.1 and 25.10)

        1. The Adrenal Medulla

        2. The Adrenal Cortex

        3. Structure of Steroid-Secreting Cells (Fig. 25.11)

    E. The Pineal Gland (p. 758)

    F. The Pancreas (pp. 758–759, Fig. 25.12)

    G. The Thymus (p. 759)

    H. The Gonads (p. 759)

III. *Other Endocrine Structures (pp. 759–760)*

IV. *Disorders of the Endocrine System (pp. 760–761)*

    A. Pituitary Disorders (p. 760)

    B. Disorders of the Thyroid Gland (p. 760)

    C. Disorders of the Adrenal Cortex (p. 760, Fig. 25.13)

    D. A Disorder of the Pancreas: Diabetes Mellitus (p. 761)

V. *The Endocrine System Throughout Life (pp. 762–763, Fig. 25.14)*

Lecture Hints

1. Present an overview of the function of the endocrine system and list major endocrine organs, using Figure 25.1 to identify their locations.

2. Remind students of the difference between an endocrine gland and an exocrine gland.

3. Define *hormone*.

4. Stress the anatomical and functional relationships between the endocrine and nervous systems, explaining how both work to maintain homeostasis and coordinate physiological functions throughout the body.

5. Name several examples of hormonally regulated processes.
6. Emphasis the concept of feedback mechanisms for control of the synthesis and release of hormones.
7. List organs that function purely as endocrine glands; list other organs that combine endocrine function with other activities.
8. Discuss how hormones are classified chemically.
9. Explain the basic interaction between hormones and their target cells, noting that although hormones freely circulate through the body, all tissues are not susceptible to all hormones.
10. Describe three mechanisms that control hormone secretion: humoral stimuli, neural stimuli, and hormonal stimuli. Refer to Figure 25.2.
11. Describe the location and basic divisions of the pituitary gland (hypophysis), including its major vessels. Refer to Figures 25.3 and 25.4.
12. List the cell types in the adenohypophysis, the hormones secreted by each cell type, and the basic functions of each hormone.
13. Define and give examples of *tropic hormones*.
14. Explain the structural and functional relationships between the adenohypophysis and the hypothalamus, explaining how the hypothalamus controls the secretions of hormones from the adenohypophysis. Refer to Figures 25.6 and 25.7.
15. Define *releasing hormones*, and trace their path through the pituitary gland.
16. Describe the structure of the neurohypophysis and the functions of the two hormones it releases.
17. Describe the location and structure of the thyroid gland, listing its secreted hormones and their functions. Refer to Figure 25.8.
18. Describe the location and structure of the parathyroid glands, listing their secreted hormone and its function. Refer to Figure 25.9.
19. Describe the location and structure of the adrenal (suprarenal) glands, distinguishing between the outer cortex and inner medulla, and list the secreted hormones by each part and their functions. Refer to Figure 25.10.
20. Using Figure 25.11, describe the ultrastructure of a cell that secretes steroid hormones.
21. Describe the location, anatomical features, and endocrine functions of the pineal gland.
22. Describe the location and endocrine functions of the pancreas, thymus, and the gonads.
23. Point out that endocrine cells are present in several other organs of the body, including the heart, GI tract, placenta, kidneys, and skin. List the respective hormones produced and their functions.
24. Discuss disorders of the endocrine system, describing the effects of excessive or inadequate hormonal secretion by the pituitary, thyroid, and adrenal glands.
25. Discuss causes, symptoms, and treatments for diabetes mellitus.
26. Using Figure 25.14, describe basic embryonic development of some major endocrine organs.
27. Describe the effects of aging on some of the organs of the endocrine system.

Classroom Discussion Topics and Activities

1. Use a model or a chart of a human torso to exhibit the major endocrine glands.
2. Demonstrate major endocrine glands using a dissected cat or rat.
3. Use photographs illustrating people with endocrine disorders such as goiter, gigantism, cretinism, and acromegaly.
4. Present the endocrine system with a global view, using the textbook's Short Answer and Essay Questions 14–18 as a required assignment.
5. Diagram a feedback loop, beginning and ending with the anterior pituitary. The sequence will look like this: anterior pituitary → secretes → tropic hormone → stimulates → target endocrine gland → secretes → its hormone → inhibits → anterior pituitary.
6. Ask students to diagram the relationship of the pituitary to the hypothalamus in a similar diagram. It may look similar to this:

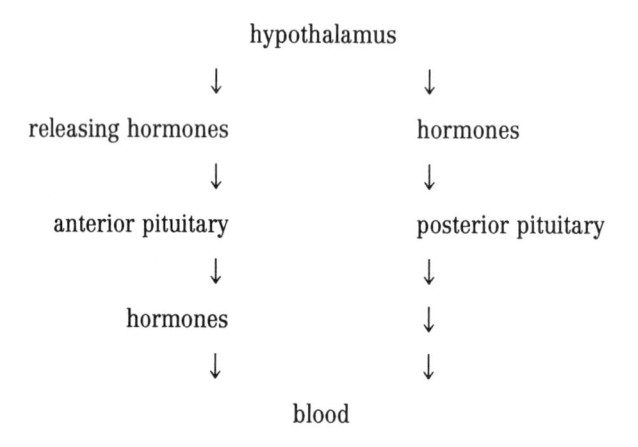

```
                    hypothalamus
                   ↓           ↓
         releasing hormones   hormones
                   ↓           ↓
         anterior pituitary   posterior pituitary
                   ↓           ↓
              hormones         ↓
                   ↓           ↓
                    blood
```

7. Continue to discuss word origins with the students:
   a. Explain that the prefix "nor-" used in noradrenaline and norepinephrine describes the lack of a certain chemical radical that is part of the adrenaline (epinephrine) molecule.
   b. Explain that pituitary in Latin means "phlegm" because historically it was believed this gland was the source of the mucus in the nasal cavity.
   c. *Lact* = milk, *infundibulum* = funnel, and so on.
8. Discuss why the pancreas, ovaries, testes, thymus, digestive organs, placenta, kidneys, and skin are considered to have endocrine functions. Relate the endocrine functions to the non-endocrine functions of these organs.
9. Discuss the role of the endocrine system in stress and stress responses.
10. Ask students to construct a list of all endocrine organs that are not controlled by the pituitary gland and the hypothalamus.
11. Some endocrine structures are whole organs, others are tissues within organs, and others are isolated cells. Ask students to give examples of each of these.
12. Discuss why the capillaries supplying all endocrine organs are either fenestrated capillaries or sinusoidal capillaries, but they are never typical, continuous capillaries.
13. Ask students to explain how an adult could be a giant and have acromegaly as well.

14. It is known that occasionally students of human anatomy go out on Friday nights and drink beer with friends. Ask students how they explain to their uninformed friends the common repercussion of very frequent urination.

Clinical Questions

1. Mr. Swami made an appointment to see his doctor for pain in his loin area. Tests and X rays revealed kidney stones and bones with a moth-eaten appearance throughout his skeleton. The lab technician botched the measurement of his blood-calcium levels, and these are being remeasured, but the phosphate concentrations in his body fluids are very high. While waiting for the lab results, what tentative diagnosis does the doctor make?

   Answer: The problem is probably hyperparathyroidism resulting from a tumor of the parathyroid gland. Hypersecretion of parathyroid hormone has probably stimulated a massive reabsorption of bone mineral (calcium and phosphate) from the skeleton, and blood-calcium levels are expected to be as highly elevated as the phosphate levels are. The treatment of Mr. Swami's condition is removal of the tumorous parathyroid gland.

2. Butch, a high school wrestler who is trying to "make weight" before his wrestling match, buys diet pills off the shelf. He takes them as recommended and experiences a quick weight loss. What could cause his sudden loss of weight? (The label on the pill bottle lists a chemical known to be a strong diuretic.)

   Answer: The diuretic antagonized the effect of antidiuretic hormone, causing water to be flushed from the body through excessive urination. The "weight loss" was simple water loss.

3. A woman with excessive body hair, a deep voice, and an enlarged clitoris shows the outward symptoms of which hormonal dysfunction?

   Answer: The dysfunction is hypersecretion of androgens, possibly from a tumor of the adrenal cortex.

4. The parents of 14-year-old Megan are concerned about her height because she is only 4 feet tall, and they are both close to 6 feet tall. After tests by their doctor, certain hormones are prescribed for the girl. What are the probable diagnosis, hormones prescribed, and the reason why the girl might expect to reach normal height?

   Answer: The diagnosis is hyposecretion of growth hormone. The prescription is commercial pituitary growth hormone. The reason the girl might reach her growth potential is that the epiphyseal plates of her bones have not yet closed, allowing additional growth of the skeleton and body in response to the hormone.

5. Paula, a 28-year-old woman, has been in the first stage of labor for 15 hours. Her uterine contractions are weak, and her labor is not progressing normally. Since Paula and her doctor desire a vaginal delivery, the physician orders that Pitocin (a synthetic oxytocin) be infused. What will the effect of this hormone be?

   Answer: Pitocin and oxytocin stimulate contraction of the smooth muscle of the myometrium, thus strengthening the uterine contractions to expel the baby.

ART RESOURCES
Transparency List

Figure 25.1 Location of the major endocrine organs of the body.

Figure 25.2 Control of hormone release.

Figure 25.3 The pituitary gland (hypophysis).

Figure 25.4 The major vessels of the pituitary gland.

Figure 25.6 Structural and functional relationships between the adenohypophysis and the hypothalamus.

Figure 25.7 The neurohypophysis.

Figure 25.8 The thyroid gland.

Figure 25.9 The parathyroid glands.

Figure 25.10 The adrenal gland.

Teaching with Art

Figure 25.6 Structural and functional relationships between the adenohypophysis and the hypothalamus.

Textbook p. 750; transparencies; Digital Archive CD-ROM.

Checklist of Key Points in the Figure

- Remind students of the precise locations of structures located in the figure.
- Review examples of hormones secreted by the adenohypophysis, mentioning why the anterior pituitary is no longer called the "master" gland.
- Stress that hormonal secretion by the adenohypophysis is controlled from the hypophysis of the brain.
- Define and distinguish between *releasing hormones* and *inhibiting hormones*.
- Explain that both releasing hormones and inhibiting hormones must travel through the hypophyseal portal system to control hormonal secretions from the adenohypophysis.
- Compare and contrast the locations and functions of both sets of capillaries making up the hypophyseal portal system.
- Point out successive stages in which the releasing hormones signal secretion of adenohypophyseal hormones.

Common Conceptual Difficulties Interpreting the Art

- Distinguish between functions of the adenohypophysis and the neurohypophysis.
- Explain the significance of capillary networks.
- Explain the location of the median eminence.
- Identify the infundibulum.

Art Exercises

1. Provide unlabeled copies of Figure 25.6, and instruct students to label and color code arteries red, veins blue, and capillaries a third color, identifying the parts of the hypophyseal portal system.

2. Ask students to look at the Figure 25.6 and list the successive steps in the pathway from the secretion of releasing hormones to adenohypophyseal hormones to target organs, as can be deduced from this figure.

Critical Reasoning

Again ask students to study Figure 25.6. Ask them to speculate why the adenohypophysis and the neurohypophysis—both of which are functionally unrelated—came to be so tightly mated together in the body, almost to the point that they appear to constitute a single organ. What is the *functional advantage* of this configuration?

(Note: Before asking this question, it is sometimes helpful to stress the different origins of both structures by pointing out that the adenohypophysis originates in tissues that form the roof of the mouth and that the neurohypophysis originates from brain tissue.)

Answer: The close proximity of the adenohypophysis and neurohypophysis allows the hypophyseal portal system to be as short as possible—a situation that enables releasing hormones to travel rapidly to their target cells in the adenohypophysis.

SUPPLEMENTAL COURSE MATERIALS
Library Research Topics

1. Research the role of hormones in the treatment of nonhormone-related disorders.
2. Research the inheritance aspect of certain endocrine disorders, such as diabetes mellitus, and certain thyroid disorders. Research the new treatments for Type I diabetes.
3. Research the current information on the function of the diffuse neuroendocrine system (DNES), in the digestive tube and the DNES derivatives.
4. Just as some athletes abuse steroid hormones, other young athletes take growth hormone to increase their size. Investigate this illegal procedure and the effects of growth hormone on athletic performance.

Audiovisual Aids/Computer Software

See Preface of the Instructor's Guide for Key to Audiovisual Distributors

Videotapes

1. *Diabetes* (FHS, 19 min., 1991). Covers both Type I and Type II diabetes mellitus.
2. *Dwarfism: Born to Be Small* (FHS, 52 min., 1997). Examines symptoms and treatment of pituitary dwarfism.
3. *Endocrine Control: Systems in Balance* (IM, 30 min., 1997)
4. *The Endocrine System* (IM, 20 min., 1993). Covers hormone classes, control mechanisms, and functions.
5. *The Endocrine System* (EBE, 20 min., 1993)
6. *The Endocrine System (Anatomy and Physiology Series)* (CAP/HCA, 28 min.)
7. *Endocrine System*. 2nd ed. (EBE, 20 min.)
8. *The Feedback Cycle* (FHS, 10 min.). Examines the feedback mechanisms controlling homeostasis. Covers hormone modulation of cellular activity; examines different endocrine glands and their hormones.

9. *Glands and Hormones* (IM, 24 min., 1994)
10. *Glands and Hormones* (*Body Atlas Series*) (CAP/HCA, 30 min.)
11. *Homeostasis* (*New Living Body Series*) (FHS, 20 min., 1995)
12. *Hormones* (*Human Body Live Action Video Series*) (CAP, 28 min., 1993)
13. *The Hormonal Control* (FHS, 10 min). Examines the roles of hormones in homeostasis.
14. *The Human Body: Endocrine System* (COR, 16 min., 1993)
15. *The Living Body: Messengers* (FHS, VHS, or BETA). Describes the role of hormones including the role hormones play in response to sudden emergency.
16. *The New Living Body: Homeostasis* (FHS, 20 min., 1995). Examines hormones and feedback systems in the body.
17. *Regulatory Systems* (PLP, 30 min.)
18. *Seasonal Affective Disorder* (EBEC, 25 min.). Examines causes and treatment of SAD.
19. *Selected Actions of Hormones and Other Chemical Messengers* (BC, 25 min., 1994)
20. *Your Body, Part 3: Endocrine System* (PLP, CH-140203, VHS, 51 min.)

Computer Software

1. *Biochemistry of Hormones* (CSBC). Covers the chemical nature of hormones.
2. *Body Language: Digestive and Endocrine System* (CBSC, Mac only). Examines the digestive and endocrine systems in terms of organs, chemicals, and functions.
3. *Diabetes and Hypoglycemia* (PLP, Apple II, IIE, II+, IIC 48K). Topics include symptoms, causes, tests, complications, and the role of diet in the treatment of diabetes mellitus and hypoglycemia.
4. *Dynamics of the Human Endocrine System* (EI, Apple II or IBM PC, 1988). View of endocrine organs both anatomically and functionally, with emphasis on hormone actions and interactions.
5. *Hormones* (EI, Apple II, 1987). Emphasizes the basic principles of hormone action rather than exhaustively surveying hormone effects.
6. *The Human Body, Part II* (CL, Disk for Apple II/Mac/Win)
7. *The Human Body, Part II* (HCA, Disk for IBM, 1995)
8. *Learning About the Human Body* (Mac/Win, 1996)
9. *The Living Body* (Queue, Win)
10. *Nervous and Hormonal Systems* (Queue, Disk for Apple II/Mac/IBM). Examines homeostatic control of nervous and endocrine systems over body functions.

Slides

1. *The Endocrine System and its Function* (EI, Slides). This diverse and complex system of hormone-producing organs is viewed anatomically and functionally with emphasis on hormone action and interaction.
2. *The Chemistry of Life: Hormones and the Endocrine System, Parts 1–3* (HRM)

Suggested Readings

Anderson, I. Self-vaccination halts march of diabetes. *New Scientist* (August 10, 1991): 19.

Aunis, D. Exocytosis in chromaffin cells of the adrenal medulla. *International Review of Cytology* 181 (1998): 213–320.

Axelrod, J., and T. Reisine. Stress hormones: Their interaction and regulation. *Science* 224 (1984): 452.

Belchetz, P.E., and P. Hammond. *Mosby's Color Atlas and Text of Diabetes and Endocrinology*. St. Louis: Mosby, 1999.

Cormack, D.H. *Essential Histology*. Philadelphia: J.B. Lippincott, 1993.

Crapo, L. Hormones: Messengers of life. New York: W.H. Freeman & Co., 1985.

Fackelmann, K. Elusive amylin. *Science News* 138 (October 20, 1990): 250–251.

Fawcett, D.W. *A Textbook of Histology*. 11th ed. New York: Chapman & Hall, 1994, Chapters 17–21.

Geriatrics. Special Issue: Endocrine Functions and Aging. Various articles and authors. 50 (April 1995).

Hall, R., and D.C. Evered. *Color Atlas of Endocrinology*. 2nd ed. St. Louis: Mosby, 1990.

Horvath, E., and K. Kovacs. Fine structural cytology of the adenohypophysis in rat and man. *Journal of Electron Microscopy Technique* 8 (1988): 401–432.

Inoue, K., et al. The structure and function of folliculo-stellate cells in the anterior pituitary gland. *Archives of Histology and Cytology* 62 (August 1999): 205–218.

Junqueira, L.C., et al. *Basic Histology*. 9th ed. Stamford, Conn.: Appleton & Lange, 1998.

Karasek, M., and R.J. Reiter. Morphofunctional aspects of the mammalian pineal gland. *Microscopy Research and Technique* 21 (April 1, 1992): 136–157.

Klawans, H. *Toscanini's Fumble and Other Tales of Clinical Neurology*. Chicago: Contemporary Books, 1988, Chapter 12, p. 161.

Kurosumi, K. Ultrastructural immunocytochemistry of the adenohypophysis in the rat: A review. *Journal of Electron Microscopy Technique* 19 (September 1991): 42–56.

Lefabvre, D., et al. Oxytocin gene expression in rat uterus. *Science* 256 (June 12, 1992): 1553.

Marshall, P. The heart as a gland. *Nursing Times* 86 (February 14–20, 1990): 42–43.

McEwen, B.S., and T. Seeman. Protective and damaging effects of mediators of stress. Elaborating and testing the concepts of allostasis and allostatic load. *Annals of the New York Academy of Sciences* 896 (1999): 30–47.

Moore, K.L. *Clinically Oriented Anatomy*. 34th ed. Philadelphia: Lippincott Williams and Wilkins, 1999.

Porterfield, S.P. *Endocrine Physiology*. St. Louis: Mosby, 1996.

Robbins, S.L., V. Kumar, and R. Cotran. *Basic Pathology*. 6th ed. Philadelphia: W.B. Saunders, 1997.

Sapolsky, R.M., et al. How do glucocorticoids influence stress responses? Integrating permissive, suppressive, stimulatory, and preparative actions. *Endocrine Review* 21 (February 2000): 55–89.

Scheithauer, B., et al. Ultrastructure of the neurohypophysis. *Microscopy Research and Technique* 20 (1992): 177–186.

Swain, R., and B. Kaplan. Practices and pitfalls of corticosteroid injection. *The Physician and Sportsmedicine* 23 (March 1995): 27–40.

Unsicker, K. The chromaffin cell: Paradigm in cell, developmental and growth factor biology. *Journal of Anatomy* 183 (Pt 2) (October 1993): 207–221.

Williams, P.L., et al. *Gray's Anatomy*. 38th ed. New York: Churchill Livingstone, 1995.

Young, M.W. The tick-tock of the biological clock. *Scientific American* 282 (March 2000): 64–71.

ANSWERS TO TEXTBOOK QUESTIONS

Answers for multiple-choice and matching questions 1–10 are located in Appendix B of the textbook.

Short Answer and Essay Questions

11. (a) *Pituitary*: inferior to the diencephalon in the sella turcica, where the anterior lobe (pars distalis) lies anterior to the posterior lobe (pars nervosa); *pineal*: roof of diencephalon; *thyroid gland*: anterior neck; *parathyroid*: on the posterior surface of, or imbedded within, the lobes of the thyroid gland; *adrenal*: on the superior surface of the kidney. (b) *Pituitary*: growth hormone, thyroid-stimulating hormone, adrenocorticotropic hormone, melanocyte-stimulating hormone, follicle-stimulating hormone, luteinizing hormone, antidiuretic hormone, and oxytocin; *pineal*: melatonin; *thyroid gland*: thyroid hormone and calcitonin; *parathyroid*: parathyroid hormone; *adrenal*: catecholamines, mineralocorticoids (aldosterone), glucocorticoids (e.g., cortisol), and sex hormones.

12. The hypothalamus is the "master" of the pituitary gland. Releasing hormones and inhibiting hormones from the hypothalamus control the release of hormones from the anterior pituitary.

13. The thyroid gland contains parafollicular (not parathyroid) cells in its follicles, and the parafollicular cells secrete calcitonin. The parathyroid glands are distinct glands, although they may be imbedded in the thyroid gland. Parathyroid cells secrete parathyroid hormone.

14. (a) Hormones are messenger molecules that are secreted by endocrine cells and travel through the circulation to target cells elsewhere in the body. Hormones signal physiological responses in their target cells. (b) Renin is a hormone secreted by smooth muscle cells in the kidney, and atrial natriuretic hormone is secreted by cardiac muscle cells. Hormones secreted by neurons include all releasing hormones and inhibiting hormones from the hypothalamus, as well as oxytocin and antidiuretic hormone.

15. (a) thyroid gland. (b) pancreas. (c) adenohypophysis of the pituitary. (d) adenohypophysis. (e) pineal. (f) ovary. (g) adrenal cortex.

16. Students should draw lines and arrows from (a) skin (source) to liver to kidney to intestine (target). (b) pancreas to liver. (c) kidney to bone marrow. (d) neurohypophysis (and hypothalamus) to breast, uterus, and all smooth musculature of the reproductive tract.

17. (a) adenohypophysis. (b) neurohypophysis (hypothalamus is also correct). (c) thyroid gland. (d) parathyroids and thymus. (e) adrenal medulla.

18. (a) adrenal gland. (b) thyroid gland. (c) pituitary gland. (d) pancreatic islets/pancreas. (e) ovary or testis. (f) thyroid gland.

19. The first set of capillaries, in the median eminence, receives the releasing hormones. The second set of capillaries, in the pars distalis, distributes the releasing hormones to the endocrine cells of the adenohypophysis, then receives the hormones from these cells (e.g., GH, FSH, LH, TSH), and distributes these hormones to the general circulation.

20. (1) Zona glomerulosa: mostly mineralocorticoids (e.g., aldosterone). (2) Zona fasciculata: mostly glucocorticoids (e.g., cortisol). (3) Zona reticularis: glucocorticoids and androgens (DHEA).

Critical Reasoning and Clinical Applications Questions

1. In response to stress, corticotropin-releasing hormone is secreted by axon terminals into the primary capillary plexus in the median eminence, travels down the infundibulum within the hypophyseal portal veins, and reaches the secondary capillary plexus in the pars distalis. The releasing hormone exits this plexus, binds to the corticotropic cells of the adenohypophysis, and signals these cells to secrete adrenocorticotropic hormone (ACTH) into the secondary capillary plexus. From there, the ACTH circulates in the bloodstream to the adrenal cortex, where it signals the secretion of cortisol into the blood.

2. (a) The hypersecreted hormone is growth hormone. (b) The disorder is called gigantism.

3. Dense particles of calcium in the pineal make this gland radiopaque and visible on X-ray images.

4. The surgeons should look for the parathyroids in the anterior thorax or inferior neck, for these glands occur in such places in some people.

5. *Fat man*: People with abnormally low metabolic rates, caused by hyposecretion of thyroid hormone (hypothyroidism), use food energy slowly, gain weight easily, and may become obese. *Dwarf and giant*: Hyposecretion of growth hormone from the anterior pituitary during childhood leads to dwarfism, and a tumor that causes hypersecretion of this hormone during youth causes gigantism. *Bearded lady*: the zona reticularis cells of the adrenal cortex secrete androgens, and a tumor formed by these cells will secrete excess androgens into the blood, causing a beard to grow on a woman. *Eye-protruding person*: Graves' disease, characterized by an excessive secretion of thyroid hormone, causes the eyes to protrude, perhaps due to edema in the orbital tissue behind the eyes or perhaps through an effect on the extrinsic eye muscles.

SUPPLEMENTAL STUDENT MATERIALS TO HUMAN ANATOMY, THIRD EDITION
Chapter 25: The Endocrine System

To the Student

It's Saturday night, and your friends want to go out and eat pizza and drink beer. During the course of the evening, a friend asks the question, "Why do you urinate more frequently after a couple beers?" You confidently answer, "Because of the alcohol in beer, you have very successfully suppressed your ADH!" You are able to answer this question, as well as celebrate, because you understand the basics of how the endocrine system works. This chapter explores anatomical and functional relationships between the endocrine and nervous systems, explaining how both work to maintain homeostasis and coordinate physiological functions throughout your body. There are several organs that are purely endocrine in function, as well as several other organs that have endocrine cells but belong to other organ systems. All these organs produce hormones that function as chemical messengers, going to specific target cells and causing specific effects.

Step 1: Examine an overview of the endocrine system, describing glands and hormones.

- ☐ Define an *endocrine gland* in terms of its basic structure and function, listing all endocrine glands covered by your textbook.
- ☐ Define *hormone*.
- ☐ List several hormonally regulated processes.
- ☐ Explain similarities between the endocrine system and the nervous system.
- ☐ Describe how hormones are classified based on chemical structure.
- ☐ Explain the basics of hormonal action, defining target cells.
- ☐ Describe the mechanisms that control hormone secretion: humoral stimuli, neural stimuli, and hormonal stimuli.

Step 2: List and describe the major organs of the endocrine system, including hormones produced and hormonal effects.

- ☐ Using a chart format, list the location and structure (region/area) of the pituitary gland, including all the hormones secreted, their targets, and hormonal effects.
- ☐ Diagram a simplified feedback loop representing the endocrine interactions between the adenohypophysis and a target endocrine gland.
- ☐ Explain how the hypothalamus controls the secretion of adenohypophyseal hormones.
- ☐ Define *hypophyseal portal system*, explaining its significance.
- ☐ Define and distinguish between *releasing hormones* and *inhibiting hormones*.
- ☐ Trace the path of releasing hormones through the pituitary gland.
- ☐ Describe the location and structure of the thyroid gland and the parathyroid glands, including hormones secreted, their targets, and hormonal effects.
- ☐ Describe the location and name the two divisions of the adrenal gland, explaining their structure (region/zone) and including hormones secreted, their targets, and hormonal effects.

- ☐ Describe the ultrastructure of a cell that secretes steroid hormones.
- ☐ Describe the location and structure of the pineal gland, pancreas, thymus, and gonads, including hormones secreted, their targets, and hormonal effects.

Step 3: Describe disorders of the endocrine system and describe changes associated with aging.

- ☐ Distinguish between hyposecretion and hypersecretion of hormones and name disorders associated with each.
- ☐ Describe diabetes mellitus.
- ☐ Describe the embryologic development of major endocrine glands.
- ☐ Describe the effects of aging on some endocrine glands.

Step 4: Solve short answer and essay questions in the textbook for an excellent overall understanding of the endocrine system.

- ☐ Answer textbook questions 15–18, using photocopies of respective textbook diagrams.

CHAPTER 26
Surface Anatomy

LECTURE AND DEMONSTRATION
Student Objectives

1. Define *surface anatomy*, and explain why it is an important field of study. Define *palpation*.
2. Describe the major surface features of the cranium and face.
3. Describe and define the *important surface features of the neck*, including the anterior and posterior triangles.
4. Describe the easily palpated bony and muscular landmarks of the back. Locate the vertebral spines on the living body.
5. List the bony surface landmarks of the thoracic cage, and explain how they relate to the major soft organs of the thorax. Explain how to find any rib (second to eleventh).
6. Name the important surface features on the anterior abdominal wall.
7. Identify and explain the following: linea alba, umbilical hernia, examination for an inguinal hernia, linea semilunaris, and McBurney's point.
8. Explain how to palpate a full bladder and the bony boundaries of the perineum.
9. Locate and palpate the main surface features of the upper limb.
10. Define and explain the significance of the *cubital fossa, pulse points in the distal forearm*, and the *anatomical snuff-box*.
11. Describe the surface landmarks of the lower limb.
12. Explain exactly where to administer an injection in the gluteal region and in the other major sites of intramuscular injection.

Suggested Lecture Outline

I. *Introduction (p. 770, Figs. 26.1–26.4)*

II. *The Head (pp. 770–774, Figs. 26.5 and 26.6)*
   A. Cranium (p. 770)
   B. Face (pp. 770–774)

III. *The Neck (pp. 774–777, Figs. 26.7–26.9)*
   A. Skeletal Landmarks (p. 774)
   B. Muscles of the Neck (pp. 774–776)
   C. Triangles of the Neck (p. 777)

IV. The Trunk (pp. 777–783)

    A. The Back (pp. 777–779, Fig. 26.10)

        1. Bones of the Back

        2. Muscles of the Back

    B. The Thorax (pp. 779–780, Figs. 26.11 and 26.12)

        1. Bones of the Thorax

        2. Muscles of the Thorax

    C. The Abdomen (pp. 781–783, Figs. 26.11 and 26.13)

        1. Bony Landmarks

        2. Muscles and Other Abdominal Surface Features

    D. The Pelvis and Perineum (p. 783, Fig. 26.14)

V. Upper Limb and Shoulder (pp. 783–789)

    A. Axilla (p. 783, Fig. 26.11)

    B. Shoulder (p. 783, Figs. 26.15 and 26.16)

    C. Arm (p. 783, Figs. 26.15 and 26.17)

    D. Elbow Region (pp. 783–787, Fig. 26.18)

    E. Forearm and Hand (pp. 787–789, Figs. 26.19–26.22)

VI. Lower Limb and Gluteal Region (pp. 789–793)

    A. Gluteal Region (pp. 789–791, Fig. 26.23)

    B. Thigh (p. 791, Figs. 26.24–26.26)

    C. Leg and Foot (pp. 791–793, Figs. 26.24–26.26)

Lecture Hints

1. Define *surface anatomy*, explaining that internal structures as well as external structures may be located by surface anatomy.

2. Explain that surface anatomy reflects a regional approach to the study of anatomy as opposed to a systemic approach.

3. Define *palpation*.

4. Explain that females have more fat than males, commenting on the clinical significance.

5. Instruct students to review bones and muscles, using Figures 26.1–26.3.

6. Using Figure 26.4, ask students to review major points for palpation of an arterial pulse.

7. List and palpate the major surface features of the cranium and face. Refer to Figures 26.5 and 26.6.

8. Describe the relationship of the cranium to the scalp, explaining why scalp wounds bleed profusely.

9. List and palpate the major surface features of the neck, including skeletal landmarks, cartilaginous features, and muscles. Refer to Figure 26.7.

10. Describe the boundaries of the anterior and posterior triangles of the neck, naming structures associated with each triangle. Refer to Figure 26.8.
11. List and describe the easily palpated bony and muscular landmarks of the back.
12. Identify the location of the triangle of auscultation, using Figure 26.10, and explain its clinical significance.
13. Define *trunk*, including the comprehensive term *back*.
14. Identify the bony landmarks of the back, naming the most easily located ones.
15. Distinguish between the posterior median furrow and the supracrestal line. Refer to Figure 26.10.
16. Explore with students the surface of the anterior thorax, identifying the sternum, explaining how to count ribs, and naming major superficial anterior muscles. Refer to Figures 26.11 and 26.12.
17. Describe the bony landmarks of the thoracic cage, distinguishing between the midaxillary line and midclavicular line, and identifying the locations of soft organs in the thoracic cavity.
18. Explain the clinical importance of the costal margins as landmarks.
19. Using Figure 26.11, identify and list the surface landmarks on the anterior abdominal wall.
20. Explain why the umbilicus, linea alba, linea semilunaris, and McBurney's point are important clinical landmarks. Refer to Figure 26.11.
21. Define and explain how to palpate the *bony landmarks of the perineum* and a *full urinary bladder*. Refer to Figure 26.14.
22. Identify important superficial structures associated with the axilla. Refer to Figure 26.11.
23. Identify skeletal landmarks of the shoulder area, explaining the site of intramuscular injections. Refer to Figure 26.15.
24. Define *arm*, and identify the surface landmarks (bony, muscular, venous, and arterial) associated with the arm, forearm, and hand. Refer to Figures 26.15–26.22.
25. Define *cubital fossa* and *anatomical snuff-box*. Refer to Figures 26.18 and 26.21.
26. Define the *gluteal region*, naming prominent bony landmarks and muscles. Refer to Figure 26.23.
27. Distinguish between the natal cleft and the gluteal fold.
28. Define *leg*, and identify the surface landmarks (bony, muscular, venous, and arterial) associated with the thigh, leg, and foot. Refer to Figures 26.24–26.26.
29. Distinguish between the femoral triangle and the political fossa.
30. Using Figure 26.16, identify three major sites of intramuscular injections.

Classroom Discussion Topics and Activities

1. Invite a muscular male and female to come to class as models, and demonstrate various features of surface anatomy on these people. The students can palpate along on their own bodies. Provide a human skeleton during this exercise for reference.
2. Pass out a list of body structures that the students should palpate on themselves and on each other. (Of course, the list should be heavily weighted toward the head, neck, and limbs because students will not want to feel structures on the thorax and abdomen that they consider embarrassing to palpate in public.)

3. Ask for student volunteers to permit counting of their ribs. The trick is to find the costal cartilages of the second ribs at the sternal angle, then count down along the sides of the sternum.

4. Ask for a student volunteer to permit a demonstration of auscultation sites of the thorax and abdomen. Provide stethoscopes for students to listen to the body sounds of each other.

5. Discuss clinical conditions that usually can be diagnosed through palpation and those conditions that are not detectable through palpation techniques.

6. The skin forms the body surface, yet the study of surface anatomy is very different from the study of skin structures. Ask students to identify the differences between studying skin and studying surface anatomy.

7. A total body regional summation may be used at this time. Choose a body region and ask students to name all systems represented in that body region, followed by names of specific structures of that system. For example, students may list the following systems and structures for the head: nervous: brain; circulatory: internal carotid artery; and muscles: temporalis. The list of structures may be as specific or as general or as inclusive as the instructor desires.

Clinical Questions

1. On his first day of nursing school, Calvin learned an easy way to locate the pulse point of the radial artery in the anterior distal forearm. How did Cal locate this pulse point?

    Answer: It is directly lateral to the tendon of flexor carpi radialis, which is visible deep to the skin of the anterior distal forearm when the hand is flexed against resistance.

2. Kay was stuffing garbage into a garbage can and cut her wrist on a piece of broken glass that she had forgotten was in the trash. The wound bled more than she expected. At the emergency room, the doctor told Kay that the cut was across the "snuff-box." How does this explain the relatively large amount of bleeding?

    Answer: The main trunk of the radial artery runs through the anatomical snuff-box in the lateral wrist (on its way to form the deep palmar arch in the hand).

3. After Tina was born, her parents saw a cherry-sized bulge in the skin of her navel that enlarged when she cried. What is it, and should it be corrected surgically?

    Answer: This was a congenital umbilical hernia, and the bulge is formed by a loop of the small intestine that has pushed through a circular weakening in the anterior abdominal wall. Small umbilical hernias like this usually correct themselves before the child's second birthday.

4. Nine sorority sisters were talking and realized that all of them had had appendectomies. They compared the locations of their appendectomy scars. Two of them had their incisions in the pubic region of the abdomen ("bikini cuts") so that the scar would not be noticeable when they wore swimwear, but the other seven women had their incisions on the right side of the anterior abdominal wall, about one-third of the way between the anterior superior iliac spine and the umbilicus. What is this latter point called, and why is it such a common site of appendectomy incisions?

    Answer: The point is McBurney's point, and it is the point on the skin directly superficial to the base of the appendix. It is easiest for the surgeon to locate the appendix when cutting into the abdomen at this point.

5. During a physical examination, Hilda, a heavy woman, was noticed to have a large bulge below the skin of the anterior surface of her superior thigh, several centimeters inferior to the inguinal ligament. What is the probable diagnosis?

Answer: The bulge is in the skin of the femoral triangle, so Hilda probably has a femoral (not inguinal) hernia. In such hernias, intestines push inferiorly deep to the inguinal ligament and raise a bulge in the superior thigh. Incidentally, femoral hernias are more common in women than in men because of the greater width of the female pelvis.

ART RESOURCES
Transparency List

Figure 26.5 Surface anatomy of the lateral aspect of the head.
Figure 26.6 Surface structures of the face.
Figure 26.7 Anterior surface of the neck.
Figure 26.8 Lateral surface of the neck.
Figure 26.9 Anterior and posterior triangles of the neck.
Figure 26.10 Surface anatomy of the back.
Figure 26.11 The anterior thorax and abdomen.
Figure 26.12 The bony thoracic cage as it relates to the underlying lungs and pleural cavity.
Figure 26.14 Surface features of the perineum.
Figure 26.15 Shoulder and arm.
Figure 26.17 The three heads of the triceps brachii muscle, which insert on a large tendon.
Figure 26.18 The cubital fossa on the anterior surface of the right elbow.
Figure 26.19 A way to locate the styloid processes of the ulna and radius.
Figure 26.20 The anterior surface of the forearm and fist.
Figure 26.21 The dorsum of the hand.
Figure 26.22 The palmar surface of the hand.
Figure 26.23 The gluteal region.
Figure 26.24 The lateral surface of the lower limb.
Figure 26.25 The anterior surface of the lower limb.
Figure 26.26 The posterior surface of the lower limb

Teaching with Art

Figure 26.7 Anterior surface of the neck.
Figure 26.8 Lateral surface of the neck.
Figure 26.9 Anterior and posterior triangles of the neck.
Textbook pp. 776–777; transparencies; Digital Archive CD-ROM.

Checklist of Key Points in the Figure
- Identify the skeletal landmarks of the neck.
- Review the muscles of the neck.
- Review the blood vessels of the neck.
- Review the larynx.

Common Conceptual Difficulties Interpreting the Art
- Explain a regional approach to the study of the neck as opposed to a systemic approach.
- Review the importance of the study of surface anatomy.

Art Exercises
1. Palpation Exercise: Provide students with unlabeled copies of Figures 26.7–26.8. Instruct students to read about palpation techniques of the neck, on textbook p. 776, and to label each structure discussed as they find it. Students may work individually or in pairs. Alternatively, provide students with a checklist of required structures for palpation and instructions to label work sheets as structures are palpated.
2. Neck Structures Drawing Exercise: Instruct students to sketch the following structures as they relate to the sternocleidomastoid muscle:
   a. Sternal head
   b. Clavicular head
   c. Cervical lymph nodes
   d. External jugular vein
   e. Pulse point of the external carotid artery
   f. Subclavian artery
   g. Brachial plexus
   h. Mastoid process of the occipital
3. Regional Anatomy Exercise: Ask students to list every body system represented in the neck and then to expand their lists to include specific neck structures of each system they have learned during their study of anatomy.

Critical Reasoning
1. Ask students why trauma to the posterior triangle of the neck may interfere with breathing.

   Answer: The phrenic nerve leaves the cervical plexus within the posterior triangle to innervate the diaphragm.
2. Ask students to name the chambers that blood may potentially flow into in the case of a severe blow to the side of the neck and head that results in a ruptured internal carotid artery.

   Answer: Spaces of the temporal bone.

SUPPLEMENTAL COURSE MATERIALS

Library Research Topics

1. Research the basic steps by which a physician proceeds through a physical examination, and consider how surface anatomy is used in each step.
2. Research the ways in which athletic trainers use surface anatomy.

Suggested Readings

Basmajian, J.V. *Surface Anatomy: An Instruction Manual.* Baltimore: Williams and Wilkins, 1977.

Donnelly, J.E. *Living Anatomy for Physical Educators, Coaches, and Athletic Trainers.* Champaign, IL: Human Kinetics Publishers, Inc., 1982.

Keogh, B., and S. Ebbs. *Normal Surface Anatomy.* Philadelphia: J.B. Lippincott, 1984.

Moore, K.L. *Clinically Oriented Anatomy.* 3rd ed. Baltimore: Williams and Wilkins, 1992.

Romanes, G.J. *Cunningham's Textbook of Anatomy.* 11th ed. London: Oxford University Press, 1972.

Williams, P.L., et al. *Gray's Anatomy.* 38th ed. New York: Churchill Livingstone, 1995.

ANSWERS TO TEXTBOOK QUESTIONS

Answers for multiple-choice and matching questions 1–9 are located in Appendix B of the textbook.

Short Answer and Essay Questions

10. Feeling internal body structures through the skin with the fingers is called palpation.

11. (a) One way to locate the ventral gluteal site is to draw an imaginary line laterally from the posterior superior iliac spine to the greater trochanter, and then proceed 5 cm superiorly from the midpoint of this line. (b) Intramuscular injections are often given into the deltoid muscle, about 5 cm inferior to the greater tubercle of the humerus.

12. C7 is the first prominent spinous process that is felt as one runs a finger down the neck in the posterior median sulcus; T3 is the spinous process that lies at the same level as the medial end of the spine of the scapula; T7 lies at the level of the scapula's inferior angle; L4 lies at the level of the supracrestal line (line connecting the highest points of the two iliac crests on the back).

13. A femoral hernia will always lie inferior, and an inguinal hernia will always lie superior, to the inguinal ligament. A femoral hernia is evident as a bulge in the superior thigh, and an inguinal hernia may be represented as a bulge in the groin. Placing a finger in the superficial inguinal ring and asking the patient to cough, as explained in Figure 26.13, may detect an inguinal hernia that does not raise a distinct bulge.

14. The posterior superior iliac spine forms a distinct dimple in the gluteal region. In a bone marrow biopsy, the aspiration needle is inserted into the iliac bone 1 cm inferolateral to the dimple.

15. The apex point of the heart is in the fifth left intercostal space, in the midclavicular line. (See Figure 18.2a on p. 523.)

16. *Appendix*: McBurney's point, one-third of the way along a line from the right anterior superior iliac spine to the umbilicus (p. 781). *Gallbladder*: intersection of the right linea semilunaris with the costal margin (p. 781).

17. See Figure 26.9 and the text on p. 777.

18. The borders of the triangle of auscultation are formed by the latissimus dorsi, trapezius, and scapula.

19. (a) On the lateral side of the hip, just anterior to a hollow and about one hand's breadth inferior to the iliac crest (p. 790). (b) Medial thigh (Figure 26.25a). (c) Lateral anterior thigh (Figure 26.25b). (d) This is the ischial tuberosity, just superior to the medial part of the gluteal fold (p. 790).

20. The *facial artery* is a branch of the external carotid artery. The *common carotid artery* is a branch of the brachiocephalic artery (right) or the aorta (left). The *brachial artery* is a continuation of the subclavian artery (which branches from the brachiocephalic artery or aorta). The *radial artery* is a branch of the brachial artery. The *femoral artery* is a continuation of the external iliac artery (which branches from the common iliac). The *popliteal artery* is a continuation of the femoral artery (which branches from the common iliac). The *posterior tibial artery* is a branch of the popliteal artery. The *dorsalis pedis artery* is a continuation of the anterior tibial artery (which branches from the popliteal artery).

Critical Reasoning and Clinical Applications Questions

1. Mrs. Schultz has both a Colles' fracture of the wrist and a proximal dislocation of the ulna at the elbow. The force of landing on her outstretched hand has driven the distal end of the radius proximally into the radial shaft, which explains why the styloid process of the radius lies more proximally than normal. The same force also dislocated the ulna superiorly by 2 cm, for the olecranon process normally lies directly in line with the two epicondyles of the humerus.

2. The buckshot had severed both sciatic nerves deep to the gluteus maximus muscles. These nerves innervate the entire lower limbs, except the anterior parts of the thighs.

3. The hamstrings were injured.

4. The cut had apparently severed many important structures in the posterior triangle of the gang member's neck. Paralysis of the limb indicated that important parts of the brachial plexus were cut. Lack of sensation in the skin of the neck indicated that some nerves of the cervical plexus were severed. The fact that blood flowed freely from the wound but did not spurt suggests that the external jugular vein had been cut, but no major artery had been opened. His inability to turn his head or shrug his shoulders indicated that the sternocleidomastoid and trapezius muscles were weakened, meaning the accessory nerve was severed. Finally, he was gasping for breath because a phrenic nerve had been cut and half his diaphragm was paralyzed.

5. The child's case was not unusual. Scalp wounds tend to bleed profusely but heal quickly.

6. The cancerous lymph node itself was not sore or inflamed. However, as it enlarged, it exerted pressure within the narrow confines of the popliteal fossa, which is covered by a strong roof of fascia that resists expansion. This pressure in the popliteal fossa caused Gabrielle's pain.

SUPPLEMENTAL STUDENT MATERIALS TO HUMAN ANATOMY, THIRD EDITION
Chapter 26: Surface Anatomy

To the Student

Primarily, your study of anatomy incorporated the systemic approach, until this chapter. Now you have the unique opportunity to combine everything you have studied by using an anatomical regional approach. There is a chance you looked at the skeleton and muscle information in this chapter when your instructor covered those topics earlier. Nevertheless, a wonderful summary and "put-it-all-together" concept pervades this chapter. The regional approach of this chapter enables you to better understand the relationships between muscles, bones, blood vessels, lymph nodes, nerves, internal organs, and sites of injections, drawing blood, and inserting tubes. Whether your career goal is a health care profession or not, it is to your advantage to be able to understand the normal body in order to detect something that is abnormal. Careful observation and knowledge of palpation techniques will aid this understanding. And, do not forget, your own body is the best "cheat sheet" possible in anatomy. It is the one thing you cannot leave behind when you go into the classroom for your exam!

Step 1: Describe surface anatomy as a field of study.

☐ Define *surface anatomy*.

☐ Explain the importance of surface anatomy to the "living" body.

☐ Define *palpation*.

☐ Distinguish between systemic and regional approaches to the study of anatomy.

☐ List several ways surface anatomy provides information for a clinician.

Step 2: Describe the major surface features of the head.

☐ Distinguish between the cranium and the face.

☐ Palpate major surface features of the cranium as described by your textbook.

☐ Distinguish between the cranium and the scalp.

☐ Palpate major surface features of the face as described by your textbook.

Step 3: Describe and palpate the major surface features of the neck.

☐ Palpate the major skeletal landmarks of the neck as described by your textbook.

☐ Palpate the major muscles of the neck.

☐ Define and describe the *anterior* and *posterior triangles*.

☐ Using the triangles of the neck as a reference, describe locations for palpations of a pulse, the larynx, cervical lymph nodes, and the trachea.

☐ Sketch the anterior and posterior triangles, labeling important surface features.

☐ List at least three vitally important structures that lie deep in the neck, explaining why they are so important.

Step 4: Describe and palpate the major surface features of the trunk.

- ☐ Define the *back*, and count and palpate vertebral processes, naming the easy ones to find as landmarks.
- ☐ Distinguish between the posterior median fissure and the supracrestal line.
- ☐ Define and describe the posteriorly located *triangle of auscultation*, explaining the clinical significance of this area.
- ☐ Explore the anterior thoracic surface, palpating all bony and muscular features described in your textbook.
- ☐ Distinguish between the midaxillary line and the midclavicular line.
- ☐ Map the location of the pleural cavities, the lungs, and the heart using the ribs as a reference.
- ☐ List and palpate all features of the anterior abdominal wall listed in your textbook.
- ☐ Define *umbilicus*, and explain the examination for an inguinal hernia.
- ☐ Define *linea alba*, explaining why this is a site of clinical significance.
- ☐ Describe the location of McBurney's point, explaining why this is a site of clinical significance.
- ☐ Distinguish between linea semilunaris and tendinous intersections.
- ☐ Explain the clinical significance of a physician placing a stethoscope on the abdominal wall, describing the sites of placement and the clues various sounds provide.
- ☐ Describe how to palpate a full urinary bladder.
- ☐ Describe the bony boundaries of the perineum.

Step 5: Describe and palpate the major surface features of the upper limb and shoulder.

- ☐ Define *axilla*, naming important superficial structures associated with this part of the body.
- ☐ Explain why women should palpate the axilla during a breast self-examination.
- ☐ Identify and palpate the bony landmarks of the shoulder.
- ☐ Identify an upper limb location for an intramuscular injection.
- ☐ Identify and palpate the bony and muscular surface features of the arm.
- ☐ Identify and palpate the bony landmarks of the elbow region.
- ☐ Explain where and why you feel a tingling sensation if you bump your elbow, or in more common vernacular, "hit your crazy/funny bone." (And, be careful with your explanation because the reference is not to your "humerus.")
- ☐ Define and describe the *cubital fossa* and explain the clinical significance of the median cubital vein.
- ☐ Describe and palpate the bony and muscular structures of the forearm and hand listed in your textbook.
- ☐ Assume the anatomical position, then pronate your hand and identify which forearm bone remains more stationary.
- ☐ Make a clinched fist, and identify either one or both of the tendons evident on the anterior wrist.
- ☐ Describe and palpate pulse points in the distal forearm.
- ☐ Identify an important site for drawing blood and administering an IV distally on the upper extremity.

Step 6: Describe and palpate the major surface features of the lower limb and gluteal region.

- ☐ Identify and palpate the bony landmarks of the gluteal region.
- ☐ Distinguish between the natal cleft and the gluteal fold.
- ☐ Explain the clinical procedures and concerns for administering intramuscular injections in the gluteal region, i.e., the "safe area."
- ☐ List and palpate the bony and muscular landmarks of the thigh.
- ☐ Explain the femoral triangle and describe the clinical significance of this area.
- ☐ Define and palpate the *popliteal fossa*.
- ☐ List and palpate the bony landmarks of the leg and foot described in your textbook.
- ☐ Identify the location of the pulse of the posterior tibial artery and the dorsalis pedis artery.